D1082852

# HARVARD EAST ASIAN SERIES

HARVARD EAST ASIAN SERIES, 11

# CHINA AND CHRISTIANITY

The East Asian Research Center
at Harvard University
administers research projects
designed to further
scholarly understanding
of China, Korea, Japan,
and adjacent areas.

PAUL A. COHEN

# CHINA AND CHRISTIANITY

*The Missionary Movement and the
Growth of Chinese Antiforeignism*

1860–1870

HARVARD UNIVERSITY PRESS

CAMBRIDGE, MASSACHUSETTS

1963

FOR ANDREA OPPENHEIMER COHEN

# PREFACE

THE sealing off of the Chinese mainland in 1949 from all but a handful of Westerners brought to an abrupt halt a century-long era of intensive Western activity in the Middle Kingdom. Also, it provided the Western historian with an unusual chance to look backward and try to gain a fuller, more balanced understanding of the complex forces that played such a decisive part in the molding of modern China. One of these forces was the Christian missionary movement. Much has been written about it both by participants and by outsiders. But, with very few exceptions, the quantity of the literature has not been matched by its quality. And, even in the exceptions, there has been a strong tendency to view the history of Christian missions in China as but one phase of the history of Christian missions the world over; an example of this is Kenneth S. Latourette's monumental work, *A History of Christian Missions in China* (1929). The focus, in effect, has been on missions history, not on Chinese history.

With the coming of age of the field of modern Chinese studies in recent years, the inadequacies of this old Western-centered approach have become apparent, and a new approach has been suggested which is more concerned with understanding and evaluating the role played by Christian missions in Chinese history. Noteworthy in this connection is John K. Fairbank's exploratory study, "Patterns behind the Tientsin Massacre" (*Harvard Journal of Asiatic Studies,* 1957). This approach may be profitably applied to various phases of the impact of the missionary movement on modern China. Thus, much remains to be done in appraising the role played by the missionary in the introduction of Western secular thought and material culture, the evolution of modern Chinese education, the transformation of certain traditional Chinese social customs, the development in China of Western medical techniques and standards, and so on. What weight should be given to the missionary's influence in these areas, as compared with the influence in the same areas of other Westerners and of Western-oriented Chinese? How did the Chinese respond to these contributions at different times and among different social groups? During what periods, in what circumstances, and to what extent was there a constructive effect on modern Chinese development? a negative, disruptive effect? The answers to such questions would reveal a great deal about the impact on modern Chinese history of certain aspects of the missionary movement which were *intentionally* promoted by the foreign missionary.

This same basic approach may also be applied to other developments on which the influence exerted by the missionary, although equally significant to the historian, was less conscious and not at all intended. One such development, which has attracted widespread notice among past and present observers of the Chinese scene, was the growth of a violent, uncompromising antiforeignism in nineteenth-century China, and its subsequent embodiment in an equally violent and uncompromising nationalism in the twentieth century. General statements about this complex phenomenon have been made in abundance. The time has come, it would seem, for historians to take a closer look at Chinese antiforeignism — its nature, the forms it took, and the factors that helped to shape its growth. Scholarly considerations aside, the practical value and relevance of such an undertaking for our understanding of present-day Chinese actions and motives is too obvious to require elaboration. The roots of contemporary Chinese xenophobia are long and deep. Moreover, if today Chinese xenophobia is, in a certain sense, the handmaiden of Chinese modernization, during the nineteenth century this same xenophobia acted as a major inhibition on modernization; as such, it must be better understood if we are to gain a fuller appreciation of the slow and painfully reluctant manner by which China responded to the West in those years.

A related phenomenon on which the foreign missionary exerted a significant, though subtler, influence during the closing decades of the nineteenth century was the gradual breakdown and eventual collapse of Chinese political authority. One of the chief causes of this breakdown was the powerlessness of the Chinese government to cope with xenophobia at the grassroots level and its consequent inability to carry out the unequal treaties in the interior with any degree of effectiveness. The breakdown reached critical proportions at the time of the Boxer rebellion, when a group of high provincial officials openly disregarded imperial orders; it culminated in 1912 with the overthrow of the dynasty. Since this decay of centralized power was decisive in the shaping of modern Chinese history, it is imperative that all of the contributory influences be studied.

The present book falls into two parts. In an introductory chapter I have attempted to place the nineteenth-century Chinese reaction to Christianity in historical perspective. The native tradition of anti-Christian thought is viewed within the broader context of traditional Chinese attitudes toward alien systems of thought generally. Extensive translations from the original Chinese are incorporated into this chapter, with a view to introducing the Western reader both to the lore of the Chinese anti-Christian tradition and to the content and flavor of the various types of arguments stemming from it.

The remaining chapters are devoted to an examination of the relationship, over a limited but crucial span of time, between the Christian missionary movement and two of the phenomena outlined above—the growth of Chinese anti-foreignism during the latter part of the nineteenth century and the gradual breakdown of the Chinese government's political authority as a result of its inability to cope with this antiforeignism. My reasons for concentrating on the period from 1860 to 1870 are many and will be made clearer in the ensuing pages. Suffice it to say here that this decade marked a critical turning point in modern Chinese history and in the history of Christianity in China. The year 1860 signaled the beginning of a last major effort, on the part of a dynasty seriously shaken by internal revolt, to come to terms with the foreigner without sacrificing any of the essentials of Chinese tradition and, at the same time, regain popular support. The signing in the same year of the Treaties of Tientsin and the Sino-French Convention of Peking enabled the foreign missionary, for the first time in over a century, to reside and preach legally in the Chinese interior. This new circumstance, coupled with many others, created serious problems for the Chinese—problems which had a debilitating and in some cases an altogether paralyzing effect on the power of the Chinese government. The government wrestled with these problems valiantly throughout the 1860's. But the Tientsin Massacre of June 1870 made it abundantly and tragically clear that, in the end, the government could not surmount them. The Massacre and its aftermath have therefore been taken as a fitting terminal point to my investigations.

A word should be said here about the nature of the materials used in this study and the approach adopted in dealing with them. Most of these materials center on what the Chinese call *chiao-an*. This is a general term denoting anti-Christian outbreaks, along with the whole gamut of legal cases and other difficulties involving Christian subjects and foreign missionaries. It is translated here as "missionary cases," with the implicit understanding that missionaries themselves were not always directly involved in *chiao-an*. Some missionary cases were of minor importance; others had international repercussions. The immediate causes behind them were complex, and the varied circumstances of time, place, and personality under which they took place offer little solace to the historian, ever in search of simple patterns. Nevertheless, looking at this same situation from another vantage point, one is struck by the bare fact that so many missionary cases did occur. Is it not highly probable that this profusion of incidents was indicative of certain general problems which followed in the wake of the missionary's bold intrusion into the Chinese interior? Or, put in another way, might it not be legitimate to view the particular incidents as discrete and transitory reflections of a widespread and growing undercurrent of tension in Chinese society after 1860? In this book an effort will be made to approach the missionary cases of the 1860's from two standpoints. On the one hand, they will be viewed in more or less chronological sequence, so that full justice may be done to the dramatic build-up of Sino-foreign tension over the decade. At the same time, the cases will be studied within an analytical framework, so that the problems which they brought into focus (and in some instances fostered) may be better understood. For obvious reasons, detailed treatment cannot be given to all the missionary cases which took place during the 1860's, or even to all the "serious" ones. Moreover, since the seriousness of a case was not necessarily commensurate with its significance, sometimes I have dealt with less serious cases quite fully, treating more serious ones (occasionally involving loss of life) only in passing.

March 1963                                                P.A.C.
Ann Arbor, Michigan

# ACKNOWLEDGMENTS

THIS study began as a seminar paper a few years back. It then grew into a dissertation and finally, after several revisions, reached its present form. Throughout each of these stages I have been immeasurably indebted to my teacher at Harvard University, Professor John K. Fairbank.

At an early point the manuscript was read, in part or in its entirety, by Professors Benjamin I. Schwartz, Mary C. Wright, and Lloyd Eastman, all of whom were very helpful in their comments. Others who assisted me in a variety of ways were Professor Lien-sheng Yang, Professor Kwang-Ching Liu, Mr. Arthur A. Cohen, Father Fang Hao, Professor Sasaki Masaya, and Mr. Michael Wai-mai Lau. To these individuals also I am extremely grateful.

Since the manuscript in its preliminary form was based extensively on materials in the Chinese collection at Harvard, I owe a special debt of gratitude to the assembler and director of that fine collection, Dr. K'ai-ming Ch'iu. At a later stage I had the good fortune to be able to make use of several important archival collections abroad. In this connection, I should like to express my indebtedness to Professors Kuo T'ing-i and Chang Kuei-yung of the Institute of Modern History, Academia Sinica (Taipei), for granting me free access to the Tsungli Yamen archives, and to Messrs. Wang Erh-min and Lü Shih-ch'iang for expediting my use of the archives. I should also like to thank the people in charge of the archives at the Public Record Office (London) and the Quai d'Orsay (Paris) for making pertinent diplomatic correspondence available to me with a minimum of red tape.

Parts of Chapters 1 and 10 were originally published in *The Journal of Asian Studies*. I wish to thank the editor, Rhoads Murphy, for permission to use this material here.

It takes many persons to see a book through to completion, and, although some of them are not mentioned here, I hope that they will not take this as a sign of ingratitude on my part. One who deserves special recognition is my wife who, in addition to performing many of the more unpleasant tasks associated with the making of a book, has at all times been both my severest critic and the most generous source of encouragement. It is to her that the book is dedicated.

# CONTENTS

# ILLUSTRATIONS

*following p. 140*

Title page of the 1871 edition of the *Pi-hsieh chi-shih* (A record of facts to ward off heterodoxy).

Title page of the *Pi-hsieh shih-lu* (A true record to ward off heterodoxy).

T'ien Hsing-shu (1837–1877). The photograph is taken from Ling T'i-an, *Hsien-T'ung Kuei-chou chün-shih shih*, ts'e 1, p. 12.

Seven anti-Christian posters circulated in China during the late nineteenth century. The posters are taken from *Chin-tsun sheng-yü pi-hsieh ch'üan-t'u* (Heresy exposed in respectful obedience to the Sacred Edict: A complete picture gallery); this pamphlet was reproduced in *The Cause of the Riots in the Yangtse Valley: A "Complete Picture Gallery"* (Hankow, 1891).

# I
# THE ANTI-CHRISTIAN
# TRADITION

But are we not much superior to them? Are we not more manly, more intelligent, more skilful, more humane, more civilised, nay, are we not more estimable in every way? Yes, according to our way of thinking. No, emphatically no, according to theirs.

Griffith John, China missionary, *1869*

The people of the world are bigoted and unenlightened. Invariably they regard what is like them as right and what is different from them as wrong, resulting in mutual recrimination and a state of near enmity. They do not realize that the types of humanity are not uniform and that their customs also are not one, that it is not only impossible to force people to become different but also impossible to force them to become alike.

The Yung-cheng Emperor, *1727*

# CHAPTER 1

# THE ANTI-CHRISTIAN
# TRADITION IN
# CHINESE THOUGHT

IT IS a fact of singular note that, in the nineteenth century, the vast majority of the educated classes of China either passively or actively rejected Christianity. Passively, they did so by remaining coldly indifferent to Christianity's message; the percentage of officials and literati who embraced the foreign religion was infinitesimally small. Actively, they expressed their hostility by writing and disseminating inflammatory anti-Christian literature; creating countless stumbling blocks for the Christian missionary; issuing threats of retaliation against any who dared enter the religion or have dealings with its foreign transmitters; and by the direct instigation of and participation in anti-Christian riots.

The extent of this anti-Christian activity is suggested by the situation in the 1860's. At one time or another during this decade vast sections of China appear to have been flooded with anti-Christian propaganda. Moreover, although the exact number of cases of open or veiled opposition to the missionary and convert will never be known, one Chinese bibliography lists over fifty incidents important enough to require top-level diplomatic treatment,[1] and the record indicates that the number of less important cases, which were settled locally, may well have run into the thousands. (Thus, an east Chihli Catholic missionary wrote in the mid-

1860's: "More than two hundred minor local persecutions . . . came this year to hamper the movement of conversions." [2]) Naturally we have no way of proving that the great majority of these cases were directly or indirectly inspired by the educated classes. But the evidence available and the almost unanimous opinion of contemporary foreigners both tend to support such an assumption.

In part, of course, this intense hostility to Christianity arose in response to peculiarly nineteenth-century circumstances: Christian influence on the ideology of the Taiping rebellion (a revolt which devastated large sections of China from 1851 to 1864 and came perilously close to toppling the Ch'ing dynasty), Christianity's identification with the use of foreign force and gunboat diplomacy after 1840, the interference of some missionaries in Chinese administrative affairs, and so forth. It is seldom recognized, however, that above and beyond these immediate factors there was a *tradition* of anti-Christian thought in China,[3] going back at least as far as the early seventeenth century. Its literature was abundant. And it proved to be a major influence on the anti-Christian attitudes of the nineteenth-century Chinese intellectual.

## THE HETERODOXY-ORTHODOXY ANTITHESIS IN CHINA

Before examining this tradition it may be well to place it in historical context. The Chinese, long before the coming of Christianity, possessed a well-established cultural category which they used to label teachings and practices that deviated from a particular ideal or norm. This category has been designated by such words as *i-tuan*, *tso-tao*, *hsieh*. All these terms share a common meaning which may be roughly (if somewhat ambiguously) rendered "different from the way of the sages." *Hsieh,* the most colloquial and richest in meaning of the three, in some contexts has additional overtones of a supernatural, uncanny power which gains ascendancy over the individual and leads him astray; in other contexts it plainly refers to the gamut of excesses and irregularities in the sexual sphere. *I-tuan, tso-tao,* and *hsieh* are frequently used in opposition to *cheng,* meaning "right, straight," or *cheng-tao,* "the right (or straight) path." In the past, Western writers, notably J. J. M. de Groot, have used the words "heterodoxy" and "orthodoxy" to characterize this antithesis. Although these words, for the Westerner, have certain connotations derived from our own history, etymologically and semantically they are similar enough to the Chinese terminology to justify their continued use.

*I-tuan, hsieh,* and *tso-tao* were all used well before the Christian era, the first two terms going back at least as far as the time of Confucius (551–479 B.C.).[4] Naturally their precise connotations varied, depending upon who used them, when they were used, and what they were used against. But whether employed by Mencius in the fourth century B.C. to characterize the schools of Yang Chu and Mo Ti or by Han Yü in the ninth century A.D. to vilify Buddhism, the basic meaning of the words seems to have remained intact. Invariably they were used by the upholder of one philosophical or cultural norm to stigmatize the beliefs and practices of those who professed allegiance to other and divergent norms. Presumably they could be used by Buddhists against Confucians or by Taoists against Buddhists. But in actual practice they seem to have been employed most frequently by Confucians, either to attack an existing social order with which they were dissatisfied (as in the case of Mencius and Han Yü) or to defend the status quo against all teachings which threatened to subvert it (as in the case of orthodox Neo-Confucians of the Ming and

Ch'ing periods). The orthodoxy defended could, in other words, be an orthodoxy which existed in the form of an un-realized ideal only or one which had an objective basis in fact. But the semantic basis underlying the application of the terminology remained constant.

There was also a considerable degree of continuity in the specific arguments used to support these labels. It may be instructive, therefore, before launching upon our examination of the anti-Christian tradition, to survey briefly some of the arguments used against another foreign religion — Buddhism — by those who regarded it as heterodox.

The Indian religion entered China shortly before or after the beginning of the Christian era and grew rapidly in influence from the third century A.D., reaching its apogee in the T'ang dynasty (A.D. 618–906). It was frequently supported by the state during this period and enjoyed a large following among all classes of Chinese. Nevertheless, even at the height of its power, Buddhism was confronted with detractors. These men could not, as did some later Confucians, brush the religion aside with the disdainful epithet of "heterodoxy" and leave it at that. It was not, after all, until the Sung period (A.D. 960–1279) that a genuine Confucian orthodoxy became firmly established in China. On the contrary, the arguments of the early anti-Buddhists were hammered out in the thick of ideological combat. And, as a result, they laid much of the groundwork for future anti-heterodox thought in general and anti-Christian thought in particular.

One of the earlier anti-Buddhist thinkers whose writings have been preserved was Hsün Chi (d. 547), who wrote during the period of the Southern Dynasties (420–589).[5] Hsün Chi's main thesis was that Buddhism undermined the imperial state. But before he was through he had forged a whole arsenal of weapons with which to attack the foreign religion. In the political sphere, he claimed that Buddhism subverted the power of the throne, usurped imperial authority and ceremonial, and destroyed the Confucian concept of government by discouraging the members of society from performing their proper functions. In the realm of economics, Buddhism did disservice to the state by withdrawing men and women from worthwhile occupations and squandering wealth on unproductive activities. Because of its neglect of the natural human relations, moreover, the Indian religion was detrimental to social harmony and, because of its advocacy of celibacy, was harmful to the family. Finally, in the realm of morals, Hsün judged the Buddhists to be guilty of hypocrisy, avarice, infanticide, and sexual perversion. Hsün Chi concluded that as a result of all these evils a dynasty which wedded itself to the religion of the Buddha was destined to be short-lived. In his own words: "The [Liu] Sung and [Southern] Ch'i were two dynasties which esteemed the Buddha, honored the monks, changed their national customs, and converted their temples. But the Buddha was evil and the monks deceitful. They were intent on falsehood, they practiced abortion and murdered their offspring, they indulged in wanton promiscuity, and brought confusion to the teachings. Therefore they caused the Sung and Ch'i dynasties to be crushed and destroyed." [6]

During the Sui-T'ang (581–906), Buddhism maintained its firm grip on the Chinese masses and on many of the literati. But at the same time, Confucianism slowly began to reassert itself as a state ideology. Emperor Yang of the Sui took a first step in encouraging this tendency when, immediately after usurping the throne in 605, he set up an examination system with a pronounced Confucian bias. A further impetus was provided in the early T'ang with the establishment by the gentry of schools having a Confucian curriculum. Against this background, the scholar-official Fu

I (555–639) presented in 621 and 624 two groups of proposals for the suppression of Buddhism. In a sense, there was little in Fu I's arguments that had not been said before. But, in addition to elaborating upon certain of Hsün Chi's theses (such as the political and economic liabilities of Buddhism), his thinking shows some subtle shifts in emphasis. Whereas Hsün had focused on the political subversion of the Buddhist elite — the monks and nuns — Fu I seems to have been more sensitive to the general social disintegration which resulted from Buddhism's influence over the masses. The people, he felt, had been terrorized and deluded by the Buddhist doctrines of heaven and hell and of retribution beyond the grave, with the consequence that, feeling themselves assured of happiness after death, they had become contemptuous of temporal authority.

Another change in stress from the earlier arguments of Hsün Chi may be found in Fu I's virulent xenophobia. Chinese thought and institutions were, in his eyes, incomparably superior to those of India, while Buddhism, which he disparaged as "the barbarian miasma," could not even lay claim to a measure of originality, being "nought but magicians' lore which mean and depraved people have ornamented by copying the profound words of Chuang-tzu and Lao-tzu." [7]

The Sinocentric and rationalistic tendencies so marked in Fu I's thought came to the fore again in the often quoted representation against Buddhism of Fu I's later-day fellow in arms, Han Yü (768–824). Han Yü's famous memorial was written in 819 as a protest against the honor paid by the emperor to a religious relic, the finger bone of the Buddha. It is significant less for the comprehensiveness or novelty of its argumentation than for its literary quality and timeliness. For the great influence of Buddhism over the intellectual classes of China waned rapidly from the ninth century onward. And a new Confucian orthodoxy, marked from the outset by a strong undercurrent of antiforeignism, emerged and flourished, with but brief intervals of interruption, until the early years of the present century.[8] Han Yü, widely regarded as a patron saint of the new orthodoxy, voiced sentiments against Buddhism which later achieved broad acceptance among the educated classes. His first argument was that in ancient times, before Buddhism's penetration into China, the empire had been at peace, sovereigns had reigned for long periods, and the people had been contented and happy. With the religion's entry during the reign of Emperor Ming of the Han, however, war and disorder followed in rapid succession, and dynasties became short-lived. Han Yü then voiced the fear, suggested earlier by Fu I, that the stupid and easily deceived masses, upon seeing the tribute paid to the Buddha by the emperor, would flock to the monasteries, upsetting the normal order and destroying the age-old customs. Following this he portrayed the barbarian origin of the Buddha, whose language and clothing differed from those of the Chinese and who failed to abide by the relationships between prince and subject, father and son. In terms of later antiheterodox thought, it is Han Yü's rationalistic, antimystical outlook which especially strikes the reader. This is seen in his acknowledgment of Confucius' dictum, "Worship the spirits, but keep them away." It is superbly expressed in the question which he addressed to the emperor regarding the Buddha bone: "How could a sublime intelligence like yours consent to believe in this sort of thing?" [9]

During the Sung and succeeding dynasties, Buddhism, though losing its grip over the lettered classes of China, remained a powerful force in the lives of the uneducated masses. "The modern period," in effect, "saw a striking cleavage between the rational ethic of the elite and the religious ethos of the peasantry." [10] Since certain strands of the religion remained a major component in the ideologies of rebel movements and the rites of secret societies, its practice and propagation were clearly circumscribed by dynastic laws. These laws, as seen in the Ming (1368–1644) and Ch'ing (1644–1912) codes, were not overtly directed against Buddhism, being grouped under the general title, "Prohibition of the sorcery of wizards and witches" (*Chin-chih shih-wu hsieh-shu*). But the practices which they condemned were ones which had commonly come to be associated with Buddhism in its popular forms. Activities such as incanting charms, scribbling characters in sand in order to invoke supernatural assistance, burning incense, concealing pictures and images, fabricating canonical writings, gathering disciples, holding meetings at night, deceiving the people under the guise of cultivating good works, and joining such Buddhist-tinged sects as the White Lotus Society and the White Cloud School were all clearly marked as heterodox and were punishable with death in the case of principal offenders.[11] The political, as opposed to religious, concern of these statutes is self-evident. It is further brought out by the injunction that leniency be applied to "those good subjects who, while attending to their occupations, chant the Buddhist sutras and abstain from meat in order to invoke blessedness, but who do not study or practice heterodox teachings, fabricate and transmit to their disciples canonical writings and charms, take up collections, and deceive the masses." [12]

Unquestionably the most widely publicized document in the history of antiheterodox thought in China was a sermon composed by the Yung-cheng Emperor (r. 1723–1735), taking as its text part of the so-called *Sacred Edict*. The *Sacred Edict* (*Sheng-yü*) consisted originally of sixteen brief maxims set down by the K'ang-hsi Emperor (r. 1662–1722) in 1670.

Upon the death of K'ang-hsi they were amplified by his son and successor, Yung-cheng, and published (in 1724) for popular edification under the title *Sheng-yü kuang-hsün*.[13] Examination officials even in the nineteenth century occasionally asked candidates to write them down from memory. Students in Chinese schools studied them. And twice monthly the local officials and gentry throughout the empire were supposed to expound them to the illiterate populace.[14] There were few Chinese, therefore, who were not at least familiar with the general contents of these maxims.

The sermon which concerns us directly is based on the seventh maxim entitled, "Destroy heterodox doctrines in order to render honor to orthodox learning" (*Ch'u i-tuan i ch'ung cheng-hsüeh*). The argument is grounded almost entirely on two philosophical principles emphasized by Mencius and later incorporated into the Neo-Confucian philosophy of the Sung. They are, first, that man's nature is inherently good and, second, that his conduct in life is determined not only by his nature but by external influences as well. All too easily the purity of his original condition is besmirched by his environment and he is led astray. The practical problem which results from these principles is one of controlling man's environment in such a way that the turbid influences which run counter to the primal purity of mind and heart are reduced to a minimum, while, conversely, the pure and the good are maximized. Mencius had dealt with this problem chiefly by stressing the twin influences of the virtuous ruler and the good education, and the Yung-cheng Emperor faithfully attempts to represent both.

First he points out that the way of the early kings and the achievements of the sages of the past were rooted entirely in orthodox learning. The tenets of heterodox thought, by contrast, bring fear into the hearts of men and disorder into the world, eventually eating away at the material well-being of the people. From ancient times, Yung-cheng continues, three teachings have been handed down in China — Confucianism, Buddhism, and Taoism. The last two are obviously inferior to the first, dealing as they do exclusively with the individual heart and spirit. But they are not to be spurned on this count alone. The main reason for rejecting them is that they provide a haven for all the bad classes of society: rabble-rousers, scum, "shiftless ne'er-do-wells." These classes pervert the original tendencies of Buddhism and Taoism (which might in themselves be tolerable), and "seize upon situations involving calamity and good fortune to peddle their foolish nonsense. At first, they only entice away the wealth [of others] with the object of fattening themselves. Then, gradually, it reaches the point where they hold meetings for the burning of incense at which men and women mingle together promiscuously, and peasants and artisans forsake their occupations to meet with these folk who babble so about strange things. Finally, what is worst of all, rebellious, pernicious people furtively enter their midst, forming cliques and contracting alliances."

After reeling off this indictment of heterodox sects, the emperor then singles out as illustrations the White Lotus and Wen-hsiang societies (they were apparently closely related) and the Western religion of the Lord of Heaven (t'ien-chu), that is, Catholicism. He also makes it clear that deceiving the masses by these heterodox ways is not pardoned by the law, the very intention of which is "to dispel heterodoxy and elevate orthodoxy." Finally, toward the end of the piece, Yung-cheng re-emphasizes the basic harm effected by such tenets and practices: "The injuries worked by natural calamities and by brigands go no further than the body, but the injuries resulting from heterodox principles extend to man's mind. The mind, in its original condition, is wholly orthodox. If [you people] will exercise full mastery over [your minds] you naturally will not be led astray, your character and conduct will be upright, and no heterodoxy will ever be able to overcome orthodoxy." [15]

Although the emphasis thus far has been placed on Buddhism, the label of heterodoxy could be, and indeed was, applied to almost any teaching or practice that departed from the orthodox path. In no place is this better indicated than in a little known edict issued by the same Yung-cheng Emperor in 1727. It is a remarkable document, not only for the forthright manner in which it comes to grips with the problem of defining heterodoxy, but also for the unusual degree of cultural relativism that it displays. In the context of the present study it is significant enough to be quoted at some length:

Hitherto Buddhists and Taoists have maligned the religion of the West, and the Westerners have heaped discredit upon the falsehoods of Taoism and Buddhism. Each has slandered the other, calling attention to its heterodox ways. According to both of these views, everything which is in agreement with "me" is the orthodox way, while everything which differs from "me" is heterodox. This is hardly what the sages meant by "heterodoxy." Confucius said, "To apply oneself to the study of heterodox ways [i-tuan] is indeed harmful." But did Confucius thereby castigate all [teachings and practices] which differed from his own as heterodox?

All teachings established by China or by foreign countries which are put into operation without regard for the truth and which are injurious to the ways of the world and to the sentiments of man are heterodox. Take for example the Westerners' worship of the Lord of Heaven. Now, heaven, by means of yin and yang and the five elements, transforms and produces all things. Therefore it is said that all things have their origin in heaven. It, then, is the "Lord" — the controlling power. From ancient times on have there ever been people who did not know to revere heaven, or teachings which did not do so? What difference is there in the case of the Western religion's revering of heaven? [The difference emerges] when they say that heaven came down to earth and transformed itself into a man in order to save mankind. It appears that these farfetched words merely use the name of heaven in order to beguile the rash and ignorant into following their religion. This then is the heterodoxy of the West . . .

The Buddhists originally regarded purity and nonaction as fundamental, and the search for understanding of one's Buddha-nature as the task to which one should apply oneself. On this basis their activities of self-cultivation and self-fulfillment are unparalleled in virtue. But when they say that one should ignore the obligations existing between ruler and minister and disregard those between father and son, abandon the proper human relationships and return to Nirvana; when, moreover, some of them talk wildly about misery and bliss in order to agitate and deceive the ordinary people, and avail themselves of Buddhism to cover up their treachery — this then becomes the heterodoxy within Buddhism.

The Confucians guard the way of the early kings and study the writings of the sages and paragons of virtue. All of them are held up as models by the masses. When, however, they use their [knowledge of] literature to grasp for the accouterments of honor, and regard their [mastery of] the examination curriculum as a means of spreading their reputations; when they rely on rumors and heterodox doctrines to get the ear of the people, and fashion captivating stories and lewd songs in order to agitate their minds — this then becomes the heterodoxy within Confucianism . . .

"When the Master was very ill, Tzu Lu asked leave to perform the rites. The Master said, My expiatory rites began long ago." [16] Now, the rites which Tzu Lu [wished to perform] were heterodox, whereas the rites [performed by] Confucius constituted the orthodox way. In the very same thing, right and wrong, heterodoxy and orthodoxy, were differentiated — right and orthodox constituting the orthodox way, and wrong and unorthodox making up the way of heterodoxy. Hence what they were talking about consisted only in the gap between right and wrong, heterodox and orthodox; it had nothing to do with the subjective differences existing among men.

The Yung-cheng Emperor closed with a general summation of his thesis that the people of the world tended to make judgments not on the basis of an objective standard of right and wrong, but on the basis of their personal beliefs. Each group had its excellences and each its shortcomings. "If they would but preserve the former and abandon the latter . . . they could be at peace with each other and everyone would perform his [proper] function." Only at this point would they "obtain wise emperors and virtuous kings, and, clearly comprehending the way which is all-embracing, achieve a world of universal harmony." [17]

From this survey, certain general features of the Chinese notion of heterodoxy and of the antiheterodox tradition can be tentatively identified. In the first place, the meaning and content of the term was influenced to no small degree by historical context and personal bias. Even the Yung-cheng Emperor's attempt to impart an objectively valid meaning to "heterodoxy" was marred by the very subjectivism which he recognized and decried. For, although ostensibly it was his view that the element of good in all teachings was to be preserved, in the last analysis his standards for measuring this good conformed to the Chinese predilections of his own time and were suspiciously Confucian in tone.

Again, the arguments employed against heterodoxy were profoundly affected by the strength and self-confidence of the reigning orthodoxy and, conversely, by the specific character of the enemy and its position in Chinese society. Thus, in the case of Buddhism, the argument based on xenophobia, which formed such an important part of the polemics of Fu I and Han Yü, became increasingly ineffective as Buddhism was domesticated. Moreover, the economic argument so forcefully wielded against the Indian religion in its heyday diminished considerably in importance with the decline in Buddhism's economic strength.

Nevertheless, there were significant continuities in the antiheterodox tradition, at least insofar as this tradition was directed against Buddhism. One was the belief that heterodox teachings and practices fostered social unrest. When men and women mingled indiscriminately at public gatherings, and peasants and artisans were enticed away from their work by the seductive babbling and obscene literature of religious impostors, normal human bonds were shattered and the harmony of the social order was disrupted. Hsün Chi's charges of deceit, abortion, and adultery were thus echoed more than a millennium later by a nineteenth-century Kansu magistrate, Huang Yü-pien, who accused the Buddhists of sexual promiscuity and avarice;[18] and Kiangsu governor Ting Jih-ch'ang's (1823–1882) statement in the 1860's, that "we may fairly attribute the rebellions of late years to the impure literature now prevalent," [19] immediately brings to mind the Yung-cheng Emperor's injunction against "captivating stories and lewd songs."

Another continuity in the antiheterodox tradition was its rationalistic or skeptic bias. The authors of the Ming and Ch'ing laws against heterodoxy, continuing in the footsteps of Fu I and Han Yü, showed themselves to be deeply apprehensive of such popular practices as invoking spirits, incanting charms, burning incense. Popular beliefs such as that of rewards and punishments beyond the grave were equally suspect.[20] This rationalistic bias continued unabated in the nineteenth century, and the *P'o-hsieh hsiang-pien* (A detailed refutation of heterodoxy) of the above-mentioned Huang Yü-pien is a case in point. Following an introductory section in which he quotes the sixteen maxims of K'ang-hsi and the provisions of the Ch'ing code against heterodoxy, Huang details a whole series of heterodox beliefs and practices drawn chiefly from works of Buddhist-tinged sects. Addressing himself in particular to the gentry, who he hopes will inform the masses of the book, Huang is at great pains to point out that whatever strength heterodox groups have is derived from their ability to deceive the ignorant commoner. Tenets which are essentially heterodox are passed off as orthodox, while the propagation of good is merely used as a camouflage for evil-doing.[21] Huang's skepticism is dramatized by his punctuation of each section with the closing refrain, "this is not to be believed [or trusted in]" (pu k'o hsin yeh).

Closely related to the above two points, and more important perhaps than either, was the abiding notion that heterodoxy was a political threat. This aspect was, quite naturally, given greatest stress in imperial edicts and dynastic laws, but, as shown by the arguments of Hsün Chi, Fu I, and Han Yü, it also occupied an important place in writings of a less authoritative nature. If the chief interest and aim of a dynasty was its continued existence, its greatest source of anxiety was bound to spring from those groups or activities which most threatened it. Since the rebellions which jeopardized the political lives of dynasties were so regularly associated with heterodox teachings, what could be more logical than to ban these teachings and place the severest limitations on all varieties of popular organization?[22] Conversely, the Neo-Confucian devotee who was eager to express his loyalty to the reigning house could do so in no better way than by indoctrinating the commoners within his sphere of influence with orthodox tenets. Such indoctrination was regarded, at least during the Ming and Ch'ing periods, as a major instrument of political control.

Now that we have a somewhat clearer notion of the variety of connotations implied in the Chinese terminology for "heterodoxy," it may be fruitful to consider the comparative functioning of the heterodoxy-orthodoxy antithesis in China and in the West. From a purely semantic standpoint, the resemblance is quite close, since the antithesis is used in both cultures to characterize a polarity between a norm and certain departures from that norm. Again, etymologically, the evolution of the two sets of terms exhibits a striking parallelism. "Orthodoxy" stems from the Greek *orthos* signifying "right, straight" (primary meanings of *cheng*) and *doxa* signifying "opinion," while "heterodoxy," also from the Greek, has the literal meaning of "other opinion" — a close approximation to *i-tuan* ("other [or different] strand").[23]

The historical settings in which the antithesis operated were very different in the two cases, however, and led to certain concrete differences in the use of the terms. (That this need not be so, given a suitable historical context, was clearly indicated by Hsü Chi-yü when, in referring to the Protestant Reformation, he remarked: "[The religion of Jesus (Protestantism)] styled itself the orthodox religion [*cheng-chiao*] and reviled the religion of the Lord of Heaven [Catholicism] as heterodox [*i-tuan hsieh-shuo*]."[24])

In the first place, although there have certainly been exceptions, the concept of heterodoxy in Western history has tended to have strong religious-theological connotations, while in Chinese history, *i-tuan*, *hsieh*, and so on, were always applied very broadly and were never limited to any particular sphere, much less the theological.* This contrast can be carried a step further. In the West the antithesis has generally been used to denote two variants within a single system of religious dogma, the Roman Catholic,

---

* The most obvious exception to this generalization was perhaps the Greek case in which the term "heterodoxy" was broadly applied to all peoples who refused to be assimilated into the Greek cultural order. It must of course also be recognized that, although the notion of heterodoxy within the order of Christendom was rooted in religious-theological preconceptions, its ramifications spread into many other spheres.

for example, regarding himself as orthodox in contrast with the Protestant. Religions completely outside of the Judeo-Christian (and in some cases, Moslem) complex have not been treated as heterodox but, at least from the Christian standpoint, as heathen or pagan. Moreover, particularly after the Middle Ages, wholly nonreligious categories of thought — political, social, philosophical — have had no definable relationship whatever to the orthodoxy-heterodoxy antithesis in the religious sphere. One strand of socialist thought might be regarded as heterodox by the proponent of another. But from the religious point of view, both are quite simply regarded as secular.

When we turn to China, the contrast is immediately apparent. An "orthodox" Confucian could indeed stigmatize the thought of an "unorthodox" Confucian as *hsieh*. But he was just as apt to go farther afield and apply the label to Buddhism, Taoism, Christianity, or any form of activity subversive of the political and social status quo. The Chinese application of the category was in effect broader on all fronts than its Western counterpart, extending beyond the realm of one thought system into other and completely different systems, and extending beyond the realm of thought altogether into the sphere of action. The reasons for this broadness of application are, I think, several. First, as postmedieval Western society became more and more pluralistic in nature, an increasing number of heterodoxies developed, each referring back to a different orthodoxy. In Sung and post-Sung Chinese society, on the other hand, as Confucianism to an ever-increasing extent became the only orthodoxy worthy of the name, *all* departures from the Confucian norm became heterodox.

Second, Confucianism, whether in power or out, always looked upon itself as a state ideology as well as a personal ethic. Thus it was just as sensitive to incursions in the political sphere as it was to threats of a purely doctrinal nature, and it could with perfect consistency characterize suspicious practices as heterodox as well as noxious beliefs.

Finally, the Chinese world view was an all-encompassing one, with China — the seat of all civilization — situated in the center and all other peoples on the periphery. When other countries submitted to this world view and dutifully carried out their obligations toward China, they were graciously permitted to retain their strange ways and harmony prevailed. But when one or another of these peoples became "rebellious" and attempted not merely to carry on their own way of life, but to superimpose it on the Chinese way, friction developed, and a new heterodoxy-orthodoxy orientation emerged, centered on intercultural lines. Thus, when Buddhism was introduced from India, Taoists and Confucians became codefenders of Chinese (as opposed to Confucian) orthodoxy. And when the Western religion, Christianity, made its first concentrated effort to penetrate the Middle Kingdom more than a millennium later, *Chinese* thought became orthodox vis-à-vis the heterodoxy of the new *foreign* invader. The Chinese categories for heterodoxy and orthodoxy were therefore relative, in addition to being broad. Just as Jesus could be regarded as heterodox in relation to the Judaism of his day and yet later become the founder of a new orthodoxy, Chinese Buddhism could be, at one and the same time, heterodox with respect to Confucianism and orthodox in contrast with Christianity.

CHRISTIANITY AS HETERODOXY: THE
SEVENTEENTH AND EIGHTEENTH CENTURIES

After earlier efforts about which we know little, but which ultimately proved abortive, Christianity was again established in China in the late sixteenth century,[25] but it was labeled almost immediately with the stigma of "heterodox." Like Buddhism earlier, its foreign origin, its fundamental nonadherence to Confucianism (particularly in its Sung and post-Sung guise), the miraculous content of some of its doctrines, and its suspected motives of political subversion all combined to cast it in this undesirable role. Although this did not prevent the religion from making considerable headway at times, its general and legal position was rarely secure. The edict of toleration granted by the K'ang-hsi Emperor in 1692 was abruptly withdrawn by the Yung-cheng Emperor in 1724, and it was not until the treaties of 1858–1860 that the propagation of Christianity in the Chinese interior was once again authorized. Before, as well as during, the nineteenth century, moreover, severe persecutions were frequently carried out against the religion at the local level and, in some instances, throughout the empire.[26] And even when Christianity escaped the active hostility of the government, it was always subject to the disapprobation of the Chinese author — official and nonofficial alike. It is to the writings of these individuals that the remainder of this chapter will be addressed.

To the best of my knowledge, the earliest work of importance to be directed exclusively against Christianity and other aspects of Western civilization was the *P'o-hsieh chi* (An anthology of writings exposing heterodoxy).[27] This work, compiled by a Chekiang literatus, Hsü Ch'ang-chih, and with a preface dated 1640, contains almost sixty essays, memorials, and other short pieces written by some forty Buddhist and Confucian scholars of the late Ming. The intention of the work, as stated by its compiler in a brief introduction, is to uphold orthodoxy by refuting heterodoxy. Since it is a large book and contains enough material on early Sino-Western intellectual conflict to merit monographic treatment,[28] a brief résumé of some if its more prominent arguments is all that can be attempted here.

As in some of the early anti-Buddhist writings, the argument based on reason and common sense is employed in the *P'o-hsieh chi* with considerable effectiveness. If, one writer asks, God is really as good and as powerful as the Catholics claim, how could He permit Adam and Eve to commit a sin so contaminating that it was transmitted to all subsequent generations? If even man, in his weakness and impotence, can to some extent guard against evil, should not an all-powerful God have been capable of rooting out this evil altogether? [29]

Another form of argument, based more on skepticism than on reason per se, is the argument which demands "proof." One writer in the *P'o-hsieh chi* remarks: "[The Catholics] chide the Buddhists and Taoists on the ground that their statements about attaining Buddhahood are obscure and cannot be investigated, and their doctrines of cause and effect and transmigration are vague and unsusceptible of proof. Is [the Catholic doctrine] that those who worship God are assured of going to heaven . . . while those who reject God are certain to enter hell . . . alone capable of being examined into and proven?" [30] In addition to the skepticism suggested in this statement, one detects a curious note of defensiveness regarding the teachings of Buddhism and Taoism. This is confirmed a few lines later: "The *Tao-te ching* of the Taoists and the Buddhists' *Yin-kuo ching* . . . have always taught men to serve their rulers loyally and their parents filially, to revere the gods in the spiritual sphere and to love others in the temporal. These [precepts], moreover, complement Confucianism. There is nothing in them comparable to the statements of the Catholics, which would have our emperors and princes do away with all sacrificial rites and our gentry and people cast off all ceremonies pertaining to ancestor worship." [31]

This phenomenon of comparing Catholicism unfavorably with Buddhism and Taoism is one which is seen again and again in the *P'o-hsieh chi* and other anti-Christian works of the Ming and Ch'ing. On doctrinal grounds alone, the orthodox intellectual of these periods frequently tended to reject Buddhism and Taoism as heterodox or, at least, to place them in a lower position vis-à-vis Confucianism. But when it came to defending Chinese culture as a whole, the two traditional teachings were, more often than not, drawn protectively to the bosom of orthodoxy in an attempt to marshal all available forces against the new foreign invader.[32]

From the point of view of a modern Westerner (but not necessarily a seventeenth-century Chinese), the least convincing mode of reasoning in the *P'o-hsieh chi* is the argument which rests its case on established authority. A Fukienese contributor to the work illustrates this approach clearly: "In the open [the Catholics] publicize their doctrines in such a way that they do not seem to be greatly at odds with the teachings of our Confucian sages, Yao, Shun, the Duke of Chou, and Confucius. But in fact they secretly set forth their own religion, rejecting Buddhism, reviling Taoism, repressing Confucianism, and pronouncing their doctrines to be superior to those of Yao, Shun, the Duke of Chou, and Confucius." The same writer points out, a page later, that in the Catholic religion it is not necessary to perform sacrifices to one's ancestors and deceased parents. He then remarks: "What sense does this make? The *Book of Rites* states: 'The son of heaven sacrifices to heaven and earth, the feudal lords sacrifice to the hills and streams within their fiefs . . .'" [33] In such cases the author is clearly less interested in exposing possible contradictions *within* Christianity than he is in showing where Christian beliefs run counter to established Chinese beliefs. To invalidate Christianity, therefore, it is only necessary for him to invoke the Chinese classics.

A final argument of consequence employed against the Catholics in the *P'o-hsieh chi* is the legalistic argument. Here the provisions of the Ming code proscribing praying to heaven by private individuals (presumably to gain divine support for one's evil schemes), the incantation of charms over water, the assembling of crowds in nocturnal gatherings, and such, are pitted against the suspicious practices of the Catholics, demonstrating that the foreign religion could be viewed as heterodox for political as well as doctrinal reasons.[34]

The next great literary outburst against Christianity came from the pen of the early Ch'ing official, Yang Kuanghsien (1597–1669).[35] Yang's reputed violence of temper, his antiforeignism, and his jealousy of the power held in Peking by the prominent Jesuit astronomer, Adam Schall (1591–1666), all combined to make him a self-appointed antagonist of the Western religion. Yang's attacks on Christianity and on the calendar devised by Schall began in 1659. Six years later, during Schall's trial (prompted by Yang's accusations), these attacks were collected and published under the title, *Pu-te-i* (I could not do otherwise). The arguments voiced in this work are the product of an acute, if not entirely dispassionate, mind. Moreover, they indicate that Yang took the trouble to familiarize himself with at least the basic elements of early Christian history and doctrine. For us, however, the importance of the work lies chiefly in the emotional fervor with which it is saturated and in the fact that it was widely disseminated, in somewhat abbreviated form, in the last century.[36] The most pertinent question, then, is that of Yang's later appeal. What was it about his writings that made him the favorite of the nineteenth-century opponents of Christianity?

Central to Yang Kuang-hsien's way of thinking was his ardent xenophobia. He vented this in politics in his crusade against Schall. It was also unleashed in the intellectual sphere against the theories of the Catholic convert, Li Tsu-po (d. 1665). Li, in 1663, had published a pamphlet entitled *T'ien-hsüeh ch'uan-kai* (A summary account of the early worship of God in China), in which he sought to develop certain ideas about the history of the Christian Church in China and the origin of the Chinese race. Man, according to him, had originated in Judea. A branch of this early human family had then migrated to China under a leader whom Li tentatively identified as the legendary Chinese ruler, Fu Hsi. Li maintained that the Christian God had been worshiped in ancient China under the name of T'ien or Shang-ti and that this worship, known as *T'ien-hsüeh,* had been lost in the Chou period and later revived by Matteo Ricci (1552–1610) and other missionaries.[37] It is not hard to imagine Yang Kuang-hsien's response to these views: "Schall's book says that one man and one woman were [created] as the first ancestors of mankind. He was not so bold as to state contemptuously that all the people of the world are the descendants of his religion. According to Li's book, however, our China is nothing but [an offshoot] of Judea; our ancient Chinese rulers, sages, and teachers were but the descendants of a heterodox sect; and our classics and sage teachings, propounded generation after generation, no more than the remnants of a heterodox religion. Are there no limits to foolishness?"

Yang expresses his morbid dislike of foreigners in other ways also. The censor, Hsü Chih-chien, in his preface to Li Tsu-po's book, had accused the Buddhists and Taoists of ignoring the relationships between ruler and subject, father

and son, and had stated that even Confucians were sometimes remiss in their behavior. To this Yang replied:

Alas! What kind of talk is this? The establishments of the
Buddhists and Taoists present offerings to the imperial ancestral tablets, thereby [showing] that they still recognize the relationship between ruler and subject. The Buddhists say that
waiting upon the Pratyeka Buddhas is not comparable to being
filial toward one's parents, thereby [showing] that they still
recognize the relationship between father and son. How much
the more do we Confucians base our teachings on these natural
relationships? But the Lord of Heaven, Jesus, was nailed to
death because He broke His country's laws. This was no case
of recognizing the relationship between ruler and subject. Jesus'
mother, Mary, had a husband called Joseph. But they say that
Jesus was not begotten by His father. Moreover, the people
who take refuge in their religion are not permitted to present
offerings to the ancestral tablets. This is no recognition of the
relationship between father and son.

Yang's enthusiastic vindication of Buddhism and his cultural patriotism are further evinced when he accuses Christian writers of plagiarizing the Buddhist doctrines of
heaven and hell and then, hypocritically, turning around
and attacking the native religion.

Yang Kuang-hsien was, by philosophical conviction, an
orthodox Confucian and appears to have had little real sympathy with Buddhism or Taoism. But when confronted
with the foreign religion, Christianity, these traditional intellectual distinctions became less important to him and all
but collapsed before his emotional commitment to Chinese
culture. In Yang's view, Christianity, even in the seventeenth century, was a real menace to the Chinese way of
life. It was bad enough that the Europeans flouted the age-
old social conventions and elevated their teachings above
those of Confucius. But when they held positions of influence in the capital and roamed at will through all the

provinces, making careful maps of Chinese military installations, was it not high time to sound the bell of warning?

Here, I think, we have a clue to Yang's later appeal. Huang Tsung-hsi (1610–1695), Ku Yen-wu (1613–1682), and other of his contemporaries were convinced that the fall of the Ming dynasty had been occasioned, in large part, by the fact that its intellectuals had lost touch with reality. To combat these ruinous metaphysical tendencies, they immersed themselves in empirical studies. Yang, however, more in the tradition of the early anti-Buddhist thinker, Hsün Chi, ascribed the collapse of the Ming to the relaxation of the laws restricting intercourse with foreigners.[38] Unlike Huang and Ku, his great concern was with the problem of China and the West. Of course, at the time, this was Yang's fantasy. The West was in no position to threaten China, even if it wished to. But the sense of urgency which Yang imparted to the question and the violence of his proposed solution appealed strongly to later Chinese for whom the problem of Western invasion had become a paramount reality. And the name, Yang Kuang-hsien, became, more than any other, associated with the most uncompromising hostility to Christianity and the foreign missionary.

Although it was not until the second half of the nineteenth century that Yang Kuang-hsien found a true disciple, there is no want of references uncomplimentary to Christianity in the intervening period. Chang Yü-shu (1642–1711),[39] the famous compiler of the *P'ei-wen yün-fu* and *K'ang-hsi tzu-tien*, wrote, sometime after 1675, a short essay entitled *Wai-kuo chi* (A record of foreign countries). In it he refers to the teachings of Matteo Ricci and other early missionaries as "ridiculous and unorthodox" and hence not heeded by Confucians. Moreover, feeling that the influence of the foreigners was based solely on their knowl-

edge of geometry, Chang launches into a critical discussion
of the Western calendar, prefacing his remarks with a brief
reference to the charge of heterodoxy leveled against Adam
Schall by Yang Kuang-hsien.[40]

In the *Ming-shih* (History of the Ming dynasty), compiled between 1679 and 1739, a few pages in the section on
Italy are devoted to the history of Catholicism in China.
In recounting Matteo Ricci's initial presentation of tribute,
the authors stigmatize the objects offered as unorthodox
(*pu-ching*) and compare them disparagingly with the Buddha relic denounced by Han Yü. Further on, the charges
brought against Christianity during the late Ming by Shen
Ch'üeh and others are briefly summarized.[41] In these accusations the foreign religion is clearly labeled as heterodox. Christians, moreover, are charged with deceiving the
masses, violating the dynastic laws against heterodoxy, and
following in the footsteps of the White Lotus and other
secret societies. In no part of this short account, however,
are Christian doctrines themselves subjected to examination.[42]

Sometime during the K'ang-hsi reign prior to 1702, a
Chinese scholar, Tung Han, included a reference to Christianity in his miscellany, *Ch'un-hsiang chui-pi* (Scribblings
by Tung Han). Entitled "T'ien-chu-chiao" (The religion
of the Lord of Heaven [Catholicism]), this brief item is
based largely on parts of the geographical work, *Chih-fang
wai-chi* (Notes supplementary to the geography of the ancients) by the Italian Jesuit, Giulio Aleni (1582–1649).[43]
Tung Han, after quoting from Aleni various tenets of
Christianity — such as the creation of heaven, earth, and
mankind by God, God's descent to earth in the person of
Jesus, the miraculous powers of Jesus and His disciples,
Jesus' ascent to heaven, the doctrines of heaven and hell,
the sinfulness of man — concludes by remarking: "[Aleni's]

words are largely of this nature — ridiculous, wild, and without foundation. If we let the petty barbarians from across the seas pour into China with their heterodox teachings and, in addition, build palatial residences in order to house them and provide them with rich emoluments to sustain them, when they beguile men's hearts into rejecting the orthodox way whose fault will it be?" [44]

In 1709 the devoted Confucian scholar-official, Chang Po-hsing (1652–1725),[45] prepared a memorial in which he implored the K'ang-hsi Emperor to take decisive action against Catholicism. Only a few years earlier, the famous rites controversy, centering on whether Chinese Catholics should be allowed to perform the traditional sacrifices to ancestors, had reached an acute stage when the papal legate, Cardinal de Tournon, arrived in Peking in late 1705 and took a position diametrically opposed to that favored by the Chinese emperor.[46] Chang Po-hsing, noting the growing influence of the Catholic religion, was fearful lest its irreverence toward the ancestors and former sages, its elevation of God above heaven, and its indiscriminate mixing of the sexes should lead to the disintegration of public morals. In order to guard against such a catastrophe, he recommended that all foreigners be sent back to their native lands, that their religious disciples be dispersed, and that their churches be converted into free schools.[47]

Although Chang Po-hsing's draft memorial was never actually presented, its spirit was soon embodied in the *Sacred Edict* of the Yung-cheng Emperor (1724) which clearly and authoritatively stamped Catholicism as heterodox. Moreover, it was given wide publicity by its inclusion in the *Ao-men chi-lüeh* (A brief record of Macao), a frequently reproduced work written by two officials who served successively in Macao, Yin Kuang-jen and Chang Ju-lin (1709–1769), and first printed in 1751.[48] The *Ao-men chi-lüeh* was not the earliest account of Western ways written by a Chinese.[49] But it was certainly one of the most comprehensive to date. Fully one half of the book is devoted to a description of the maritime trading countries of the southeast (such as Portugal and Holland) and a detailed account of the way of life, religion, calendar, and language of the Portuguese at Macao. Significantly, in their description and explanation of the various religious practices observed by the Macao Catholics, the authors invariably employ Buddhist terminology for such words as "church" (*ssu*) and "priest" (*seng*).[50] Moreover, noting that in certain portions of the Bible doctrines were expounded which, in their view, did not differ very greatly from the Buddhist doctrines of heaven and hell, Yin and Chang proceed to construct a theory which will account for this curious phenomenon. According to this theory, the countries of the West were originally Buddhist and Moslem. Because of the Westerners' characteristic fondness for novelty, their clever scholars appropriated the Moslem nomenclature of "serving heaven" (*shih-t'ien*) and stole the Buddhists' doctrine of heaven and hell, in order that they might incorporate them into their own religion.[51]

Of course, the genesis of this bizarre theory can be partly explained by the Catholics' use of traditional Chinese religious terminology to characterize their own doctrines and by certain superficial similarities which actually did exist among the three religions. But nineteenth-century Chinese who were much more familiar with the West — Wang T'ao (1828–1897), for example — developed theories of the origin of Christianity which were not substantially different.[52] It would appear, rather, that this was a subtle instance of the same sort of xenophobia or Sinomania suggested earlier in the *P'o-hsieh chi*[53] and *Pu-te-i*, and still earlier in Fu I's view that (foreign) Buddhism was but a corruption of (Chinese) Taoism. By characterizing Christianity as a religion which, far from adding anything new to the "traditional" religions of China, was actually taken from them, Christianity was placed in a position in China which was at best superfluous.

Another author who criticized Christianity on the basis of his experiences at Macao was the Fukien literatus, Chang Chen-t'ao (1713–1780). Chang was confident that Chinese subjects would never actually believe in the foreign religion. The doctrines of the Catholics were, after all, hardly worth mentioning, and their writings were even shallower than those of the Buddhists and Taoists. The problem was that, while all other heterodox sects made use of their religions in order to acquire wealth, the barbarians alone used wealth in order to spread their religion. Either because of impoverishment or greed, Chinese could not resist the annual stipends granted them if they joined the religion. Hence, in spite of the prohibition against Christianity, its adherents steadily grew in number.

How did the Catholics get their seemingly unlimited supply of money? In part, according to Chang, they inherited it through the donations of deceased laymen. In part they made it by means of an alchemical process which was to achieve far-flung notoriety in later anti-Christian writings. The procedure was as follows. When a Chinese convert was on the verge of death, the Catholic priest came and, covering the convert's head with a piece of cloth, pretended to pronounce the absolution. In reality, however, he secretly made off with the eyes of the dying man. These were then mixed with lead and mercury to create silver, none of the original quantity of lead being depleted. The eyes of the barbarians of course were useless in this technique — hence the motive for seducing so many Chinese into the foreign religion.[54] The importance of Chang Chen-t'ao's writings, it

seems to me, is that they foreshadowed later anti-Christian
literature by placing less stress on refuting Christian doctrines than on identifying the Western religion with practices calculated to repel most Chinese. This shift in emphasis was necessary if such writings were to become effective
stimulants to mass action.[55]

The theory put forward in the *Ao-men chi-lüeh,* that
Christianity was originally an offshoot of Buddhism and
Islam, was given further impetus in the *Ssu-k'u ch'üan-shu
tsung-mu,* the mammoth Chinese bibliographical work compiled under imperial auspices by Chi Yün (1724–1805) and
others and completed in 1782. In the *Ssu-k'u* a number of
books by early Catholic missionaries — Ricci, Aleni, Didace
de Pantoja (1571–1618), and others — were summarized
and subjected to critical examination. The compilers,
clearly recognizing the early Jesuit policy of attacking Buddhism and upholding Confucianism, attempted to expose
the theory behind this policy by identifying Christianity
as a corrupt form of the Indian religion. Originally, according to their argument, the Western religion possessed
only Buddhist writings. Europeans then seized upon the
ideas in these writings and changed them deceptively. But
they still could not conceal the true source. When they
came to China, however, and familiarized themselves with
the language of the Confucians, they were able to polish
their doctrines. At this point, their Buddhist origins being
no longer discernible, they claimed that their religion was
superior to the three religions of China. Although this particular thesis is propounded at only one point in this chapter of the *Ssu-k'u,* the notion that some of the most important tenets of Christianity were borrowed from Buddhism
is alluded to elsewhere.[56] In fact, this notion, in one form
or another, was by now well on its way to becoming the

generally held belief of almost all Chinese who wrote on Christianity from the point of view of the nonbeliever.

Most of the above writers examined and criticized Christianity from the standpoint of Chinese culture. The foreign religion was heterodox, in their view, because it contradicted certain fixed cultural norms; it was anathema because it consciously opposed the traditional Chinese religions, especially Buddhism, and placed itself above them. With the exception of Yang Kuang-hsien and several others, these writers were not specifically concerned with Christianity as a *political* menace. That it was so regarded is, nonetheless, clearly indicated in official writings. The imperial edicts dealing with the 1784–1785 persecution of Catholics may be taken as a case in point. The most important factor behind this persecution was the Moslem rebellion which raged in China between 1781 and 1784. Because the Christian religion was regarded as being either the same as or similar to that of the Moslems, foreign missionaries were suspected of being in league with the rebels. Many of them were, as a result, apprehended and brought to Peking for trial. Although the Catholics proved during the trial that they were motivated only by religious aims and had no connection with the Moslems, they were still convicted on obviously political grounds.

In part, fear of the political motivation of the foreign missionaries in this case was a direct consequence of the Chinese view of Catholicism as heterodox and the suspicions which generally attended the propagation of any heterodox teaching. This was suggested in an edict of December 31, 1784, in which the Ch'ien-lung Emperor stated that "Occidentals propagating their religion and misleading the masses are of greatest harm to the morality and the conventions of the people." It was further suggested in an interesting passage that occurred in the document announcing the sentences for the convicted Catholics: "Though it is not forbidden that Chinese go overseas for trade, yet, if these culprits make this a pretext and go to the Occident to study for the priesthood we must necessarily take measures to prevent this and stop the further spread of this religion."

In assessing the motivations which lay behind the drastic measures taken by the Chinese government on this occasion, however, the time factor must not be overlooked. This was the end of the eighteenth century. And, as suggested by Bernward Willeke in his study of the 1784–1785 persecution, the government's action may well have been prompted in part by the fact that Christianity was the religion of those foreign nations which had conquered the Philippines, the East Indies, and India, and which wielded considerable influence in other parts of Asia. Who could say that China was not also involved in their master plan? [57]

## CHRISTIANITY AS HETERODOXY: THE NINETEENTH CENTURY

The nineteenth century ushers in a new phase in the history of Christianity in China. The great expansion of Protestant missionary activity in this century was first felt in the Chinese empire with the arrival of Robert Morrison in 1807. From then on, Protestants of many nationalities streamed into the Middle Kingdom in response to the challenge of China's millions. In similar fashion, Catholic missionary operations in China were stepped up considerably. Along with this intensification of missionary activity, the nineteenth century bore witness to an unprecedented expansion in European trade the world over. Here again the

vast population and resources of China provided a major
incentive for Western intrusion. These two conditions, together with the general spread of European political domi-
nation in Asia, greatly complicated the impact on China
of the West, in general, and of Christianity, in particular.

Changes in impact, however, are not always matched by
corresponding changes in response. Certainly this was true
of China where, by various means, the actual complexity
and seriousness of the new Western impact was for decades
persistently minimized. The Chinese government's initial
response to Western commerce was the traditional one
of confining it geographically and imposing upon it a
multitude of legal restrictions.[58] Similarly, the first response
of the Chinese intellectual to Protestant Christianity was,
much to the dismay of the Protestants, to regard it as identical with "traditional" Catholicism. The propagation of
Christianity in any form remained illegal, and Catholic
missionaries who resided clandestinely in the interior continued to be persecuted severely.[59]

The tensions resulting from this unhappy combination of
revolutionary impact and traditional response became particularly acute in the 1830's, culminating at the end of this
decade in the first Anglo-Chinese War (1839–1842). The
unequal treaties ending this war did not alter radically the
legal status of Christianity in China. Christian missionaries,
like other foreign subjects, were permitted to reside in the
five treaty ports. Moreover, the emperor, in December 1844,
granted virtuous Chinese subjects permission to practice
Christianity. But the Yung-cheng Emperor's prohibition on
foreign preaching was still in force, and, with the exception
of brief and sporadic itinerant journeys in the vicinities of
the open ports, foreign missionaries were not legally permitted to go into the interior to preach or live. Nevertheless, the treaties did introduce a long and turbulent era of

Sino-Western contact. And a new interest in the foreigner and his religion was awakened in the minds of a small handful of Chinese scholar-officials.

One of the most celebrated of these was the Hunanese historian-geographer, Wei Yüan (1794–1856),[60] whose *Hai-kuo t'u-chih* (An illustrated gazetteer of the maritime countries) was widely read in both China and Japan. The *Hai-kuo t'u-chih* was first issued in 1844 in fifty *chüan;* in 1847 it was expanded to sixty *chüan* and finally in 1852 to one hundred *chüan*. Since the section on Christianity in the first edition is only slightly less complete than that in the last, the first edition is used here with one or two exceptions. This section has been all but ignored by Western scholars, although the work as a whole has received some attention.[61] This is all the more remarkable because it contains one of the most comprehensive compendia of anti-Christian lore to date, and it was to become a leading source book for future anti-Christian thought.

Wei begins by noting the references to Judea in the T'ang, Sung, and Ming dynastic histories. From the *K'un-yü t'u-shuo* (An illustrated discussion of the earth) by Ferdinand Verbiest (1623–1688), he then quotes the account of the building, during the Ch'un-ch'iu period (722–481 B.C.), of a magnificent "Catholic church" (*t'ien-chu-t'ang*, lit., "church of the Lord of Heaven") by the two sage kings, David and Solomon.* Here, the subtleties of the Christian doctrine of the Trinity, together with the difficulties of translating Christian terms into Chinese, get the better of Wei. "If the Lord of Heaven [*t'ien-chu*] was born in the

---

* This, of course, is a reference to the first temple of Jerusalem, erected by Solomon in the tenth century B.C., well before the beginning of the Ch'un-ch'iu period. The Ch'un-ch'iu date and the designation of the temple as a *t'ien-chu-t'ang* were, however, not the inventions of Wei. See Nan-huai-jen (F. Verbiest), *chüan-hsia*, p. 2a-b.

Yüan-shou period of the Han [2 B.C.–A.D. 1]," he asks in bewilderment, "how could there nevertheless have been kings who built a church of the Lord of Heaven during the Ch'un-ch'iu period?"

Wei next makes use of Aleni's *Chih-fang wai-chi* to describe (without comment) such elements of Christianity as the notion of a single, all-powerful, all-knowing God, the miracles worked by Jesus, Jesus' ascension, the ability of His disciples to converse in all tongues without ever having studied them, and so on. He follows this up with a résumé of facts concerning the Nestorian Tablet and several other items of no special interest to us.[62]

Next the reader is presented with some Chinese lore about the foreign religion. From the *Lieh-huang hsiao-shih* (A sketch of the last Ming emperor) by Wen Ping (1609–1669) comes an account of how the famous convert, Hsü Kuang-ch'i (1562–1633),[63] upon entering government service, vigorously advanced the doctrines of Christianity and smashed to fragments the Buddhist images in the temples. Also from this work comes a story about the Catholics of Peking who, before accepting new converts, had them bring their Buddhist images to the church, destroy them, and throw them into the church pond. One day, however, just as they were beginning to melt down the images, there was a sudden clap of thunder and all of the idols vanished. The people who had assembled broke into a sweat, clasped their palms together, and chanted "A-mi-t'o-Fo" (Amida Buddha). Henceforth there were no more such gatherings.[64]

Quoting from the *Ao-men chi-lüeh*, Wei next recites the story of the king of Annam who killed all the Christians in his country because they would not follow him. Again from this book comes an account of a Javanese port city, at the entrance to which there was a stone cross lying on the road.

The road was guarded by armed soldiers, and entering merchants had either to tread upon the cross or forfeit their lives.[65] "Even Westerners dared not disobey."

The next item of interest presented by Wei is an excerpt from the brief essay, "T'ien-chu-chiao lun" (On Catholicism) by Yü Cheng-hsieh (1775–1840),[66] in which this well-known scholar attempts to prove that Christianity was originally the religion of the Rakshasas (evil demons of Hinduism); that this religion was then transmitted to Jesus; and that Jesus' death was caused not by the crucifixion (as stated in the writings of Catholics), but by His wife's betrayal (as depicted in a Moslem work which Yü names). "If Jesus had really been put to death on a cross," Yü asks in wonder, "how could [His followers] bear to treasure the object on which He was so cruelly punished, and revere it so highly?"[67] Wei Yüan provides a fitting conclusion to this section on quotations by giving two long selections from Yang Kuang-hsien's *Pu-te-i*.

The final part of Wei Yüan's account is his often referred-to "T'ien-chu-chiao k'ao" (An examination of Catholicism). The first two portions consist of a fairly straightforward exposition of the ten commandments, the Christian doctrines of heaven and hell, the Golden Rule, the belief that Jesus died in order to redeem man's sins, and so on. In the final portion, Wei reproduces the sections of the *Ssu-k'u ch'üan-shu tsung-mu* dealing with works by Western Catholic authors.

It is only at the end of the "T'ien-chu-chiao k'ao," where Wei interjects a commentary, that the reader is first given a direct indication of the author's own views on Christianity. Wei accepts without hesitation the notion that Islam and Christianity were derived from the ancient Indian religion of the Brahmins. The Christians, although they prohibited ancestor and idol worship, nevertheless hung the cross and images of Jesus and His mother in their homes. Was this not the same as the idol worship of the Brahmins? From the standpoint of Buddhism, Wei is critical of Christian opposition to the injunction to abstain from killing, while as a Chinese he deplores the double standard of Christian morality which forbids a childless man to take a concubine, but permits a rich one to keep countless female slaves. Wei is again confused by the Christian assertions that man's store of goodness or evil and his fate beyond the grave are unalterably determined before the end of his lifetime, and that there is no rebirth or transmigration. Why, if these things were true, didn't the Lord create only good people at the beginning and forgo the creation of depraved (hsieh) and wicked persons? Finally, Wei expresses his indignation that the Christian should scoff at both the Buddhists and the Moslems. Was not the virtue of the Buddha immeasurably greater than that of Jesus? Mohammed and Jesus were both emissaries of heaven. Why was it then that when the one acted on behalf of heaven it was right, whereas when the other did so it was wrong? [68]

In the 1852 edition of the *Hai-kuo t'u-chih*, Wei Yüan inserts a final note in which he summarizes some of the current lore about Christians. All converts are supported throughout their lives by the foreigner and are, in addition, each provided with three payments of one hundred and thirty taels to be used as trading capital; fellow religionists of both sexes lodge together in the same buildings; pastors are notified when death approaches so that they can come and gouge out the eyes of the dying. Wei spices up his account with several tales, one of which relates the trials of a doctor in Peking who thought that he might be able to relieve his financial distress by joining the heterodox sect. The missionaries made him swallow a pill which caused him, on his return home, to throw away the ancestral tablets and mumble incoherently. His wife, as previously instructed by him, forced a special medicine down his throat. Some time later when he awoke from his stupor, he saw wriggling in the privy a tiny female form. On the following morning one of the missionaries arrived with a knife and demanded the return of the object, telling the doctor that it was the Holy Mother of God.

A second tale tells of a Chinese who entered the religion on false pretenses so that he could learn the various techniques of the foreigner. Feigning illness he summoned the pastor. The pastor was just about to cut out his eyes when the impostor sprang out of bed and struck him roundly. Wei's account closes finally with a characterization of the mysterious process by which foreign missionaries made silver from lead and Chinese eyes. With more than a touch of bitterness, he likens the practice of not using Westerners' eyes in this technique to that of distributing opium only among the Chinese people and not among the barbarians.[69]

Wei Yüan's commentary on Christianity contains a mixture of fact and fable, of straightforward exposition and unconcealed prejudice. This harmonizes with the general object of the *Hai-kuo t'u-chih*, which was to provide information on the barbarians that could then be used to attack them. From this point of view, it is interesting to compare Wei's account with the approach to Christianity taken in the *Ying-huan chih-lüeh* (A brief description of the oceans' circuit), completed in 1848 by another geographer-official, Hsü Chi-yü (1795–1873).[70] On the surface, Hsü's account is much more objective, and he appears to be more interested in scholarship for scholarship's sake than in influencing public policy. But Hsü also is no friend of Christianity. Sometimes he discloses his hostility more or less openly: the writings of the Christians are vulgar and unpolished, for instance, and the spread of Christianity to China is superfluous in view of the fact that China already has Confucianism. Much more often, however, Hsü's distaste for Christianity is expressed indirectly. Whatever claims it might hold to a separate identity are belittled by his assertions, at various points, that it is an offshoot of Buddhism, that some of its most important doctrines were established by Moses long before Jesus, and that the only difference between Christianity and Islam is that the followers of the latter did not eat pork.

In recounting the history of the various countries of Europe, Hsü's high degree of selectivity again bears witness to his inner feelings. He carefully notes the supreme power of the Pope and lesser religious leaders in temporal affairs, a church-state relationship which was hardly calculated to appeal to most Chinese.[71] In the section on Italy, he describes the militant intolerance of the early European Christians who proselytized by the sword and killed off all opponents.[72] In several places, he gives an account of the charges of heterodoxy brought against Catholicism by Luther and the subsequent hatred which prevailed between Protestants and Catholics.[73] To the uninitiated these references could hardly avoid giving the impression of a religion which was warlike in its attitude toward others, sharply divided within its own ranks, and, most of all, un-Christlike. The Anglo-Chinese War, the importation of opium into China, and the intolerance sometimes exhibited by the Christian missionary did little to dispel this impression.

One of the most interesting, if not the best known, of the anti-Christian works of the 1840's is a piece by Liang T'ingnan (1796–1861),[74] entitled *Yeh-su-chiao nan ju Chung-kuo shuo* (A discussion of the obstacles confronting the entry of Christianity into China; 1844). Liang T'ing-nan was a Kwangtung scholar with unusually broad interests. In 1838, while compiling his famous *Yüeh-hai-kuan chih* (Gaz-

etteer of the Canton maritime customs), he became concerned with China's foreign relations. This eventually inspired him to write a number of treatises on the West, four
of which, including his critique of Christianity, were collected and published under the title, *Hai-kuo ssu-shuo*
(Four discourses on the maritime countries; 1846). In the
preface to this work, Liang refers to the teachings of Christianity as being too shallow for men to take seriously and
to the acts of its founder as being so hollow that they can
only make people suspicious. Even the Buddhists, he claims,
regard Christian teachings as empty, while the miracles attributed to Jesus differ little in essence from the magical
performances of the Taoists.

The *Yeh-su-chiao nan ju Chung-kuo shuo* itself appears
to be devoted in large part to a fairly detailed summation
of the origins of Christianity, Old and New Testament lore,
Christian rites, the differences between the religions of
Moses and Jesus (the most important of which are, in
Liang's estimation, the Christian doctrines of the resurrection and the last judgment), and Christianity's relationship with other Western religious teachings. Of more
interest to us, however, is the critical discussion which is in-
terjected toward the end. Here Liang remarks that the doctrines of Christianity which he regards as most incompre-
hensible are the resurrection and the last judgment. He is
baffled by the dualism which claims, on the one hand, that
man turns to dust, while, on the other, he is endowed with
a spirit enabling him to live forever. He is likewise mysti-
fied by the doctrine of a final-judgment day when all people, living and dead, shall come before the Lord's tribunal.
If the Christians are so certain that this day is to come,
why are they ignorant of the appointed time? What place,
moreover, could possibly be large enough to hold all the

spirits awaiting judgment and still enable them to hear and understand the Lord's sentences?

The most trenchant part of Liang T'ing-nan's critique is his belief that, whatever worth Christianity may have, it is incompatible with the traditional values of Chinese culture. In China, to be without descendants is considered unfilial. But Jesus does not permit people to take concubines even if it means cutting off their posterity.[75] Again, the sages and religious worthies of China express their reverence for heaven by practicing virtue. They do not, as do the Christians, secretly pray to and ingratiate themselves with God, beseeching His blessings and protection. As for the foreign missionaries, they, like the Chinese merchants, are governed exclusively by the profit motive. It is therefore quite impossible to prevent Chinese, with their traditional disdain for the merchant, from being suspicious of them. More crucial, finally, than any of these specific differences is Liang's conviction that the rich Confucian tradition is so deeply ingrained in Chinese culture that it cannot possibly be uprooted by Christianity.[76] Although some may question the ultimate validity of this view, it can hardly be overlooked in any appraisal of factors influencing the fate of the Christian enterprise in China.

With the passing of the 1840's, two events occurred which significantly shaped the course of the Christian Church in China. These were the Taiping rebellion (1851–1864) and the second Anglo-Chinese War with its resulting treaties (1858–1860). If for no other reason than that it was perhaps the most serious domestic upheaval in the world at this time, the Taiping rebellion would probably have left its mark on Chinese Christianity during the 1850's and 1860's. But the publicly proclaimed adherence of the rebels to a form of Christianity, together with the fact that their ideology was considerably influenced by Christian beliefs and practices,[77] served to accentuate this effect. Although it is often stated that the rebellion failed partly because its bizarre ideology lacked appeal for the educated classes, it is less frequently noted that the traditional antagonism of these classes toward Christianity was hardened by the Taiping experience. For some, the rebellion provided conclusive proof of what they had been saying all along, that the foreign religion was a heterodox sect of the worst possible sort. For others, who had no preconceived notions regarding Christianity or who were entirely ignorant of its tenets, it was only natural to identify the Taipings with Christians in general and transfer hatred of the former to the latter. This was especially so when, during the early stages of the rebellion, Protestant missionaries hesitated in disclaiming affiliation with the insurgents and, quite to the contrary, actually went so far as to establish communication with them in order to ascertain the degree of their commitment to Christianity.[78]

Coming close on the heels of the Opium War and at a time when the Chinese government had its hands full in putting down the Taipings, the Anglo-French invasions of 1858–1860 were hardly conducive to the bolstering of Sino-Western amity. From the Christian missionary's standpoint, however, the negative psychological impact of this war was probably much less important than the positive institutional changes introduced by the foreigners' victory. The Treaties of Tientsin and the Sino-French Convention of Peking permitted the foreign missionary for the first time in over a century to live, own property, and preach in the interior of China. The problems generated by this novel situation will be explored in subsequent chapters. For the present it is enough simply to note the physical changes in the position of Christianity made possible by the new treaties. In 1858, after a half century in China, the total number of

Protestant missionaries had grown to a scant eighty, and with sporadic exceptions, their work was confined to the five treaty ports and Hong Kong.[79] Fifty years later, in 1905, the Protestant missionary force had multiplied forty times and was engaged in work throughout the Chinese empire.[80] The growth of the Catholic missionary enterprise after 1860, while less phenomenal than that of the Protestant, also was considerable, both in numbers and in extent of territory covered.[81] The foreigner's presence in the lives of ordinary Chinese was, therefore, much more pervasive than it had ever been before.

As a result of these new conditions, China's traditional hostility to Christianity was greatly exacerbated and, from 1860 on, the empire was deluged with a growing torrent of violently anti-Christian pamphlets and tracts. The most notorious of these was the *Pi-hsieh chi-shih* (A record of facts to ward off heterodoxy). Written by "the most heartbroken man in the world" (T'ien-hsia ti-i shang-hsin jen) and first produced in 1861, the *Pi-hsieh chi-shih* was reissued again and again in a variety of forms and, together with its derivatives, for decades ranked supreme in the annals of Chinese anti-Christian literature.[82] One abridged version of the work, entitled *Pi-hsieh shih-lu* (A true record to ward off heterodoxy), was considered important enough by a group of Shantung missionaries to be translated under the title *Death Blow to Corrupt Doctrines*.[83] (To avoid confusion, this title will be italicized when it refers to the translation and placed in quotation marks when it refers to the original Chinese work.) Moreover, the work was so explosive in content that it was banned by the Chinese authorities in at least three provinces.[84] Some idea of the extent of its influence and of the foreign reaction to it may be garnered from the comments of contemporaries.

American Board missionaries in Peking in October 1870 described it or a similar work as "an abominable book recently issued by the literary class against Christianity and widely circulated in several provinces. It is filled with the most loathsome obscenity and the grossest misrepresentations and falsehoods. Nothing could be more calculated to foment disturbances in the minds of the ignorant people." [85] At around the same time, the inspector-general of the Chinese Maritime Customs Service, Robert Hart, remarked: "We have got hold of a book . . . very clever and . . . a queer mixture of truth and error . . . It is evidently the work of a well-read man, and I have no doubt but that the literati have it, and many more like it, on their shelves. The opposition to Christianity seems to be mainly owing to stories of what priests do with female converts, etc." [86] In Shantung in 1869–1870, "a printed pamphlet of considerable size, entitled 'The Overthrow of Evil set forth in Authentic Extracts' " was widely circulated. It included "a reissue of every attack . . . from the comparatively serious and dignified arguments of Yang Kwan-sien, in the 17th century, and the sacred edict of Yung Chêng, in the 18th, to the foul and obscene calumnies" of later writers. In Laichow fu, according to the Rev. J. L. Nevius, copies of the pamphlet "were sent by the local officials to the schoolmasters of the city, with directions to impress its contents upon their pupils. At other places it has been read aloud . . . in public day after day." The tract professed to be "published by the gentry and people." [87] Clearly, this was the *Pi-hsieh shih-lu* — the work translated by the Shantung missionaries (one of whom appears to have been Nevius) in August 1870.[88]

Referring to the "Death Blow to Corrupt Doctrines," the Protestant missionary, Gilbert Reid, stated in 1890 that "many of the anonymous placards that appear, reviling

Christianity, are based on this foul tract," while another Protestant missionary, Timothy Richard, during the same year wrote that "a prefectural professor encouraged . . . students to write essays on the model of the 'Death-blow.' " [89]

As to the circulation of the book (and its derivatives) beyond the confines of Shantung, in 1868 the gentry and people of Nanyang, Honan, reported having seen the *Pi-hsieh chi-shih*,[90] and the French minister to Peking wrote in 1873 that the antimissionary disturbances in Honan were entirely the result of its distribution there.[91] Again, in September 1870, an anti-Christian riot in Wu-ch'eng, Kiangsi, was apparently inspired by the *Pi-hsieh shih-lu* ("Pi-hsieh-shi-lu"), which was reported to have achieved widespread distribution in the province and was described as "a farrago of obscene calumnies against Christians of all denominations . . . similar to one published in 1861 or 1862, copies of which were sent to the various district magistrates in Hoopeh for gratuitous circulation." [92] Some years later, finally, the Protestant missionary, Griffith John, learned from a Chinese official that the "Death Blow to Corrupt Doctrines" was to be found in every city, village, family, monastery, and bookshop in Hunan.[93]

The origin of the *Pi-hsieh chi-shih* poses a rather thorny problem and is dealt with separately in Appendix II. Suffice it to say here that there is considerable evidence, both internal and external, that the original edition of the work was compiled by a man from Hunan province, possibly as part of an officially inspired effort to stimulate opposition against the Christianity-tainted Taipings. Thus, the Chinese Catholic scholar, Fang Hao, attributes the work to a Hunanese attached to Tseng Kuo-fan's (1811–1872)[94] military staff. If true, this would provide a very interesting commentary on both the relationship of the Taipings to anti-

Christian activity and the ideological program instituted by Tseng to combat the rebels.[95] Kenneth S. Latourette, the distinguished historian of Christian missions, has stated that "Hunan was more bitterly anti-foreign than any other section" of China, and that "because of the intense anti-foreign feeling, no [Protestant] residence could be established" there before 1900.[96] In the view of some Chinese scholars, this xenophobia was generated in part by Hunan's unpleasant experience with the Christianity-influenced Taipings and its pride in having led in their suppression.[97] Given this situation, the surprisingly small number of antimissionary disturbances which took place in Hunan in the nineteenth century must be attributed to the paucity of foreign missionaries residing there.[98] For, in the field of anti-Christian propaganda, as we shall see, Hunan's leadership was quite unrivaled. Beginning with Wei Yüan in the 1840's, but especially after 1860, hostile literature emanated from the province in all directions and provided the spark for an untold number of antimissionary disturbances.[99] In these circumstances, if the *Pi-hsieh chi-shih* were indeed a product of Hunan, as seems to be the case, its significance would be all the more enhanced.

The *Pi-hsieh chi-shih* opens on a note of official sanctity with the Yung-cheng Emperor's *Sacred Edict* on heterodoxy. Following two prefaces, the author gives an account which, though professing to be a compilation of the teachings of the heterodox Christian* religion ("T'ien-chu hsieh-chiao chi-shuo"), is actually a curious patchwork of Christian his-

* Although *T'ien-chu-chiao* (Catholicism) is the expression most commonly used in the *Pi-hsieh chi-shih* to denote the foreign religion, there is no question but that it is also intended to embrace Protestantism (*Yeh-su-chiao*) and should therefore be translated "Christianity," even when specifically Catholic practices are described. The author himself remarks that the distinction made in the treaties between Catholicism and Protestantism is merely a camouflage designed by the barbarians to mislead people (see *PHCS, chüan-shang*, p. 5b).

tory and practices, tales of the lascivious behavior of priests and converts, weird and obscene barbarian customs, and esoteric terminology. Because the factual portions of this account almost invariably consist of Western practices unfamiliar to the Chinese, the mode of presentation is uniquely suited to confusing the uninitiated reader and making it difficult for him to judge just where fact ends and falsehood begins. After announcing, for example, that priests are castrated in their youth and that converts commit sodomy with them intrepidly, the author launches into a discussion of Christian Sunday worship: "On this day work ceases entirely and old and young, male and female, all assemble at the Christian church. The pastor takes his seat at the front and extols the virtue of Jesus, describing Jesus as the primal head of the Church [*hui chih yüan-shou*] and the believers as the Church's aggregate body [*hui chih ch'üan-shen*]. The whole group mumbles through the liturgies, after which they copulate together in order to consummate their joy. They call this '*ta-kung*' ['supreme dispassionateness'?] or '*jen-hui*' ['the assembling of the beneficent'?]."

This skillful blending of truth and falsehood is again encountered in the author's description of Western marriage procedures. He notes justly that in the West go-betweens are not used and that young men and women marry people of their own choice. But immediately after this we are told that the bride must spend the night with the pastor before being married (called *sheng-yü lo-fu**) and that a father can marry his daughter-in-law, a son his mother, and so on.[100]

Another device used by the writer to outrage his readers' sensibilities is that of attributing to the foreigner practices which in most cultures (including China's) would be strin-

---

* It is possible, given the context, that *lo-fu* here may be a transliteration of the English word "love," in which case the entire phrase could be rendered, "love-making commanded by the holy one."

gently tabooed. Here again the grain of truth that lends credibility to all effective slander is adroitly introduced. The author, for example, correctly observes that Western women are (at least in the amenities of everyday social intercourse) esteemed more highly than men and that Western rulers are not infrequently women. But the rationale for this topsy-turvy state of affairs, he proceeds to tell us, lies in the menstrual flow of women. This periodic discharge is regarded by Westerners as the most precious gift conferred by God upon mankind, without which human propagation would be impossible. Therefore, when a woman's period arrives, the barbarians vie with each other to obtain some of her menses and drink it — thus accounting for the unbearable stench which many of them have.[101]

Other malpractices noted in this section revolve chiefly around the foreigners' use of sorcery. By means of charms and strange pills they bewitch people into becoming Christians joyfully and cause women to indulge in promiscuous relations. Similarly, by gouging out the eyes of dead converts, concealing the hair and nails of women under mats, doing bodily injury to little boys and girls, and such, they implement their evil designs.[102]

The next section of the *Pi-hsieh chi-shih* consists of a brief and not particularly interesting account of the entrance of the heterodox religion into China ("T'ien-chu hsieh-chiao ju Chung-kuo k'ao-lüeh"). This, in turn, is followed by two selections from Yang Kuang-hsien's *Pu-te-i*.

The second *chüan* begins with a fairly long section containing excerpts from Christian and non-Christian works, interspersed with the critical commentaries of "the world's most heartbroken man." As in the later section, "An-cheng" (Evidence from cases), the author is scrupulous in giving his sources. From all indications, moreover, he seems to have done little tampering with the original works.[103] The subject matter of the quotations ranges from Christian history and practices (real and unreal) to a whole galaxy of evils said to have been introduced into China by the West. Again, as the following excerpt suggests, the salacious sexual practices of the foreigner furnish a major motif:

"During the first three months of life the anuses of all [Christian] infants — male and female — are plugged up with a small hollow tube, which is taken out at night. They call this 're-tention of the vital essence' [liu-yüan]. It causes the anus to dilate so that upon growing up sodomy will be facilitated. At the junction of each spring and summer boys procure the men-strual discharge [ching-shui] of women and, smearing it on their faces, go into Christian churches to worship.* They call this 'cleansing one's face before paying one's respects to the holy one' [chieh-mien ch'ao-sheng], and regard it as one of the most venerative rituals by which the Lord can be worshiped. Fathers and sons, elder and younger brothers, behave licen-tiously with one another, calling it 'the joining of the vital forces' [lien-ch'i]. They say, moreover, that if such things are not done, fathers and sons, as well as brothers, will become mutually estranged. There are all sorts of things of this nature which cannot be fully related. Hard as it may be to believe, some of our Chinese people also follow their religion. Are they not really worse than beasts?" (Quoted from the Feng-t'u kuang-wen.)

The world's most heartbroken man comments: To commit sodomy already severs the principles by which men are regu-lated. How much more so [when it involves] the newly born! To say that it is in preparation for committing sodomy when full-grown is particularly monstrous. The menses is at bottom a filthy substance. To smear the face with it and then worship the Lord, and yet to regard this as a clean and reverential ceremony — is this not still more meaningless? When fathers and sons and brothers indulge in mutual license, the principles underlying human relationships are utterly destroyed. To call [this sort of activity] "the joining of the vital forces" is to

* It seems conceivable that here ching-shui is intended by the author to have the double meaning of "menstrual discharge" and "holy water."

beautify unduly its name. All such evils are indeed things which [even] beasts do not do. It is utterly amazing.[104]

The next section, entitled "A critique of heterodox doctrines" ("P'i-po hsieh-shuo")[105] consists of a fairly intensive examination of Christian teachings, as represented in four Christian works. In view of the persistent efforts of Griffith John to determine the authorship of the "Death Blow" (see Appendix II), it is interesting to find that the work which comes under heaviest attack in this section is his *Yüeh t'ien-lu chih-ming* (An examination of the evidences of the heavenly path).[106] As evidenced by the *Pi-hsieh chi-shih* account, John's exposition in this essay of such doctrines as the Trinity, redemption, and the final judgment is aggressive in tone and a model par excellence of the type of missionary literature which made little or no effort to adapt to Chinese surroundings. In this light, the item-by-item rebuttal of an admittedly hostile Chinese intellectual assumes peculiar significance. The following extracts will give some idea of the flavor of the author's arguments.

[John] says, "God is the great Father; one's own father is a mortal father. God loves the people as His own children. His mercy is many, many times greater than that of mortal fathers." He states further, "The power of the rulers of all countries is conferred upon them by God alone."

Let me ask: since God loves the people as His own children, and His mercy is many, many times greater than that of mortal fathers, why is it that from ancient times on there has been no lack of tyrannical rulers? And why does God [have to] confer unlimited authority upon brilliant sages in order to safeguard His children?

[John] says, "The rewards and punishments of God are like the laws of the rulers of states, transgressors [in both cases] being punished." He further states, "All men are steeped in sin and wickedness, and it is impossible for them [by their own efforts] to avoid perdition and everlasting suffering. If there had not been established a measure for the redemption of sin there could be no salvation at all. Fortunately there was within the Trinity a second figure — the Holy Son, Jesus — who was sent down into the world from heaven to suffer for us the pain which we should have suffered. God saw this good work and forgave men's sins."

Let me ask: [John says that] the rewards and punishments of God are like the laws of the rulers of states, and that those who are steeped in sin and wickedness, being the beneficiaries of the suffering undergone by Jesus on their behalf, obtain forgiveness for their sins. If today there should be thousands of rebels revolting, who could not be pacified and who had [committed crimes] which were unpardonable by the laws of the land, and if suddenly a minister of great merit were to memorialize requesting that he alone be blamed and that there be no punishment of the crimes of the thousands who had revolted, on the ground that his merit was sufficient to equalize [their crime], would this be right?

[John] says, "There will come a day when all heterodox teachings will be utterly destroyed and every evil entirely cleansed, when the lands and seas will be transformed into a new world in which everyone will revere God and love others as themselves. These are things which will surely come to pass."

Let me ask: are the heterodox teachings which shall be utterly destroyed the teachings of Confucius and Mencius? The teachings of the Buddha and of Lao-tzu? The teachings of Confucius and Mencius are surely as bright as the sun and stars. Even the unorthodoxies of Buddhism and Taoism — are they to be likened to the extreme depravity and evil of *their* religion? As to everyone's revering God, this can only mean that we must, as in their religion, equate smearing the face with menstrual discharge when worshiping God with "cleansing the face before paying one's respects to the holy one." As to loving others as oneself, this simply means forcing others to follow their heterodox religion. With respect to his statement that these are things which will surely come to pass, the rebellion of the Taiping rebels is a close approximation to the fulfillment of which he speaks.

[John] says, "Recently Protestant missionaries have come to your China and have spent over fifty years preaching the Holy Way and commending the Scriptures. The people throughout the land should all have repented and believed in the Lord. But, in the end, the believers are few and the nonbelievers many. This, again, is an obvious sign of human depravity. Hence you Chinese, according to the laws of God, are all truly sinful."

Let me ask: this evidence of human depravity, this sinfulness of the Chinese, does it consist in the moral obligations which we uphold, the Confucian teachings? Fortunate it is that the believers are few and the nonbelievers many! If [the Christians] were to get their way in China and draw us all into their evil fold, there would no longer be any place for our posterity.[107]

The tone and content of the polemics in this section is decidedly different from that in previous portions of the *Pi-hsieh chi-shih.* The charges of atrocious practices, licentious behavior, and sexual perversion are kept at an absolute minimum. The author confronts John's statements directly and, at times, with considerable forcefulness. In the final chapter of the *Pi-hsieh chi-shih,* however, there is a reversion to the earlier mode of argumentation. The "An-cheng" section, containing over four dozen items drawn from written and oral sources, is a compendium of weird, salacious, and vicious activities allegedly indulged in by Christians. The purpose of the section, as a few examples will suffice to show, is twofold: first, to catalogue these malpractices and, second, to suggest that calamity will be visited upon all who participate in them.

"Ch'en Yüan-i of Kweilin, Kwangsi was very covetous by nature. When he heard that by entering the Christian religion he could acquire great wealth, he immediately joined. Afterwards it was discovered that he had taken money from the public treasury, and he was cut open in the market place." (Quoted from the *Kuang-chien lu.*)

"Ho Ta-hai was a Fukien man. He had talent but was ill-mannered. Ta-hai studied with an Englishman, Pa-li-ta, who was versed in calendrical calculation, and as a consequence he was beguiled into following the Christian religion. He acquired recipes for making love and committed incest with his mother. Before a year had passed he was struck dead by lightning." (Quoted from the *Hu-t'u chi* and the *Ch'ung-cheng lu*.)

Tso Tsung-te, a disciple of the barbarian rebel, Griffith John, arrived in Kiangnan and bought ten or so young girls from people who were in distressed circumstances. He placed them in a large residence. Each night, shortly after midnight, Tso, accompanied by two others, lit a lantern and stood in the middle reciting charms while all the young girls took positions around them. Presently blue smoke would emanate from the mouths of Tso and the others, the lantern light would suddenly brighten, and all of the young girls' clothing would fall off [mysteriously]. Tso and his associates, while standing, would then copulate with each of them in turn and blow on the girls' genitals. Hand in hand they would then dance around in circles several times and all go to sleep. In time the owner of the house got wind of these goings on and promptly drove them out . . . This was seen by a certain Yin . . . and related to me in this manner.

In Lichow [Hunan], recently, there was a rebel who had the power to make himself invisible and who, by means of black magic, cut off the queues of men, the nipples of women, and the testicles of little boys . . . Were you to ask [the victims] about this, they would in some cases say, "I saw a priest wearing a cross on his chest. When he struck me I fell to the ground and, immediately becoming dizzy, could not stop him from doing what he did." All the women and little boys who were thus injured suffered terribly upon reviving, and often died before a day had passed. This was observed personally by a certain Feng of Changsha and a certain Yang of Shanhwa [hsien in Changsha fu], both of whom were in Lichow. Fearing that injury would befall them, they returned home and told me this in great detail.[108]

An appendix to the *Pi-hsieh chi-shih* opens with a ballad of about three hundred seven-character lines. It is entitled "Pi-hsieh ko" (A ballad to ward off heterodoxy) and repeats in condensed form much of the inflammatory material in the book proper. In accordance with the author's professed aim that the ballad be suited for popular consumption (see his first preface), it is cast in rhymed form and written in semicolloquial style.

Of considerably greater significance is the next section of the appendix entitled "Measures for militia defense" ("T'uan-fang-fa"). Here, in great detail, an entire action program is proposed by the author to implement what has been broadly suggested throughout — that the pestilence of Christianity be rooted out of China. Provision is made for the setting up of head and subsidiary offices; the manner in which the militia units will be financed; the supply and storage of weapons; the establishment of ancestral shrines (together with quarterly inspections of all homes and punishment of all who disregard this injunction); the carving of crucifixes and crosses on city walls and on all thresholds (with a detailed description of the crucifix and specific measures for enforcing the compliance of converts); a mutual security system (similar to the *pao-chia*) to sit in judgment over all who continue to follow the heterodox sect; careful investigation of all suspicious characters and strangers, with capital punishment for those who are found to be members of the Christian religion or who conceal such persons, and rewards for those who apprehend them; periodic inspection of militia units and militia leaders to guard against negligence; the establishment of clan militias; a conscription system; regular drills for militiamen, with lectures on the evils of Christianity and the virtues of the *Sacred Edict;* naval militia and marine police, along with a river customs system to finance them; capital punishment for all who have business dealings with Christians; the salary and rations to be allotted to each militiaman; and so on. In the last of his twenty proposals the author stresses that the resulting militia system should not limit its activities to defending the region against the inroads of the foreigner, but should also eliminate all traces of local robbers and assist the government troops in rounding up escaped remnants of the Hung-chin tsei (Taipings?).[109] In closing, he makes a spirited plea for the adoption of his program and attempts to reconcile it with the imperial edicts tolerating Christianity.[110]

The ultimate significance of these proposals and their relationship to a possible "anti-Christian movement" is yet to be determined. In the materials for the 1860's, there is no indication that these specific proposals were ever actually implemented, although similar ideas were advanced in other quarters.[111] It seems to be the case, however, that the *Pi-hsieh chi-shih* and its relative, the *Pi-hsieh shih-lu*, achieved wide circulation only after this decade, and, as we have seen, there is concrete evidence that the two works *in their entirety* inspired anti-Christian disturbances in the 1870's. A solution to this problem, therefore, awaits the study of these later years.

The final section of the appendix consists of an illuminating six-page essay on the Elder Brother Society, which need not concern us except to note that the author is quite as avid in his denunciation of it as he was of the Christian heterodoxy.

The book closes with an extremely valuable catalogue, listing two hundred and twelve works (more than a hundred of which the author claims to have seen), a few written by missionaries and converts, but most by anti-Christian Chinese. One would have to go a long way to find more impressive evidence than this of the existence of a rabid and prolific anti-Christian tradition in China.

This brings us to the final question of the place which should be assigned to the *Pi-hsieh chi-shih* in this tradition. In particular, should it be viewed as a revolutionary departure because of its highly scatological content? I think not. The earlier works examined in *this* survey, it is true, have tended to cast opprobrium on Christian malpractices in the sexual sphere more by implication — such as in the often repeated charge that Christians of both sexes mingled together indiscriminately during worship — than by direct description. But the *Pi-hsieh chi-shih* makes extensive reference to earlier works which were much more graphic, indicating that the problem is essentially one of availability of materials. I would suggest, rather, that the unique significance of the *Pi-hsieh chi-shih* lies less in its content than in its aim. For, unlike many of its predecessors, its intent is overwhelmingly propagandistic. It is designed for one purpose only, to excite mass action. Here, moreover, I think we have one explanation of its emphasis on scatology. Scatology has always been an eyecatcher. And charges of sexual license and perversion have always, in the most varied cultural milieus, been the favorite devices by which indignant upholders of the orthodox order have sought to incriminate their real or imagined foes.[112]

From the preceding it is apparent that in traditional Chinese society Christianity was viewed as heterodox for a variety of reasons, most of which had been applied to Buddhism centuries before Christianity ever entered the Middle Kingdom. In some cases, as in the *P'o-hsieh chi*, it was attacked on grounds which were primarily doctrinal. In other instances, Yang Kuang-hsien's work providing the most obvious case in point, it was denounced because of its foreign origin or because its adherents were regarded as a political menace. In still other cases, as in the *Pi-hsieh chi-shih,* the religion was identified with Western civilization as a whole and was condemned because it seemed to threaten the very base of Chinese culture and society. Similarly, the arguments used to support the label of heterodoxy varied widely in quality and tone, depending to a considerable extent on whether the writer's main purpose was to communicate with other intellectuals or to stimulate mass action.

One question remains at least to be raised, if it cannot be satisfactorily answered. The succeeding chapters all deal, in one way or another, with Chinese opposition to the Christian missionary enterprise during the decade from 1860 to 1870. To what extent can this opposition, as well as the opposition examined in the present chapter, be characterized as anti-Christian, and to what extent can it be characterized as antiforeign? This question does not ordinarily arise in the context of intranational or intracultural religious conflict, where the issue is more clearly drawn along doctrinal lines. But in the Chinese case, where the teachings opposed were the fruit of a foreign civilization, the question becomes critical.

It seems clear that — at least until the last years of the nineteenth century, when the Chinese response to Western culture became less monolithic and hence more complex — opposition to the missionary enterprise was dictated in most cases by a mixture of both motives, but with the anti-Christian motive plainly subordinate to, and dependent upon, the antiforeign. Of course, in the sense that Christianity was viewed as a heterodox doctrinal alternative to Confucianism or as a heterodox political threat to the dynasty, presumably it would have been attacked almost as vigorously if it had been an indigenous teaching. But it was not an indigenous teaching. Because Christianity was viewed as an external force which aspired to revolutionize the entire spiritual foundations of Chinese culture, a force moreover which was transmitted by outsiders and which after 1860 enjoyed outside political-military backing, antiforeignism naturally became an ingredient of overriding importance in all opposition to it. For many Chinese of the period, Christianity was simply the most conspicuous and irritating expression of a civilization which, in *all* its dimensions, they heartily detested. And although, in the remainder of this book, the term "anti-Christian" is frequently used interchangeably with the term "antiforeign," it must be understood in this very special sense.

# II
# THE ANTI-CHRISTIAN
# TRADITION
# IN ACTION, 1860–1870

# CHINA, CHRISTIANITY, AND THE FOREIGN POWERS IN 1860

IT MAY be said with some justice that, prior to the nineteenth century, Christianity and its missionary transmitters did not pose a serious problem for China. This is demonstrated, perhaps most clearly, by the simple circumstance that the response of the Chinese intellectual classes and government to the foreign religion was mixed and uneven. Some highly placed officials and scholars, as we have seen, viewed Christianity with genuine concern and opposed it vigorously. Others, however, who were just as prominent — Hsü Kuang-ch'i, Li Chih-tsao (d. 1630), and Yang T'ing-yün (1557–1627),[1] to name only the most well known — became devout Christians. It may be assumed, moreover, that in between these two extremes lay a third segment of China's intelligentsia — probably by far the largest — which did not feel the necessity of confronting Christianity one way or the other and remained quite indifferent to its tenets. Individual Chinese, in effect, could reject, accept, or ignore the religion with impunity, and the Chinese government could, at its pleasure, tolerate or persecute it without regard for the consequences of its actions. The dynasty acted from a position of strength and self-confidence. The missionary stood alone and unaided before "the forces of evil."

During the nineteenth century this whole situation changed drastically. Chinese society was severely wrenched by a series of domestic problems ranging from bureaucratic decay and corruption to antidynastic rebellion and, in its foreign relations, by the unprecedented advance of Western imperialism. After 1860, moreover, the missionary finally achieved his long-sought goal of full official toleration and, more important still, was for the first time in a position to demand that this toleration be enforced. One result of this new set of circumstances was a considerable broadening and intensification of the tradition of Chinese hostility toward Christianity. This was expressed in writing, as we have already seen. It also took more active forms, as subsequent chapters will indicate. In the last analysis, it was perhaps best demonstrated by the incontrovertible fact that, despite the immensely increased forces which Christianity brought to bear upon the evangelization of China, the educated classes now, with few exceptions, steadfastly refused even to sympathize with the religion, much less embrace it.

## THE SITUATION IN 1860

The position of the missionary enterprise in China from 1860 on was based upon the Sino-French agreements of 1858 and 1860, which in turn represented the culmination of long-standing French efforts to secure the legalization of Christianity's status in the empire. France, unlike Great Britain, did not have a significant commercial stake in China, and her Far Eastern policy generally, as has been admirably shown by John F. Cady, was rooted in political rather than in economic considerations.[2] The fact that her course in China was dictated more by European power rivalries — an inherently unstable basis for the formation of policy — than it was by permanent and enduring interests in China itself accounts to a large extent for the indecisiveness and secrecy which frequently marked France's actions.

A further consequence of her lack of real interests in the empire was that she was forced to create unreal ones in order to counter the prestige and influence of Great Britain. The French protectorate of Roman Catholic missions was established, then, less because these missions were Catholic than because they were French.

Although it is beyond the scope of this study to present a full account of this aspect of Sino-French relations, the protectorate's modern development may be briefly summarized.[3] The first portent came in 1844–1846, as a consequence of the negotiations between Théodose de Lagrené and Ch'i-ying (d. 1858) in Canton. The original impetus for Lagrené's mission had been France's desire to share in the spoils of the Opium War and keep up with England by making a commercial treaty. Upon his arrival in China, however, Lagrené found that the French object had already been achieved by virtue of the Chinese notion of according equal privileges to all the "barbarians." For a variety of reasons, both personal and political, he therefore concentrated his efforts in the ensuing negotiations on getting China to legalize the practice of Christianity. Ch'i-ying did not offer too much resistance and repeatedly applied to the throne, asking that Chinese subjects who believed in Catholicism sincerely and did not excite disturbances, seduce people's wives and daughters, or deceitfully gouge out the eyes of the sick, be permitted to practice the religion freely. After three such requests the throne, on December 14, 1844, handed down an edict to the effect that Chinese who accepted Christianity for good purposes would thereafter be exempt from punishment. Lagrené, by resorting to threats and intimidation, was able to wrest a further edict from Peking in February 1846, which explained the new toleration policy to the provinces and granted the additional concession that old church buildings, dating from the time of the K'ang-hsi Emperor, if still standing and not otherwise in use, should be restored to Christian ownership. In these edicts the political content of the Chinese notion of heterodoxy was clearly evidenced. Catholicism itself was not to be regarded as heterodox, but only those groups which used the religion to do evil.[4]

During the remainder of the 1840's, Catholic missionaries continued at their own peril to penetrate the Chinese interior, wearing Chinese clothing and living on Chinese fare. By pursuing their work unostentatiously they were usually able to avoid harassment. If apprehended by Chinese authorities and conducted to the nearest French consul (as stipulated in Article 23 of the French treaty of 1844), they invariably returned to their stations in short order and continued as before. The contrast with the Protestant missionaries of the time who lived comfortably with their families in the treaty ports, made periodic trips back to Europe, and devoted their efforts chiefly to translation work was striking.

Toward the end of the Guizot ministry (October 1840–February 1848) official French policy took a turn toward moderation, and the first accredited resident chargé d'affaires for China, Baron Forth Rouen, was instructed not to allow the aggressive spirit of French missionaries to involve France in difficulties with the Chinese government. This policy was never applied, however, partly because the new French vice-consul at Shanghai, Charles de Montigny, began to implement his own policy soon after his arrival in January 1848. Montigny, although personally inclined toward religious skepticism, regarded the cause of religion as a prime instrument for the extension of French political and moral influence in China. Since France had no commercial interests to jeopardize, and her missionaries would no doubt ignore any attempted restraints anyway, he embarked upon a successful course of active personal intervention on behalf of both native Christians and Catholic missionaries over a wide radius around Shanghai. Overriding Forth Rouen's protests, he developed an "enormous popularity" in missionary circles; and when the new Napoleonic regime eventually got around to formulating a Far Eastern policy, "Montigny's performance at Shanghai was one of the few shining examples of the enhancement of French prestige in that part of the world." [5]

In the meantime missionary pressure to obtain French governmental assistance in China went on unabated. In early 1851 the French chargé at Canton submitted for Paris' consideration a long memorial prepared by Bishop Mouly of Chihli asking France to aid in the protection of missionaries and restoration of ancient church properties. A Catholic missionary assembly held in Ningpo later in the same year petitioned the French foreign minister for similar ends; another conclave at Shanghai, toward the end of 1851, asked the Pope to assign France the role of protecting Catholic missionaries in China. Finally, in mid-1852, eight Catholic bishops in the Far East addressed a concerted appeal for increased French protection directly to Napoleon III. Such protection, in their view, was necessary as much for the honor of France as for the interests of missions.

In France, the dovetailing of clerical pressure (to which Louis Napoleon was peculiarly susceptible because of his dependence on clerical support) and the need to bolster dynastic prestige was rapidly culminating in a revival of imperialist sentiment. Although a variety of circumstances prevented this sentiment from being immediately translated into action in China, it had become firmly ingrained in French policy by mid-1853.[6]

The spark which eventually ignited this new policy was the judicial execution of a French missionary, August Chapdelaine, in Kwangsi province on February 29, 1856.[7] Being at once a tangible challenge to French political prestige and an attack on Catholic missions, Chapdelaine's death served to bring about a coalescence of French political and clerical objectives. At the same time, by representing a flagrant violation of Article 23 of the French treaty, it provided a convenient pretext for France's participation in the joint expeditions of 1857–1860.

The story of the 1857–1858 expedition, the negotiations at Tientsin, the resumption of fighting in 1860, and the further negotiations at Peking has been told well and need not detain us here.[8] Suffice it to say that, if the French Foreign Ministry appeared somewhat cool in 1858 to the establishment of a vigorous protectorate in China,[9] two years later it did an almost complete about-face. Baron Gros's secret supplementary instructions in 1860 devoted considerable attention to Church affairs, and in the end the "only important material beneficiary from the French war with China was . . . the Catholic missionary interest."[10]

The benefits which accrued to the missionary as a result of the war were substantial indeed. Article 13 of the Sino-French Treaty of Tientsin (which was ratified in 1860) secured for the Catholic missionary the right to preach and practice his religion freely anywhere in the Chinese empire, under the effective protection of the Chinese authorities. It further guaranteed Chinese subjects the right to practice Christianity, without being liable to punishment. Finally, it abrogated all previously written official documents that had been directed against the Christian religion.[11]

At Peking in 1860 the allied armies forced the Chinese authorities to consent to additional agreements which buttressed still further the privileges of the Christian missionary and convert. Article 6 of the French text of the Sino-French Convention affirmed the imperial edict of February 20, 1846, which had promised to restore to the Catholics all confiscated religious and benevolent establishments. The Chinese text went a great deal further than this,[12] apparently due to the duplicity of one of the interpreters on the French side.[13] It promised that Catholicism would be tolerated throughout China; that those who arrested Christians illegally would be punished; that churches, schools, cemeteries, lands, and buildings which had been previously seized from Catholics would be handed over to the French representative at Peking for transmission to the Catholics concerned; and, most important, that French missionaries would be permitted to rent and purchase land in all the provinces and to erect buildings thereon at pleasure. The Chinese, either unwittingly or because they were helpless to do otherwise, accepted the Chinese text as authoritative and attempted, at least halfheartedly, to put it into force.[14]

Thus the legal basis for the French protectorate was established. It was effectively confirmed by the issuance on October 29, 1860, of the first passports, duly visaed by the Chinese government, for delivery to twenty-eight Catholic missionaries in the Chinese interior. The passports stipulated that the Chinese provincial authorities were to protect the missionaries and permit them to preach, reside in any locality, rent or purchase land, and construct buildings.[15]

In addition to being applicable to all Catholic missionaries, under the French protectorate, these privileges were also applicable to all Protestant missionaries, by virtue of the most-favored-nation clauses in the earlier treaties.[16] The missionaries of both faiths guarded their newly won rights as precious possessions and applied constant pressure upon their governments to see to it that they were vigorously enforced. None, at the time, seemed to have any compunctions concerning the manner in which these privileges had been gained.[17]

The new treaties also, by opening up the Chinese interior,

provided the necessary legal conditions for the spectacular growth experienced by the missionary movement after 1860. In 1870, at the end of the decade with which we are dealing, estimates put the total number of Chinese Catholics at anywhere from 369,441 to 404,530, with about two hundred and fifty European priests. Szechwan, which in the eighteenth century had been the scene of the chief triumphs of the Société des Missions-Étrangères in China, was still in 1870 the leading province in terms of total numbers of Catholics (about eighty thousand) and foreign missionaries (forty-four). Other provinces containing sizable numbers of converts and missionaries were Kiangsu (under Jesuit direction), Chihli (under the direction of the Jesuits and Lazarists), and Fukien (Dominicans). The provinces in which, by the end of the 1860's, Catholic missionaries had made the poorest showing were Hunan, Anhwei, Kwangsi, and Kansu.

The number of Protestants, starting from a reported eighty-one missionaries in China in 1858, grew by leaps and bounds during the sixties; by 1874 the total missionary force was claimed to be four hundred and thirty-six. Unlike the Catholics, however, they had to start from scratch in their penetration of the interior in the 1860's and, as late as 1877, had missionaries residing in only three inland provinces: Kiangsi, Anhwei, and Hupeh. For this and other reasons, the total number of Chinese Protestant communicants by the summer of 1869 was a scant 5,753, and most of these seem to have been located in the southern coastal provinces of Fukien, Kwangtung, and Chekiang.[18]

Because of the rudimentary state of Protestant activities in the sixties, and also perhaps because of the differences in approach and method between Protestant and Catholic missionaries generally, the vast majority of anti-Christian incidents and legal cases in this decade involved Catholic missionaries and their converts. One may in fact go a step further and assert that, when the average Chinese of this time *thought* of Christianity, he generally had in mind Catholic Christianity, its missionary proponents, and its official protector, France. Moreover, in the rare instances in which a qualitative distinction was made in official writings between Protestants and Catholics, it was almost invariably against the latter that the memorialist vented the brunt of his hostility.

## THE T'UNG-CHIH RESTORATION, THE TSUNGLI YAMEN, AND CHINA'S NEW FOREIGN POLICY

Most of the ensuing discussion concerns events of the T'ung-chih reign (1862–1874). This period was officially classified by the Chinese as a restoration (*chung-hsing*), suggesting an eleventh-hour attempt on the part of the dynasty to re-establish and revitalize its severely shaken institutional foundations.[19] During the critical days of the autumn of 1860, when Peking was threatened by the allied forces and the Chinese court had fled northward, certain leading figures in Chinese government circles, in true restoration spirit, came to the clear realization that China would have to modify drastically the framework in which she conducted her foreign relations if she intended to revive and preserve the old order. The leaders of this group — Prince Kung (I-hsin; 1833–1898), Wen-hsiang (1818–1876), and Kuei-liang (1785–1862)[20] — were individually prominent Manchu officials who had been delegated by the court to handle the peace negotiations. Early in 1861 they memorialized, pointing out the need for a new type of foreign policy to cope with a barbarian problem which had no precedent in Chinese history.[21] On January 20, 1861, the throne approved Prince Kung's proposal that a formal office be established to handle foreign affairs. Thus was born what has been regarded as "the most striking institutional innovation of the Restoration period" — the Tsungli Yamen.[22]

The Tsungli Yamen, from its inception, had to grapple with problems which were nothing short of gigantic. In part these were mechanical. The Chinese government had decided upon a course of strict adherence to the treaties. But in many areas the treaties were either ambiguous or silent. And if the Chinese wished to hold their own against the foreigners in these areas, they had to become acquainted with Western concepts of international law and foreign diplomatic techniques. Similarly, if they were to lessen their dependence upon the foreign diplomatic corps in Peking, they were obliged to study European languages and cultivate their own channels of information on current European developments.

Some of these difficulties were overcome simply by the fact that, under the new treaty system, greater experience with foreigners and their ways was inevitable. Constant personal contact with the envoys in Peking enabled the members of the Tsungli Yamen to assimilate rapidly the types of reasoning and argumentation to which the foreigner was most receptive.[23] This acquired skill was soon supplemented with the presentation to the throne (in 1865) of W. A. P. Martin's completed translation of Wheaton's *Elements of International Law*, the printing of which had been subsidized by the Chinese government.[24] Again, with the establishment in the early 1860's of a small number of foreign-language training centers, the Chinese gradually began to build up a reservoir of specialized talent to assist in implementing the new foreign policy.[25]

What precisely was this new foreign policy? It was neatly summed up in the ancient saying referred to by Prince Kung, Wen-hsiang, and Kuei-liang in their joint memorial of January 1861: "Resort to peace and friendship when temporarily obliged to do so; use war and defense as your actual policy." With the Nien rebellion (1851–1868) ablaze in the north and the Taipings still going strong in the south, China's military situation was at a low point in 1860–1861. She was in no position to devote all, or even most, of her energies to getting the European barbarians under control. The important thing was to keep new foreign demands at an absolute minimum until China had re-established domestic political control and was again able to direct her military potential exclusively against the foreigners. This was to be accomplished through the treaties. When, after the completion of the peace negotiations of October 1860, the British and French forces promptly withdrew from the Chinese capital and sailed back south, the Chinese negotiators clearly saw that the allies were not covetous of Chinese territory; they also noted that when the foreigners made demands they based themselves on the treaties. Consequently, if China herself observed the treaties faithfully, she could insist that the foreigners do likewise. In this way, the treaties, instead of being so many foreign fetters on the Chinese, would become a Chinese instrument for controlling the foreigner.[26]

This policy was, from the outset, consistently applied to the whole question of Christianity and foreign missions. Christianity, the Tsungli Yamen wrote in a confidential letter to the governor of Hunan early in the decade, was no less harmful to people's minds and to social customs than the teachings of Yang Chu and Mo Ti during the Warring States period, Taoism during the Han, or Buddhism during the Chin, Wei, Liang, and Sui dynasties. But China needed a breathing spell and, however loathsome the foreign religion might be, for the time being it would have to be suffered. The local officials, moreover, would have to observe strictest justice and impartiality in all their dealings

with the Christians, and culprits who violated the treaties
would have to be punished. If, the letter concluded, the
common people could be made to sympathize with the government's plight and not continue to harbor resentment, in
the future, when the situation in the southeast had calmed
down and China's military might had been restored, means
would once again be found "to extol orthodoxy and destroy
heterodoxy." [27]

Consistent with the basic nature of China's new foreign
policy — a policy dictated by expedience — the radical institutional innovations proposed in January 1861 were regarded as decidedly temporary in character. With respect
to the Tsungli Yamen, in particular, Prince Kung and his
associates had plainly stated: "As soon as the military cam-
paigns are concluded and the affairs of the various countries
are simplified, the new office will be abolished and its functions will again revert to the Grand Council for management so as to accord with the old system." [28] Temporary or
not, however, the Yamen, if it was to fulfill its new functions effectively, had to be invested with a substantial
amount of independent authority. It had to be able to
exercise judgment on its own without constant recourse to
the emperor for sanction.

The whole question of authority was a two-pronged one,
having both legal and political implications. First, the
Yamen needed the legal authority to make decisions on
the spot with a reasonable degree of certainty that these
decisions would be seconded by the throne. This problem
was promptly settled during the first year of its existence,
when the Prussian representative asked the Yamen to request permission for foreigners to enter the walled cities of
Canton and Chaochow. The imperial edict in reply evinced
concern lest foreigners think that the Yamen was lacking in
authority to take action, and instructed it to correct this im-

pression by taking appropriate measures on its own initiative.[29] The extent of the Yamen's *de jure* authority was also seen in the fact that all through the sixties its recommendations in matters involving Christian missions were almost invariably approved by the throne, with little or no modification.[30]

The political aspect of the problem of authority became of paramount importance for the Tsungli Yamen when the points at issue in China's foreign relations affected the empire internally. The Yamen had to have a reasonable amount of assurance that its decisions, once arrived at in Peking, would be promptly and effectively carried out by Chinese officials in the provinces. If this assurance was lacking, the office's ability to deal with the representatives of the foreign powers was bound to be seriously compromised, no matter how much legal authority the throne conferred upon it.

The area in which this enforcement problem loomed largest in the 1860's was that of Christian missions, since the missionary was, to all intents and purposes, the only foreigner residing in the Chinese interior at this time. If the problem was to be avoided or reduced to manageable proportions, a variety of conditions would have to be met. The provincial official would have to do his utmost to implement the treaties on the local scene, overcoming whatever prejudices he himself might cherish and, at the same time, firmly suppressing all signs of antiforeign or anti-Christian feeling among the gentry and populace. For his part, the foreign missionary would have to occupy his new privileged position with all the sensitivity and tact required of an exceptional situation, he and his converts overcoming all temptations to abuse their treaty rights and, perhaps more important still, taking advantage of these rights in a manner sufficiently quiet and unobtrusive that local friction would be reduced. Finally, France and the other powers, aware of the difficult situation the Chinese government was in, would have to exercise great patience and forbearance in their dealings with this government, supporting it at all times and in all possible ways in its efforts to carry out the treaties in the interior. This meant placing a firm check on missionary excesses; it meant further that when friction did erupt in the interior, everything possible would have to be done to avoid quick settlements through the local application of foreign force, thereby subverting the authority of the Chinese central government.

As it turned out, unfortunately, none of these conditions was consistently fulfilled during the 1860's. The Chinese provincial officials were either unwilling or unable to carry out the treaties effectively. The antiforeign sentiments of the gentry, in particular, could not be suppressed. The missionaries and converts all too often exercised their privileges in a less than judicious manner. And the foreign powers, although at times cooperating with the Tsungli Yamen, on other occasions were not averse to undercutting the Yamen's position and taking matters into their own hands. The result was that friction on the local scene instead of being reduced mounted steadily as the decade progressed, and Sino-foreign relations were plagued almost incessantly by antimissionary outbreaks.

# CHAPTER 3

# GENTRY OPPOSITION TO CHRISTIANITY

SCARCELY had the ink dried on the new treaties when it became apparent that the major obstacle to their implementation on the local scene would be the virulently antiforeign gentry — a class which, in both the cultural and social spheres, felt itself to be threatened by the new foreign missionary of the post-1860 era.

## THE MISSIONARY'S THREAT TO GENTRY CULTURAL HEGEMONY

The *shen-shih* or gentry (a term which, in spite of its inadequacies, is used here *faute de mieux*) were the social group most deeply and consciously wedded both to Chinese civilization and, more generally, to the notion that China was the seat of all civilization. The members of this class were schooled from early childhood in the traditions and values of Confucianism, and their social position and prestige rested, to a very considerable extent, on their active identification with these traditions and values. Consequently, when Confucian civilization came under attack, as it did in the nineteenth century, the gentry stood to lose the most. And their position became particularly vulnerable when the attackers announced that *they*, and not the Chinese, were the custodians of civilization.

When viewed in this perspective, the hostility vented against Christianity and the foreign missionary by the gentry becomes more easily intelligible. For, more than any other Westerner of the time, the missionary was in a position to make his views known to the Chinese intelligentsia. And not only did the missionary reject out of hand the idea that China was the seat of all civilization, but, going a step further, he took a very dim view of much of Chinese culture itself, to say nothing of its ardent apostles, the gentry.

The Protestant and Catholic missionaries of mid-nineteenth-century China, if they agreed on little else, seem to have been virtually unanimous in many of the judgments which they passed on Chinese culture and society. The reasons for this are not hard to find. In the first place, the missionaries were all Westerners and all subject to the prevailing prejudices of their countrymen back home, where the romantic idealization of China, which had enjoyed such a vogue in the eighteenth century, had been replaced in most quarters by a distinctly less favorable image. In the second place, the missionaries in China, regardless of the form of Christianity which they professed, were confronted with certain common obstacles, and the frustrations they experienced could not but lend a degree of uniformity to their responses to the Chinese setting. Finally, China in the middle of the nineteenth century can scarcely be said to have been clothed in her finest raiment. The increasing weakness and lack of popular support of the dynasty, coupled with the relatively low ebb to which Chinese cultural life had fallen, were glaringly apparent to all Europeans, whose countries were, by contrast, surging with vitality in every sphere.

Why was the missionary in China? Theological differences aside, few missionaries expressed the driving force that urged them on with greater poignancy than Hudson Taylor, the inspired founder of the China Inland Mission: "Shall not the low wail of helpless, hopeless misery, arising from one-half of the heathen world, pierce our sluggish ear, and rouse us, spirit, soul, and body, to one mighty, continued, unconquerable effort for China's salvation? that, strong in God's strength, and in the power of His might, we may snatch the prey from the hand of the mighty, may pluck these brands from the everlasting burnings?" [1]

If the aim of all missionaries was to achieve China's salvation, however, the obstacles they met were great. A Jesuit missionary wrote in 1855 of the "abject materialism in which the mass of the nation is entombed, and which perverts its moral sense much more than superstition and idolatry." [2] Another Jesuit, Father Leboucq, some years later expressed the view that the greatest obstacles to the conversion of the Chinese were pride, materialism, and moral decadence.[3] Monsignor Aguilar, a Dominican in Fukien, commented pessimistically in 1862 on the avarice which "reigns supreme over all these people, who think and act only for cash. How could they embrace the religion of He who had no place to rest His head?" [4] Griffith John, in a letter home, expressed the acute anguish which the missionary experienced in the wake of these frustrations:

The people are as hard as steel. They are eaten up, both soul and body, by the world. They don't seem to feel that there can be reality in anything beyond sense. To them our doctrine is foolishness, our preaching contemptible, our talk jargon, our thoughts insanity, and our hopes and fears mere brain phantoms. . . . Think of the conversion of four hundred millions of the most proud, superstitious, and godless people of the human race. Sometimes I am ready to give up in despair and think that China is doomed to destruction, that to raise it out of its state of moral and spiritual degradation is a matter of impossibility.[5]

When the missionary looked one level deeper, however, he saw quite clearly that the real enemy of the Christianization of China was less materialism, superstition, and pride than the pervasive influence of Confucianism. In the opinion of William Muirhead of the London Missionary Society, "until the incubus of Confucianism is removed we have no hope in reference to China." [6] And, quoting again from a letter of Griffith John, "though the influence of idolatry on the general mind is superficial, that of Confucianism is far from being so. On the contrary, it penetrates the very depths of their soul, entwines itself around all their thoughts and affections, and holds them with a tenacious grasp." The attitude of many Chinese intellectuals was summed up pithily by a Confucian scholar who reportedly said to John, "I assure you I would rather go to hell with him [Confucius] than with Jesus to heaven." [7]

If Confucius was the enemy, it was natural that the missionary should vent his frustrations, disappointments, and anger on the most direct embodiment of Confucius' influence, the gentry-scholar class. The Protestant missionary, John Chalmers, could thus remark: "Under the outward show of politeness and refinement imparted to the educated Chinese chiefly by Confucianism, there lies almost nothing but cunning, ignorance, rudeness, vulgarity, obscenity, coupled with superstition, vainglory, arrogant assumption and inveterate hatred of everything foreign." [8] In Griffith John's view, "the anti-foreign, anti-progressive, exclusive, self-satisfied, proud, and supercilious spirit of this class is *the* resisting medium in China," [9] and in Muirhead's, "the pride and prejudice, the bigotry and self-conceit of the Chinese scholars are unbounded; and while their ideas are of this kind, there can be no progress on their part in the right direction." [10] This resentment against the educated classes seems generally to have been shared by Catholic missionaries, some of whom wrote in 1869: "These Pharisees of China, irreconcilable enemies of the Christian faith, completely

eaten up with pride, are neither able to nor wish to understand a religion of humility and penitence." [11]

Although it was the upper stratum of Chinese society
which took the brunt of the missionaries' criticism, the society as a whole was frequently treated in a contemptuous
and, in some cases, arrogant fashion. To one missionary of
Catholic persuasion, Chinese society was "decrepit," [12]
while to another of the Protestant faith, it was "in large
measure vitiated, corrupt, and depraved," its social life being "marked by principles and practices, which place them
in a low position as compared with our Christian civilization." [13] Chinese society was frequently dismissed as stereo-
typed, unprogressive, and somewhat beyond the pale of civilization (which in this case meant nineteenth-century European civilization).[14] In the same vein, the Chinese people
were regarded by more than a few Catholic and Protestant
missionaries as children who "must be treated as children." [15]

It is only fair to add that there was also a small contingent of missionaries, largely Protestant, who were unusually
tolerant and even appreciative of many facets of Chinese
culture. But, ironically enough, the missionaries who went
farthest in this direction — such as Timothy Richard,
W. A. P. Martin, Joseph Edkins — were precisely those
who were most deeply committed to revolutionizing the
bases of Chinese life and ways.[16] This paradox suggests a
more general question: Can a missionary be *genuinely* tolerant of a society which, to a greater or lesser extent, he
wishes to change? However sympathetic he may be, is not
the element of rejection at the heart of his Weltanschau-
ung? Timothy Richard felt that the purpose of the missionary in China should not be "to destroy, but to fulfill." [17]
But could he fulfill without at the same time destroying?

When the above paragraphs are juxtaposed with the first chapter of this book, one gets some idea of the tremendous intellectual tension and cultural clash which emerged from the confrontation of the foreign missionary and the educated Chinese of the mid-nineteenth century and after. Where the Chinese viewed the missionary, particularly the Catholic, as motivated chiefly by material interests, the missionary responded by viewing the Chinese as hopelessly ensconced in the things of this world. Where the missionary regarded the Chinese as superstitious, the Chinese replied with profound skepticism toward the most cherished beliefs of the missionary. Each viewed the other as unfathomable in his ways. Each felt that the other belonged to a lower order of civilization. It would be difficult, indeed, to imagine a more violent nonmeeting of minds.

### THE MISSIONARY'S THREAT TO THE GENTRY'S SOCIAL POSITION

In the social sphere also, the missionary represented a marked threat to the gentry's position of dominance. The gentry in the nineteenth century were a clearly defined social group with "legally recognized and socially accepted" privileges and, also, certain well-established social functions.[18] Membership in the gentry was generally obtained either by passing the government examinations or by purchasing educational titles and degrees. The former (and most prestigious) method of entry required a considerable amount of leisure time, which was derived in most cases from the ownership of land. The gentry, in contrast with the commoners, were generally regarded as the social equals of the local officials (who for the most part came from the gentry class) and had free access to them. Also, like the officials, their status was marked by special modes of address, decorations, hat buttons, and garments. Certain ceremonial functions could be participated in only by members of the gentry class. Finally, the gentry's favored position was buttressed by very substantial legal immunities and economic privileges. Through exploitation of their privileged position, the gentry frequently extended their power beyond its formal limits. Although such abuses were most common in the economic sphere, they extended to other areas as well. Thus, the gentry frequently infringed upon the judicial functions of the local officials by actively interfering in legal suits — a practice which was repeatedly forbidden by the emperor.

Quite apart from their special privileges, the gentry also performed a variety of functions on the local or regional scene. They frequently participated in welfare activities, arbitration, the planning and supervision of public works, and the collection of taxes. In time of crisis, as during the Taiping rebellion, they organized local militia corps for the defense of the locality. At all times, as we have already seen, they acted as the principal repository of traditional Confucian moral and intellectual values, in which capacity they served as teachers; contributed to the establishment of local private schools; subsidized promising young students; constructed and repaired the examination halls; contributed to the upkeep of Confucian temples, shrines for virtuous people, and such; compiled local gazetteers; and assisted the authorities in indoctrinating the common people of the area with the official ideology.

In relation to the two other important social groups on the local scene, the commoners and the officials, the gentry occupied a strategic middle position. Sometimes they cooperated with the officials in oppressing the common people. At other times they placed themselves at the head of the commoners and made trouble for the local officials. Because the official was generally not a native of the locale, and rarely held office in the same area for more than a few years, the gentry were frequently called upon for advice and assistance. Their activities in this regard naturally expanded during periods of emergency (such as the 1850's and 1860's), when the local official's authority weakened at the same time that the problems besetting him multiplied greatly.

The gentry's position on the local scene in the nineteenth century was clearly one of great power and prestige. Traditionally, it was the only *nonofficial* social group which possessed such sources of influence. This situation, however, underwent a radical change after 1860 in many of the areas in which the foreign missionary lived and operated. To say that the missionary actually usurped the prerogatives and powers of the gentry would, in most instances, be an exaggeration. What he did do was to edge in on the gentry's exclusive possession of these prerogatives, thereby setting himself up as a rival source of influence.

The missionary, especially the Catholic, frequently adopted the garb of the Confucian literatus.[19] He was the only person on the local scene besides the gentry who could and did address correspondence to the local official and visit him as a social equal.[20] There are at least two instances in the 1860's in which Catholic missionaries advised or assisted the Chinese administration in connection with military matters.[21] The Catholics, with their orphanages, and the Protestants, with their famine and flood relief work, participated in welfare activities traditionally undertaken by the gentry. The Catholic missionaries, in particular, frequently interfered in litigation in which their converts were involved and were probably in many cases more effective than the gentry. Finally, all missionaries enjoyed an extraterritorial status in the interior, which made them more immune to Chinese laws than the gentry had ever been.

One could go on almost indefinitely in listing these concrete ways in which the missionary assumed the prerogatives of the gentry. More important than any of them, perhaps, was the simple fact that he was a teacher and, worse, a teacher of a doctrine which took open issue with Confucianism and the whole range of popular cults. He was educated, at least to the extent that he could read and write — skills which traditionally in China had been the monopoly of the gentry class and a few wealthy merchants. He preached in public, frequently engaging in open debate with the literati and occasionally taking considerable delight in exposing their "ignorance." [22] Again, especially in the case of the Protestants, he wrote and distributed a voluminous amount of literature, further establishing his role as a teacher. The effect of all this on the literati was summarized by Griffith John, in words which highlight both the perceptiveness and the biases of this extraordinary missionary: "It is impossible not to displease them. To preach is to insult them, for in the very act you assume the position of a teacher. To publish a book on religion or science is to insult them, for in doing that you take for granted that China is not the depository of all truth and knowledge. . . . To propound progress is to insult them, for therein you intimate that China has not reached the very acme of civilisation, and that you stand on a higher platform than they." [23]

Again, as a teacher and as a person of considerable influence on the local scene, the missionary subverted the gentry's traditional role as leader, adviser, and opinion former of the common people and as mediator between the latter and the officials. For, although the native convert was still a Chinese subject, he now frequently turned to the missionary when faced with legal or other difficulties, and it was often to the missionary that he now rendered obedience, sometimes in return for protection.

## THE GENTRY'S RESPONSE

The gentry's natural aversion to Christian doctrine was thus buttressed and intensified by their resentment of the missionary's incursions upon their traditional status and prestige. In response, they sought, through a variety of means, to excite local opposition against the missionary and convert, doing this either in defiance of the expressed wishes of the local authorities or with their tacit approval and, in some cases, open encouragement. The human material for this active opposition was generally provided by the populace of the area or, somewhat less frequently, by the transient literati who gathered periodically for government examinations in the major urban centers of each province. The instrument most effectively and extensively used by the gentry to arouse these groups was the written word.

The record indicates that during the 1860's the circulation of inflammatory anti-Christian literature was closely linked with anti-Christian incidents in at least fourteen of the eighteen provinces of China proper.[24] This literature may be roughly divided into two types. The first, general in nature and found typically in the form of manifestoes (*hsi-wen*) and brief pamphlets, was designed more for the purpose of generating an atmosphere of anti-Christian sentiment than for that of provoking specific anti-Christian acts. A direct outgrowth of the anti-Christian literary tradition surveyed in Chapter 1 (particularly works of the *Pi-hsieh chi-shih* variety), this kind of writing contained lengthy recitals of the absurdities of the foreign religion and the perverse practices indulged in by its adherents, and it frequently concluded with a general call for action on the part of all loyal Chinese to protect China from degenerating into a land of beasts and barbarians.

A second type of anti-Christian literature, very brief and usually appearing in the form of anonymous placards, handbills, and notices (*ni-ming chieh-t'ieh*), adapted the contents of the first type to concrete situations and did so in such a way as to be highly effective in inciting mass action. Some pieces of this sort mentioned specific missionaries by name; others referred to specific places. Many of them gave directions for carrying out some act of destruction. Moreover, in a number of instances, the issuance of such writings was timed to take advantage of specific occasions, one of the more common being the assembling of the literati for the examinations.

This anti-Christian literature was either posted in prominent places or reproduced in quantity and distributed. The manner in which it exerted its effect on the illiterate masses was dual in nature. On the one hand, it created an explosive climate of rumor and suspicion concerning the activities of the foreigner. On the other, it activated suspicions, fears, and resentments which the non-Christian populace accumulated on its own through direct, personal experience with the missionary and convert. An interplay of forces was thus set up which could, given the necessary spark, lead to violence.[25]

This dual process was clearly illustrated in a missionary case which broke out in Nanchang, the provincial capital of Kiangsi, in 1862. The Nanchang case and a cluster of incidents which took place shortly afterward in neighboring Hunan provide considerable insight not only into the means by which the gentry resisted the spread of Christianity after 1860, but also into the control problems created for the local official.

THE HUNAN-KIANGSI INCIDENTS OF 1862

*The Nanchang incident: A model case*

On the night of March 17, 1862, a crowd suddenly assembled at the Catholic orphanage in Nanchang and destroyed it, along with several tens of shops and homes owned by Chinese Catholics. On the following evening, another mob destroyed the old Catholic church outside the city, and four days later two more homes belonging to converts were ransacked and torn down.[26] During these outbreaks the expectant magistrate of Nanchang hsien was Hsia Hsieh (1799–1875), a native of Anhwei. Although Hsia was by no means free from the antiforeign prejudices common to his generation, his xenophobia did not keep him from taking an active scholarly interest in Sino-foreign relations.[27] One result of this interest was a work entitled *Chung-Hsi chi-shih* (A record of Sino-Western affairs), compiled by Hsia from 1851 to 1865, under the pseudonym of "the lame old man on the river" (Chiang-shang chien-sou). In one essay of this book, Hsia narrates in detail the events which culminated in the March incidents at Nanchang. The following account is based both on this and on the memorials and edicts dealing with the case.

In January 1862, a French missionary of the Lazarist order, Antoine Anot,[28] arrived in Nanchang to re-establish the Catholic mission there and negotiate for the return of Catholic properties which had been confiscated during the fifties. Anot's Chinese assistant, Fang An-chih, had come to the city a month earlier to make preliminary preparations for the establishment of an orphanage and for Anot's arrival. At the time, the governor of the province, Yü-k'o, requested his subordinates to inquire into the correct mode of procedure for receiving Anot. Hsia Hsieh, after a careful

examination of the sections of the new treaties concerning
intercourse between Chinese and foreign officials, recommended to Yü-k'o that Anot be treated as equivalent in
rank to a foreign consul. When the missionary arrived,
however, the somewhat presumptuous inscription "acting
on behalf of the minister plenipotentiary" (*tai-li ch'üan-
ch'üan ta-ch'en*) had unexpectedly been added to his visiting card, and Hsia, resentful of this arrogant gesture, urged
the governor to reject Anot's petition for an interview. Unfortunately, Yü-k'o had already instructed other local officials to give Anot a full-dress welcome of the sort ordinarily provided for a governor or governor-general. When
the gentry and people of Nanchang heard about this they
became alarmed, and their excitement increased when Anot
asked the governor to have the newly won toleration proclamation publicly displayed.[29]

Around the time of Anot's arrival in Nanchang two inflammatory writings penned by the gentry of Changsha,
Hunan, filtered into the Kiangsi capital.[30] These pieces
were reprinted again and again during the 1860's, enjoyed
wider distribution perhaps than any other writings of the
same genre, and were the subject of several angry communications from the British and French representatives. The
first document, entitled "Public summons [*kung-hsi*] issued
by the entire province of Hunan," commenced with a dia-
tribe against the "English dogs," whose ruler was at times
a man, at times a woman, and whose racial background was
half-human, half-beast. Seven "absurdities" of the Christian
religion were then subjected to scrutiny. If Jesus, merely
by virtue of His power to heal the sick, could be classed as
a god with infinite wisdom and spiritual force, did this not
make Pien Ch'üeh (of the Warring States period), Hua T'o
(eastern Han), and all the other famous doctors in Chinese
history sages of the first rank? If Jesus was really heaven-

sent, how could He have been crucified by a mortal ruler after having spent a scant thirty years on earth? The narration of these "absurdities" was mild in comparison with the catalogue of strange and harmful Christian practices that followed. The Christians violated the most sacred family relationships and ignored their ancestors. Christian men and women displayed their total indifference to evil by bathing together in communal tubs and revealed their complete lack of respect for the bodies given them by their parents by cutting out people's hearts and gouging out their eyes. Finally, they duped young lads in order to rob them of their vital powers and did untold harm to women by extracting their menstrual discharge. Whatever the Christians might say, their underlying intentions were crystal clear. If prompt action were not taken to defend China, this country which for several thousand years had been the home of civilized human beings would soon become transformed into a wasteland of uncultured savages. The proclamation closed with specific suggestions as to what should be done if the barbarians made their way into Hunan.

The second document was divided into ten sections, in each of which an example of the perverse and wayward behavior of the Christian missionary was recounted in lurid detail. The contents and the strange terminology employed bear a suspiciously close resemblance to parts of the *Pi-hsieh chi-shih*, a pamphlet which, it will be recalled, was first published at about the same time and very possibly emanated from the same place. The document accused the missionaries of achieving ascendancy over the minds of converts by making them drink a mysterious potion, concocted by mixing the remains of dead priests with a stupefying drug. After consuming this, a tiny demon attached itself to the convert's heart, whereupon he became insane and was willing to die rather than change his convictions. The missionaries gave the female members of the religion pills which, though called "elixir of life," were in fact aphrodisiacs. Once these were taken, the fires of lust burned within, and the women, contrary to their usual inclination, chased after the missionaries. The latter then initiated them into the pleasures of sex, causing them henceforth to hold their husbands in very low regard. The missionaries were further charged with excising a tiny portion of the wombs of women, thus preventing them from bearing children; sucking out the semen of young lads, whereupon they weakened and died within a few days; and so on. Toward the end of the piece, the missionaries were branded as rebel spies — a charge which, as will soon be seen, did not fall on deaf ears in the rebel-ridden Nanchang region.[31]

These writings, filled with salacious accusations and assuming a threatening posture toward Catholics in general, arrived in Nanchang at a time when popular suspicions concerning the newly founded Catholic orphanage were mounting. According to the local officials' report, the missionaries connected with the orphanage had from the start barred the main door and gone in and out through the small rear door. On occasion they purchased girls from other places and took them into the orphanage. Since anyone who did not practice the religion was not permitted to go inside and look around, it was difficult for anyone besides the members of the Church to have a very intimate knowledge of how the missionaries operated. The sources of friction described in this report were supplemented by later investigations, which revealed that the girls in the orphanage far outnumbered the boys and that the children ranged in age from five or six to ten or eleven, all well past the suckling stage.[32]

Such procedures could not but strike the Chinese as strange. Female offspring in traditional China were not as

highly prized as male offspring and were occasionally abandoned by families in straitened circumstances. Thus, the
fact that Catholic orphanages frequently took in more girls
than boys, while easily explainable when looked at from the
point of view of existing social conditions, was subject to
misconstruction when seen from the point of view of contemporary Chinese values. Second, the traditional Chinese
"orphanage" was closer to what people in the West would
call a foundling home and was concerned with infants
rather than older children. In this context, practices that
were perfectly normal in Western society aroused suspicion
and apprehension among the Chinese.[33] And these fears
were easily compounded by the aura of secrecy which reportedly surrounded the management of the orphanage at
Nanchang. In these circumstances, the contents of the Hunan proclamations were all the more likely to achieve their
calculated effect.[34]

Just at this juncture, during the early months of 1862,
government examinations were convened in Nanchang.
Gentry and literati from the whole area were assembled in
the capital, and the air was buzzing with excitement. According to Hsia Hsieh's account, two of the gentry, Hsia
T'ing-chü and Liu Yü-hsün, together with others, took up
a collection and sent the Hunan proclamations to the
printer. Tens of thousands of copies were soon off the press
and distributed throughout the area. With this the inhabitants of Nanchang became still further aroused, and the
Catholic missionaries, in alarm, attempted to communicate
their fears to acting Governor Li Huan (1827–1891). The
Chinese official of the time, however, as will be seen again
and again in this narrative, was reluctant to compromise
himself by having any more to do with the foreigner than
was absolutely necessary. Li would not see the missionaries
on the ground that the new governor, Shen Pao-chen (1820–

1879), was soon to arrive in the city. But when Shen did arrive, he too turned a deaf ear to their pleas. On March 17 anonymous handbills appeared, setting a time for all to meet at the Catholic orphanage and demolish it. The stage was thus set for the acts of violence which took place that night.[35]

With the posting of the handbills, the local officials of Nanchang were faced with a dilemma which was common during the 1860's and which Mary Wright describes thus: "Responsible local officials were torn between their duty to the Throne, which insisted on observance of the treaty provisions, and their duty to the people under the Confucian system. Many an official was faced with the necessity of destroying his own effectiveness as a magistrate by issuing orders that alienated the gentry and ran counter to popular custom." [36] Although public order had been threatened prior to March 17, Li Huan and Shen Pao-chen had pursued a policy which was tantamount to ignoring the situation. But now some attempt, however innocuous, had to be made to prevent a potentially serious incident from taking place. The local officials therefore took two lines of action. First they started to draft a proclamation to the gentry and populace warning them against being overly credulous of hearsay and suddenly exciting disturbances. Then they tried to reach the influential member of the gentry, Hsia T'ing-chü, who, it was felt, could stop the disturbance.[37] Unfortunately there was no time to put into effect either of these two measures, and on the evening of the seventeenth the previously threatened action against the Catholics was successfully carried out.

Following the initial outbreak of the incidents, Hsia Hsieh and several other local officials went to notify Governor Shen Pao-chen. Shen's response, as quoted by Hsia Hsieh, is of interest: "The barbarians have for a long time been doing what they wanted with us; they never expected our people to take action in revenge. Even though we, ourselves, must shoulder the responsibility for the mismanagement [of this affair] I hope that no arrests will be made." Shen then reported the facts of the matter to the throne and requested that he himself be severely dealt with. But he impeached none of the local officials; nor were any arrests ever made in connection with the case.[38]

### The Hunan incidents

In less than a month after the Nanchang disturbances, a series of incidents broke out in neighboring Hunan. At the time, the Hunan Braves, under Tseng Kuo-fan's leadership, were still taking a major part in putting down the Taiping rebellion. Moreover, as was noted in Chapter 1, the Taiping forces had met some of their bitterest opposition in Hunan, and in view of the fact that the rebels practiced a form of Christianity, however corrupt, it was natural for the Hunanese to transfer their fears and hatreds to the foreign religion. This transfer was clearly evidenced in the Hunan manifestoes of March. It was also pointed out by the governor of the province, Mao Hung-pin (1806–1868), who added that the veil of mystery and secrecy which surrounded the preaching and practice of Catholicism made it extremely easy for the gentry and people to confuse the false "Catholicism" of the Taipings with its real counterpart.[39]

Against this general setting, several events occurred which seem to have furnished the immediate occasions for the Hunan incidents. First, it may be assumed that news of the Nanchang riots reached the gentry and people of Siangtan hsien in nearby Hunan before April 12, the date on which the first of the Hunan incidents occurred in that hsien. This is even more probable since the gentry of Hunan, as their March manifestoes demonstrated, were obviously interested in all forms of anti-Christian activity.

Second, the recently promulgated toleration proclamations permitted the Chinese Christians of Hunan to acknowledge their religion more openly and, in some cases, to abuse the increased power and influence which naturally accrued to them as a result of their new status. Mao Hungpin noted, in particular, the anger and jealousy aroused among the gentry and populace of Siangtan when a native convert temporarily in charge of the Christian community there began to ride about in a four-carrier sedan chair and to visit the local officials. The Chinese in question was only a commoner and clearly had no right to act in this manner.[40]

Again, as in Nanchang, government examinations were being held in Changsha prefecture, of which Siangtan hsien was a part. On April 5 the vicar apostolic of Hunan, Michel Navarro, was warned by a Christian literatus, who had come to Changsha to take the examinations, that the other candidates were talking about destroying the church and killing the Europeans.[41] The excitement was undoubtedly intensified by the posting of notices demanding the death penalty for all missionaries.[42] A concrete focus of friction was provided, finally, by the approaching completion of a new Catholic church in this district.

As the news reaching the missionaries in Siangtan became increasingly grave, Bishop Navarro informed the local officials and requested their protection. This protection was not forthcoming and on April 12 the initial disturbance broke out. A mob of literati and commoners set fire to the new church. They then placed crosses in the streets and at the entrances of houses and, according to Navarro, trampled on them, "blaspheming against our Lord Jesus and cursing the Europeans." The following night another mob assembled and, after pillaging the home of a well-to-do Christian family, demolished it entirely, burning to death five children.

Shortly after this, further destruction was visited upon the prefecture of Hengchow, just south of Siangtan. Here, late in April, the churches of Hengyang and Tsingchüan districts, Navarro's residence in Hengchow, several church buildings, and the homes of a large number of native Catholics were all destroyed by mobs.[43]

## Chinese management of the Hunan-Kiangsi incidents

In the spring of 1862, both Anot and Navarro journeyed to Peking to seek redress. Because, as we have seen, it was the express policy of the Chinese government to comply in every possible way with its treaty obligations, the foreigners would have to be compensated. Moreover, a conciliatory policy was all the more mandatory since the French at this very moment were helping the Chinese to suppress the rebels in Shanghai, Ningpo, and other places.[44] At the same time, the Chinese government was unable, for both strategic and ideological reasons, to go too far in its efforts to be amicable. This was a government committed to the restoration of Confucianism, and it was therefore unable to alienate itself in principle or in fact from the local gentry and populace.

The French demands were received by the throne on October 17, 1862. The most important of them stipulated that Shen Pao-chen and Mao Hung-pin were to post proclamations (composed by the French) alongside the toleration edict issued by the emperor on April 5, 1862; that the Catholic properties destroyed in Hunan (evaluated at forty thousand taels) were to be restored by the Chinese within six months; that the three Hunan magistrates, who had been impeached for their failure to prevent or suppress the riots, were to raise an additional indemnity of five thousand taels to compensate Bishop Navarro and his converts; that the damage done in the Nanchang case (evaluated at seventy thousand taels) was to be compensated for by transfer of the public orphanage outside Nanchang to the Catholics and an additional indemnification of seven thousand taels; and that compensation was to be made for the Catholic church in Wu-ch'eng (in Nanchang fu) which had been destroyed during the Tao-kuang period, and for the churches and other properties destroyed during the K'ang-hsi and Ch'ien-lung reigns in Siangtan hsien and Heng-chow fu, Hunan.[45]

These demands were transcribed and sent to Governors Shen and Mao, both of whom objected strenuously to most of the items. Significantly, the ground for rejection voiced in almost every instance was that acceptance of the items in question would arouse the anger of the local populace. This was good Confucian reasoning, to be sure. But it was also an attitude dictated by the local situation confronting the two governors, and it cannot simply be written off as official recalcitrance.[46]

Nevertheless, the uncompromising stand taken by Shen and Mao was acceptable neither to the Chinese central administration nor to the French representative, Count Michel A. Kleczkowski. Again and again, in his communications to the Tsungli Yamen, Kleczkowski put pressure on the Chinese, relating the manifold benefits gained by China in the past as a result of Catholic missions, emphasizing France's present support of the Chinese government in its campaign against the rebels, and, finally, threatening to go himself to Nanchang and Changsha with French gunboats, if the Chinese remained obdurate.[47] Foreign pressure was undoubtedly increased by the presence in Peking of Anot and Navarro and by a serious antimissionary incident which had occurred in Kweichow in February 1862.

The Chinese government, resisted on the one hand by its highest provincial officials and pressured on the other by the French, was in a difficult predicament. But because it had to adopt a conciliatory policy toward the French, the imperial edicts repeatedly expressed impatience with Shen and Mao and urged them to conclude immediately and with strict justice their management of the cases. In edict after edict the throne expounded the general policy of controlling the foreigner by placating him until such time as China had built up her own defenses and was no longer dependent upon him.[48]

Following the outbreaks in Hunan and Kiangsi, the governors concerned were ordered by the throne to find out the causes of the incidents and the identities of the men who inspired them. Nothing of particular interest emerged from the Hunan investigations. During the course of Shen Pao-chen's inquiries in Nanchang, however, the charge was widely circulated that the officials were taking advantage of the foreigner's influence to annoy the common people. Shen, fearing that these accusations might lead to another disturbance, asked several of his trusted intimates to masquerade as traveling merchants and visit the teashops and wineshops in the Nanchang area, in an effort to find out why the populace was so antagonistic. In one of the resulting conversations — a transcription of which was submitted by Shen to the throne — the people accused the officials of giving in to the foreigner in all matters, of timeserving and turning their backs on troublesome situations, and of showing little concern for the lives of the common people.

The people's disenchantment with the local officials was further suggested by their uncooperative attitude during the investigations. It was conclusively shown in an incident which occurred on May 27, 1863, the date of Anot's return to Nanchang from Peking. Shen Pao-chen, in addition to providing Anot with an official escort from Kiukiang to Nanchang, took the precaution of instructing the local officials to quiet the populace before the missionary entered the city. Nevertheless, encouraged by gentry placards, a mob gathered around Anot's boat immediately upon its arrival and stoned the occupants, forcing them to return downstream. The official attendants whom Shen had assigned to make preparations for Anot's entry into the city were also stoned and upbraided by the rioters for having had dealings with the foreigner.[49] Better evidence could hardly be found of the difficulties which the provincial official encountered after 1860 when he attempted to implement measures that were favorable to the foreigner's interests.

In a memorial of June 29, 1863, Governor Mao Hung-pin announced that the construction of the new Catholic church in Siangtan had been completed and that the crosses had been removed from the streets. The same results were reported for Hengyang and Tsingchüan districts in Hengchow prefecture, and an additional five thousand strings of cash were granted to the converts of these districts for repairs. In the same memorial Mao pleaded successfully for the reinstatement of two of the three officials who had earlier been impeached.[50] In September 1864, after Navarro had returned safely to Hunan under proper escort, the French representative expressed his gratitude to the Hunan governor for his satisfactory management of the cases.[51]

The further disturbance that occurred when Anot returned to Nanchang led the French to stiffen their demands in the Kiangsi case. An indemnity of seventeen thousand taels was finally settled upon and paid by the Chi-

nese; the public orphanage outside the city gates was transferred to the Catholics; and compensation was made for the
destruction during the Tao-kuang period of the Catholic
church in Wu-ch'eng.[52]

### Common elements in the Hunan-Kiangsi incidents

According to Bishop Navarro, the Hengchow destruction
was prompted by letters from literati in Siangtan. He emphatically states that none of the incidents was popular in
origin and that the common people only followed along
after much prodding by the literati, whom he castigates
bitterly.[53] Although Navarro was hardly a disinterested by-
stander in this case, his contention nevertheless rings true,
particularly when one takes into account the strong likelihood that the bitterly anti-Christian writings emanating
from Changsha in March had been penned by members of
the gentry class.

In the Nanchang case, the evidence implicating the gentry is even more conclusive. Moreover, thanks to Hsia
Hsieh's account, we know the names of two of the men
who, though they may not have actually directed the outbreak of March 17, by printing and circulating the inflammatory Hunan writings clearly played a key role in setting
the stage for it. Who were Hsia T'ing-chü and Liu Yü-
hsün, the two men named by Hsia Hsieh? Hsia T'ing-chü
was a native of Sinkien hsien, which together with Nanchang hsien made up the prefectural city of Nanchang. He
passed his *chin-shih* examinations in 1833, held office in
Kweichow as an assistant grand examiner, and at the time
of the incidents was a Hanlin graduate on leave.[54] Hsia was
unquestionably a person of great influence in the area. He
was a lecturer at Kiangsi Academy (Yü-chang shu-yüan) in
Nanchang, and when the local authorities were deliberat-
ing over what to do to prevent the March 17 outbreak, one

of them said to Hsia Hsieh, "although [Hsia T'ing-chü] did not have a hand in planning [this disturbance] he can put a stop to it." [55]

Unquestionably, Hsia T'ing-chü was also a local trouble-maker. Shortly after the riots occurred, with the evident intention of fanning the anger of the people, he transmitted to Governor Shen Pao-chen several suspicious items — some dried blood, a copper tube, and a package of bones — which he claimed to have found on the premises of the Catholic orphanage in the city. Hsia reported that the dried blood had been refined from the bone-marrow of orphans, that the copper tube was used by the missionaries to gouge out eyes, and that the bones had been retrieved from the yard behind the orphanage.[56] Since there was no corroborative evidence, Shen took little stock in the stories about the first two items, and subsequent investigations revealed that the bones probably belonged to soldiers who some years before had died defending the city walls behind the orphanage. Nonetheless, rumors about the articles gained currency in Nanchang, and in order to pacify the inhabitants Shen Pao-chen had to send the suspicious items to the Tsungli Yamen so that it could question the French representative concerning them.[57]

On Liu Yü-hsün (1806–1876) we have more biographical data, but all Hsia Hsieh tells us of his activities in connection with the Nanchang incident is that he participated in the reprinting of the Hunan manifestoes. Liu was born in Nanchang hsien in the early years of the century. He became a provincial graduate (chü-jen) during the Tao-kuang period and held various minor posts until the outbreak of the Taiping rebellion. In the early fifties he distinguished himself as a militia leader, and in 1855 Tseng Kuo-fan appointed him commander of the newly created Kiangsi naval force. Liu continued to fight the Taipings until their ultimate defeat some nine years later. He proved an able commander and was cited by the emperor several times for bravery. The top civil position he held was that of provincial judge in Kansu.[58] His high standing among the Nanchang gentry was reflected by the fact that he was one of the principal compilers of the 1870 edition of the *Nanch'ang hsien-chih* (Nanchang hsien gazetteer).

Although Nanchang was one of the few cities in the Yangtze valley below Changsha which never fell into Taiping hands, it had lived in constant dread of the rebels for a decade. In 1853 it had been besieged and almost occupied. And as late as January 1862, when Anot first came to the city, it was only a scant one hundred and twenty-five miles from rebel-held territory.[59] It is not surprising, then, that the people of Nanchang confused Taiping and Catholic, and strongly feared that the presence of Catholic missionaries in the city would attract rebel believers and result in serious harm.[60] Whether or not Liu Yü-hsün shared in these convictions, his long years of campaigning against the Taipings undoubtedly taught him to hate anything even remotely associated with the rebels, Christianity included.

Perhaps what is most significant about Liu and Hsia T'ing-chü is that they were both members of the so-called "upper" gentry group.[61] Both had gone beyond the licentiate (*hsiu-ts'ai*) level and both had held responsible positions in the bureaucracy. There is no way of determining whether it was the rule or the exception that the more active opponents of the foreign missionary during the 1860's came from this group. But if it was the rule, it would underscore the tremendous difficulties facing the Chinese government in its efforts to enforce the new treaties. For, in the last analysis, this enforcement could be carried out only by the local official. And the local official, in turn, especially in times of internal distress, could rule effectively only with the cooperation of the more prominent gentry under his jurisdiction.

This leads us to a second phenomenon witnessed in both the Nanchang and Siangtan cases, namely that the local officialdom (including the two governors in the Nanchang case) did nothing to prevent the incidents, although in each instance ample advance warning had been given. Since this problem of official paralysis recurred frequently during the 1860's, it deserves our close attention. The local official, because the size of the civil bureaucracy in nineteenth-century China was minuscule in proportion to the size of the population[62] and because government "troops were stationed only at a relatively small number of widely separated strategic points," [63] was dependent to a great extent upon the consent of the governed. This consent was obtained partly through indoctrination and partly through state-sponsored welfare activities for the relief of the peasantry. But the key role was played by the local gentry, whose influence over the peasantry in traditional China was proverbial;[64] without their active support the local official frequently could not discharge his duties.[65]

However, though the official could ill afford to alienate the gentry, after 1860 he also had definite obligations to the foreigners living within his jurisdiction. When a missionary requested protection and the need for such protection was obvious, the official was required both by treaty and by imperial command to provide it to the best of his ability. Under these conditions, the choice which many a local official had to face was the none too pleasant one of disobeying imperial orders and running the risk of being punished for administrative negligence or obeying the throne and risking the perhaps even greater danger of losing gentry and popular support. Since neither of these alternatives was particularly attractive, the most natural thing for the local official to do was to take no action, or at best only token action, on behalf of the missionaries. In this way he retained the affections of the gentry and people and stood a fairly good chance of not being punished by his superiors, unless considerable foreign pressure was exerted.[66]

That this dilemma actually existed for local officials cannot, of course, be conclusively proven. It is put forward here simply as a hypothesis which reasonably accounts for the behavior officials exhibited on certain occasions. Provided that the dilemma did exist, one would expect it to have operated most acutely in those areas where antiforeign feeling was normally strongest and at such times when this feeling was most easily activated. For it was then that the local official could least afford to set himself in opposition to public opinion. Viewed in this light, it is perhaps more than coincidental that the classic cases of "official paralysis" in the 1860's (among which may be cited the Nanchang and Siangtan incidents) took place in important urban centers — traditionally the strongholds of Confucian orthodoxy — and while government examinations were in progress — when the geographical concentration of the antiforeign gentry class was at its highest.[67]

In both the Nanchang and Siangtan cases, government examinations were being held when the riots broke out, and young examination candidates participated in the disturbances. It is a familiar enough fact that even in Western countries unusually severe tensions frequently erupt during examination periods. In China, however, the examinations represented the culmination of years of intensive preparation. And success was likely to be the sole channel to social advancement. In view of the severe pressures under which the candidates labored, some form of release was, if not quite desirable politically, very understandable from the psychological standpoint. Given the decided aversion felt by so many educated Chinese for the West in general, the form that this release took on certain occasions was that of direct action against the representative (if not the sole) repository of Western influence on the local scene — the foreign missionary.[68]

The missionaries were well aware of the dangers they might encounter at examination time. Later in the decade, a Miss Bowyer of the China Inland Mission wrote: "I would ask you to pray that we may be guided in the coming year, when about 60,000 students are expected in Nankin for the examinations. Our houses are but a short distance from the place where they will meet. The Lord can keep us. We are in His hands, and it is a joy to know it." [69] Even more to the point was the fateful comment of the unfortunate Szechwan missionary, Jean-François Rigaud, shortly before he was killed: "Our anxieties have been dissipated and calm has been restored to the district [Yuyang]. The period of the examinations, so dreaded by our Christians and by those of the pagans who are preparing to embrace the faith, ended about twenty days ago, without causing any fresh conspiracy to burst forth." [70]

If the foreign missionary had real cause for anxiety during examination periods, his presence created problems for the local authorities which were no less real. The Chengtu Tartar general, Ch'ung-shih (1820–1876), wrote that it was impossible for the local officials to arrest the culprits on the spot following the Yuyang outbreak of 1865, because the chou examinations were about to start in Yuyang, the literati from the whole area had gathered there, and firm suppressive measures might touch off an even bigger disturbance than the one that had already occurred.[71] Similarly, Kiangsi governor Liu K'un-i (1830–1902) went to great lengths in the winter of 1869–70 to keep Catholic missionaries from re-entering Nanchang until after the approaching *chü-jen* examinations had been completed.[72] Again, in 1870, the governor-general at Nanking, Ma Hsin-i (1821–1870), is reported to have cautioned the foreign missionaries in the southern capital to be particularly circumspect during the forthcoming provincial examinations.[73]

If the missionaries cooperated with the local officials, their chances of averting trouble were considerably enhanced. Thus, when Bishop Navarro returned from Peking to his residence in Hengchow in 1864, he was persuaded not to enter the city until the examinations then in progress were over. Trouble was thereby prevented in a city that was still smarting from the reparations exacted by the French for the Hengchow riots.[74] On the other hand, in an incident which occurred in Anking, Anhwei, late in the decade, the two British missionaries involved were officially advised, prior to the examinations, that it might be best for them to leave the city temporarily. The missionaries replied that this was both unnecessary and out of the question,[75] and an incident that could have been serious broke out.

The foreign missionary was of course perfectly within his rights if he chose to remain in a city during examination periods. And indeed, for those Protestant missionaries who were intent upon bringing the Gospel to the educated classes of China, the strategic value of such occasions was too great to be ignored. It is also true that, in the major urban centers where examinations were held, the local authorities probably had the physical means at their disposal to prevent or suppress disturbances. We come back, then, to the problem originally posed. Could they implement these means in direct defiance of gentry and popular sentiment and still retain their effectiveness as officials, an effectiveness which, *in most cases*, depended more upon persuasion than upon force? This, I would suggest, seems highly unlikely.

Brief mention, finally, may be made of another element which appears to have played a prominent role in both the Hunan and Kiangsi cases: popular identification of Taiping Christianity with the Catholicism of the Westerner and the belief that the foreign missionary was in some way associated with the rebels. This was clearly exhibited in the manifestoes which emanated from Changsha in March 1862 and in Mao Hung-pin's comments on the Hunan incidents. It was also evidenced in Nanchang, as we have seen.

This transference of popular hatred and fear of the Taipings to the foreign missionary was obviously conditioned by temporal and geographical factors and was not a widespread phenomenon during the 1860's. But during the period when the rebellion was still in progress, and in regions, such as the Hunan-Kiangsi area, which had experienced long and bitter fighting against the rebels, it appears to have played a significant part in generating anti-Christian sentiment.

## RESIDUAL PROBLEMS

Whereas we can be fairly certain that the gentry inspired much of the active opposition to Christianity and the foreign missionary in the sixties, and that they did so in large part through a skillful use of the written word, when we try to delve more deeply into their anti-Christian activities we meet pitfalls on all sides. For example, what other means did they use to excite local opposition? Did the more active opponents of the missionary come chiefly from the upper ranks of the gentry (as in the Nanchang case) or from the lower ranks — those who had only obtained the *hsiu-ts'ai* degree or who had entered the gentry class through purchase (*chien-sheng*)? Again, to what extent was the gentry's effort

to expel the missionary an organized effort, as was claimed
by so many foreigners at the time? [76]

These questions are extremely hard to answer. Contemporary anti-Christian and antiforeign literature is available
in abundance, both in the original and in translation. However, although these materials give us great insight into some
of the means used to excite popular opposition, their authorship and the circumstances surrounding their distribution are almost always well suppressed. The two other major
categories of materials — Chinese official, and foreign official
and nonofficial documents — give us far more specific data,
but this information is all too often supported by evidence
which is either flimsy and circumstantial or conflicting. A
few examples will illustrate the difficulties.

In a case which took place in Yangchow, Kiangsu, later
in the decade, a number of prominent gentry were accused
by foreigners. But according to Tseng Kuo-fan, who managed the case, such responsible former officials would never
have acted in defiance of an imperial treaty and were certainly not guilty. In the final reckoning, moreover, "nothing
could be proved against the gentry. The one overt rabble-
rouser, who had seemed to be of that class . . . when eventually produced and identified proved to be a 70-year-old
half-wit, not even a *hsiu-ts'ai*." [77]

Again, in an incident which broke out in Tsunyi, Kweichow, during the sixties, the principal instigator was regarded by the Catholics to have been a certain Kien-in
(Chien Yin, 1828–1873), "one of the persons of standing of
Tsunyi, who had acquired a great reputation fighting the
rebels, and had in reward received the title of taotai." [78]
But the Chinese officials who were charged with the management of the case obviously felt otherwise about Chien
Yin. Far from punishing him, Li Hung-chang (1823–1901),
regarding him as "just and incorruptible," sent him to assist

in calming down the Tsunyi populace. And Ch'ung-shih also delegated responsibilities to Chien in connection with the case, judging him to be an "intelligent and experienced" individual who was "looked up to in his native district." [79] To the foreigner this would have been regarded as a flagrant instance of official connivance, which may in fact have been true in this case as well as in the Yangchow incident. But on the basis of the conflicting evidence, we cannot be certain.

The root of the problem, of course, lies in the fact that both the Chinese and the foreigner were too deeply involved in these events to be able to view them with Olympian detachment. The missionary was not always concerned with "fair procedures" when he had an opportunity to embarrass his detractors. And the Chinese official, in his reports to the throne, did not savor the idea of implicating members of the gentry class, upon whose support his effectiveness as an official materially depended.

If the gentry's role in exciting opposition to the missionary during the sixties is to be understood in greater depth, the types of materials most needed are contemporary nonofficial Chinese documents, such as Hsia Hsieh's eyewitness account of the Nanchang case. Although Hsia was an official at the time, his account was written in a private capacity and was meant to be seen by neither the emperor nor the foreigner. As a consequence, he was willing to divulge details, such as the identities of the leading gentry instigators, which were suppressed in the official accounts. Unfortunately, to the best of my knowledge, Hsia's essay is a lone exception in the period with which we are dealing.[80] And until it is supplemented by materials of a similar nature, we must be content with only a partial understanding of gentry anti-Christian operations.

# CHAPTER 4

# OFFICIAL OPPOSITION
# TO CHRISTIANITY

IF THE records left by the foreigner are to be credited, the Christian missionary enterprise in the 1860's was resisted not only by the gentry but also by Chinese officials at all levels and in virtually every province. In Anhwei and Kiangsu, a Jesuit missionary reported that the Christians' efforts to obtain property were repeatedly and energetically contested by the subprefects, the prefects, and the governor-general himself.[1] Again, in Yunnan, a Catholic father wrote that not a single official liked the Christians or would protect them and that several made trouble for them under a variety of pretexts.[2] In 1865, the bishop in charge of Shansi asserted that the number of conversions in that province would have been considerable had it not been for the unjust and violent opposition of the magistrates.[3] During the same year, a French consul reported that the local officials of Fukien province were extremely uncooperative in their attitude toward the missionaries.[4] Many other general statements to this effect can be found.[5]

The means by which the local and provincial authorities resisted Christianity were manifold. In a few instances, as in Kweichow during the early sixties, they resorted to the gentry strategy of writing and circulating inflammatory anti-Christian literature.[6] More often, however, they took advantage of the power and influence of their official positions either to discriminate against the Christians or to harass them openly. One missionary reported that when Christians became involved in difficulties with the native guilds (as a result of the idolatrous demands placed on them by these institutions), the officials invariably sided with the guilds because of their importance as a source of revenue.[7] In another instance, a Christian from Sungkiang (Kiangsu) was molested by an official for speaking out against him when, instead of delivering the usual bimonthly exhortation to the populace, the official heaped abuse upon the missionaries and converts.[8] In 1867 in Hupeh, a magistrate declared that he would no longer suffer the practice of the Christian religion in his district and thereupon arrested three Christians, one of whom reportedly died in prison because of brutal treatment.[9] In still another case, this time in Chihli, a group of Christian subjects was attacked and harassed by a mob, and when the official in charge appeared on the scene, instead of arresting the culprits, he placed himself at their head and attempted to force the converts to trample on a cross, as a sign of their apostasy.[10] A more veiled instance of official opposition to Christianity was provided by Li Hung-chang (who, incidentally, was repeatedly accused by Westerners of being violently anti-Christian).[11] Li, shortly after he became governor-general of Hupeh and Hunan, apparently issued a proclamation against secret societies in which, after naming several of these, he added, "and all others which call upon you to worship on any day other than the Emperor has fixed."[12]

## THE PHENOMENON
### OF BUREAUCRATIC DECLINE

Why did so many Chinese officials — in particular the lower-ranking ones — oppose Christianity? The simplest and most direct answer is that all officials were, in the broadest sense, members of the gentry class. The vast majority came directly from the gentry, while the few non-degree-holders who were appointed to office automatically became gentry as a result. The significant distinction which must be drawn between the gentry and the official, therefore, is a relative one. When, as was the rule, an official occupied a post in a province other than his own, his role in the locality in which he was serving was that of an official, not of a member of the gentry. But when he returned to his native place, either on leave or to retire, his role reverted to that of gentry. A clear illustration of this dual role was provided by Hsia T'ing-chü in the Nanchang case. Although Hsia had served as an official in other parts of the empire, while he was in Nanchang he functioned as a member of the local gentry class.

One might go a step further and suggest that the role of the gentry *qua* gentry was essentially local in character — their loyalties and obligations centered on their native districts or, in rarer instances, their native provinces. The role of the gentry member *qua* official, however, was an imperial role. He functioned as a member of a bureaucracy which derived its power from a central source. His primary loyalties presumably were directed not to his home province or the province in which he served, but to the throne. And it was to the throne that he was ultimately responsible.

To the extent that the official shared the cultural and intellectual commitments of the gentry class, then, it was natural that he too would be vigorously opposed to the spread of Christianity. But to the extent that he took his responsibilities to the throne seriously, it might be expected that he would do his best to overcome this personal antipathy and earnestly implement the treaties. This was the situation *in vacuo*. In practice there were at least three different forces at work tending to encourage the natural opposition of the official to Christianity and to discourage him from fulfilling his imperial obligations. First and perhaps most important, there was the gentry opposition examined in the preceding chapter, an opposition which the official could ignore only at the risk of compromising his own position. A second force, which is explored more fully later, was the missionary's exploitation of his privileged legal status and consequent challenge to the prestige and authority of the official. A third force was the phenomenon of bureaucratic decay and the concomitant weakening of central authority in many parts of the empire.

During times of peace and dynastic vigor, the Chinese bureaucracy was beset by a variety of evils, some of them common to all bureaucracies. During times of internal stress and dynastic decline, such as the mid-nineteenth century, these evils multiplied in geometric proportion. Corruption became more rampant than ever. To finance imperial military operations, the sale of offices to persons whose only qualification was cash increased significantly. Because of the unusually high priority given to military requirements, moreover, people with primarily military backgrounds were frequently given high posts in the civil bureaucracy. Again, the precarious Chinese system of local control, based to a high degree on popular consent and cooperation, all but collapsed in areas plagued by revolt.[13]

### THE T'IEN HSING-SHU CASE, 1862

It is against this background of bureaucratic dislocation that we may most profitably view the most serious case of open and clear-cut official opposition to Christianity in the entire decade of the 1860's.[14] First, it occurred in Kweichow, one of the provinces in which the central government's grip was least secure. Although this western province was not directly involved in any of the great rebellions of mid-nineteenth-century China, it had been the scene of almost continual unrest since the late Tao-kuang period and revolt was widespread during most of the sixties.[15] Second, it took place at a time when the authority of the Chinese government was still being threatened by the Taiping and Nien rebellions in the east, and when its prestige had not yet recovered from the humiliating defeat suffered at the hands of the Anglo-French forces. Together with the Kiangsi and Hunan missionary cases, albeit in a somewhat different fashion, the Kweichow incident dramatized with swiftness and clarity the tremendous problems which the government would be up against in its efforts to carry out the treaties in the interior. Finally, the Kweichow case was inspired by a young man from bitterly antiforeign Hunan, who had risen high in the ranks of Chinese officialdom almost exclusively because of his military successes against the Taipings.

T'ien Hsing-shu (1837–1877) was typical of the sort of man who, though lacking the usual qualifications for high office in China, was nevertheless able to achieve a considerable amount of power because his talents were peculiarly suited to the needs of the time. Unlike Tseng Kuo-fan, P'eng Yü-lin (1816–1890),[16] and other great mid-nineteenth-century military figures, he had received little education. Through his bravery and daring, however, he was able to advance with astonishing rapidity from the position of a rank-and-file soldier in the early fifties to the concurrent posts of provincial commander in chief and imperial commissioner in charge of Kweichow military affairs by 1860 (and even acting governor of the province for a brief spell during the winter of 1861–1862).[17] These were high positions for a young man who had not yet reached his twenty-fifth birthday, and unfortunately T'ien's reckless and irresponsible behavior soon proved a fair match for his abilities as a warrior. In 1861 he was twice impeached for having reported falsehoods to the throne and for having failed to protect the lives and property of the Kweichow population. Lo Ping-chang (1793–1867), who was ordered to investigate T'ien's conduct, memorialized that ever since his appointment to the post of imperial commissioner he had acted arrogantly and had repeatedly initiated unjust impeachment proceedings against his subordinates. T'ien was relieved of his duties as imperial commissioner, but was permitted to retain his other posts in view of his past merits and as an inducement for him to reform his ways.[18]

But T'ien did not reform. Instead of leading his soldiers into battle, he remained in Kweiyang (the provincial capital), lording it over the officials and inhabitants of the city and giving himself up to a life of self-indulgence and debauchery. (According to the Kweichow missionaries, the young commander, in June 1861, took his eleventh wife.[19])

Just at this juncture, in April 1861, the passports authorized in Article 8 of the new French treaty arrived in Kweiyang by special courier. For Catholic missionaries who had spent long, precarious years living clandestinely in the Chinese interior, the arrival of these new credentials was, understandably, an event of moment. To celebrate their new status, therefore, the bishop of Kweichow, Louis Faurie (1824–1871), decided that the missionaries should present their passports to the high authorities of Kweiyang with a great show of ecclesiastical pomp and splendor. After suitable preparations, this decision was effectively carried out on a fine afternoon in late May when, to the accompaniment of fireworks, music, streaming pennants, and a large crowd of curious Chinese, the bishop and his colleagues were sumptuously conveyed to their prearranged rendezvous with the governor. After this visit was over, the procession continued to the yamen of the provincial commander in chief, T'ien Hsing-shu. T'ien, however, refused to receive Faurie, saying that he was occupied with important business. This precedent once established, the missionaries were similarly rebuffed by many other officials, none of whom, apparently, wished to incur T'ien's wrath.[20]

The pomp with which this visit was conducted was much discussed among the missionaries and Chinese of Kweichow, and even had reverberations in Peking, Paris, and Rome. Kleczkowski, the French chargé d'affaires, wrote the Kweichow bishop, asking: "What good can be produced by such gratifications of the sentiment of personal dignity, if they have as their primary result to shock and wound the pride of the authorities?"[21] The importance of the incident is that it served as a pretext for T'ien Hsing-shu to vent his hostility against Christianity and the foreigner. This he did by a succession of maneuvers which began in the summer of 1861, continued on into the following year, and eventually led to his punishment and fall from power.

The first overt manifestation of T'ien's hatred came in May when, shortly after the missionaries' presentation of their passports, his soldiers forced their way into the Catholic chapel in Kweiyang and absconded with the sacred images inside. On this same day Faurie learned that the young provincial commander had written a libel against the Christians and was having it distributed gratis in all the houses of the city. Early in June, T'ien's soldiers created further annoyances in the Catholic convent at Kweiyang, and a few weeks later they stole some objects from the church there.[22]

On June 12, 1861, a much more serious incident took place when some soldiers, apparently under T'ien Hsing-shu's orders, arrested three Chinese seminarists in Chaochia-kuan, a village just south of Kweiyang. Faurie's complaints to the governor of the province were ignored, and on July 29 the three prisoners, along with a fourth convert, were unceremoniously beheaded. With this, Faurie ordered one of his co-workers, S. Mihières, to go to Canton (where Kleczkowski was at the time) to register a complaint with the legation and obtain redress. Faurie directed Mihières, above all, to seek the transfer of T'ien Hsing-shu from Kweichow. But Kleczkowski, in view of the new era in Sino-foreign relations, was intent upon giving as little offense as possible to the Chinese authorities, and he arrived at a settlement which was far milder than what Faurie wished and which took no action whatever against T'ien. The French chargé's defense of his action, in a letter to the bishop, demonstrated an acute awareness of China's difficulties and of the responsibility of the foreign powers not to compound them:

As respects the present, what is particularly important in the management of all our religious affairs in China, always so difficult and complicated, is that none leaves behind it the germs of hatred and future discord; what is essential is that nowhere and especially in the farthest reaches of provinces which are inaccessible to our representatives of any kind, should either the authorities or the populations ever imagine that our worthy bishops and our hard-working missionaries are agents of our policy, enemies of China, detractors of their government and their customs, and more or less willing instruments of the ruin and eventual subjugation of their land. If such were the case, no human power could prevent the evil which would result from it.

. . . . . . . . . . . . . . . . . . . . . .

With tact, conciliation, patience, and modesty, we will gradually make a great deal of headway. I know from experience. *But above all let us not pose as conquerors. Let us not flout the authorities and the literati.*[23]

During the latter months of 1861, as T'ien Hsing-shu became apprised of Mihières' trip to Canton, of the settlement negotiated there, and of the attempt made by Faurie to obtain his transfer, his hatred of the foreign religion and its missionaries seems to have doubled in intensity. An anti-Christian pamphlet, containing language which even "the meanest people in the market place would disdain to utter," was reprinted by T'ien and widely circulated in the Kwei-yang area.[24] In December, he flagrantly violated imperial orders by sending to all the local officials of Kweichow a secret letter denouncing the heterodox foreign religion and threatening to take reprisals against any official who countenanced its preaching and observance in his district.[25]

In the wake of these events, on February 18, 1862, three Chinese Christians and a French priest, Jean-Pierre Néel, were arrested and dragged before the authorities in Kaichow, just north of the Kweichow capital. Néel sought to justify his presence in the area by showing his credentials to the Kaichow magistrate, Tai Lu-chih. Tai, however, is reported to have remarked, in the presence of the crowd assembled, that these credentials were meaningless and that Prince Kung, whose seal was affixed to them, had betrayed China to the foreigners. He then asked the prisoners to renounce their religion and, when they refused to do so, wrote out a brief sentence stating: "I have uncovered a conspiracy prior to its occurrence, and do [hereby] punish the authors of it with death." The four condemned were then stripped of their clothing, led to the execution grounds, and beheaded in the presence of Tai Lu-chih and the other local authorities. On the following day a Christian woman was executed in similar fashion, again on the formal orders of the Kaichow magistrate.[26]

It would appear to be a strong possibility that Tai Lu-chih's actions were inspired by T'ien Hsing-shu's December letter.[27] Tai's anti-Christian sentiments had already been conclusively demonstrated in 1858, when he executed four native Christians in Anshun fu,[28] and it would be hard to find a likelier candidate for the implementation of T'ien's designs. But Tai's own account of the incident, as conveyed to the throne in a memorial penned jointly by T'ien and acting Governor Han Ch'ao, gives a quite different picture. According to this report, the militiamen of Kaichow were resentful of the refusal of Néel and the others to participate in the annual festival of the dragon lantern. They therefore seized the Catholics, conducted them to the yamen, and insisted that Tai Lu-chih sentence them to immediate death. Tai, seeing that popular feeling was running high and being, moreover, completely dependent upon the militia for the defense of the locality against the ever-present rebels, was left with no alternative but to accede to the wishes of the people. This account was received by Peking in February 1863, accompanied by another memorial penned by Han Ch'ao alone, in which the Kweichow governor sought to absolve T'ien Hsing-shu from all connection with the Kaichow incident.[29]

By this time, T'ien's punishment for persistent recalcitrance in military matters had long since been ordained by the emperor. Moreover, in December 1862, the French legation in Peking had formally demanded his execution, along with that of Tai Lu-chih and another official.[30] It seems quite probable, in the circumstances and in view of T'ien's past record of misconduct, that the provincial commander, in order to save his own skin and perhaps that of Tai Lu-chih, deliberately misrepresented the true motives underlying Tai's actions in the Kaichow case, and pressured Han Ch'ao into seconding this falsification. Such, in fact, was the charge leveled by the French representative in Peking, and it was readily echoed by the throne.[31]

The details of the events succeeding the outbreak at Kaichow need not concern us here, except to note that all through 1862 and right up to his departure from Kweiyang in May of the following year, T'ien Hsing-shu appears to have continued to harass the Catholics in the capital and to circulate inflammatory pieces directed against them.[32]

Of considerably greater interest and importance are the difficulties which emerged in the Chinese management of the T'ien Hsing-shu case. As we have already seen, the central government had, since late 1860, firmly committed itself to a policy of scrupulous adherence to the Tientsin treaties, and it was especially anxious, at this early date in the new treaty era, to show both the foreigner and the country at large that it meant business. Thus T'ien Hsing-shu, Tai Lu-chih, and the other Kweichow officials who had violated the treaties would have to be punished. The only question was what form these punishments should take. The demands of the foreigner had to be met, but in such a way that the price paid was not too steep.

In these circumstances, the death penalty sought by the French representative (but not, it is only fair to add, by the Kweichow missionaries[33]) was unthinkable. T'ien Hsing-shu was still something of a popular hero in certain areas of Hunan and elsewhere and had been commended by the emperor personally for his military exploits. Whatever his errors may have been, for the Chinese government to punish him with death would be tantamount to playing with dynamite at a time when, plagued by revolt and in dire need of popular support, it could least afford to do so.[34] (At no time during the 1860's, incidentally, was capital punishment administered to a Chinese official — high or low in rank — because of his implication in anti-Christian activities.[35]) The course followed by the Chinese in order to extricate themselves from this difficulty was twofold: on the one hand, they argued vigorously with the French legation, willingly accepting its lesser demands but steadfastly rejecting its demands for the death penalty; on the other hand, they proceeded to take action against T'ien and the other Kweichow officials independently, according to Chinese law.[36] Kleczkowski continued to press his initial uncompromising stand. In April 1863, however, he was replaced as head of the French legation by Jules Berthemy, and one of Berthemy's first acts was to relax somewhat the original French demands. In a communication of June 5 the death penalty was requested for T'ien Hsing-shu only. Tai Lu-chih's sentence was to be reduced to lifelong exile, while a third official, whose death Kleczkowski had demanded, was not even mentioned.[37]

This turned out to be the break that the Chinese government was looking for. In October Bishop Faurie intimated to the high provincial officials of Kweichow and to Berthemy that it was not his desire to see T'ien Hsing-shu punished with death.[38] The new governor-general of Yunnan and Kweichow, Lao Ch'ung-kuang (1802–1867), and Kweichow governor Chang Liang-chi (1807–1871) seized upon this opening to write immediately to the Tsungli Yamen, suggesting that since T'ien's crimes were nevertheless serious, the penalty of death should be reduced by one degree only, and he should be exiled to Sinkiang, never again to be employed in any official capacity. In November, Berthemy wrote to Faurie that he would be willing to relax his position regarding T'ien. The throne, in February 1864, also indicated its desire to settle the matter on the basis suggested by Lao and Chang, and after numerous delays, in March 1865 T'ien was finally sentenced to exile.[39]

A second difficulty confronting the Chinese in the management of the Kweichow case may be briefly noted. This was the strictly administrative problem of obtaining the final execution by the provincial authorities of T'ien Hsing-shu's sentence. In March 1865, T'ien was situated in Siu-shan hsien, in the southeastern corner of Szechwan. The emperor therefore ordered the governor-general of Sze-chwan, Lo Ping-chang, and Ch'ung-shih immediately to depute officials to proceed to Siushan, take T'ien into custody, and start him off on his journey to Sinkiang. Seven months later, in October, the Tsungli Yamen reported anxiously that T'ien was still in Fowchow, Szechwan (a short distance northwest of Siushan), and that he refused to leave on grounds of "illness." The throne issued a further edict, instructing Lo Ping-chang and Ch'ung-shih to see to it that T'ien was forwarded to Sinkiang at once, illness or no illness, and warning them that they would be held responsible for any complications with the French which resulted from this delay. In November, Ch'ung-shih replied that he had received a report from the deputy to the effect that T'ien's health was somewhat improved and that an early date had been set for his departure from Fowchow.[40] T'ien, nevertheless, did not cross the Szechwan border into Shensi until July of the following year,[41] and he was evidently still in Kansu in September 1867,[42] over two years after his exile had originally been ordered.

This excessively long delay in the execution of imperial instructions has something almost ludicrous about it when viewed from a distance. But, at the same time, it underlines the glaring weakness of the central government's authority in the western provinces during this era. That the Chinese government was sincere in its efforts to achieve T'ien Hsing-shu's punishment is not open to question. (When Tso Tsung-t'ang [1812–1885], then governor-general of Shensi and Kansu, requested that T'ien, a fellow Hunanese, be permitted to lead troops against the rebels in Kansu under an assumed name, Tso was firmly rebuffed by the throne.[43]) But when it came to implementing this good faith, the regime was largely at the mercy of the provincial bureaucracy. And to the extent that it could not make the provincial officials toe the line in matters pertaining to foreign intercourse, its own position vis-à-vis the foreign powers was bound to be seriously impaired.

## EARLY CHINESE EFFORTS TO REGULATE MISSIONARY ACTIVITIES

Prompted by the difficulties which it had experienced in managing the Kweichow, Hunan, and Kiangsi cases, the Tsungli Yamen, in September of 1862, proposed to the French representative three regulations to cope with a missionary problem that already, at this early point in the new treaty era, was assuming threatening proportions. First, the Yamen urged that foreign missionaries, in their selection of converts, employ greater care and discretion, permitting only law-abiding subjects to enter the religion. If the missionaries persisted in being concerned as much with the quantity as with the quality of their followers, unsavory characters were bound to infiltrate the religion freely for the sake of foreign protection. Christianity's reputation would decline, and the hostility against it would intensify, giving rise to further outbreaks.

Since this charge of indiscriminate selection of converts was to be repeated again and again, it bears comment. Since 1724, it will be recalled, the foreign religion had been officially regarded as heterodox, with all the unpleasant connotations of political and social subversiveness implied in this classification. As a result of the *Sacred Edict* of the Yung-cheng Emperor, it was closely linked in the minds of many Chinese with that most feared of secret societies — the White Lotus.[44] Moreover, throughout the 1860's, it was still listed as a forbidden sect in the Ch'ing code. (Not until the reissuance of the code in 1870 were the articles prohibiting Christianity specifically expunged.[45]) Under these conditions, the 1860 abrogation of the prohibition against Christianity created a paradoxical situation. Incapable of undoing in a single day the work of more than a century, the Western religion found itself in the awkward position of being both heterodox and not heterodox, of being at once prohibited and tolerated. Regardless of the fact that it was legally permitted, in actuality it was on the strictest probation. And if it was to counter effectively the strong prejudices which existed against it, it had to present itself as totally incorruptible, as a teaching fundamentally different in nature from the heterodox teachings (such as Taiping Christianity) which at this very moment were creating havoc over large portions of China. This was no easy burden to bear for an organized movement that was as subject as any other to human frailty and the desire for quick results. At times, as we shall see, the Christian enterprise (in particular its Catholic component) did in fact show itself to be less than discreet both in its choice of converts and in its methods of attracting them. The Tsungli Yamen's proposal, therefore, was legitimate enough; but it was also clearly unenforceable, in the absence of complete missionary accord.

The Yamen's second proposal was that a sharp distinction be drawn between the foreign and the native practitioners of Christianity and that this distinction be recognized and preserved by both missionaries and local Chinese officials. The missionaries were guests in China and were to act and be treated as such. When an important matter arose, the officials were obliged to receive them in accordance with the general rules of propriety. At the same time, however, the missionaries were to abstain scrupulously from all interference in official affairs. Chinese subjects, on the other hand, were still Chinese subjects, even though they joined the foreign religion. Becoming Christian did not give them the right suddenly to magnify their importance vis-à-vis non-Christians or to usurp Chinese official prerogatives. Moreover, while foreign bishops and priests might wear Western or Chinese dress, as they pleased, Chinese Christians were to continue to wear native garb.[46]

The Yamen proposed, finally, that all litigation involving Christian and non-Christian subjects be decided impartially by the local authorities, on the basis of right and wrong, irrespective of the religious commitments of the litigants, and that Christian subjects, when they had legitimate grievances, take them to the officials and not to the missionaries.[47]

These three proposals were seemingly cooperative in spirit and placed limits not only on the actions of Christians — native and foreign — but also on those of Chinese officials. Kleczkowski told the Yamen that he would give them careful consideration.[48] The difficulty was that the proposals were too general in nature. Without further elaboration, possibly including the establishment of some sort of regulatory agency, they could hardly be effected. And yet if they *were* spelled out more fully, it is hard to imagine that they would have been acceptable to the foreigner.

In the early months of 1863, a series of measures similar to that outlined by the Tsungli Yamen was proposed to the throne by Ch'ung-shih. In a memorial received in March, Ch'ung observed that, prior to the relaxation of the prohibition against Christianity, Christian and non-Christian subjects had lived together peacefully but that, with the establishment of the treaties, this relationship had deteriorated and opposition to the religion had increased. In part this increased opposition was a result of agitation by narrow-minded Chinese who refused to adjust to the new situation. In part it stemmed from the bad reputation which the religion earned for itself by taking in unsuitable subjects and by paying scant heed to traditional Chinese customs and mores. To mitigate these evils, Ch'ung urged, on the one hand, that circular instructions be issued to all Chinese officials to the effect that they should deal with cases involving Christians in an impartial manner and, on the other hand, that the Tsungli Yamen request the French representative to instruct all bishops to avoid transmitting their doctrines to disreputable persons. If these proposals could be implemented, Ch'ung felt, Chinese orthodoxy would be safeguarded against the incursions of the foreign religion. And the latter, by actually putting into practice its exalted aims, might be able to leave the ranks of the heterodox! [49]

In April 1863, Ch'ung-shih presented two more memorials on the missionary problem, in which he placed special stress on the abuses with which Christianity was becoming associated. Ordinary subjects, upon entering the religion, became arrogant and boastful and suddenly began "to ride about in sedan chairs." Taking advantage of foreign protection, moreover, they treated the local officials with contempt and in some cases even evaded government service. Clearly, in Ch'ung's view, something had to be done if the traditional Chinese social order was to be preserved and chaos prevented. He suggested, first, that foreign missionaries be assigned ranks and titles appropriate to their status, thereby differentiating them sharply from their native converts, who were still subject to Chinese jurisdiction. More generally, Ch'ung proposed that the Tsungli Yamen, in conjunction with the French minister, devise a basic set of ground rules to prevent Sino-foreign discord in the interior.[50] Ch'ung's proposals were referred to the Tsungli Yamen. Apparently, however, the Yamen took no action, and it was not until several years had passed that it renewed its efforts to gain foreign acceptance of restrictive measures.

# CHAPTER 5

# THE MISSIONARY'S ABUSE
# OF HIS POSITION

THE Kweichow case of 1862 highlighted the difficulties involved in implementing China's new foreign policy in the face of widespread bureaucratic decline and weakened central authority. T'ien Hsing-shu's hatred of Christians may have derived from his Hunanese background and his years of fighting against the Taiping insurgents. It may have sprung from his jealousy of the newly won status of the foreign missionaries of Kweichow province. But, regardless of the causes of this hatred, ultimately it was possible for him to express it in action only because of the power and influence of his office. And it is very doubtful whether a man of T'ien's background and qualifications would have held such high office in more peaceful times.

One of the major tasks confronting the leaders of the T'ung-chih Restoration, then, was to remove the evils that plagued the bureaucracy and to re-establish the prestige and power of the central government in the provinces. This would have been difficult enough in any circumstances. It was made particularly difficult after 1860 by the presence in the interior of the foreign missionary armed with his new privileges.

For just as the missionary vied with the gentry for influence in the social and cultural spheres, so too in the political sphere he represented a significant threat to the authority of the local official. In some cases this threat was a simple consequence of the missionary's treaty rights. For example, when his life or property was endangered, he was empowered to seek the protection of the Chinese authorities. If this protection was not forthcoming and he suffered injury or damage as a result, he was further empowered to go over the head of the local authority and bring the matter to his government's attention. Invariably, his claims were then presented to the Chinese government, and he obtained material satisfaction for the wrong done him. If the case was sufficiently serious, moreover, the foreign government often proved powerful enough to see to it that punishment was inflicted upon the local Chinese authorities who had failed to carry out their treaty obligations. In such cases the missionary exercised an authority which, at bottom, was greater than that of the local official.

In other cases the missionary made his power felt on the local scene by abusing his treaty rights or by using them with a minimum of discretion. Catholic and Protestant missionaries accepted, at times with considerable delight, the application of force to obtain redress.[1] The Catholics, furthermore, often demanded excessively large indemnities for injuries sustained. (In the province of Szechwan alone, between 1863 and 1869 they collected 260,000 taels in reparations.[2]) Since these sums usually had to be raised by the gentry and officials of the localities concerned, they were hardly conducive to the lessening of tensions.[3] Again, the Catholics, during the early sixties, took full advantage of the sweeping terms of Article 6 of the Sino-French Convention, which, it will be recalled, provided for the return of previously confiscated Church properties to their original owners. The sites involved had long since been purchased and occupied by Chinese, and had in many cases undergone extensive renovations. The missionaries, moreover, seldom possessed legal proof of prior ownership, and arbitrary methods of dispossessing the owners and turning the sites over to the foreigner were not uncommon. The Franciscan fathers even went so far as to demand, in addition to the return of their former properties, reimbursement for house and land rents collected during the preceding hundred-year period.[4] Catholic missionaries also demanded, as restitution for injuries sustained in antiforeign riots, buildings which had been constructed with public funds and which were of great symbolic importance to the Chinese. Since Catholic indiscretions in this whole area of real estate transferals aroused intense hostility on the part of the resident populations,[5] a few examples may be cited.

In partial compensation for the property damage sustained in the Nanchang incident of 1862, the French, as we have seen, demanded and received the public orphanage outside the city gate. In 1861 a former Shanghai church edifice, long used as a temple of the god of war, was returned to the Jesuits through the influence of General Montauban; the ancient residence of the missionaries in Shanghai, which had since been transformed into a meeting hall, was also retrieved through the general's influence, despite the protests of some of the literati who used it.[6] At Chengting, Chihli, the site of an imperial palace, then in ruins, was obtained by the Catholics, who proceeded to erect on it a church, an orphanage, and several schools.[7] In 1861 various ancient Catholic properties in Peking were restored to the foreigners, among which was the site of the Pei-t'ang (North Church), given to the French Jesuits by K'ang-hsi. The new Pei-t'ang erected by the Catholics during the 1860's proved a source of continual friction because of its great height and its proximity to the imperial palace.[8] Friction also resulted in Nanyang, Honan, because of Catholic efforts to retrieve a former Church property which had been converted into a merchants' guildhall.[9] Somewhat later in the decade, finally, Monsignor Anouilh reported that as a result of recent persecutions in his diocese (western Chihli) fourteen temples and a large municipal building, among other items, were surrendered to the Church.[10]

In some cases, at least, French missionaries, in their demands for compensation, showed themselves to be acutely conscious of their role of furthering the prestige and power of France, as well as that of the Church. Monsignor Guillemin, vicar apostolic of Kwangtung, Kwangsi, and the island of Hainan, wrote to the French foreign minister in 1859 that since the missionaries were the sole Frenchmen living in Canton (which at this time was occupied by British and French forces), it was up to them and their converts to "counter balance the English influence" in the city. Guillemin could think of no finer way to accomplish this than by building a church in Canton that would be "one of the finest souvenirs of France in this distant land." Napoleon III was interested in the project and promised that 300,000 francs would be made available for it. When Guillemin asked the Chinese authorities for a suitable site, they were very conciliatory and offered large areas both inside and outside of the city. The bishop, however, would accept none of their offers and insisted upon one of the three finest locations in Canton — the imperial treasury, the former site of the governor-general's yamen, or a Taoist temple. In spite of the fact that even the French commander at Canton felt that Guillemin's demands were unnecessarily harsh, the presence of French troops in the city had the ultimate effect of intimidating the Chinese into yielding. Guillemin, ironically enough, ended up by acquiring the site of the yamen which had been occupied by the intensely antiforeign governor-general of the forties and fifties, Yeh Ming-ch'en (1807–1859), and on it there was eventually erected a large Gothic structure that loomed over the city as a visible symbol of French power.[11]

In still other instances, Catholic missionaries encroached upon official authority more directly. In Kweichow the missionaries of the Société des Missions-Étrangères repeatedly pressed the French legation to obtain the transfer, first, of Governor Chang Liang-chi and, then, of Governor Tseng Pi-kuang (d. 1875).[12] Bishop Faurie later in the decade committed the unprecedented act of sending a communication (chao-hui) directly to the Tsungli Yamen to request that a taotai, To Wen, and several other officials who had shown favor to the Catholics, be pardoned for their former misconduct.[13] Bishop Pinchon of Szechwan at one point announced to the Chinese authorities his decision to employ an official seal (kuan-fang) in all future correspondence with them,[14] while in Shantung a missionary was accused by the Chinese of actually having adopted the title of governor (hsün-fu).[15] Catholic missionaries repeatedly aroused the ire of provincial officials and the Tsungli Yamen by employing forms of correspondence reserved for official use only.[16] Again, in numerous instances the missionaries assumed a position of de facto equality with the local authorities by negotiating settlements directly with them.[17]

## MISSIONARY INTERFERENCE
### IN OFFICIAL AFFAIRS

In the view of almost all Chinese officials, the most serious and widespread abuse committed by Catholic missionaries in the 1860's was their tendency to interfere in local official affairs either on behalf of their converts or in order to gain converts.[18] Since this was, in some respects, one of the most delicate and complex problems arising out of the new treaty framework, it merits our close attention. As we have seen, one of the clauses in Article 13 of the new French treaty granted Chinese subjects freedom to practice Chris-

tianity without being liable to punishment *for this reason.*
This item does not seem to have met with much opposition
from the Chinese officials who negotiated the treaty.[19] It
was, after all, no more than a reaffirmation of the earlier
edicts of the Tao-kuang Emperor (1844 and 1846). In reality, however, it proved to be what may well have been the
most serious infringement upon Chinese sovereignty in the
whole treaty system. It was much more than a mere repeti-
tion of the earlier edicts. These, it will be recalled, had
specifically refused the missionaries permission to enter the
interior to preach and live. And without missionary aid,
the Chinese Christian, though he had been granted "religious liberty" on paper, was usually helpless to enforce
this right. Under the new treaty, however, the missionary
was right on the spot and since the local official, in Latourette's words, "did not wish to become embroiled with foreigners who through their consuls and ministers could
make trouble for him with his superiors," [20] the missionary
was frequently able to provide his converts with protection
of the most efficacious sort.

An incident which took place in 1863 in Kiaoho hsien,
Chihli, clearly illustrates the power which the missionary
could now wield vis-à-vis the local official. A band of counterfeiters pillaged a temple in the district to obtain copper
statuary for their trade. The literati immediately cried
"profanation, sacrilege," and before long complaints were
lodged against three Christians "whom people were sure
they had seen leaving the temple during the night." Father
Leboucq, the Jesuit priest in charge of the area, continues
the narrative:

They had just pinioned my 3 Christians when I arrived at
the yamen. "Pardon me," I said to the mandarin, "if I do not
salute you and employ polite usage . . . I have just one word
to say to you . . . , but listen closely. If you had in your sub-

prefecture a counterfeiters' workshop, and the emperor had knowledge of it, would you not expect soon to receive the silk cord with orders to hang yourself?" — "Yes," answered the magistrate pale and trembling. — "Well then, follow me; at the very moment that I talk to you, people are making cash 15 *li* from your tribunal." — "Impossible!" — "You will see." — "Then I will send soldiers." — "No," said I, "it is you who must go there. Since in the future it will be impossible for Christians to vindicate themselves before your tribunal, I insist today on vindicating, myself, those whom you have just enchained." The mandarin did not answer a word but, turning toward his henchmen, said to them: "Go and set free the Christians whom you have placed in irons and arrest their accusers." [21]

This case was, if Leboucq's account is accepted, a clear instance of persecution. Hence, even though his brusque manner might have left something to be desired,[22] he was perfectly within his rights in seeking the acquittal of his converts. But what of those cases in which a convert sought a missionary's assistance in matters that were basically nonreligious? Leboucq admitted, at another time, that Chinese often requested his support for purely temporal matters and had the adroitness, when doing so, to link their grievances either closely or distantly with the cause of religion. This naturally complicated the missionary's position. He might regard it, as Leboucq did, his "scrupulous duty" not to occupy himself with temporal affairs.[23] (Just how scrupulous Leboucq really was in this regard is not at all certain. One Catholic author points to him as a prime example of the type of missionary who, after 1860, adopted the "perilous" method of assisting Chinese in lawsuits, provided that they first agreed to become Christians along with their whole families.[24]) But often, obviously, it was unclear whether the real reason why a Christian had been accused was his religious association or the fact that he had indeed violated the law. In these borderline cases, the missionary risked the alienation of the neophyte if he did not intervene with the Chinese authorities, while if he did intervene, he ran the danger of alienating the authorities.

Some Catholic missionaries, either to protect or to acquire converts, actually went so far as to use their political influence in clear contravention of Chinese law. In the early sixties, for example, a Christian woman of Kuan hsien, Szechwan, was charged with a long list of crimes including swindling and murder. According to the Chinese legal code, she was punishable by death. The French bishop, Eugène Desflèches, however, apparently spoke out in her favor, and Ch'ung-shih, in order to appease Desflèches, closed the case by sentencing her to banishment.[25] (It is worth noting in passing that Desflèches, for some twenty years, led bands of armed Christians against the authorities and non-Christian inhabitants of Szechwan. By the late 1870's his activities had become so outrageous that the Chinese government requested his removal from China as a condition for the maintenance of peace and order in the province — a request which was promptly accepted and executed by Paris.[26])

Whatever short-term gains the Catholic missionary may have won by exercising political influence in local Chinese affairs, in the long run the damage done to his position in Chinese society was probably far in excess of any dubious benefits. Chinese subjects in trouble with the law frequently turned to the missionary for protection, causing more than a few Chinese officials to accuse the Church of being a refuge for the scum of society.[27] Other subjects relied upon the Church's influence to act arrogantly toward their non-Christian neighbors, resist payment of taxes, trump up false legal charges, and commit all sorts of other unlawful acts.[28] The extent to which the power of the Church was feared by the people is somewhat amusingly illustrated by an incident recounted by the Jesuits of Kiangnan. A blacksmith in the vicinity of Soochow, finding that his anvil was not bringing in enough cash, decided to supplement his income through more devious means. He traveled all about the area and, falsely claiming that he was Christian, fleeced numerous heathen families by threatening them with the wrath of the Catholic religion if they did not pay him a certain sum of money. It was not until after he had collected from 300,000 to 400,000 cash in this manner that he was finally exposed.[29]

Although a good many Chinese, perhaps a majority, probably joined the Church from the purest of motives, committed no crimes, and never applied to the missionary for assistance in temporal affairs, the Christian community as a whole fell heir to the bad reputation fostered by the more mischievous of its members and became the butt of the hostility generated by this smaller group. More serious still, the missionary, to the extent that he was successful in shielding Chinese subjects from the law, removed them from Chinese jurisdiction, creating *imperia in imperio* and stirring the fires of hatred in a bureaucracy that was unwilling to relinquish any of its prerogatives.

### Bishop Faurie in Kweichow: A case study in missionary interference

The most notorious case of missionary interference in Chinese political affairs in the 1860's took place in Kweichow.[30] This case, though in some respects atypical, reveals with unusual clarity the motives which inspired the missionary to involve himself in local affairs as well as the Chinese reactions which this interference produced; it also provides a curious footnote to the as yet unwritten history of Kweichow's political troubles in this period.[31]

During 1863–1864 in rebel-infested Anshun prefecture (just west of Kweiyang), a great popular movement in favor of Catholicism suddenly erupted, in which whole villages evinced a desire to embrace the faith. François-Eugène Lions, the missionary of the Société des Missions-Étrangères in charge of the area, wrote an urgent letter to the Catholic bishop in Kweiyang, begging him to send the human and financial assistance needed to cope with the situation. The bishop, Faurie, in a burst of enthusiasm, communicated to Paris requesting substantial reinforcements. These, however, were unavailable at the time, and Lions asked Faurie himself to come to Anshun to assist him. The bishop consented.[32]

What was behind this sudden upsurge of pro-Catholic sentiment? Subsequent events reveal that a number of elements were involved, the least important of which was religious zeal. In 1861 and 1862, as we have seen, the Catholics in the vicinity of Kweiyang had been severely persecuted by the military commander and former acting governor of the province, T'ien Hsing-shu. When the French proved themselves influential enough to obtain T'ien's exile to Sinkiang, and to acquire his plush yamen in the Kweichow capital for Church purposes,[33] the foreigner naturally came to be viewed as a powerful force in the province. This notion was reinforced by the great favor shown to the Catholics by the new governor-general of Yunnan and Kweichow, Lao Ch'ung-kuang. (Lao had previously gained the confidence and respect of the French at Canton, where, as governor-general, he negotiated the transfer of the former site of Yeh Ming-ch'en's yamen to the missionaries in 1861. In 1863, he took the unusual step of issuing a proclamation in favor of Christianity which he allowed to be drafted by a Catholic official on his staff.[34])

In these circumstances, it was only natural that the distressed inhabitants of Anshun and nearby areas should turn to the Catholics for help. The government had been pursuing a policy of extermination against the rebels in southwestern Kweichow, and although the latter genuinely desired peace, they dared not enter into direct negotiations with a Chinese officialdom which, from all indications, was thoroughly corrupt and oppressive. Consequently, when the Moslem and Miao rebel chieftains heard that the Catholic leader was going to visit Anshun they communicated with Faurie and requested him to act as mediator for them with Governor-General Lao, the only man in whom they had confidence. Faurie, in the spring of 1864, took the matter up with Lao and offered his services "on the essential condition that the whole of the past be forgotten, that no one be killed, and that the region be exempted from taxation for one year, since the levying of taxes on a disorganized region would lend itself too much to the extortions of greedy mandarins." Lao promptly accepted these conditions and, along with acting Governor Chang Liang-chi, gave Faurie full powers in writing to act as mediator and surety with the rebels.

The bishop departed on his unique mission on July 11, escorted during the initial part of the journey by an armed guard of one hundred soldiers.[35] We need not be concerned here with his attempt to pacify the rebels, except to note that he returned to Kweiyang on September 30 without having accomplished this task.[36] More important are some of the incidents that occurred en route — incidents revealing the altogether astonishing amount of political power which had accrued to Faurie as well as the Chinese response to this fact.

At one point a group of "pagans" were journeying to the market of a town through which Faurie was passing. One of the men remarked that he was going to cure himself of his opium addiction and then worship "the true God." Another in the party responded with a volley of

curses and calumnies against the Christians, whereupon
his companions warned him that "this was not the time
to speak in that vein" and that if he did not watch his
tongue they might cut it out. When this threat failed to
have the desired effect, they promptly tied up the detractor
and took him to the lodgings of the bishop. Here one of
Faurie's Chinese assistants set up court, took depositions,
and terminated the affair by condemning the "culprit" to
prison. Faurie, however, upon hearing the poor wretch's
cries for mercy, pardoned him so that his family would
not have to suffer "from his stupidity." "As his entire
punishment, I condemned him to go back to his little city
. . . and make honorable amends there in public." Faurie
then commented:

Do they, then, place people in prison for having spoken ill
of the Religion? — To be sure! — Why? — 1. Because all the
mandarins strongly prize being among my friends, on account
of my influence with the viceroy and governor, and because
they fancy that in avenging the slightest offense against the Religion they make themselves very agreeable to me; 2. because
the Christians, in particular the neophytes, are very touchy on
this point. As soon as someone permits himself to say anything
which is amiss, they tie him up and conduct him to the mandarin.

In another city there lived a militia chief, Ouy (Wei?),
who had been represented to Faurie as a persecutor of
Christians. Faurie's neophytes insisted that he have the
man thrown into prison, but the bishop, preferring a more
Christian course, sent for him. Ouy, fearing that Faurie was
going to have his head, came before him trembling and
prostrated himself on the ground. The missionary bade
him rise and from the ensuing conversation it was revealed
"that schemers had sown discord between him and us.
They told him that I sought to have him assassinated; that

I had in my retinue a regiment of French soldiers; that we came with the design of taking possession of his region, etc. In consequence, he permitted no one within his jurisdiction to become Christian. Now that he has seen my peaceful disposition, he is completely reassured. He made some fifteen prostrations, and begged me to stop at his home on my return. He wants to become a Christian along with his whole family."

Faurie next recounts the story of two feuding families in yet another village. One family, all of whose members had been wounded and whose house had been pillaged and destroyed, prepared a formidable bill of indictment against the second. Moreover, "to be more certain of success, it started by declaring itself Christian, hoping through this to obtain the support of the bishop." The second family, "perceiving the danger, also became Christian via the same motive." Faurie arrived while this feud was going on, and the two families accused each other before him. The bishop counseled them on the merits of Christian charity and forgiveness and got them to desist from any legal action. They confessed that previously they had not understood the religion, but that now they would like to become real Christians.[37]

All along Faurie's route he was received with great fanfare. Cannons were fired, music was played, flags were flown, and all the notables came out to welcome him. It was the sort of reception usually reserved for governors-general and governors (a thought which at one point occurred to the bishop, much to his discomfort). The only touch needed to complete the picture was for Faurie to remit the punishments of those who had been cast into prison because of their offenses against Christianity. This he succeeded in doing on at least three different occasions, commenting in one instance, either with dry humor or incredible naïveté: "It is remarkable that every one of the individuals implicated for flagrantly insulting the Religion, embraces the faith with ardor upon leaving prison." [38]

One of the persons whom Faurie had tried to contact during his journey was Ma Chung, the Moslem rebel chieftain of Hingi (Hsing-i), a prefecture southwest of Anshun. Ma Chung was much more sympathetic to the idea of mediation than the other rebel leaders were. However, the envoys whom he sent to meet with Faurie did not overtake the bishop until after he had returned to Kweiyang. Faurie immediately announced their presence to the governor-general and governor, both of whom wanted him to mediate with Ma. The missionary, however, was too busy at the time and delegated a trusted subordinate, Léonard Vielmon, to go to Hingi and act in his place. Vielmon's sojourn with the rebels lasted from November 1864 to September 1865. Superficially, his mission was successful. He obtained the submission of Ma Chung, and the area was temporarily pacified.[39] From the standpoint of the Church, however, the mission was a failure in several important respects and was clearly recognized as such by the missionaries.

Faurie gave the following reasons for his initial agreement to become involved in these affairs:

the hope that this mission of pacification, well carried out by a missionary, would accrue first, in general, to the honor of Christianity and would win for it the sympathy of the high mandarins and of the government, as a result of the signal service which the Church would be found thus to have rendered to the imperial cause; second, and especially as regards Hin-y-fou [Hingi fu], the hope of reforming there the Christian community of yore which the rebellion had almost entirely annihilated, and even perhaps of establishing there with one fell swoop a collection of Christian communities of considerable size and solid constitution, thanks to the influence which would naturally accrue to the Church from the success of this expedition.[40]

Title page of *Pi-hsieh chi-shih*     Title page of *Pi-hsieh shih-lu*

T'ien Hsing-shu (1837–1877)

*Title:* The [Foreign] Devils Worshipping the Incarnation of the Pig [Jesus].

*Text in center:* The heir apparent Jesus was the incarnation of the pig of heaven [the Lord of Heaven]. He was very licentious by nature. Of all the wives and daughters of the high officials of the country of Judea there was not one who did not fall prey to his lust. Subsequently his licentiousness extended to the king's concubines and he schemed to usurp the throne. Therefore a high official memorialized, making known his crimes. He was bound upon a cross and fastened to it with red-hot nails. He emitted several loud cries, assumed the form of a pig, and died. Frequently he entered people's homes, where he did unnatural things and engaged in illicit relations. As soon as a woman heard his pig's grunt her clothes would unfasten of themselves and she would let him satisfy his lust before coming to her senses. The followers of the pig therefore exhort people to worship him, making use of this as a pretext for satisfaction of their greed and lust. But if crosses are chiseled into your doorsills and steps, the pig incarnate and his followers will be seized with fear and will not approach. This is a special announcement for the benefit of people throughout the empire, that they may be apprised of [the danger] and take precautions against it.

*Text on right:* This beast is the one in whom the foreign devils take refuge. He has not yet discarded his earthly form [lit., his skin and hair].

*Text on left:* If human beings take the pig of heaven [the Lord of Heaven] as their lord, how will they have any face left?

*Note:* The character for "pig" is homophonous with that for "Lord," although the tones are different. The character for "grunt" is homophonous with that for "religion, teaching." Thus, the "religion of the Lord of Heaven" (Catholicism) becomes the "grunt of the pig of heaven." The character I have translated as "incarnation, incarnate" literally means "essence, spirit, semen." In this context, especially in view of the erect state of the pig's genital organ, a play on "semen" seems likely. The characters printed on the pig's side are those for "Jesus," those on the backs of the two kneeling foreigners "missionary" and "convert," respectively. In this picture, as well as others in the series, all characters referring to Christianity or the foreigners are printed in green in the original, and foreigners and converts are depicted wearing green hats. "Green hat" (lü-mao) in the Chinese vernacular is an epithet for "cuckold."

*Title:* Beating the [Foreign] Devils and Burning Their Books.

*Text on right:* The heterodox grunt of the pig incarnate [the heterodox religion of Jesus] has been transmitted from abroad. [Its adherents] insult heaven and earth and destroy the ancestral cult. Even if they are [punished] with ten thousand arrows and a thousand swords, it will be difficult for their crimes to be expiated.

*Text on left:* Their nonsensical [lit., dog fart] magical books stink like dung. They slander the sages and worthy ones and revile the Taoist immortals and Buddhas. All within the nine provinces and four seas [the empire] hate them intensely.

*Title:* [The Practitioners] of the Grunt of the Pig [the Religion of the Lord] Removing the Fetus.

*Text on right:* All men are anxious in regard to the three unfilial acts. Therefore they amass good deeds and beseech the gods, that they may be blessed with sons.

*Text on left:* Everyone hates conscienceless cuckolds. Hasten therefore to sweep away heterodoxy and exterminate the [foreign] devils; be on your guard lest the grunt of the pig [the religion of the Lord] insult heaven.

*Note:* According to Mencius, the greatest of the three unfilial acts was to be without male heir. The foreign missionaries were frequently accused of extracting the fetus and placenta from pregnant women for medicinal and alchemical purposes. The foreigners in the picture are again wearing green hats, suggestive of their cuckoldry.

*Title:* [The Practitioners] of the Grunt of the Pig [the Religion of the Lord] Gouging Out the Eyes.

*Text on right:* The gods naturally know when they are being insulted. If you gouge out [the eyes] of others, others will gouge out yours.

*Text on left:* You dead devils who have just become followers of the devils' grunt [the foreign religion], [do not forget] that, while those with sight may seek to become blind, only in vain can the blind seek [to recover] their sight.

*Note:* The foreign missionaries were repeatedly accused of gouging out the eyeballs of dying or dead converts for alchemical and other purposes. The term "dead devils" here clearly refers to native Christians, who presumably have become dead to all virtue. Note that the kneeling figures in the foreground are two converts whose eyes have already been gouged out by the foreigners, after whom they now crawl submissively.

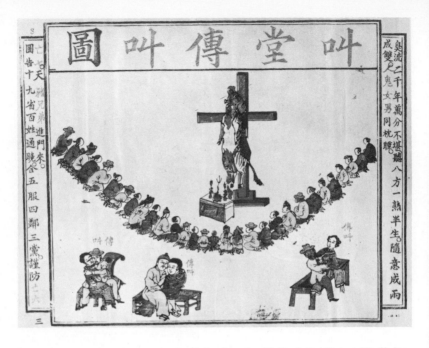

*Title:* Propagating the Grunt [Religion] in the Hall of the Grunt [Religious Hall or Church].

*Text on right:* The stench of [Christianity] has flowed through two thousand years of time. It is utterly intolerable. From all quarters people who hardly know each other freely mate and pair, human beings and devils, women and men, sleeping upon the same pillows.

*Text on left:* This illustrated announcement is for the information of all the people of the nineteen provinces [China]. Let all join with their relatives, their neighbors, and the members of their parents' and wives' clans in taking stringent precautions against the entry of the cuckolds — the brothers of the pig of heaven [the Lord of Heaven] — into their homes.

*Note:* The characters for "Jesus" are faintly printed on the belly of the crucified pig. The characters adjacent to the three couples in the foreground, although literally (in this context) signifying "the propagation of the grunt," are homophonous with the Chinese word for "preaching." This, in other words, is what the writer would have us believe the foreigners really did under the guise of their missionary labors. All of the males in the picture are wearing green hats — the sign of the cuckold.

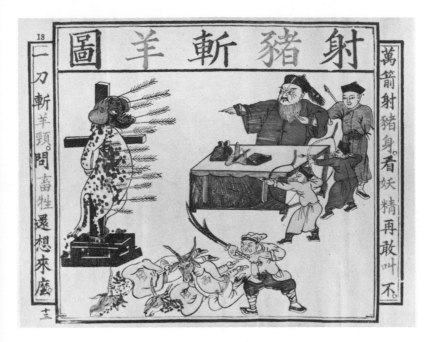

*Title:* Shooting the Pig [Jesus] and Beheading the Goats [the Foreigners].

*Text on right:* After we have pierced the pig's [Jesus'] body with ten thousand arrows, will this monster again dare to grunt?

*Text on left:* After we have beheaded the goats [foreigners] with one stroke of the sword, will these beasts still entertain thoughts of coming [to China]?

*Note:* Faintly inscribed on the body of the pig are the characters for "Jesus." The characters on the goats' bodies are those for "Westerner." Foreigners in these pictures are often represented as goats, the characters for "goat" and "foreigner" being homophonous.

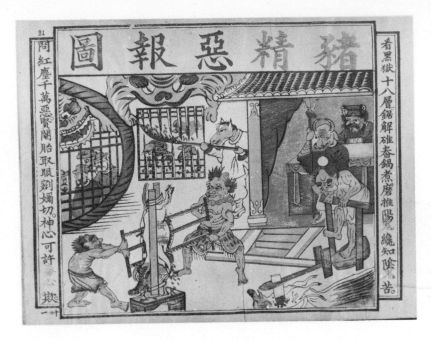

*Title:* The Terrible Punishment of the Pig Incarnate [Jesus].

*Text on right:* Only after seeing the saws cutting, the pestles pounding, the caldrons boiling, and the grindstones grinding in dark hell's eighteen levels, will the [foreign] devils of this world know the suffering endured by the [foreign] devils of the world below.

*Text on left:* You who in this life have committed a thousand times ten thousand malicious acts, who have castrated boys, removed the fetuses from pregnant women, gouged out people's eyes, and cut off women's nipples — do you think that the gods will permit themselves to be taken in by your wickedness?

*Note:* Jesus (being sawed in two) and a missionary (being pounded with the pestle) are again portrayed as pigs because of the partial homophony of the Chinese words for "Lord" and "pig."

In all of these hopes Faurie was sadly and overwhelmingly disappointed. The number of adult baptisms in 1863 had been one hundred and fifty, in 1864 around two hundred, and in 1865 three hundred. From France the directors of the Société wrote in consternation, "You announced one hundred thousand conversions, and you register 511 catechumens and 300 baptisms. What does this mean?" One of the missionaries, Eugène Lamy, provided an answer in his "Journal de Gan-chouen [Anshun]": "During the years 1863, '64 and '65, the natives worshiped *en masse,* but scarcely knowing why, they followed the general tide. They thought that in embracing the religion they would be sheltered from the harassings of the Chinese, and that in their lawsuits the bishop and his missionaries would be their powerful protectors." Faurie himself seems to have been aware of this problem well in advance of Vielmon's expedition. On July 23, 1864, en route to Anshun, he wrote to one of his missionaries, "the trouble with these regions is that we allowed too many persons to worship who were saddled with lawsuits, resulting in the alienation of the good people." And a few days later, to another missionary: "Among the worshipers there are many who come to find support in their temporal affairs; some to evade the all too just consequences of some serious accusation." [41] What Faurie does not seem to have realized, of course, was that as long as he continued to take full advantage of his position of power and influence in provincial political affairs, the Church was bound to attract the worst elements of society — the ones most needing protection — and, as a consequence, repel the "good people."

For the future of the mission in Kweichow, the more serious consequence of the Catholics' ill-advised flirtation with high politics lay in the response it drew from the officials of the province. True, some of these, seeing the high esteem in which Faurie was held by Lao Ch'ung-kuang, did all they could to put themselves in the bishop's good graces. Others, however, became more hostile than ever toward the Catholics. In December 1864, Vielmon wrote that a military official of Hingi hsien, one Liu Hung-k'uei, had thrown nine Christians into prison because of their refusal to leave the area. A month later, he reported the machinations of an official of Puan t'ing (just north of Hingi), Ch'ien Hsün. Ch'ien had given orders to arrest Vielmon if he passed through Puan. When the missionary, discovering this, took an alternate route, Ch'ien issued a proclamation ordering the confiscation of all Catholic property within his jurisdiction and making it a capital offense for anyone to embrace the Christian faith.[42] In March 1865, the above-mentioned Liu Hung-k'uei killed four Christians in Hingi and made an attempt on Vielmon's life when the missionary tried to enter his district. Again, in August of that year, a Chinese priest and five converts were massacred in Yungning (in Anshun fu), while the officials stood by and did nothing.[43]

The missionaries repeatedly laid the blame for the instigation of these incidents on the acting governor of the province, Chang Liang-chi. Vielmon was certain that Chang wanted to prevent the success of his mission, while in Faurie's view the governor was "the eternal enemy of order, of religion and of the Europeans," and "the devil of the whole province." [44] Chang was, indeed, partially successful in frustrating the efforts of the missionaries to obtain the punishment of Liu Hung-k'uei and the transfer of Ch'ien Hsün.[45] Moreover, it is true that in 1865–1866 he memorialized the throne several times, angrily accusing Faurie of interference in government affairs; of blindly and obstinately adhering to the unfeasible policy of pacification, so as to obtain more converts; of shielding culprits from the law and preventing local officials from administering justice.[46] Whether or not the governor was really behind the anti-Christian incidents of 1864–1865, it is incontestable that he hated the religion and despised its missionaries.

Chang's motives for feeling and acting as he did were complex, and the pat explanation that he was an irresponsible official must be rejected. In the first place, some of the charges he brought against Faurie contained a substantial measure of truth. Faurie, as we have seen, confessed privately that one of his chief motives for consenting to the missions of pacification had indeed been to increase the influence of Christianity in the province. Moreover, the Catholics freely admitted that hoards of Chinese had flocked to them for assistance in lawsuits and that, in the words of one of them, "the number of fish is so great and the good ones are so rare." [47] If, as charged by Faurie, Chang did secretly hinder the efforts of Vielmon to negotiate the submission of the rebels, he undoubtedly had his reasons. It is possible that as a result of his previous experience with Moslem rebels he genuinely felt that a policy of fighting (rather than negotiating) was wisest in this instance.[48] If he did feel this way, however, there was little he could do in the face of the contrary views of his superior, Lao Ch'ung-kuang. On the other hand, it is quite probable that Chang's views were also colored by his personal attitude toward Lao and toward the latter's relationship with Faurie. The governor-general, though one of the most just and competent officials of the Restoration period, was unusually "proforeign" — a characteristic which, in the context of the times, was not calculated to endear him to his fellow officials. When Lao gave, first Faurie and then Vielmon, sweeping powers to negotiate with the rebels, a function which was the exclusive prerogative of the officialdom, Chang's resentment and envy may have become irrepressible. And when Lao, in January 1866, memorialized the throne vindicating Faurie of the charges which Chang had leveled against him,[49] Chang, in June, replied with a bitter denunciation of Lao.[50]

Chang's initial accusation against the Catholics had farreaching repercussions. The Tsungli Yamen, infuriated with Faurie, spoke to the French minister and requested him to instruct the bishop to refrain henceforth from interfering in Kweichow's political affairs.[51] The French minister wrote Faurie, warning him of the grave risks he was incurring by not confining his actions to the sphere of religion. In Paris the superior of the Séminaire des Missions-Étrangères, hearing of the accusations leveled against the missionary, felt it his duty to inform the French Foreign Ministry of them. Even a cardinal in Rome wrote to Faurie inquiring about the matter.[52]

Faurie, of course, defended himself as best he could. Although he probably had little trouble clearing himself with the Church, it was not as easy to sweeten the bitter taste left in the mouths of Kweichow officials. Many years later, in 1882, a Kweichow missionary wrote that "today still, if the memory of M. Vielmon's expedition is altogether honorable and respected in appearance, the mandarins and literati are jealous at bottom of the trust which was given by the government to a foreigner."[53] Perhaps it was as Vielmon said at the time, that many officials of the baser sort could "not see without jealousy that a missionary, with cross in hand, can do in one day for the good of the people what they themselves cannot do in several years with their armed soldiers."[54] This, in the circumstances, would have been an all too human response. But it is not unlikely that officials of a better stamp also resented the missionaries' usurpation of authority. For, in the end, the influence that accrued to the foreigner as a result of this usurpation was bound to confuse the traditional lines of authority in the revolt-torn province and make all the more difficult the ultimate restoration of Chinese jurisdiction there.

## FRENCH EFFORTS TO RESTRAIN MISSIONARY EXCESSES

Count Kleczkowski left Peking in April 1863, upon the arrival of the new French plenipotentiary, Jules Berthemy. His departure can scarcely be said to have grieved the Kweichow Catholics, one of whom (Vielmon) felt that the count "wanted to obliterate the missionaries completely." [55] Although, in contrast, Berthemy was regarded as a stout friend of missions, during his brief tenure in Peking (April 1863–June 1865), he consistently adopted measures that tended to place limits on missionary aspirations. In this he had Paris' full support. Shortly after arriving at his post, he received instructions in connection with the excessive claims put forward by the Szechwan priest, Louis Delamarre: "It is important that we do not allow our missionaries to exaggerate the protection with which our treaty authorizes us to cover them. In order to preserve in this protection the moral force which alone renders it effective, we must act with prudence and opportunity and not provoke, by misplaced and incessant demands, a resistance over which it would afterwards be impossible for us to triumph by simple diplomatic measures." [56]

Profoundly convinced that Catholic missionary abuses were a fundamental cause of the antagonism which the missionary enterprise encountered,[57] Berthemy again and again counseled French bishops on the wisdom of this approach. When the vicar apostolic of northern Szechwan, Pinchon, requested authorization to intervene, *in an official capacity,* with the local authorities in affairs that concerned the Christians of his vicariat, Berthemy (in January 1864) refused the request, adding:

The powers with which your Grace would like to be invested can be conferred upon him only by the Government of the Emperor or by the Chinese Government; now He will easily understand that the first cannot delegate to a person not accountable for his actions and situated outside of its control a protectorate the exercise of which might in certain cases involve its policy, while the second, determined to attenuate as much as possible the operations of a propaganda against which it is already only too inclined to take umbrage, will always resist acknowledging to the missionaries the *right* to interfere in matters which concern its own subjects.

Berthemy went on to remark that intervention of a friendly, unofficial sort was the only kind to which missionaries might have recourse when they felt it desirable to bring influence to bear on the local authorities. A letter, almost identical to this one, was sent in February to the vicar apostolic of Honan, J. H. Baldus, who had put forth similar claims.[58]

In March 1864 the French representative returned to this same theme in a letter to the vicar apostolic of southeast Chihli, J. B. Anouilh, "whose ill-considered zeal," according to Berthemy, had "created numerous difficulties for the Legation." [59] Anouilh was one of the prime exponents of the dangerous strategy of assisting Chinese in lawsuits in return for the conversion of themselves and their entire families to Christianity.[60] Berthemy asked him to remind the missionaries under his authority that if this sort of extrareligious intervention resulted in a multiplication of conversions, the sincerity of which could often be doubted, it tended at the same time to create an antagonism of which their protégés were the most frequent victims, wounded the susceptibilities of the magistrates who regarded it as an encroachment on their prerogatives, and, by arousing the suspicions of the Chinese government, occasioned "for the present and for the future a considerable prejudice against the work which Catholic missions [were] pursuing in China." [61]

For Catholic missions, the most noteworthy event marking Berthemy's stay in China was the signing, in February 1865, of the convention which bears his name. We have already seen the extremes to which Catholic missionaries went in demanding choice locations and properties from the Chinese as restitution for grievances going back in some cases to the K'ang-hsi era. Berthemy took the position that Article 6 of the Sino-French Convention was not intended to facilitate a real estate grab for the profit of foreign clergy, but rather to provide the land needed for missionary purposes. The Berthemy Convention, therefore, while affirming the right of French missionaries to rent and purchase property in the interior, at the same time provided that the properties in question were not to be held in the name of individual missionaries or converts, but as part of the collective property of the Catholic mission of the area. The provincial authorities appear to have added to the official text of the convention the stipulation that each sale was to be preceded by a local investigation to see whether local Chinese subjects approved of the transfer. Ultimately, therefore, the Berthemy Convention tended to hamper Catholic missionaries in their subsequent property transactions.[62]

Whereas it is true that Berthemy's tenure in Peking was generally marked by restraint and tact, the missionary excesses which occurred during this period were clearly based upon the foreign protection offered by the unequal treaties. Although an ever-growing number of later missionaries came to feel that Christianity would be much better off if it dispensed with such protection altogether,[63] during the 1860's the overwhelming tendency of Catholic and Protestant opinion was to regard it as both necessary and desirable. Chinese official opinion, as might be expected, provided a sharp contrast to the missionary viewpoint. As the members of the provincial bureaucracy and the Tsungli Yamen became increasingly aware of the insoluble difficulties presented by the missionary problem within the existing framework of regulations governing Sino-foreign relations, a series of proposals was made to alter this framework, and in so doing to mitigate the difficulties. Perhaps these proposals were prompted in some cases by hatred, but more often, it would appear, there was a genuine desire to reduce friction. Although none of the proposals was ever accepted by the foreigners, they provide an unusual insight into the Chinese official's own views of the problems besetting him, after a half decade of troubled intercourse with the foreign missionary under the aegis of the new treaties.

# CHAPTER 6

# CHINESE PROPOSALS
# FOR THE REGULATION OF
# MISSIONARY ACTIVITIES

IN ADDITION to the Kweichow disturbances of 1865 in which at least ten Chinese Christians were martyred, a serious incident, involving the killing of a foreign missionary, occurred during the same year in the neighboring province of Szechwan.[1] It comes as no surprise, then, to find that when the Chinese government made its first serious attempt to regulate missionary activities, the provinces of Kweichow and Szechwan and their missionaries were deeply involved.

## THE CASE OF THE SPURIOUS
## TEN ARTICLES, 1866

On January 14, 1866, the Tsungli Yamen addressed a note to the new French representative, Henri de Bellonet, requesting him to examine and take under consideration ten articles for the regulation of Christian activities. The articles, originally fourteen in number, had been sent to the Yamen by Ch'ung-shih who claimed that they had been jointly drafted by the authorities at Chengtu and the vicar apostolic of northern Szechwan, Pinchon. The Yamen extracted the ten items that did not relate specifically to Szechwan and suggested to Bellonet that they might well be applied to the empire as a whole.

The articles may be summarized as follows. (1) The aims and activities pursued by the Christian religion are exalted ones and harmonize with those of the sages of China; but those who use the name of the religion in order to commit reprehensible acts must be severely punished upon discovery. (2) Missionaries are men of highest character and must therefore be treated with utmost respect by the local authorities; if, however, a missionary commits acts which are blameworthy and contrary to the principles of the religion, the bishop of the province in which he resides should be notified and should take steps to depose him. (3) Serious cases involving the religion should be brought to the attention of the Chinese authorities, who, after coming to a decision, will immediately announce it to the bishop in question. (4) When missionaries are confronted with an urgent matter they must study it conscientiously and try to unravel the truth, before bringing it to the attention of the local authorities. If the case cannot be settled on the spot, the complaint should be taken to the provincial capital; but the bishop must be certain first of the accuracy of the facts presented in the charge. If the local authorities who initially examine the case demonstrate partiality, the matter should be taken up with the high provincial authorities. (5) Missionaries must carefully guard against interference in the temporal affairs of their converts and must not provide them with illegal protection in cases at law. The authorities shall be free to apply to Christians the penalties prescribed by law; Christians convicted of criminal acts must be ejected from the religion. (6) The names of missionaries shall be registered each year with the provincial authorities to prevent misrepresentation; similarly, announcement shall be made of all changes in missionary personnel. (7) The names of converts shall also be registered with the authorities whenever circumstances permit; when circumstances do not permit such registration, the bishops shall be obliged to present the names of their converts upon the request of the Chinese authorities. (8) When Chinese wish to join the religion, the missionaries must carefully examine them beforehand to ascertain that they are law-abiding subjects and that they are not involved in any criminal proceedings. Prospective converts who fail to meet these standards shall not be allowed to join the religion; likewise, Chinese who are already members of the religion shall be expelled if found unworthy. (9) Christians found guilty of misdemeanors and crimes shall be duly punished by the local authorities and immediately ousted from the religion. (10) Christians, when lodging extrareligious complaints, shall do so according to a specific procedure (as spelled out in the article).[2]

Bellonet's initial response to the above articles was somewhat ambiguous. He had misgivings regarding the phrasing of some of the items and felt that in their existing form they might open the door to misapplication. Moreover, he would have liked to have consulted with the bishops before giving his approval. But Bellonet had only praise for the fair-mindedness of Prince Kung, head of the Yamen, and, in view of the long delay which would result from having to communicate with the bishops in the provinces, he announced his provisional acceptance of the articles. At the same time, however, he informed Prince Kung of his intention to invite episcopal comment on the new regulations and suggested that the Chinese provincial authorities also be ordered to transmit their observations.[3]

On January 25 Bellonet sent copies of the ten articles to each of the Catholic bishops residing in China, requesting their detailed opinions and, at the same time, making known his own feeling that the articles were potentially dangerous and might legitimize many abuses.[4] A short time

later he expressed similar misgivings in a dispatch to Paris,
stressing the fact that acceptance of the articles would be
tantamount to surrendering the extraterritorial status assured the missionaries by the French treaties. The peren-
nial confusion of France's China policy and the lack of accord between the Foreign Ministry in Paris and its representatives in Peking were convincingly demonstrated by
Paris' reply in May. Bellonet's apprehensions were taken
into account and the proposed regulations judged to be disappointing in some respects. But the view of the Foreign
Ministry was that all such observations were in a sense superfluous at a time when the missionaries and the Chinese
government seemed to have found a common area of agreement. In view of the serious difficulties that the French
legation had encountered in conciliating its missionaries
with the Chinese authorities, the new arrangement might
even be considered as constituting a "genuine improve-
ment." The legation was given permission to accept the
ten articles, provided that missionary sentiment was found
to be in accord.[5]

Missionary sentiment, far from being in accord, was outraged. When Bishop Faurie of Kweichow received Bellonet's January letter, with the accompanying text of the
articles, he could not believe that certain of the items had
been drafted by one of his colleagues. Observing, moreover, that certain references to Christianity in the Chinese
text were pejorative, he wrote to both Pinchon and the
vicar apostolic of eastern Szechwan, Desflèches, to obtain
confirmation of his suspicions. On April 1, before receiving
replies from the other two bishops, he addressed a letter to
Bellonet, informing him of his doubts regarding the origin
of the articles and voicing certain specific objections to
their contents. Soon afterward letters from Desflèches and
Pinchon completely confirmed Faurie's suspicions and an-

nounced that the articles had been exclusively the work of Chinese officials, who had but one end in view: to hamper the activities of the Christians and prevent the diffusion of the Gospel. The declaration of the bishops was materially confirmed when it was discovered that the Chinese engraver charged with the fabrication of Bishop Pinchon's Latin seal had reversed the proper word order.[6]

The finale to this dramatic exposure was necessarily anticlimactic. Bellonet, on July 7 and 9, addressed two curt and angry communications to the Tsungli Yamen, demanding the punishment of the Szechwan officials responsible for the chicanery and retracting the provisional adherence to the articles that he had given in January.[7] The Szechwan local officials, in turn, made a rather halfhearted attempt to show that it was not they who had acted in bad faith, but Pinchon himself.[8] Nevertheless, the Tsungli Yamen, which had long since instructed the high provincial officials to put the articles into operation,[9] was placed in the embarrassing position of having to disavow them officially and withdraw its previous orders.[10] In December Bishop Faurie wrote to the French representative thanking and congratulating him, on behalf of the Kweichow missionaries, for the "brilliant" manner in which he had unmasked and confounded the "dangerous trap" set for missionaries and missions in China.[11] The Chinese government, which at the start of 1866 thought it had come significantly close to a partial solution of its missionary problem, was by the end of this year farther away than ever from any solution.

### MISCELLANEOUS PROPOSALS, 1866

Several other proposals made in this year merit passing notice. In March, the governor of Anhwei, Ch'iao Sungnien (1815–1875), presented two memorials the main substance of which was that, while China could not prevent her subjects from practicing Christianity, she could and should take immediate steps to prohibit them from propagating the religion.[12] Ch'iao's view of the foreign religion flowed directly from the main stream of Chinese antiheterodox thought. He denounced Christianity because of its opposition to ancestor worship and idolism and its subversion of the natural human relationships. Moreover, he felt that the injurious influence which it exerted on public morals and on the social order was no trifling matter. The problem, as with all heterodox sects, was one of preventing the Christians from becoming so numerous and powerful that the local officials could no longer keep them in check. If the Chinese were allowed to preach as well as practice the religion, Christianity's prestige would soar, with a consequent upward surge of its membership; Christians would gradually infiltrate the yamens and the military; and there was no telling but that some clever rogue might again (evidently alluding to the Taipings) set himself up as their leader and raise the standard of revolt. Ch'iao observed that forbidding Chinese to preach Christianity would in no way conflict with the treaties, which simply permitted them to practice the religion freely. He suggested, finally, that if a total ban on Chinese preachers was at present impracticable, the Chinese government might come to an agreement with the foreign ministers to limit the number of such preachers to ten or twenty.

Ch'iao Sung-nien's two memorials were referred to the Tsungli Yamen, which, although commending Ch'iao's good intentions, found his proposals unacceptable for a variety of reasons. First, the Yamen reasoned (in a memorial of late March), while it was true that there was nothing in the thirteenth article of the French treaty expressly permitting Chinese people to preach the foreign religion, there was also nothing in the article prohibiting them from doing so. The foreigners would certainly argue that if the practice of Christianity was to be tolerated, its preaching would of necessity have to be countenanced. Second, the Yamen contended, the former Church properties in Shensi, Nanking, and elsewhere had not yet been restored, a fact which gave rise to repeated complaints on the part of the French and English (?) ministers. If, at this time, China haggled over restrictive measures, the foreigners would only be further irritated, providing the seeds for future discord.

More fundamentally, the Yamen strongly implied that Ch'iao's distinction between Chinese preachers and practicers of Christianity was of little relevance. If the local officials were unjust in their management of affairs, those who practiced the religion would be just as hard to handle as those who preached it; if the local administration was fair, on the other hand, there was no reason why those Chinese who preached Christianity should prove particularly obstructive. Chinese people, whether they preached or merely practiced Christianity, were still Chinese subjects. If, as stated by Ch'iao, there were Chinese preachers who used the religion to resist official orders and refuse payment of taxes, there was nothing in the treaties to prevent the authorities from dealing with such cases according to law.

Finally, the Yamen recalled, a set of regulations had already been agreed upon in conjunction with the French chargé d'affaires and had been communicated to all the high provincial officials. (Bellonet's provisional acceptance of the spurious ten articles had not yet been retracted.) If these regulations were strictly adhered to by the local authorities and enforced impartially, the foreign missionaries would no longer have any grounds for unreasonableness,

and the Chinese could hold them to the virtuous pronouncements they made so much of, thus defeating them at
their own game. Unstated, but uppermost in the Yamen's
reasoning, was the sound assumption that, having just obtained one significant concession from the foreigners in
the sphere of regulating Catholic missions, this was no time
to press for another.

In the course of the discussions of the Wade-Hart proposals of 1865–1866,[13] the governor of Kiangsi, Liu K'un-i,
memorialized (in May 1866) suggesting a means by which
entry into the foreign religion might be legally discour-
aged. Foreign commerce, Liu felt, merely diminished China's choicest local products. But the spread of the foreign
religion was capable of undermining Chinese customs and
opinions. Missionaries invariably indulged their converts
by intervening in public affairs and coercing the authorities. Worst of all, local ruffians assumed false identities and
created disturbances, and yet, because of the power of the
missionaries, the chou and hsien officials were unable to enforce the laws. Liu proposed that, on the pretext that persons using false names were being investigated, missionaries
should be required to turn over to the local officials the
names of all their converts. The lists thus handed in could
then be compared with the population registers, so that
those who joined the religion would have something to fear
in the future.[14]

Liu K'un-i's proposal received no imperial comment.
But it is virtually certain that if it had ever been put into
effect, it would have met great opposition from the French.
In his communication of July 9, 1866, in which he retracted his provisional adherence to the spurious ten articles, Bellonet singled out two items which would in any
case have been inadmissible — the one requesting that missionaries notify the authorities of each change in their resi-

dence and the one requiring the registration of converts. He granted that the latter item was a police measure common enough everywhere but in China. "But here, where we are convinced of the ill will of the mandarins, of their firm resolve to evade the treaties and to cause every possible injury to the Christian religion, we cannot be a party to the compilation of a list which would in their hands be a proscription list." [15]

## THE SECRET CORRESPONDENCE OF 1867–1868 [16]

The British Treaty of Tientsin provided for optional revision after ten years. Since negotiations were to start early in 1868, the Tsungli Yamen on October 12, 1867, presented for the throne's inspection a circular letter in which it outlined and commented upon the chief issues which were likely to come under discussion. The throne ordered the Grand Council to send copies of this letter to eighteen high provincial officials experienced in foreign affairs for their comments. Because the entire correspondence was, with the exception of one leak, cloaked in complete secrecy, it provides a useful barometer of contemporary official opinion. [17]

The part of the Tsungli Yamen's letter which dealt with the missionary question was the last of its six sections, entitled "On the extension of missionary activities." The Yamen began by observing that even though China might wish to prohibit these activities altogether, since they were clearly authorized in the treaties such prohibition was impossible. It went on to assert that if the thirteenth article of the French treaty and the circular instructions sent out the previous year — evidently alluding to the Yamen's letter of December 1866 to the high provincial officials, re-

tracting the spurious ten articles and enjoining the officials
to revert to the old method of dealing with missionary difficulties "on the basis of reason and in accordance with
the treaties" — were faithfully observed, there should be
no trouble, for these items stipulated that Chinese laws
were to be obeyed and that missionaries were not allowed
to interfere in local public affairs. The Yamen recognized,
however, that there were missionaries who were inclined
to extend improper protection to their converts and to assist them in their lawsuits. This occasioned great difficulty
for the local officials who, though unable to yield to the foreigners, at the same time were not in a position to control
them. When such cases arose the local officials complained
to their superiors who, in turn, complained to the Yamen.
The Yamen then protested to the foreign envoy in question, but its protests always came to nought, partly because
the envoy was unable to keep the missionaries in check
and partly because he would invariably shield the missionary at fault by raising extraneous issues.

The circular letter proposed two possible means by
which this unfortunate situation might be ameliorated.
One was to establish a system of official supervision of the
activities of Christians, analogous to that under which Buddhism and Taoism had long been regulated. The Tsungli
Yamen recognized, at the same time, that there were pitfalls in this method, not the least of which was the danger
that it would serve to institutionalize Christianity — that
far from discouraging people from joining the religion it
would do the very opposite. The Yamen's second suggestion, more general and enigmatic than the first, was that
the local gentry and people — the only classes in close daily
contact with the Christians — should, while appearing to
accept the existing situation, quietly renew the moral fiber
of those Chinese who had been led astray by the foreign

religion, exposing their errors and laying bare their per-
fidies. This would be "a prohibition which did not appear
to be a prohibition" (*pu chin chih chin*).[18]

Before reviewing the responses of the provincial officials
to the Tsungli Yamen's secret letter, it is interesting to
note the extent to which the Yamen's specific suggestions
were apparently influenced by the earlier memorial of an
obscure expectant chou magistrate of Szechwan, one Yang
T'ing-hsi. During the heated battle between the archcon-
servative Wo-jen (d. 1871) and the Tsungli Yamen in
1867,[19] Yang, another extreme conservative, took advantage
of the drought of that year to renew Wo-jen's plea for the
abolition of the T'ung-wen kuan — a school established in
the early 1860's for the study of Western learning — in the
hope that by rectifying human error the natural harmony
of the universe would be restored and rain would again
fall. The emperor's reply (of June 30, 1867) ridiculed
Yang's proposal, but at the same time sought to soothe the
powerful Wo-jen faction by inviting Yang to submit a
memorandum on self-strengthening.[20]

Yang's memorandum, received by the throne on July 8,
1867, was organized under four headings, one of which was
devoted to the means by which missionary activities should
be secretly hindered. Yang summarized the abuses frequently associated with Christianity and painted a frighten-
ing picture of what would happen if something were not
done soon. The adherents of the religion would become so
numerous that they would no longer be easy to regulate,
and in the future the religion would become so institu-
tionalized in China that it would be impossible to distinguish Christians from non-Christians or to segregate the
two groups. Yang went on to argue that since, at the time,
missionaries could not be prevented from preaching, nor
converts from practicing, the religion, the thing to do was

to devise a means of prohibiting Christianity while appearing to tolerate it. Yang's most important proposal for achieving this end was the same as that put forward by the Tsungli Yamen several months later, namely, the appointment of officials to supervise Christian activities, following the procedure already applied to Buddhism and Taoism. Chinese, he added, should be required to notify the authorities when they joined the foreign religion. In this way the gentry and populace would know at a glance who the Christians were, and the latter, by being sharply set apart from the rest of the people, would become ashamed at their difference or, if not ashamed, would at least be rendered harmless. Thus the foreign religion, without being ostensibly prohibited, would die a natural death.[21]

The similarity of the proposals put forward by Yang T'ing-hsi and the Tsungli Yamen, and even of the language used in the two cases, seems puzzling when one recalls that the Yamen had been under heavy fire from the conservative faction all during 1867. This situation is not, however, quite as puzzling as it appears. In the first place, by accepting Yang's proposals and yet, at the same time, adding significant qualifications to his specific recommendation concerning the appointment of supervisory officials, the Yamen was able to cast itself in a role that was at once conciliatory and critical with reference to the Wo-jen group. Still more important, it must not be forgotten that the members of the Yamen were at heart no more kindly disposed toward Christian missions than were the more xenophobic elements of Chinese officialdom.[22] Thus, just as Yang T'ing-hsi could share with the Yamen the knowledge that missionary activities could not be openly prohibited, so too the Yamen could join Yang in aiding and abetting all legitimate means of rendering the foreign religion impotent. Whether or not the Yamen's adoption of Yang's

slogan of "a prohibition which did not appear to be a prohibition" actually contributed to the upsurge in antiforeign
feeling witnessed throughout the empire during the years
from 1868 to 1870,[23] one thing was certain: the slogan suggested in unmistakable terms the Yamen's view that if
Christianity had to be suffered, it did not have to be encouraged.

*The provincial officials' reactions*

Of the eighteen high officials originally ordered to send
in replies to the Tsungli Yamen's letter, only seventeen actually replied (one having taken leave of absence in the
meantime), and of these seventeen two did not comment
on the missionary question. The remaining fifteen who did
comment were Tso Tsung-t'ang (governor-general of Shensi
and Kansu), Jui-lin (d. 1874, governor-general of Kwangtung and Kwangsi), Ting Pao-chen (1820–1886, governor
of Shantung), Li Han-chang (1821–1899, governor of
Kiangsu, concurrently acting governor-general of Hupeh
and Hunan), Shen Pao-chen (director of the Foochow Shipyard), Tseng Kuo-fan (Nanking governor-general), Ying-
kuei (d. 1878, Tartar general at Foochow), Liu K'un-i (governor of Kiangsi), Ch'ung-hou (1826–1893, superintendent
of trade for the three northern ports), Wu T'ang (d. 1876,
governor-general of Fukien and Chekiang), Li Hung-chang
(governor-general of Hupeh and Hunan), Ma Hsin-i (governor of Chekiang), Li Fu-t'ai (1807–1871, governor of Fukien), Kuo Po-yin (d. 1884, governor of Hupeh, concurrently acting governor of Kiangsu), and Kuan-wen (1798–
1871, acting governor-general of Chihli).[24]

Although the memorialists differed in their general estimates of Christianity, on the whole they agreed that as a
*teaching* it was no cause for worry. Kuo Po-yin, it is true,
criticized the religion for making people turn against their

parents and mistreat the gods. And many of the writers took the traditional position that Christianity was a heterodox sect even worse than Buddhism and Taoism. But Ch'ung-hou admitted to the religion's peaceful aims, and Li Fu-t'ai observed that it differed from the ordinary run of heterodox teachings in encouraging people to regard others as themselves and to act virtuously. None of the writers, moreover, evinced any fear that the Chinese educated classes had been, or would ever be, attracted to Christianity, and there was general agreement that the only persons for whom the religion had any appeal were the impoverished, the ignorant, and the disreputable.

Several of the memorialists strongly suggested that the missionary body was an arm of the state, used for political purposes. Tso Tsung-t'ang (whose departing words to his French associates in Foochow were that when they came to China in the future, they should leave their missionaries home) grouped the missionary question, along with those of imperial audience and the dispatch of Chinese envoys abroad, under the category of public affairs (kung-shih). In Tso's view, the French government's relationship to the missionaries was identical with that of the Chinese to the Tibetan Lamas. Shen Pao-chen believed that the foreign governments relied on the missionaries (and merchants), who were scattered all over the interior and were in daily contact with the officials and people, to spy out China's strengths and weaknesses. He observed, moreover, that even though the foreign representatives were fully aware of the "unrestrained and impudent behavior" of these groups, they nevertheless protected them in all sorts of ways.[25] Finally, Kuan-wen, in his proposal for dealing with unruly missionaries (see below), strongly implied that the Church was a political animal.

Almost all of the memorialists accused the foreign missionaries of the already familiar abuses of accepting bad people, interfering in local public affairs, extending improper protection to converts, and so on. In the words of Li Hung-chang's elder brother, Li Han-chang: "The converts rely on the missionaries, the missionaries rely on the foreign consuls, the foreign consuls hold the local officials responsible, and the local officials, if they are concerned with the general welfare, cannot but accommodate [the Christians]. Averting calamity in this fashion, [the local officials thus] add fuel to the fire at the same time that they would extinguish it."

To alleviate this dilemma, a number of the memorialists stressed the fact that even though Chinese practiced and preached Christianity they were still the emperor's subjects and were liable to punishment when they violated the laws. Ch'ung-hou, on the other hand, felt that the problem could be partly remedied if the local officials would be less bigoted and inflexible in their attitude toward the foreign missionaries. Similarly, Li Hung-chang, while emphasizing that the missionaries should not interfere in local affairs and that Chinese converts should remain under Chinese jurisdiction, asserted at the same time that, when Christians were oppressed by the gentry and the populace, the local officials should deal with the case fairly and promptly. Ting Pao-chen also called for greater justice in the officials' treatment of the converts, adding however that when converts stirred up trouble, the local authorities should be assisted by the high provincial officials in handling the matter. Li Fu-t'ai went even further, suggesting that when local officials mismanaged cases involving missionaries and converts they should be impeached and discharged from their posts. But, Li added, if the officials' management was irreproachable and the missionaries still interfered, the latter also should be subject to punishment. The last suggestion was elaborated by Kuan-wen who urged that when missionaries conducted themselves improperly they should be recalled by their country's representative and replaced, just as was done with Chinese officials when they were charged with maladministration.

As pointed out by Li Hung-chang, however, these were all superficial remedies. To get at the root of the evil, Li, along with Tseng Kuo-fan and others, urged that the traditional Confucian institutions — charitable, educational, and so on — be re-established at the local level and that the orthodox spirit be revitalized among the population. Only in this way could the Tsungli Yamen's "prohibition which did not appear to be a prohibition" really be effective. And only thus could Christianity ultimately be rendered harmless.

The writers who commented on the Tsungli Yamen's qualified suggestion to appoint officials to supervise Christian activities were almost unanimous in rejecting it. Shen Pao-chen pointed out that if the officials appointed were Chinese it would be impossible to control the foreign missionaries, while if they were foreigners it would be tantamount to appointing foreign ministers in the interior and would be intolerable. Shen added that since the missionaries regarded the converts' freedom to act outrageously as a major inducement for people to join the religion, they would never consent to such restriction anyway. Wu T'ang agreed with Shen that the missionaries would not submit to restriction of this sort; Liu K'un-i added that such supervision would invade the authority of the local officials. Li Hung-chang felt that the idea might work if final jurisdiction still remained in the hands of the Chinese authorities. In his judgment, however, the post would probably be filled by the missionaries themselves and would only lend itself to the spread of abuses — a view which was shared by

Li Fu-t'ai. Kuan-wen opposed the suggestion on the ground that Buddhism and Taoism were no longer heterodox and that, if the same regulations were applied to Christianity, the name of the two Chinese teachings would be tarnished. Ch'ung-hou, alone, was in favor of the idea, arguing that since the supervision of Buddhists and Taoists had never served to attract people to these teachings, there was no reason to fear that it would draw people to Christianity.

Several statements submitted by Shen Pao-chen, on behalf of persons too low in rank to memorialize the throne directly, deserve passing notice. A Kwangtung expectant taotai, Yeh Wen-lan, observed that foreign missionaries did not limit themselves to quoting the absurd words of Jesus — words which were quite sufficient in themselves to bring harm to those who heard them — but engaged in invidious activities besides. The reason why the commoners wanted to kill the missionaries was that the latter enticed and made off with women and children in order to gouge out their eyes and extract their blood. The foreigners, Yeh concluded, should be informed that henceforth only good people would be allowed to be missionaries in China — people who discoursed on astronomy and mathematics and who encouraged the populace to be loyal, filial, chaste, and righteous. Those missionaries, on the other hand, who used preaching merely as a pretext for undermining Chinese customs should be expelled. In this way only could Christianity be made innocuous.

Wu Chung-hsiang, a district subdirector of studies, also regarded the words of the missionaries as absurd and felt that their religious labors were but a mask to cover up their secret designs. Wu was alarmed at the number of ignorant common people who had already been deceived and predicted that, if missionary activities were further extended, heterodox teachings and immoral conduct would spread far and wide through China. He suggested that officials in charge of studies be ordered to go in person to all the villages, taking along with them salaried licentiates, to expound the *Sacred Edict,* the *Book of Filial Piety,* and such writings, so that orthodox learning would flourish and heterodox teachings die out.

Finally, a licentiate named Lin Ch'üan-ch'u voiced the fear that the followers of the religion, while no cause for immediate worry, would marry and in time become numerous. Lin therefore proposed that the officials establish free schools on the village level, enabling the peaceful and rectifying influence of Confucianism to be brought to all. If his proposal was carried out, Lin thought, within several decades no one would again think of entering the foreign religion.[26]

Although few of the memorialists who commented on the Tsungli Yamen's letter went quite so far as Tseng Kuo-fan did when he asserted that the harm wrought by Christianity was slight in comparison to that which would result from the introduction into the interior of railways or steam navigation, by and large the comments were surprisingly moderate in tone. The writers, it is true, were almost unanimous in opposing any further concessions to the missionaries. But at the same time they all recognized that the toleration clauses were there to stay, and none advocated that the preaching or practicing of Christianity be prohibited. No one even suggested that converts be registered or that orphanages be abolished.

Does this moderation imply that, the views of later historians notwithstanding, the missionary problem was not in fact a serious one during the 1860's or, assuming it was, that it was simply not recognized as such by contemporary Chinese officials? Mary Wright has suggested that, in view of the secret character of the correspondence, its moderate tone "tends to disprove the charge that responsible officials of the central or provincial governments either provoked or condoned . . . antimissionary outbreaks." [27] This may provide part of the answer, but it is incontestable that, at least in some cases, even responsible officials, if they did not actually provoke riots, did condone them. (Witness, for example, the statement of Shen Pao-chen when apprised of the Nanchang outbreak of 1862. Shen explicitly exonerated the Nanchang populace from all blame and exhorted his subordinates not to make any arrests.) Wright's interpretation, moreover, does not offer any explanation as to why the officials who responded to the Tsungli Yamen's letter appeared to attach so little importance to a problem which, in her own words, "was fundamentally ·the most serious problem in Sino-foreign relations." [28]

This paradox is explained in part by the form in which the Tsungli Yamen's letter was cast and the subjects it dealt with. The first five topics in the letter — receiving foreign envoys in imperial audience; sending Chinese envoys abroad; introducing railways and telegraphs; establishing foreign warehouses in the interior, arranging for inland travel and residence and allowing steam navigation on inland waterways; and importing foreign salt and developing coal mines — all dealt with new and potentially revolutionary activities which, because they had not yet been accepted by the Chinese, were eminently negotiable and of paramount concern at the moment. The question regarding Christian missionary activities, on the other hand, was not whether they should be allowed — they had already been sanctioned by treaty — but whether they should be extended. Thus, hateful as these activities might have been to the memorialists, they could not but agree with Kuanwen when he asserted: "The missionaries . . . are already operating in all the provinces without any real restrictions.

What use would there be in extending [these opera-
tions]?" [29] In the last analysis, then, one very good reason
why the Yamen and the provincial officials made light of
the missionary issue at this time was that it had, to all
intents and purposes, been removed from the arena of discussion and was, so far as the immediate negotiations were
concerned, not an issue.

But this still does not fully explain why the officials, in
commenting on the missionary problem as a whole, remained so temperate. Here, I would suggest, the immediate
circumstances of time and place and of the writers in question may have been all-important. First, it will be recalled
that the secret correspondence, in its entirety, took place
in the closing months of 1867 and in January 1868. Although serious missionary cases had taken place in Kweichow and Szechwan in 1865 and in the vassal state of Korea
in the summer of 1866, the year 1867 was almost completely
devoid of any anti-Christian incidents, much less any serious
ones, and marked a low point in antiforeign activity for the
decade as a whole.[30] This calm, so ominous from the vantage
point of the years immediately following, may well have
contributed to the resigned, almost complacent, view which
the officials took toward the missionary problem.

Second, of the fifteen officials who commented upon the
problem, only one, Shen Pao-chen, had already been actively involved in the handling of a serious Church difficulty,
and it is perhaps noteworthy that Shen's statement was one
of the strongest made of the entire group. Tseng Kuo-fan,
Li Hung-chang, Liu K'un-i, Ma Hsin-i, Kuo Po-yin, Jui-lin,
Ying-kuei, and Wu T'ang, on the other hand, did not become personally involved in serious missionary troubles
until the period from 1868 to 1870, *after* the secret correspondence was over. Tseng Kuo-fan's attitude changed

appreciably following his experience at Tientsin during the summer of 1870.[31]

Third, in the 1860's the missionary problem appears to have been especially serious in the two western provinces of Kweichow and Szechwan. Yet the high officials of these provinces were not among those called upon to comment on the Tsungli Yamen letter. It is more than conceivable that, if they had been, their replies would have been very different in tone from those of the other officials.

A more general reason, finally, why the secret correspondence concerning the extension of missionary activities was so moderate was perhaps the simple fact that this correspondence was prompted, in the first instance, by the approaching revision of the *British* treaty. At the time, British missionaries were just beginning to penetrate the Chinese interior and had not yet created any major difficulties for the local authorities. When, in the latter months of 1868, they did begin to present a problem, Chinese officials started to take a much more serious view of the situation. And when, during the early 1870's, the time for the revision of the *French* treaty became imminent, the Tsungli Yamen came forth with proposals which, had they been implemented, would have fundamentally altered the conditions under which the missionary enterprise was being conducted.

# CHAPTER 7

# OFFICIAL ACCOMMODATION
# OF THE FOREIGN MISSIONARY

AS THE decade of the 1860's drew to a close and opposition to Christianity grew more intense, it became clearer
than ever that one of the most deep-seated administrative
problems on the local scene was how the Chinese official
who wished to implement the unequal treaties effectively
was to do so in the face of this opposition. The provincial
official who showed the missionary courtesy, provided him
with protection, and managed his and his converts' affairs
in a just and impartial manner might act out of an overriding sense of responsibility to the throne. His actions
might also be motivated, in some instances, by fear of the
missionary's ultimate power in Peking or of his influence
with the higher provincial authorities. Regardless of the
motivation, however, his accommodation of the missionary
was fraught with consequences potentially dangerous to his
position as an official.

In Kweichow in 1864–1865, it will be recalled, a segment of the local officialdom went out of its way to oblige
the foreigner, because of the latter's apparent influence
with the governor-general and governor of the province.
One consequence of this was a decided increase in the ani-
mosity toward Christianity from other branches of the
Kweichow official hierarchy. A second and more fundamental consequence was the heightened tendency of many

inhabitants of the province to embrace Christianity for extrareligious reasons — chiefly protection — and the concomitant contraction of the juridical authority over such individuals of the very officials who most ingratiated themselves with the missionary. In effect, a circular process was initiated which, in its total impact, reduced the ability of the local officials to maintain law and order.

A situation similar to this also seems to have developed in sections of eastern Chihli. Here the Jesuits, in particular François Leboucq, pursued a conscious policy of courting the favor of the officials and gentry. As evidence of his success, Leboucq was decorated by the emperor for his services to the imperial cause in 1862. Moreover, in 1868, after narrowly escaping death, first at the hands of rebel and then of government troops, he won from the pen of Ch'ung-hou an apologetic proclamation which not only was highly favorable to Christianity, but which — in a manner reminiscent of Lao Ch'ung-kuang's defense of Bishop Faurie — called attention to Leboucq's fine character and praised his past services to China.[1] The fact that Leboucq had so much influence with the high authorities of Chihli undoubtedly helped him to obtain prompt and just settlements of the vast majority of legal cases in which his converts were involved.[2] At the same time, however, his effectiveness with local Chinese officialdom clearly resulted in a diminution of the latter's over-all authority. And this in turn encouraged the more unscrupulous Chinese subjects to take advantage of the missionaries' aid and protection, aggravating still further the resentment of the non-Christian population toward the Christians.[3]

In other cases, the official who earnestly sought to enforce China's treaty obligations impaired his effectiveness still more directly by exciting mob violence against himself. Thus, in Fuan hsien, Fukien, earlier in the decade the

Catholics, as a result of continual harassment, obtained redress from the Chinese authorities. But when the prefect in charge of the area tried to execute the agreement, his yamen was stormed by an angry mob and he was forced to take flight, after suffering bodily injury.[4]

A case similar to this occurred in the autumn of 1868. In June of that year the director of the China Inland Mission, Hudson Taylor, negotiated the rental of a house in Chinkiang, Kiangsu. Through the connivance of a local magistrate, however, a proclamation was issued questioning the legality of the transaction. Late in August, following the gentry-inspired anti-Christian riots in nearby Yangchow, the British consul at Shanghai, W. H. Medhurst, arrived in Chinkiang and requested the taotai in charge to obtain the issuance of a more satisfactory proclamation and secure for Taylor the peaceful possession of his property. The taotai made a thorough inquiry into the deeds of rental and, deciding that the transactions had indeed been legitimate, instructed the magistrate of the city to repair to the site in question and take the appropriate steps to transfer it to Taylor. Upon the magistrate's arrival, however, he was mobbed by a large crowd which protested vehemently against the yielding of the house. The magistrate reportedly told the crowd that the decision was not of his doing, that he was simply carrying out the orders of his superior. With this, the crowd rushed to the taotai's yamen and, forcing its way inside, destroyed some furniture and openly accused the taotai of "traitorous collusion with the foreigners."[5]

It is interesting to note that, in rare cases, the provincial official who accommodated the foreigner generated popular opposition not only against himself but against the more responsible members of the gentry class as well. As will be recalled, during Shen Pao-chen's investigation of the Nan-

chang case of 1862, popular antipathy against the local officials was expressed in a variety of ways. But, at the same
time, popular criticism was also leveled against the gentry
of Nanchang, who were accused of appeasing the foreigner
and showing little concern for the populace which had to
bear most of the suffering.[6]

A case similar to this occurred in Nanyang, Honan, in
1868. The inhabitants of Nanyang, throughout the sixties,
had stubbornly refused to transfer to the Catholics a merchants' guildhall which the Catholics insisted had been
Church property.[7] The local officials repeatedly tried to
persuade the populace to yield, but to no avail. And from
mid-decade on, a rash of anti-Christian incidents, including
at least one case of murder, broke out in the area.[8] Although
petition after petition was presented by members of the
Nanyang gentry, demanding that the missionaries carry on
their labors outside the city, it seems that a small, enlightened minority of the local gentry did try to help the officials
carry out China's treaty obligations.[9] When this became
known, two inflammatory writings were circulated in Nanyang, reviling the gentry for their shameless conduct and
accusing them of secretly collaborating in the local officials'
efforts to make the people yield the guildhall to the foreigners. Since the gentry neglected to look after the welfare
of the common people, the first piece stated, the people
would have to protect themselves by establishing popular
militia units for the defense of orthodoxy. The second writing detailed eight measures for effecting the expulsion of
Catholics from Nanyang and the punishment of persons
who rented them houses or aided them in any other way.
The last of the items stated: "If there are any vile gentry
with no sense of shame, or officials of the same ilk, who
engage in secret dealings with the Catholics, destroy *their*
homes too." [10] Clearly, Honan governor Li Ho-nien was

not bluffing when he wrote to the Tsungli Yamen in 1868 that, while he dared not cater to the gentry and populace in defiance of the treaties, at the same time he dared not oppress them in a casual manner.[11]

The Nanchang and Nanyang cases are interesting in two respects. First, they indicate that, though most of the anti-foreign activity during the sixties seems to have been inspired by the gentry, there were also cases in which individual members of this class joined with the officials in accommodating the foreigner and themselves, as a result, became the object of popular hostility.[12] In the Nanchang case, and apparently in the Nanyang case as well, members of the gentry class played a prominent role in fomenting antiforeign feeling. And yet, at the same time, the gentry in both cases came in for their share of popular criticism. Clearly, then, the mode of analysis of gentry antiforeignism presented in Chapter 3 — where particular stress was placed upon the notion of a "group interest" threatened by the missionary's presence — can be carried only so far and must be tempered by an awareness of other interests which sometimes guided the actions of individuals.

Second, the populace's criticism of the gentry in both cases seems to qualify the simple notion that the common people in traditional China invariably followed the lead of the gentry. This may indeed have been true in most situations. But the local scene was certainly more complex than this, and popular interests and responses separate and distinct from those of the gentry must also be taken into account. In other words, it is quite possible that, despite the view of most contemporary missionaries, there were more than a few instances in the 1860's in which popular hostility to the foreign religion was aroused not by the gentry, but by the people's direct contact with the missionaries and converts. Here again, it is clear that, however convenient and even necessary it may be to treat the gentry, populace, and such, as organic groups with common interests, at the same time one must not fail to recognize the exceptions to this rule — the cases in which individual members of these social groups acted in response to interests and experiences that cut across class lines.

In the Fuan, Chinkiang, Nanchang, and Nanyang cases, the efforts of apparently responsible provincial officials to carry out the treaties were compromised by popular opposition. In other cases, such efforts were undermined by a force that could prove still more powerful — the opposition of other officials. This opposition sometimes expressed itself more or less directly, as in the Kweichow cases of 1864–1865, in which Lao Ch'ung-kuang's accommodation of Bishop Faurie brought a bitter denunciation from the pen of Kweichow governor Chang Liang-chi and an intensification of the anti-Christian activities of certain local officials of the province. On other occasions, it took the form of public or private censure — a particularly potent expedient in the context of traditional Chinese social relations.

In one case, occurring in Fukien in 1868–1869, such censure actually led to the demotion of an official. This case revolved, again, around the rental of property to a foreign missionary. The site in question was a park on Ch'uan-shih-shan (Sharp Peak Island), an island off the coast of Fukien, under the jurisdiction of the treaty port of Foochow. Upon the conclusion of the negotiations for the rental of this property, the lease was sent to the Foochow prefect with a request that he instruct the magistrate of Min hsien (in Foochow) to affix his seal to it. The prefect, however, replied that the property could not be rented because doing so would stir up resentment among the populace of Ch'uan-shih-shan. The English consul at Foochow therefore brought the matter to the attention of the governor-general of Fu-

kien and Chekiang, Ying-kuei. Ying-kuei ordered the Foochow Bureau of Foreign Trade, then headed by Taotai
Hai-chung, to look into the matter and report its findings
to Fukien governor Pien Pao-ti (d. 1892).

The events which followed need not be recited in full.
Some of the gentry of the area, apparently encouraged by
Governor Pien, filed a petition requesting that the rental of
the property be prevented. In January 1869, the English
consul, without waiting for the matter to be settled, fool-
ishly told the missionaries that they might begin building
at Ch'uan-shih-shan. A scuffle then ensued between the
workmen hired by the missionaries and the villagers of
the island, whereupon an English gunboat appeared on the
scene and fired on the rioters, killing one of them. Upon
hearing of these events Governor-General Ying ordered
deputies to put down the unrest and demanded that the
English consul withdraw the gunboat from the area. Since
Governor Pien was on leave of absence because of illness,
Ying-kuei discussed the matter with the officials of the
Bureau of Foreign Trade. The latter advised him that
since English missionaries and merchants had been preaching and trading in the treaty ports for years and had leased
houses and property in many places, and because the property in question was a worthless piece of land "in the midst
of the sea," the leasing of which had already been agreed
upon, the property should naturally be transferred to the
foreigners to avoid further difficulties. Ying-kuei took this
advice and the case was soon concluded.[13]

Clearly, the conciliatory Chinese settlement of the
Ch'uan-shih-shan case was very much influenced by the
judgment of the director of the Bureau of Foreign Trade,
Hai-chung. Pien Pao-ti's conduct, on the other hand,
strongly suggests that the governor shared the intensely
antiforeign sentiments of his brother, Pien Pao-shu[14] —

sentiments that could only have been aggravated by a recent show of British military force, following anti-Christian riots in Taiwan (which at this time was under the jurisdiction of Fukien province). After the settlement of the case, Pien in April 1869 submitted a memorial accusing Hai-chung of incompetence; of having yielded to the English in the Ch'uan-shih-shan matter because of servile fear; and of having taken the unprecedented step of inviting, first the consul and then the missionaries, of Foochow to dine with him.[15] Pien concluded by requesting that the taotai be removed from his post and demoted, a request which the emperor immediately granted.[16]

The censure of officials by their fellow officials took on added significance in cases in which the accused were the highest provincial authorities. For if the court of public opinion reproached these men for justly and sincerely executing the treaties, lower and less responsible officials could hardly be expected to brave the consequences of accommodating the foreigner. One such case, though it never actually came out into the open, centered on Ch'ung-shih's handling of the Szechwan incidents of 1869. Ch'ung, as Tartar general at Chengtu from 1861 to 1871, played a prominent role in the management of the anti-Catholic outbreaks which took place periodically in Szechwan and Kweichow during this period. Although by no means proforeign in his sympathies, in his dealings with the foreigners he was generally fair-minded. Moreover, the acute intelligence exhibited in his policy suggestions won him the highest respect in Peking.[17]

In January 1869, a serious incident occurred in Yuyang chou, Szechwan, when a crowd of militiamen mutilated and burned to death a French missionary, Jean-François Rigaud, together with a sizable number of converts. Shortly afterwards a Chinese Catholic priest, T'an Ch'un-ch'ing, either in revenge or in self-defense, placed himself at the head of a group of converts and reportedly massacred well over a hundred Chinese.[18] The causes of this series of outbreaks were evidently quite complex. The missionaries placed the responsibility squarely upon the Yuyang officials and upon a prominent member of the local gentry class, one Chang P'ei-ch'ao.[19] Li Hung-chang, who was commissioned to assist Ch'ung-shih in the management of the affair, felt that the principal causes lay in a combination of official incompetence, persistent unruly behavior on the part of the converts, and, perhaps most important, the residue of resentment which still existed in Yuyang in consequence of the large indemnity that had been exacted from the inhabitants following the killing in 1865 of another French missionary, François Mabileau.[20]

Sometime during the course of 1869, a Tsungli Yamen secretary, Chou Chia-mei, penned a long letter to Prince Kung,[21] in which he reviewed the turbulent history of Church affairs in Szechwan since the start of the decade. In discussing the Yuyang incidents of 1869, Chou insisted that the massacre of non-Christians by converts (under T'an's command) was far more serious than the killing of Rigaud. Consequently, he was bitterly critical of the course being pursued by Ch'ung-shih, who felt that equivalent measures should be adopted in the settlement of the two cases. From the point of view of principle, Chou's criticism was not unjustified. According to the lists which Ch'ung had sent to the Tsungli Yamen, the number of ordinary subjects slaughtered had been far greater than the number of Christian subjects. Moreover, in the latter group there were cases of uncertain identity, so that it was by no means sure that all had been Christians. In terms of numbers killed, therefore, the two cases were far from equivalent. From the point of view of political reality, however, Ch'ung-shih's course of action could also be justified. The missionaries insisted that the non-Christians killed had been rebels who had attacked the Christians, whereas the earlier massacre of the Christians had been entirely unprovoked. Moreover, in the first incident a foreigner's life had been taken, and the French chargé d'affaires was threatening to dispatch gunboats to Szechwan if his stringent demands were not executed promptly. Ch'ung-shih might have wished to settle the cases along the lines advocated by Chou Chia-mei. But, being right on the scene, he undoubtedly had a healthier appreciation of the realities involved than had Chou. This appreciation incidentally was apparently shared by others. Chou's proposal that Ch'ung-shih be severely punished as a warning to others was evidently ignored by Prince Kung, and the ultimate settlement of the case, in which Li Hung-chang played a leading part, was overwhelmingly favorable to the foreign side.[22]

The preceding pages give some indication of the difficulties encountered by Chinese officials who made a genuine attempt to carry out the Tientsin treaties. In some instances these efforts resulted in a diminution of the official's authority. In other instances they resulted in the alienation of segments of the gentry and populace. In still others they resulted in censure by the more militantly antiforeign elements of the Chinese bureaucracy. In any event, the only substantive reward that these officials received for their efforts was the esteem and approbation of the foreigners. This, however, was a dubious (and potentially dangerous) source of gratification in mid-nineteenth-century China. To execute the treaties energetically, then, required a rare combination of political skill, courage, and a sense of justice which overrode personal feeling. All too often officials found it easier to carry out their treaty obligations in a somewhat less energetic fashion, risking light punishment for administrative negligence, but retaining the support of the gentry and populace and the approval of their more xenophobic fellow officials.

## THE ALTERNATIVE TO OFFICIAL
## ACCOMMODATION: OFFICIAL
## PARALYSIS

One of the more persistent themes running through the documentation on missionary difficulties of the 1860's was the situation in which a foreign missionary, having been apprised of an approaching anti-Christian demonstration, notified the local authorities in advance but was met with apparent indifference, as revealed in the authorities' failure either to prevent the disturbance or to provide adequate protection at the time of its occurrence. Almost invariably when this happened, the missionary accused the authorities of having connived with, or at least shielded, the culprits. And undoubtedly this was true in some instances. But in other instances one is tempted to see this inaction as a function of the complex political situation with which the local official was confronted in his efforts to implement the treaties in the interior. This certainly appears to have been so in the Hunan-Kiangsi incidents of 1862. It also seems to have been true of two missionary cases which occurred in Yangchow and Anking later in the decade and which shared many features in common with the 1862 cases.

On June 1, 1868, Hudson Taylor and other members of the China Inland Mission became the first Protestant missionaries to open a station at Yangchow, Kiangsu, a commercial center on the Grand Canal twelve miles north of Chinkiang. In early August, Taylor heard that a group of Yangchow literati had met and decided to stir up popular opposition against the missionaries, in the hope that Taylor and his party would be made to leave the city. Before long, anonymous handbills were posted, "calling us brigands of the religion of Jesus, stating that we scooped out the eyes of the dying, opened foundling hospitals to eat the children, cut open pregnant women (for the purpose of making medicine of the infants), etc." On August 14 Taylor, fearing the possible consequences of these writings, wrote to the prefect of Yangchow requesting him to take suitable steps to quiet the suspicions of the populace. The prefect, on the following day, replied that he would have proclamations issued to achieve this. Nevertheless, on August 16 a new placard was posted, opening with the words, "What a beast is this Jesus whose venom has reached to China," and calling upon the gentry and people to destroy the residence of the Europeans on August 18 — the date of the convening of the local examinations in Yangchow.

Although this particular plan failed, unrest continued to mount in the city, and on August 19 Taylor again wrote to the prefect urging him to do something. The prefect wrote back that he had already issued secret orders for the arrest of the chief troublemakers and for the issuance of proclamations to quiet the inhabitants. These promises, however, were not fulfilled. "For it was evident," Taylor later wrote, "that though the Prefect would write a polite note, *he feared the unpopularity of taking any decided steps in our favour*" (italics added).

On August 22 two foreigners from Chinkiang spent several hours in Yangchow, providing a pretext for further rumors, one of which was that twenty-four children were suddenly missing. This was all that was needed to activate the latent tensions which had been accumulating in the city. On the afternoon and evening of the twenty-second, a mob of perhaps ten thousand persons plundered, and all but destroyed, the house of the missionaries, rough-handling its occupants. During the fray Taylor and another missionary managed to escape and make their way to the prefectural yamen. Here, after being kept waiting for forty-five minutes, "it was almost more than . . . [they] could bear with composure" to be questioned as to what they had really done with the kidnaped children. The prefect was finally prevailed upon to go to the scene of the disturbance, but the damage had already been done.

At dawn of the following day, when the soldiers who had been posted at the missionaries' residence departed, crowds again assembled and Taylor again went to the yamen. At this point, according to Taylor's sworn statement, he was virtually forced by a subordinate official to write a letter to the prefect minimizing the nature of the disturbance and suggesting that the local authorities had everything under control. Only after the writing of this missive did the authorities make arrangements for the safe departure of the missionaries from the city.[23]

The diplomatic aspect of the Yangchow case went through two distinct phases. Consul Medhurst's first efforts to obtain redress from Tseng Kuo-fan (governor-general at Nanking at the time) were frustrated when the commander of the British gunboat accompanying Medhurst was forced to return to Shanghai because of illness. In November, however, Medhurst returned to Nanking with a more awesome array of British force and compelled Tseng to accede to the original British demands. Tseng saw to it that proclamations were issued, that compensation was paid, and that the Yangchow authorities were cashiered for their negligence.[24] Thus, it was made eminently clear that Chinese officials *could* be punished if they failed to provide adequate protection for the foreigners within their jurisdiction.

The Anking, Anhwei, case of November 1869 was similar in many respects to the Yangchow incident. Again the initial source of friction appears to have been the attempt of two members of the China Inland Mission, John Williamson and James Meadows, to obtain a foothold in the city. They finally achieved this objective in the spring with the rental of a centrally located house.[25] For several months the missionaries, by discreetly avoiding any activities that might create excitement or curiosity, were able to live peacefully in their new surroundings, and the district examinations came and went with no ill effects. With the convening of the prefectural examinations in late October, however, a reported fifteen to twenty thousand literati crowded into the provincial capital, greatly increasing the normal difficulties of maintaining law and order. On the morning of November 3, the missionaries suddenly learned that a placard had been posted at the examination hall, styling them "religious brigands" and calling upon all the candidates to unite on November 5 and tear down the foreigners' new residence. Williamson and Meadows, fearing the possibility of a disturbance, proceeded at once to the taotai's yamen in order to announce the existence of the placard and request protection. The taotai, however, refused to see them, sending word that he already knew of the matter and that they should take it up with the prefect. Just as the two missionaries were leaving the yamen, they were set upon by a mob of examination candidates, shouting "Beat the foreign devils, kill the foreign devils!" They rushed back in and, fearing for the safety of the house and Meadows' wife and two children, again demanded to see the taotai. In spite of the urgency of the situation, the taotai kept them waiting for almost an hour while he finished his noon meal. At this point the prefect and subprefect arrived, followed soon after by a native servant of the missionaries who told them that their house had been broken into and ransacked. Fortunately, Meadows' family escaped injury, and the party was able to leave Anking that day. No steps, however, had been taken to prevent the disturbance or to suppress it effectively once it had erupted. The taotai never even left his yamen.[26]

The outbreak at Anking had also affected the Jesuit missionaries residing in the city, and the French obtained redress from Governor-General Ma Hsin-i in December. The British also received prompt material compensation for their losses. But acting Minister Thomas Wade concentrated on the more fundamental problem of obtaining the punishment of the Anking authorities whom, he felt, could easily have prevented the incident. As a result of Wade's efforts, the four ranking local officials of Anking were severely reprimanded, but were permitted to remain in office on probation.[27]

Official paralysis, such as was displayed in the Yangchow and Anking cases, offered what was perhaps the most convenient alternative to the official who was afraid openly to oppose the foreigner in defiance of imperial instructions, but who was equally reluctant to antagonize the gentry and populace by accommodating the missionary. In the last analysis, however, such inaction was not acceptable to the Chinese central government. For the members of the Tsungli Yamen had to deal on a day-to-day basis with the representatives of the foreign powers. And the powers, as we have just seen, viewed the local official's inability or unwillingness to protect the foreign missionary as a violation of the treaties second only in seriousness to outright official opposition.

At the risk of belaboring the point, it may be worthwhile here to summarize briefly the impossible position in which the Chinese provincial official of the 1860's found himself. If he chose to oppose the foreigner or to abdicate his treaty responsibilities in any of a variety of less conspicuous ways, he excited the wrath of the foreign powers and, albeit to a somewhat less degree, of the Chinese central government. If, on the other hand, he chose to observe the treaties in a faithful and energetic fashion, he alienated powerful elements on the Chinese scene and imperiled his very position as an official. The provincial official during this era was thus faced with a crippling dilemma, the existence of which goes a long way toward accounting for the progressive deterioration of Sino-foreign relations in the interior during the 1860's and the increased tendency of the foreign powers, as the decade wore on, to resort to less friendly means in their efforts to ensure the implementation of the treaties.

# CHAPTER 8

# FRANCE, BRITAIN, AND THE MISSIONARY PROBLEM

IN AN earlier chapter certain conditions were outlined for the effective implementation of the new treaties in the interior. One of these conditions was that the foreign powers would have to exercise extraordinary patience in their dealings with the Chinese government, upholding it at all times in its difficult task and making every effort possible to avoid embarrassing it. During the first half of the 1860's the record of the powers in meeting this condition was fair. The British had not yet become involved in difficulties in the interior, and France, although supporting the rights of her missionaries vigorously, never carried out her repeated threats to use gunboat diplomacy. In the closing years of the decade, however, as the tide of Chinese antiforeignism swelled, both France and Great Britain lost patience with the Chinese government and began to take matters into their own hands. The present chapter will be devoted in part to an examination of this new turn of events. At the same time an effort will be made to compare the policies of France and Britain with respect to Christian missions and to weigh the impact which each had on the Chinese government's execution of the treaties.

## BRITISH POLICY

The bold forward policy pursued by Great Britain in China prior to 1860 underwent a complete reappraisal and

reversal during the Restoration period. The basic realization which led to this change was that, although British interests in China were indeed primarily commercial, the
nature of the Chinese economy was such that these interests
were not, and might never become, of paramount importance to England. In any event, their preservation and
furtherance were definitely not worth the risk of war. War
was too expensive and, in view of China's political weakness, might well lead to colonial responsibilities that Britain
was simply unwilling to shoulder.

Once having abandoned force or the threat of force as a
legitimate instrument of its China policy, the British government devoted itself to the promotion of those conditions
which it regarded as most essential to the *long-range* development of British commercial interests in the empire. These
conditions — peace and political stability — were to be secured through two means, both of which were enunciated in
the early sixties. First and most important, contact between
British subjects and the Chinese population of the interior
was to be reduced to a minimum, thereby eliminating, as
far as possible, situations in which friction might develop to
damage the peaceful relations between the two countries.
Closely related to this policy was the corollary one of firmly
supporting the Chinese central government and holding it
responsible for the enforcement of Britain's treaty rights. As
the British minister, Sir Frederick Bruce, had pointed out as
early as 1860, Her Majesty's interests in China were dependent upon a Chinese central authority whose jurisdiction
throughout the empire was unquestioned. The use of on-
the-spot force by consular authorities to intimidate the local
official and obtain quick settlements was at best a temporary
expedient. In the end it subverted the central government
whose strength was essential to British interests.[1]

This British policy evolved originally in response to merchant demands and not to a so-called missionary problem. With very few exceptions, British missionary work in the early sixties still centered in the open ports. The one British missionary society whose guiding purpose was to get away from the coast and into the interior — the China Inland Mission — was not formed until 1865 and did not really get under way until a few years later.[2] Nevertheless, when British missionaries did begin to create a problem for their government in the late sixties, the twin tenets of British policy were readily applied to the missionary question and were steadfastly adhered to, in theory if not always in practice and by the home government if not always by its representatives in China.

## Incidents in China, 1868–1869

By reverting to gunboat diplomacy to obtain local settlements of the Yangchow and Taiwan incidents of 1868, British consular representatives in China departed momentarily from their government's avowed China policy. But at the same time their actions provided the occasion for a strong restatement of this policy. In the Yangchow case, as we have seen, the Shanghai consul, Medhurst, after getting the facts about the incident from the missionaries involved, proceeded up the Yangtze to Nanking in the *H.M.S. Rinaldo* to obtain redress from Tseng Kuo-fan. The commander of the ship, however, suffered an attack of dysentery and promptly took his vessel back to Shanghai, leaving Medhurst, in the view of the British minister, Sir Rutherford Alcock, "in a humiliating and helpless position, obliged to take refuge in a house-boat, and deprived of all the moral influence and prestige which the presence of the ship of war gave."

Diplomacy having backfired for want of a gunboat, Alcock took the matter up with the Tsungli Yamen. But without waiting for the Yamen to act, he called upon the British naval commander, Sir Henry Keppel, "to repair the mischief" by sending a force to the mouth of the Grand Canal large enough in size to enable him to apply effective pressure both on the local authorities and populace at Yangchow and on Governor-General Tseng at Nanking. "Should the authorities," Alcock stated (in his October report to Lord Stanley), ". . . prove obstinate and recalcitrant, I have the strongest conviction the time has arrived when it will no longer be possible to avoid a collision, and a resort to such determined pressure as shall compel the local authorities to respect and uphold our Treaty rights." [3]

On November 7 Medhurst, under Alcock's orders, returned to Nanking with four British war vessels and forced Tseng Kuo-fan to yield to the original British demands. He then went back to Yangchow with two gunboats and three hundred British troops and spent the latter half of November there until the British demands had all been met. The consul's proceedings throughout were not only approved by Alcock, but received his highest praise. [4]

In November 1868, a more serious incident took place on Taiwan. [5] Because of an accumulation of merchant grievances and the destruction by mobs of Catholic and Protestant churches near Tainan (following the circulation of a rumor that mysterious drugs were being used to gain converts), Alcock made arrangements for the dispatch to Taiwan of a naval force powerful enough to threaten the Chinese into providing satisfactory redress. He did not, however, have any intention of actually resorting to battle. At the same time that he ordered the dispatch of the naval force, he arranged, through the Tsungli Yamen, for the Fukien authorities to depute the Amoy taotai to go to the island and obtain a settlement. Before either of these measures could be carried out, however, an acting consul, John Gibson, applied force on the spot and routed a Chinese force of several hundred, killing or wounding thirty-four persons.[6] Gibson's daring exploit got the British everything they demanded. Alcock, whose careful efforts to obtain peaceful redress had been frustrated, concluded that though the consul's action was "somewhat sharp and unauthorized," it had been "eminently successful" and had terminated all of Britain's difficulties with both the authorities and the people of Taiwan.[7]

The response of the Foreign Office to the British action taken in these cases is instructive. With reference to the Yangchow affair, Sir Edward Hammond, the Office's permanent undersecretary, wrote on December 6: "I do not like this very much. I think Alcock should insist at Pekin on redress and if they hesitate and are unable on their own means to afford it, he should offer British cooperation holding them responsible if they refuse it. But I cannot think it desirable for us to take direct action against the local governor unless in the last extremity. *Such a course is contrary to our policy which is to hold the central government responsible for fulfillment of Treaties.*" [8]

Lord Stanley added that he was "inclined to agree" but would leave any action to his successor, Lord Clarendon, who became the new foreign secretary on December 7. Clarendon, in his Declaration of December 28, 1868, elaborated upon the theme set by Hammond. Consular and naval officers in China were sharply commanded to refrain from all warlike acts there: "H.M. Government feel that they are acting in the interest of the Chinese Empire, when they announce their preference for an appeal rather to the Central Government than to local authorities, for the redress of wrongs done to British subjects. It is with the Central Government . . . that Foreign Powers have entered into Treaties, and it is for the interest of the Central Government that Foreign Powers should recognize its supreme authority over its provincial Governors, and that the Central Government should assume, and . . . be prepared to exercise that authority." [9]

Clarendon officially reprimanded Alcock and Medhurst for the policy they had pursued at Yangchow: "The persons of the missionaries were safe; the injury to their property had been completed many weeks before; there was no immediate emergency to be met; the question of redress due was properly debateable at Peking, and if that redress had been withheld, the pleasure of Her Majesty's Government might without any inconvenient delay have been ascertained as to the course which it would be in such a contingency expedient to adopt." [10]

He took a still stronger stand in regard to the Taiwan case, ordering Gibson's demotion, the return of the indemnity exacted, and official disavowal of the consul's action.[11] At the same time, Clarendon took advantage of the occasion of the Yangchow and Taiwan cases to issue instructions to Alcock in which he defined, in the most explicit terms possible, the precise purposes for which British naval vessels were stationed at Chinese ports and the exact limits to the authority of British consuls to intervene forceably in local affairs.[12]

Before the news of the official reassertion of Britain's conciliatory policy could reach China, a further instance of "consular chauvinism" was displayed at Ch'uan-shih-shan near Foochow, where, it will be recalled, an English consul had taken unauthorized gunboat action in early 1869. Alcock, in his communication to Clarendon, went out of his way to praise the action taken by the commander of the ship. Clarendon's reaction, privately noted on the incoming dispatch, was that "Sir R. Alcock cannot disguise his antipathy to our moderate policy. The application of force is clearly his means of overcoming every difficulty in China." [13] To Alcock he wrote: "The Consul's measures had a direct tendency to provoke, without sufficient cause, collision with the Chinese authorities and people; and I have to instruct you strongly to censure Mr. Sinclair [the consul in question] for what he did, and to caution him to be more circumspect for the future." [14]

Alcock's qualified or wholehearted approval of the gun-boat exploits which took place in the winter of 1868–69 must, in all fairness, be judged in context. The British representative was disillusioned over the lack of progress being made in the negotiations on treaty revision and was becoming increasingly suspicious that the Chinese central government was unwilling or unable to enforce Britain's treaty rights. If, moreover, he wavered on one tenet of British policy — the abjuration of local settlements by force and the support of the central government — he remained firm on the other, and perhaps more fundamental, tenet — that of discouraging friction-causing contact between British subjects and native Chinese in areas beyond consular control. In the early sixties it had been the merchants, primarily, who had insisted upon venturing into the interior with full protection. Now, with treaty revision in sight, British missionaries joined the mercantile community in vigorously demanding full rights to reside and own property inland. When, in May 1868, Lord Stanley communicated to Alcock the London Missionary Society's desire that this right be specifically incorporated into the revised British treaty, Alcock replied that this was quite unnecessary since British missionaries already possessed the right by virtue of the sixth article of the French Convention and the most-favored-nation clause. He added:

But whether it may be consistent with wisdom or prudence to seek to enforce the right, or practicable to do so in effect, having in view the safety of the missionaries themselves, and the maintenance of peace, order, and good government wherever they may elect to settle themselves, is another question.

The inclosed account of popular violence and hostility manifested in Formosa, and still more recently by the outrage of which a party of missionaries with their families were victims at Yang-chow . . . raise serious doubts as to the practicability of such establishments in the interior of China for some time to come.[15]

Alcock stated his position even more strongly in January 1869. Following the Yangchow precedent, placards had appeared in the Hankow-Wuchang area in October 1868, threatening to take action against anyone who dared rent buildings to Protestant missionaries. As the situation became increasingly tense, the British consul at Hankow, G. W. Caine, urgently requested that a gunboat be permanently stationed at Hankow. Alcock's reply was sharp and to the point: "I do not consider it either necessary or possible for Her Majesty's Government to provide a gun-boat to be permanently stationed at every port . . . if the missionaries cannot carry on their labours at Wuchang peaceably, and without an appeal to force for their protection, it seems very doubtful how far Her Majesty's Government will hold themselves justified in resorting to measures of a warlike character for their protection away from the ports."[16]

Alcock took the same position in his correspondence with the Foreign Office, questioning whether Protestant missions were justified, "by any existing prospects of success, in provoking the dangers resulting from their attempts to establish missions in the interior, and away from the Treaty ports where alone they [could] be efficiently protected."

Clarendon, in March, completely approved of Alcock's proceedings in regard to Caine's request. Once again the policies of the home government and those of its minister in China were brought into line. And Clarendon, breathing the sigh of relief that comes after awakening from a bad dream, wrote to Alcock in April: "The injudicious proceedings of missionaries in China, the violence engendered by them on the part of the Chinese authorities and people, and the excessive and unauthorized acts of retaliation to which British Consular and, at their requisition, the naval authorities had resorted, were indeed sufficient to cause Her Majesty's Government to look forward with apprehension to the intelligence which each succeeding mail might bring."

Clarendon took the opportunity to remind Alcock that he had "full power and authority to control the conduct of Consular Officers" and that if he ever felt that these powers were insufficient he should lay the matter before the home government, which would consider enlarging them to the full extent admitted by law. Clarendon could not have gone much further in expressing his confidence in the British minister.[17]

## The debate in England

Against a backdrop of growing anticlerical and anti-imperialist sentiment, the incidents of 1868 touched off a sharp reaction in England. In Parliament the Duke of Somerset wished to know just what right the British had "to be sending inland missions to China — . . . to be trying to convert the Chinese in the middle of their country?" If the home government was thinking of reducing the size of its naval forces in China, he asserted, it had better reduce the number of missionaries there too, "for every missionary almost requires a gunboat. . . . A missionary, indeed, must be an enthusiast [a quality which was decidedly out of vogue in Victorian England]; if he is not an enthusiast, he is probably a rogue. No man would go and live up one of those rivers and preach Christianity unless he were an enthusiast, and being an enthusiast he is the more dangerous." The most serious violator, in Somerset's view, was the London Missionary Society which "had much better send its missions to some other part of the world, and leave China unconverted, than pursue their present course."

Clarendon's reply to Somerset was comparatively mild. He defended the London Missionary Society and rejected the proposition that missionaries had to be either enthusiasts or rogues. In fact, he could not help admiring the spirit that animated them and the fearless zeal they displayed in the propagation of religious truth. The trouble was that this zeal often led them to court dangers which were unnecessary and which resulted in ill feeling, riot, and bloodshed: "In truth the missionaries require to be protected against themselves, and should be induced not to prosecute their labours in localities in the interior of the country, where no consul resides." The foreign secretary then proceeded to set forth in clear terms British policy regarding its China missionaries.

The day after this debate, the *Times* (March 10, 1869) commented in a lead article: "Missionaries are people who are always provoking the men of the world. . . . Parliament is not fond of missionaries, nor is the press, nor is general society. Some recent occurrences in China have tended to revive the prejudice against them."

The attack on missions did not go unanswered. In Parliament the Bishop of Peterborough (Dr. Magee) stoutly rejected the advice of Somerset that Christian missionaries should operate only in places where their work would not be prejudicial to the interests of British trade: "The youngest and least zealous of missionaries would probably reply that, important as were the interests of British trade, there was something in his eyes more sacred even than that sacred opium trade for which Great Britain once thought it worth while to wage war — namely, obedience to the command of his Master to go forth and seek to convey the Gospel to every living soul, at whatever risk to himself or others." [18]

Again, the director of the home department of the China Inland Mission, William T. Berger, wrote a long letter to the *Times* (printed on April 14, 1869) in which he sought, rather than to make an impassioned defense of the Mission's policies, to set the record straight on just what had happened at Yangchow.[19]

The storm raised in the British press was still great enough to cause the London Missionary Society to instruct its representatives in China to confine their activities to the treaty ports. Griffith John, who had been in the Hankow-Wuchang area since the early sixties, persuaded the Society to reverse its decision only after repeated and vigorous protest.[20]

### Alcock on the missionary question

The policy toward the missionary problem gradually being formulated by the British government in the late sixties was to be upheld more or less consistently for many years after. It is therefore important to understand the views of the man who, as much as any other, had a hand in shaping this policy — Sir Rutherford Alcock. Alcock, as we have already seen, was quite dubious about the immediate, or even long-range, prospects for the success of Protestant missions in China,[21] and he was definitely opposed to their extension into the interior at this time.[22] As his correspondence with the Foreign Office became known, it drew much heated comment from English missionaries, four of whom — Joseph Edkins, John S. Burdon, William H. Collins, and John Dudgeon — addressed a long and strongly worded letter to the British minister in July 1869.[23] Alcock felt that it was not consistent with his office to engage in a public debate with the missionaries. But he forwarded their letter and another by Burdon to the Foreign Office, together with an extensive and detailed defense of his own views.

Uppermost in Alcock's mind was the creation of the most desirable conditions for the development of Britain's primary concern in China — trade. "How best 'local mandarins and native gentry' can be constrained or induced to respect the Treaties into which their Government has entered, and to allow peaceable foreigners engaged in a lawful calling to reside among them or travel freely through the interior for business or pleasure, without a rupture of those friendly relations, and a resort to war, as often as those Treaties are infringed — is the problem; and a very difficult one it proves to be." Alcock felt that "the greatest obstacle to any peaceful solution" of this problem was "the missionary element." Inherent in Christianity were political and revolutionary tendencies that lay at the root of the Chinese officials' hatred of the missionaries. If this hostility could not be overcome, "it would be decidedly for the peace of China if Christianity and its emissaries were, for the present at least, excluded altogether."

As a matter of official policy, Alcock felt that there were two possible alternatives open to the British government. One was to insist upon the rights of missionaries and converts as stipulated in Article 8 of the British treaty: "The Christian religion, as professed by Protestants or Roman Catholics, inculcates the practice of virtue, and teaches man to do as he would be done by. Persons teaching it or professing it, therefore, shall alike be entitled to the protection of the Chinese authorities; nor shall any such, peaceably pursuing their calling, and not offending against the laws, be persecuted or interfered with." [24] Alcock's astute analysis of the difficulties involved in enforcing this article deserves close attention. He began by observing that to insist on any treaty stipulation's being faithfully and strictly observed required a readiness, on the part of the foreign powers, to enforce such observance by whatever means needed to secure this end. "And it is only necessary," he went on, "to read carefully the words of this Article to be aware, that, in the whole range of the Treaty from the Ist to the LVIth Article, there is nothing stipulated for so difficult to secure as the fulfillment in its integrity of this one clause." The British minister then proceeded to analyze the phrase "peaceably pursuing their calling," which referred both to the missionaries and to their catechists and converts, who were Chinese subjects:

Who is to determine when any of these three classes, but more especially the latter, are accused of offending against the laws, that they have done nothing in contravention of Chinese laws? How is false or conflicting evidence to be sifted, in a case occurring in the heart of one of the provinces far removed from any Consular authority? And supposing a Consul could proceed to the spot, how is such an officer to go behind the judgment of a Chinese magistrate and establish by unquestionable evidence that the witnesses have borne false testimony, and that the Judge has been guilty of an unrighteous judgment? And to what would such attempts to secure justice between Chinese Christians and their own authorities lead, or where could they end, save in perpetual and forcible intervention between authorities and subjects fatal to any native executive powers if successful, and fraught with infinite wrong and mischief to those whom it was desired to protect if the reverse.

With regard to the stipulation that neither missionaries nor converts were to "be persecuted or interfered with," Alcock inquired: "Who is to trace the limits between what is persecution for religion's sake and the rightful assumption of the territorial authorities to pursue crime and maintain order . . . ? or discover with certainty when the action of the Magistrate is dictated by the one or the other motive?"

Alcock here touches on the fundamental problem of enforcing Western legal and judicial standards in a Chinese context, where these standards were unknown and had no sanction in tradition. "In the end," he concluded, ". . . the whole question of missionary difficulties resolves itself into one of peace or war; the propagation of Christianity under the menace of forcible intervention by one or more foreign Powers against the will of the rulers, in defiance of the moral convictions of the nation."

The alternative course which British policy might pursue was "to abstain from Government interference for the protection of missionaries and their converts in the interior when too remote from the Treaty Ports for any efficacious intervention, except by a resort to force, — in which case it would be a plain duty to discourage, and as far as possible restrict, the operations of British missionaries within the circuit of the ports."[25] This was the policy which was strongly and repeatedly advocated by Alcock, and just as strongly and repeatedly endorsed by the Foreign Office.

British policy ultimately created a community of interest between the British official body at Peking and the Tsungli Yamen against extremist elements on both sides.[26] When, in June 1869, the Yamen, discarding its earlier misgivings, sounded Alcock out on the idea of placing missionaries and converts under some form of official supervision (shrewdly stressing the point that this was a matter which seriously affected the interests of British commerce),[27] Alcock commented in his communication to Clarendon: "I think your Lordship will see in this official opinion of the Yamên full confirmation of nearly all I have stated in reference to inland missions, and the disadvantages attending them."[28] The trouble was that in the 1860's British policy, as far as Christian missions were concerned, was not nearly as crucial as French policy. And the latter was far less conciliatory.

### FRENCH POLICY

In January 1861, when Prince Kung, Kuei-liang, and Wen-hsiang memorialized recommending a new foreign policy for China, the order of priority of their suggestions was "suppress the Taipings and Nien bandits first, get the Russians under control next, and attend to the British last." [29] France was not even mentioned. By the late sixties, this hierarchy of concerns had undergone a decided shift. The Taiping and Nien rebels had been put down; British merchants and even missionaries had proved themselves to be a minimal source of friction; and France's protection of Catholic missions had come to loom as the most persistent source of tension in Sino-foreign relations.

The view expressed by Shen Pao-chen, late in 1867, was representative of a broad segment of Chinese official opinion:

[Foreign] trade and the netting of profits are things which the feelings can still endure. But heterodox doctrines and perverse behavior [arouse] the indignation of man and god alike. Nevertheless, the religions practiced [by the Westerners] differ from each other. The Protestant religion esteems as its guiding principle purity of conduct, and although [its conception of] right and wrong runs counter to that of the sages, it can still be treated on a par with the Buddhists and Taoists. The Catholic religion, however, takes in the scum and filth and perpetrates every kind of [evil], providing a haven for fleeing culprits and constantly making trouble for the local authorities. In appearance it is [concerned only] with the propagation of its teachings. But in reality it harbors sinister motives. Upright literati and law-abiding subjects are overcome with anger and hatred, resulting in acts of violence and killing. The French seize upon these occasions to start trouble, invariably causing us in turn to be at a loss for words. Their entire store of energy is brought to bear solely on these [matters].[30]

At times during the 1860's French policy seemed to be premised on close cooperation with the other powers and on a marked attitude of tolerance toward Peking. Thus, in the middle of the decade, when the reorganization of the French concession at Shanghai was under consideration, Paris declared its opposition to "seeking triumphs of exclusive influence" and instructed the French consul to work closely with the other consular authorities.[31] Again, in 1867 it spoke of "a more exact appreciation of common interests" which was gradually being substituted "for time-honored prejudice" and congratulated Peking on its increasing awareness of "the advantage of good relations with France." Two years later, Paris emphasized the "accord which has not ceased to reign among the Powers on all questions which touch on the Far East." Moreover, minimizing in importance any complications which might have troubled its relations with China, it instructed its representatives there to preserve in their language and attitude all "the restraint required of an exceptional situation."[32]

When taken at face value, these pronouncements do not suggest any great differences between French and English policy. The tone is one of moderation; the stress is on good relations with the Chinese government and on the common interests binding the foreign powers in China. In fact, however, there was another motif running through French policy which tended to militate against the so-called cooperative policy. Although the forms in which this motif was expressed were various, its governing principle was simple: while Great Britain, realizing the situation in which the Chinese government was placed, frequently was content not to push her rights too strongly, the French government insisted upon "upholding with firmness the rights which our treaties confer upon us."[33] During the Restoration period, this subtle shift in emphasis made all the difference.

A great deal about French policy in the sixties — its inner tensions and its departures from the course pursued by Great Britain — can be explained by the nature of France's interests in China at the time. As we have seen, her commercial stake in the empire was negligible, and she took upon herself the protection of Roman Catholic missions primarily in order to counterbalance the prestige and influence that Great Britain derived from its comparatively large-scale mercantile activities. Although it is difficult to gauge precisely just how much importance Paris attached to the protectorate in relation to its over-all China policy at any one point in time, it may be stated with certainty that French diplomatic activity in China was very much preoccupied with, if not monopolized by, Church concerns during the 1860's.[34] This preoccupation only reinforced the fundamental instability and precariousness of the French position. For at the same time that France was firmly committed to the support of Catholic missions, she was unable to exercise any real control over the excesses of Catholic missionaries or antiforeign Chinese. When disturbances broke out, France's prestige was staked on her ability to obtain redress. But the sphere in which she usually had to seek satisfaction was that of Sino-foreign relations in the Chinese interior — the very area in which the Chinese central government was least able to provide it without endangering its own position vis-à-vis the gentry and populace. Consequently, the Tsungli Yamen resisted French demands wherever it could, forcing France to resort to threats and bullying tactics or, in extreme instances, to the local application of force.

Clearly this vicious cycle did not benefit the Chinese central government. Nor did it benefit the French government, which was always running the risk of overextending itself and of making demands it was not prepared to back up by force. Another tendency therefore came to play a role in

French policy, one marked by conciliation. As we have already noted, this tendency was at times displayed by support of the central government. It was also revealed in the attempts of French representatives — notably Kleczkowski and Berthemy — to restrain the injudicious zeal of certain Catholic missionaries. The trouble was that when this milder approach did not get results, France had to revert to the tougher line if she was to save face. A pendulum-like movement thus came to characterize French actions, causing consternation and distrust on the part of the Chinese and plainly revealing the uncertain ground on which French policy itself was founded.

*The French protectorate in action in the late sixties*

During the first half of the 1860's, French policy, however ambiguous at times, seems on balance to have been conciliatory. Gunboat action, while threatened on certain occasions, was never implemented. Moreover, both Kleczkowski and Berthemy appear to have premised their conduct for the most part on the axiom announced by the former, namely that the "weakness of the central government" imposed upon France "the duty to do nothing which [weakened] it more," for it was still this authority which protected Catholic missions throughout the empire.[35]

In June 1865, however, the mild-mannered Berthemy was forced to return to France because of ill health, and the French legation was placed in the hands of Henri de Bellonet, a man who was peculiarly unsuited to deal with the delicacies of the Chinese scene and who caused the Chinese government two years of unending anxiety and embarrassment.[36] Bellonet's pugnacious disposition was revealed in connection with the Szechwan case of 1865 in which the French priest, Mabileau, had been murdered. In an October communication to the Tsungli Yamen he likened the case, by implication, to the Chapdelaine incident of 1856 and threatened to revive the warlike policy of the fifties if such outbreaks were not stopped. These threats were repeated the following year when the case had still not been settled to the chargé's satisfaction.[37]

In March 1866 Bellonet wrote to the vicar apostolic of Kiangnan (Monsignor Languillat) that he had informed the Tsungli Yamen "that if the matter [of the rental of property by Catholics in Anking] was not terminated in three months, I would take possession militarily of some piece of land in the city." At the same time, however, he cautioned the bishop that this was to be regarded only as a last resort. If the French navy had to force Li Hung-chang to yield, "the English will protest sharply and complain to Paris, and the government, which is beginning to become terribly annoyed with these missions affairs . . . may very well put a flat halt, in the future, to all claims of this type."[38]

Bellonet's impatience reached its breaking point in the summer of 1866. Early in July the ten articles for the regulation of missionary activities, supposedly drafted by Bishop Pinchon in conjunction with the local officials of Chengtu, Szechwan, were proved to be a complete fabrication. Then, coming right on top of this exposure, Bellonet on July 10 was informed of a massacre of priests and converts that had taken place in Korea. Four days later he submitted two dispatches to the Tsungli Yamen, one dealing with the Korean affair, the other with unsettled missionary cases in the southern provinces. In the latter dispatch, the French chargé declared that since the officials and gentry of the southern provinces continued to oppress Catholic missionaries and converts and were unwilling to observe the treaties faithfully, he would have no choice but to use gunboat diplomacy. He had already sent instructions to the French naval commander. Wherever the gunboats went, he continued, the officials, gentry, and wealthy families would be compelled to furnish at least one thousand taels daily to compensate for the expenditures involved. In this way the Chinese tendency to be forgetful of obligations would be cured and recourse to forceful tactics would not be necessary in the future.[39]

On July 25 Bellonet, in seeming emulation of the Wade-Hart proposals of 1865–1866, presented a long communication to the Tsungli Yamen in which he outlined his own suggestions for China's reform.[40] The Frenchman touched on the advantages to the dynasty of modernizing its military, commercial, and communication systems. But the main theme of his argument was that the central government's consistent inability to settle Catholic affairs stemmed from its unwillingness to exercise firm control over a bureaucracy that was corrupt and power-hungry throughout. If China did not discard her antiquated customs of her own accord, and quickly, hostilities would again break out and the foreign powers would have to act.

Bellonet did not limit his dispatch to generalities. He threatened that, if the cases still pending in Chihli, Shensi, and Honan were not swiftly concluded, he would seize several tribute-bearing junks and reimburse the missionaries with the money realized from their sale. With regard to the still unsettled Mabileau case, moreover, the chargé issued an ultimatum: If the case was not terminated to his satisfaction within one year, he would dispatch French gunboats to Szechwan to seize the culprits and remove Lo Ping-chang and his confederates from their high offices, replacing them with officials who were more responsible.[41]

Bellonet reserved the brunt of his anger for Li Hung-chang, who at the time was acting governor-general at Nanking. Li was accused of obstructing the Jesuits' efforts to recover their ancient church site at Nanking.[42] If it had not been for the Korean affair, Bellonet stated, the southern capital would already have been occupied and Li taken prisoner. As it was, however, the French naval contingent had its hands full and there was still time to settle the matter amicably. But, he warned, the French commander already had instructions to take the city by storm if a satisfactory settlement was not arrived at soon. Bellonet went still further, urging Prince Kung to obtain the transfer of the governor-general, thereby demonstrating to Li's would-be emulators that even the most powerful officials of the empire were not immune from punishment for opposing the treaties. If this request could not be satisfied, France would either commence hostilities or recognize Li Hung-chang as an independent monarch and deal with him directly. Bellonet clearly meant business. Five days prior to the submission of this lengthy communication, he had written to Paris advocating an approach that differed little in essentials from the foregoing, and on July 25, without waiting for positive instructions, he boldly announced to the home government his plans for a punitive expedition up the Yangtze in the spring of 1867.[43]

Bellonet's unsympathetic, bellicose spirit was exhibited perhaps most strikingly in connection with the Korean massacre of March, in which nine French Catholic missionaries, along with numerous native priests and converts, were put to death by order of the Korean regent.[44] On July 14 the French chargé d'affaires addressed a curt note to the Tsungli Yamen, announcing that since China had repeatedly asserted her lack of authority over Korea, France would feel free to occupy the country.[45] Without awaiting instructions from Paris, he promptly authorized the French naval commander in the Far East, Rear Admiral Roze, to proceed to Korea on a punitive expedition. Roze left Chefoo on October 11 with a force of seven ships and six hundred troops.

He soon announced the blockade of the Korean west coast and the partial destruction of the city of Kangwha. However, when a detachment of French troops stumbled onto a fortified hill and was handsomely defeated with a loss of three killed and thirty-two wounded, the Koreans felt that they had beaten France — a feeling which was seemingly confirmed when shortly after the French force retired to its winter station.

Although the Tsungli Yamen, as Mary Wright has ably shown, was under no such illusions,[46] in the long run the Roze expedition was a complete military and diplomatic failure. For purposes of public consumption, Paris adopted the face-saving formula that "as firm as is our intention not to engage in adventurous expeditions, the situation there [in Korea] could not remain entirely unpunished." [47] Its actions, however, belied its words. On November 10, 1866, a severe reprimand was issued to Bellonet for his presumptuous conduct in authorizing the expedition in the first place,[48] and eighteen days later a new French minister, Count de Lallemand, was appointed to head the legation at Peking.

When Lallemand arrived in the Chinese capital in May 1867, France's prestige was at a new low, a circumstance which, incidentally, he attributed primarily to his predecessor's policy of trying to accomplish everything by means of intimidation.[49] In spite of the new minister's urgent pleas for authorization to reverse the Korean check, however, Paris stood firm, telegraphing in September: "As regards Korea, confine yourself to an attitude of complete abstention. As to the protection of our nationals, avoid with care anything that might create complications." [50] France had clearly overextended herself in the Far East, and Paris, just as clearly, was in no mood to countenance additional reckless undertakings.

The uneventfulness and lack of missionary complications that characterized Lallemand's brief spell in Peking proved but a momentary lull. In November 1868 he left the legation in the hands of its secretary of two years' standing, Count Julien de Rochechouart. Confronted with the rising wave of antiforeign activity that marked the closing years of the decade, Rochechouart, brother-in-law of the French liberal Catholic, Montalembert, and a convinced believer in the inferiority of the "Chinese race," quickly reverted to the Bellonet approach of threatening to by-pass the Tsungli Yamen and exert local pressure.[51]

Rochechouart, although at times irritated by the lack of restraint exhibited by individual missionaries (particularly those of the Société des Missions-Étrangères),[52] was a powerful supporter of the concept of a French protectorate of Catholic missions and quite unashamedly viewed the Catholic missionary as a prime instrument for the furtherance of French political and commercial objectives in China.[53] The French government's part of the bargain, as he saw it, was to provide the missionaries with complete and effective protection, and he was convinced that the only way to achieve this goal and "prevent serious complications from arising between the French Government and that of China [was] to employ from time to time certain extradiplomatic means, more energetic and threatening in appearance than in reality."[54]

The new chargé d'affaires did not tarry long in implementing his philosophy. On March 3, 1869, he issued an ultimatum to the Tsungli Yamen that if his demands in connection with the January killing of the French missionary Rigaud and numerous converts in Yuyang were not met by July, he would depute French officials and gunboats to Szechwan to assist the Chinese authorities in their management of the affair.[55] Prince Kung replied with a note which, although rejecting the time limit, was moderate enough in tone. On March 6, however, Rochechouart returned the prince's note as unacceptable and reaffirmed his intention to send France's Hankow consul to Szechwan. The members of the Tsungli Yamen, somewhat bewildered by the chargé's action, made an appointment to meet with the interpreter of the French legation. But before they had even begun talking, Rochechouart, according to the Yamen's account, suddenly appeared on the scene, accompanied by one of the Szechwan missionaries, and announced that if the case was not settled in accordance with his original demands he intended to leave China shortly and would place the entire matter in the hands of the French admiral; he then stalked out. On the thirteenth, moreover, the French representative presented the Yamen with a new set of demands, calling upon the Chinese government to assign an imperial commissioner to the case and insisting that the Szechwan governor-general, Wu T'ang, be ordered to Peking and interrogated to determine whether he was implicated in the incident.[56]

Consistent with his general approach of placing a minimum of faith in the Chinese central government, Rochechouart, in the summer of 1869, took an excursion into Shansi in order to settle mission and other problems. After narrowly escaping death at the hands of a mob in Taiyuan, the capital of the province, he returned to Peking in August,[57] only to find that another serious outbreak had occurred in Tsunyi, Kweichow, in June. The French representative again threatened to send the Hankow consul to the western provinces if his demands were not met. He further insisted that the Kweichow governor, Tseng Pi-kuang, be cashiered and sent to Peking for questioning.[58]

During the summer and fall of 1869, signs of increased antiforeign activity were displayed in many other provinces besides Kweichow and Szechwan. In June Rochechouart reported to Paris that he was receiving "desperate" letters from missionaries all over the empire, and in August rumors of a general massacre of foreigners were printed in the Shanghai papers.[59] By October Rochechouart had lost all patience with the Tsungli Yamen. In the middle of this month he made the extraordinary request that the Yamen submit a memorial to the throne on his behalf. The Yamen was afraid to refuse, because in an accompanying note the chargé simultaneously announced his intention of going to Tientsin to meet with the French naval commander.[60] Rochechouart's memorial was general in content. He placed the blame for the anti-Christian outbreaks in Szechwan, Kweichow, and other areas on the officials of the provinces in question and claimed that, although he had repeatedly requested the Tsungli Yamen to secure satisfactory settlements of these cases, the members of the Yamen had either pleaded impotence or, when there was a method of settling the cases, refused to apply it. Since, Rochechouart concluded, the Yamen had abdicated its responsibilities in this manner, and he himself, prior to his departure from the capital, had already exhausted all measures for the preservation of harmony between the two countries, he had no choice but to ask the emperor to accept the presentation of this memorial in which he described the situation in a straightforward manner. He also expressed his profound hope that the emperor would think over the circumstances and grant to the foreigners the equitable requests that the Chinese officials were unwilling to concede.[61]

The emperor's only response to Rochechouart's memorial consisted in a stern rebuke to the Tsungli Yamen for ever having allowed it to be presented in the first place.[62] On November 2 the French representative sent a communication to the Yamen, accusing it directly of evasive, delaying tactics and criticizing it for having deputed Li Hung-chang, a hater of Christians, to investigate and manage the Szechwan cases. He repeated his demand that Wu T'ang and Tseng Pi-kuang be transferred and announced the plans for his impending trip up the Yangtze to settle all outstanding missionary cases.[63]

It is interesting in passing to note the reflections on this expedition that Rochechouart himself made some eight years after. "The only way," he wrote, "to enforce the clauses of the treaties consented to by the Chinese government and to succeed in settling a few of the pending affairs is to address oneself by turns, according to circumstances, either to the central government or to the provincial authorities." Paraphrasing his words of 1869 to the Tsungli Yamen, he continued: "I understand and deplore your impotence; therefore, in order to avoid complicating our good relations, the government which I represent has decided to send Admiral X*** to maintain the order which you do not dare to maintain and to give assistance to the viceroy [evidently Ma Hsin-i], whose good intentions are impeded by the malevolent spirit of the population." [64]

The French foreign minister (as well as the minister of marine) was extremely anxious about the possible complications that might result from the Rochechouart expedition and, as late as December 24, expressed the hope that the chargé might have abandoned his plans.[65] Rochechouart, however, was determined to go ahead and by November 10 had already left Peking for Tientsin. At Tientsin he was informed of a new disturbance which had just erupted in Anking, and he went immediately to Shanghai. The Tsungli Yamen, meanwhile, fearing that France's coercive course would result in further incidents, addressed urgent dispatches to Li Hung-chang, Ma Hsin-i, and Anhwei governor Ying-han, pressing them to settle the missionary cases within their respective jurisdictions. It requested the throne to issue similar instructions. At the same time, the Yamen addressed a communication to the French legation, reviewing at length the action which it had taken in the Szechwan, Kweichow, Hupeh, Shansi, Honan, and Kwangtung cases and defending itself against the French chargé's accusations of negligence and incompetence.[66]

In far-off Szechwan, Li Hung-chang, hearing of Rochechouart's projected journey, exerted himself to bring about a quick termination of the Yuyang case, which he rightly viewed as being far more serious than the one in Tsunyi. By December 21 he was able to get the missionary, Mihières, to agree to terms, which were then promptly communicated to the French consul at Hankow to be passed on to Rochechouart.[67] Although privately expressing grave concern over the possibility of a French gunboat excursion into the western provinces, Li reassured the throne that in view of the rough, mountainous terrain of Kweichow and Szechwan, and the lack of land forces at France's disposal, there was little likelihood that such an expedition would materialize.[68]

The details of Rochechouart's trip up the Yangtze at the turn of the year need not concern us.[69] Backed by four French gunboats, the chargé d'affaires went to Nanking, Anking, Kiukiang, Nanchang, and Hankow, negotiating rapid settlements of all pending missionary difficulties. Careful arrangements were made by Ma Hsin-i, Liu K'un-i, and other high officials to avert any incidents along the route. (Liu, nevertheless, had to order troops out to repress the excitement of the Nanchang gentry and populace upon Rochechouart's arrival in that city.) At Hankow Rochechouart met with Li Hung-chang in late January and worked out a satisfactory arrangement concerning the Yuyang case. On January 29 he started back for Peking via the overland route.[70]

When presented with these dramatic results, Paris—mindful, one suspects, of the recent and well-applauded successes of British gunboat diplomacy and anxious, after the Korean debacle, to restore its lost prestige in China—quickly forgot any initial uneasiness and gave to Rochechouart's proceedings its full approval.[71]

Rochechouart's expedition won him a lasting place in the hearts of patriotic French missionaries, one of whom remarked: "In my opinion, it has been a long time since France has made so handsome and eloquent a demonstration on behalf of Catholic missions in the Far East. One would have to go back to Louis XIV to find something approximating it. A minister who travels through a large portion of China especially to regulate the affairs of Christians and to protect Catholic interests is indeed noble."[72]

The expedition was also applauded in the treaty ports, where impatience with the Chinese government and a desire for quick results had always been the predominant mood. Even the usually sympathetic British representative at Peking, Thomas Wade, by transmitting to the Tsungli Yamen a summary of a Shanghai newspaper article that praised the expedition, seemed to imply that if this was the only way the foreign powers could get decisive action, the cooperative policy might have to undergo considerable rethinking. Wade's note confirmed the Yamen's worst fears about the French expedition. It requested that urgent instructions be issued to all high provincial officials to terminate swiftly and impartially all British missionary cases then pending or that might later develop, in order to prevent the British from having any pretext for taking further local action. The throne acted in accordance with the Yamen's recommendations.[73]

If the Tsungli Yamen's standing was seriously compromised by Rochechouart's new strategy of settling out-

standing differences through personal negotiation with the
provincial authorities, Rochechouart's own prestige and that
of France soared. On his return to Peking in March 1870,
the French chargé became more highhanded than ever.
When the Anking authorities hesitated in carrying out the
terms that had been agreed upon, a French gunboat was
again dispatched to the city in March;[74] an attack in February on the Kweichow missionary, Lebrun, brought new
demands for the transfer of Governor Tseng Pi-kuang;[75] and
when Li Hung-chang was ordered to Shensi prior to the
termination of the Tsunyi case, Rochechouart threatened
either to resort to local force or to negotiate with Li in
person.[76]

## BRITISH POLICY, FRENCH POLICY, AND THE TSUNGLI YAMEN

How did the policies pursued by Britain and France in
the sphere of Christian missions ultimately affect the position of the Tsungli Yamen in the 1860's? It seems fairly clear
that British policy, despite occasional lapses, tended to
bolster the Yamen's position, while that of France, despite
occasional bland pronouncements to the contrary, tended
to subvert it. I have dwelt on the more or less overt ways in
which French representatives, in particular Bellonet and
Rochechouart, by-passed or threatened to by-pass the Yamen.
But more important, in the last analysis, was the subtle subversion resulting from France's determination to insist on
her treaty rights. Since French interests in China during this
epoch revolved principally around Catholic missions, the
rights which French ministers usually found themselves
attempting to protect were those of Chinese converts and
foreign missionaries in the interior. But of all the rights
granted in the treaties these were the most displeasing to the

gentry and the officials. The Chinese central government was thus faced with a fundamental problem which Mary Wright has characterized in the following terms: "The Restoration government could not possibly attempt to break down the Confucian prejudices of the literati, for the survival of the traditional state depended on the resurgence of these ideas. At the same time, the survival of any state at all appeared to depend on coming to terms with the foreigners." [77]

The Chinese government's response to this dilemma was twofold. First, it tried to meet the problem head on and reduce its proportions by gearing the gentry and the provincial officials to the needs of the times, while vigilantly holding the foreigners to the treaty provisions. Second, as we have already noted, it tried to mitigate the problem by proposing a series of measures restricting missionary activities. The trouble with the first approach was that it was ultimately unacceptable to xenophobic Chinese in the provinces. The trouble with the second was that it was rejected, time and again, by the foreigners.

Part of the difficulty, of course, was that when conflicts broke out in the provinces the foreign representatives at Peking got their information from the missionaries involved, while the Tsungli Yamen got its information from the local Chinese authorities. The two stories rarely tallied. Yet the Yamen could do little else but repeatedly urge the provincial officials to judge all cases with impartiality.[78] Since Chinese and foreign standards of impartiality often did not coincide, the problem came no closer to solution.

A related course, adopted with less frequency by the Yamen, was the typical Restoration approach of calling for higher standards of competence in the lower ranks of the provincial bureaucracy.[79] Ideally, this was perhaps the best approach. The superior magistrate, by transcending his own prejudices and using greater skill and tact, might be able to harmonize the demands of the foreigner and the sentiments of local Chinese, and thus alleviate the problems involved in handling foreign relations at the local level. The trouble here, of course, was that the supply of such supermagistrates could never meet the demand. And even when local officials were fair and competent in all other spheres, their prejudices often got in their way in matters relating to the foreigner.

If the Tsungli Yamen enjoyed scant success in getting Chinese local officials to toe the mark in foreign intercourse, it fared little better in its efforts to "harness" the foreign diplomats in the capital. True, in isolated instances it was able to win the day. But one suspects that its victories were just as often the result of forces outside its control. For example, in the Korean case of 1866 the Yamen displayed a considerable degree of astuteness in humiliating, and bringing diplomatic pressure to bear on, the fiery Bellonet.[80] But in the end the reason that the French did not pursue the affair was because Paris had never supported it in the first place. Again, in the Ch'uan-shih-shan and Taiwan cases of 1868–1869, the Yamen was incensed at the unauthorized use of gunboats by British consular authorities and demanded that these authorities be censured. But when they were, it was not in response to the demand of the Yamen (as its members apparently believed) but to that of the Foreign Office.[81]

In citing these examples it is not my intention either to ridicule the Tsungli Yamen or to impugn its skill and adaptability. The point is that, because the Yamen acted from a position of weakness, when it was effective in the diplomatic arena it could be so only in limited areas or with a substantial amount of cooperation from the powers. With respect to mission affairs, in particular, even when the Yamen was able to get the foreign powers (notably France) to modify their demands, it could not get them to eliminate these demands altogether. And finally it had to confront the fundamental difficulty of carrying them out in a hostile interior.

## DIPLOMACY AND THE LOCAL SCENE

In commenting upon the culprits in the Nanchang case of 1862, the members of the Tsungli Yamen wrote: "From the standpoint of human feeling and principle they are loyal subjects; from the standpoint of the law [the treaties] they are criminals." [82] The Yamen here put its finger on one of the most critical sources of tension in Chinese society after 1860—the abnormal cleavage existing between the values of the community and the laws governing it. In ordinary circumstances, when the laws of any community are violated and the violation is legitimately and fairly punished by the authorities of the community, tension relaxes and there is a return to normalcy. When, however, the violation is purportedly committed *in defense of* existing standards and is punished not in accordance with the will of the community but in accordance with the will of a hostile outside party, the tension which initially led to the violation tends to increase. This generalization proves particularly useful in analyzing many situations which developed on the Chinese local scene during the 1860's. Put more concretely, the foreign missionary, by insisting on his rights and repeatedly demanding that his government obtain redress when these rights were violated, tended to create a net increase in tension on the local scene. This in turn made it that much more difficult for his rights to be effectively enforced, and for the Chinese government to "normalize" Sino-foreign relations in the interior.

Chinese officials during the 1860's showed a shrewd ap-

preciation of this phenomenon. Thus, in the Anking case
of November 1869, Ma Hsin-i and Anhwei governor Ying-
han both reported that if the examination candidates responsible for the riots were apprehended prior to the
conclusion of the examinations (in mid-January 1870), it
would be difficult to prevent further riots from breaking
out.[83] Again, in the T'ien Hsing-shu case of the early sixties,
one of the more delicate problems facing the Chinese government was how to obtain T'ien's punishment without
intensifying antiforeign feeling in Kweichow and in T'ien's
native province of Hunan.[84]

More significant were the numerous instances in which
the settlement of one case actually did stimulate a discernible increase in friction, which in turn led to further outbreaks or to other expressions of antiforeign sentiment in
the same locality. This sequence was clearly noted by Li
Hung-chang and Chou Chia-mei in connection with the
Yuyang cases of 1865 and 1869. Both men felt that the eighty
thousand tael indemnity exacted after the first case had
served more as an irritant than as a sedative.[85] Again in
Nanchang, Kiangsi, as we have already seen, the management of the 1862 riots provoked considerable hostility
against both the foreigner and the local officials. During the
closing months of 1862, while Father Anot was in Peking
seeking redress, a notice was circulated in the area which
stated in part:

At the time [of the original incident] we wanted to put to
death the two rebels, Anot and Fang [An-chih], but unfortunately they fled ahead of time. Recently it has been heard
that they went to the capital to lay a charge and aroused the
consul of their country to send a dispatch in which he had the
audacity to ask of His Excellency our governor a compensation
of 70,000 taels, along with the orphanage property outside the
city, the reconstruction and return of their original orphanage
within the city, and all sorts of other unscrupulous things aimed

at blackmailing us. At present our military needs are critical. How can our Chinese wealth [be used] to make good these insatiable demands? [86]

The notice then called for the forcible ejection of Anot should he attempt to return to Nanchang, which, as will perhaps be recalled, was precisely what did happen in May 1863 when Anot's boat was stoned by a mob and he was forced back downstream. For the remainder of the decade, moreover, Catholic missionaries were unable to re-establish a foothold in the Kiangsi capital. In 1866 an itinerant missionary was attacked and robbed outside the city,[87] and as late as 1870, when the Catholics announced their intention to clear ground for the erection of a church, Governor Liu K'un-i reported to the Tsungli Yamen that the French were bitterly detested by the Nanchang gentry and populace and that he could not guarantee the peaceable re-entry of the missionaries into the city.[88]

A further illustration of this phenomenon was witnessed in Luichow (Lei-chou) prefecture in southernmost Kwangtung. Here, in 1867, a French missionary, accompanied by the local Chinese authorities, took formal possession of a newly purchased church residence. Scarcely had the officials left the scene, when an angry mob stormed the building and burned it to the ground. In May of the following year, the vicar apostolic of Kwangtung and Kwangsi, Monsignor Guillemin, went to Luichow in a gunboat donated by the governor-general and saw to it that suitable reparations were exacted from the officials and people. The chapel was then rebuilt *at the expense of the inhabitants* and was soon ready for reoccupancy. On Christmas day, 1868, however, a mob again collected and once more demolished the hated symbol of foreign intrusion, seriously injuring one of the missionaries. This in turn touched off a series of antiforeign incidents which plagued the area all through 1869 and well into 1870. Three additional chapels were destroyed, hundreds of Christians left homeless, and at least seven or eight killed.[89]

In Hunan province also, although the causes of antiforeignism were complex and varied, undoubtedly the hostility continually shown in certain areas was partly nourished by the proved ability of Catholic missionaries to obtain satisfaction for transgressions committed in these areas. It will be recalled that, after the Changsha and Hengchow incidents of 1862, Bishop Navarro journeyed to Peking to seek redress and that his requests were promptly satisfied owing to the energetic action of both Count Kleczkowski and Hunan governor Mao Hung-pin. But signs of resentment continued in these two prefectures all through the sixties. Later in 1862 another riot broke out in Changsha;[90] in 1864, when Navarro returned to the province, disturbances were narrowly averted in both Changsha and Hengchow;[91] in 1865 the bishop reported the destruction of two Christian homes in one of the districts comprising the Hunan capital; and in April of that year the unheralded arrival of some American Protestant missionaries at the time of the examinations in Hengchow stimulated the posting of inflammatory placards and a near attack on the Catholic church in that city.[92] At the turn of the decade, Hunanese xenophobia became more evident than ever. Hostile notices were spread in all directions in 1869. During the same year Protestant missionaries who attempted to establish themselves in Changsha and elsewhere were driven away and their literature burned. Again in 1869 the Italian priest, J. T. Raimondi, on an excursion through the province was advised by his Chinese companion to duck when their boat passed Changsha.[93]

The above cases — with the possible exception of Hunan

where conditions were admittedly more complicated — seem to indicate fairly clearly that foreign-dictated settlements of antiforeign incidents produced more provocation than they did peace. Far from removing the local hostility which initially gave rise to incidents, they tended to deepen this hostility and thereby foster conditions favorable to the outbreak of further trouble. Whether or not further incidents actually did break out, a snowballing effect was initiated, making it more and more difficult to establish any lasting basis for Sino-foreign harmony on the local scene.

### THE RISING CRESCENDO OF ANTIFOREIGN ACTIVITY

This accumulative process may well have contributed to the redoubling in intensity of all forms of antiforeign activity, and in particular of the predominantly gentry-inspired anti-Christian paper war[94] during the last years of the decade. In 1868 a Mr. Stott of the China Inland Mission was severely hampered in his efforts to operate a small school in Wenchow, Chekiang, by "wicked reports circulated in the city, and posted up in public places in handbills."[95] In May of the same year, the Jesuit missionary, Joseph Seckinger, reported that immediately after his departure from Hwaian prefecture (Kiangsu), two placards were posted in the city, accusing the Church of atrocious practices and warning people against having any dealings with it.[96] At about the same time, the apostolic vicar of Kiangnan, Languillat, brought to the attention of the Chinese authorities two violently anti-Christian writings which, the bishop claimed, had been distributed far and wide throughout Kiangsu province.[97] Later in the year, as we have seen, hostile notices played an important part in anti-Christian incidents in Nanyang, Honan; Ch'uan-shih-shan, Fukien; and Yangchow, Kiangsu.[98] Again, in October, a long anti-Christian notice appeared outside the east gate of Shanghai.[99]

In 1869 the Jesuit missionaries of Kiangnan wrote of "injurious and infamous placards" which had been posted in Soochow and which, among other things, accused the missionaries of using human eyes to transmute metals, make telescopes, and bewitch people.[100] In nearby Changchow the Jesuits were on the point of purchasing a favorable tract of land near the east gate of the city when suddenly "numerous and harmful placards" were circulated, declaring: "Let the devil from the Occident . . . be driven away! Let the flesh of the person who dares to sell an inch of land for the building of a church be skinned alive and eaten raw." These apparently were not idle threats, for the Chinese owner of the property and his wife were cruelly treated until they begged the missionaries to release them from their obligation.[101] Inflammatory placards were circulated in Anking during the summer of 1869 and again in the fall in connection with the destruction of the English church which took place in that city in November.[102]

In 1869 Tseng Kuo-fan's assumption of his new post as Chihli governor-general triggered the spreading of various rumors, one of which was that the throne had summoned this great administrator because it was resolved to exterminate all Europeans. The presence of ten thousand of Tseng's soldiers seemed to corroborate these stories, and the literati seized upon the opportunity to draw up and print "libels which before long were circulated even in the smallest hamlets." [103] This inflammatory literature appears to have played a role in an anti-Christian incident which occurred in Yungnien hsien, Chihli, in May.[104]

In the summer of 1869, anti-Christian pamphlets were circulated in Canton in connection with the imprisonment and pending execution of a Christian woman charged with having used sorcery on young children, gouging out their eyes, and so on.[105] Again, the succession of serious disturbances which took place during this year in Szechwan reportedly stimulated the composition and widespread dissemination of a libelous piece of writing.[106] And in southernmost Kwangsi, the martyrdom of a Chinese priest in December 1869 was apparently inspired by a "masterpiece of lies" composed and circulated by the literati of Pokpah (Po-pai) hsien in this province.[107]

A rash of anti-Catholic incidents broke out in Kweichow in the late 1860's.[108] The most serious, as we have seen, occurred in the city of Tsunyi, where in June 1869 the churches and other establishments of the Catholics were ransacked and destroyed, and a French missionary, Pierre Gilles, sustained injuries which, according to the French, were the cause of his death in August.[109] In mid-July, shortly after the outbreak, a piece of writing was distributed in the Tsunyi area which clearly revealed the intent of the gentry (and officials?) to eliminate Catholicism from the scene. Consisting of ten articles, it declared that all those who practiced the religion and were unwilling to apostatize were to be driven from the region; that their homes and possessions were to be confiscated and converted into common property; that after the expulsion, any who continued to harbor Christians would be treated in the same fashion as people who provided refuge for bandits; that the people would not allow the Tsunyi authorities to be punished for permitting the June outbreak. The populace was called upon to make ready its weapons and await a given signal. Informers who divulged the plot to the Christians were to be treated even more severely than if they had been Christians.[110] Of course, this manifesto (and an even more inflammatory one which followed it[111]) did not succeed in driving the Catholic population from Tsunyi. But it undoubtedly contributed to the continuation of anti-Christian sentiment in the area.[112]

Finally, it may be recalled, the end of the 1860's and the beginning of the seventies marked a high point in the circulation of inflammatory anti-Christian literature in Hunan, Kiangsi, Shantung, Honan, and other provinces. Aside from the *Pi-hsieh chi-shih* and its derivatives, the most important items in this barrage were two pieces that came from Hunan in 1869 and achieved widespread distribution in the lower Yangtze valley. Curiously enough, the items in question turned out to be exact replicas of the Hunan manifesto and the accompanying itemization of Christian malpractices which had played such a crucial role in the Nanchang riots of 1862.[113]

The extent to which this sudden upsurge in the writing and distribution of anti-Christian literature was part of a broad organized effort to promote antiforeign action remains an enigma.[114] For the time being, it is perhaps safest to assume that it was organized in certain instances, spontaneous in others. The result, in any event, was a sharp increase in antimissionary disturbances and Sino-foreign friction during the last few years of the decade — a trend which the British and French gunboat exploits of these years certainly did nothing to counteract.[115]

### ELEVENTH-HOUR EFFORTS TO SOLVE THE MISSIONARY PROBLEM

In February 1869 the imperial princes, the Grand Council, and the Grand Secretariat were given copies of the Chinese officials' correspondence on treaty revision. Although agreeing substantially with the course of the Tsungli Yamen, the general tenor of the advice which soon poured in was that, as a supplement to diplomacy, somewhat more emphasis should be placed on China's military preparations. With respect to Christian missions, Prince Ch'un (1840–1891),[116] who headed the opposition to Prince Kung in court politics, proposed on behalf of the grand secretaries that Catholic orphanages be abolished to avert popular suspicions and that militia units be secretly established in places where there were churches to prevent perverse subjects from precipitating disturbances and to provide good subjects with a source of encouragement for the future. The proposal to abolish orphanages was also put forward by Wo-jen.

The Tsungli Yamen deemed both sets of proposals inadvisable.[117] But, in June 1869, as we have seen, it did sound Alcock out about regulations to place relations between converts and ordinary subjects on a more viable footing. Although the British minister's private views regarding the seriousness of the missionary question seem to have coincided very closely with those of the Yamen, however, the Christian missions issue played a subordinate role in the Anglo-Chinese negotiations on treaty revision and was not even mentioned in the stillborn Alcock Convention which culminated these negotiations. Despite the existence of a large measure of agreement between the Chinese and British governments, as long as the missionaries of France and other countries continued to enjoy certain privileges in China, Britain could ill afford to restrict her own missionaries unilaterally.[118]

*An ominous warning: Hsüeh Fu-ch'eng's proposals*

Taking as his point of departure the Szechwan and Kweichow cases of 1869, the youthful Hsüeh Fu-ch'eng (1838–1894),[119] sometime during the course of this year addressed a letter to Li Hung-chang in which he outlined his views on the missionary question. Hsüeh was serving on Tseng Kuo-fan's secretarial staff, while Li had been charged with the management of the above two cases. Although Hsüeh's views were probably not made public, their extremist tone provides, on the one hand, an interesting insight into a man who two decades later was to become one of China's first envoys to Europe and, on the other, a possible indication of the mood of other intelligent lower-ranking officials of this period.

Initially, Hsüeh began, the foreigners had taken advantage of the Taiping upheaval to launch a surprise attack on China, bringing terror to the court at Peking. "At the time the Westerners fought with all their strength to preach Christianity. If [the right] to preach Christianity had not been granted the treaties would not have been concluded; if the treaties had not been concluded the [foreign] troops would not have withdrawn. We accommodated them then so that we might rid ourselves of the immediate evil. We had no choice. Circumstances [dictated our course]." In 1860, Hsüeh continued, the Treaties of Tientsin were supplemented, and again China could do nothing about it. During the following decade French missionaries established churches all over and began to seduce the ignorant people with money and drugs. The natural dispositions of those seduced were suddenly metamorphosed, and they rebelled against all normal human relationships, giving heed only to the missionaries. At first only a few extremely ignorant and impoverished subjects rushed to join the religion, grateful for its material rewards. Afterwards, however, every scoundrel came to rely on the Church as a haven from justice, and as the missionaries' power to resist the civil authorities became known, the membership of the religion steadily grew in size.

If one were to use the language of chemistry, the Church had, in Hsüeh's view, served as a precipitant, separating out the bad elements of Chinese society from the good. As this phenomenon became more and more marked, loyal Chinese became increasingly angry and resentful, and before one anti-Christian disturbance was settled another broke out to take its place, leaving the empire in a state of almost constant turmoil and conflict. The officials were helpless. If, when an incident occurred, they took the side of the people against the converts, the Westerners, appealing to the treaties, held them responsible and might even summon troops, thereby hindering China's general interests and encouraging the people to trifle with the law. If, on the other hand, the officials sided with the converts and punished the people, who was there who would not enter the foreign religion?

Viewing the missionary problem in the context of Sino-foreign relations generally, Hsüeh expressed his fear that the missionaries' penetration into the interior was but the first stage in a larger Western plan to seize complete control of China, as had been done in other Asian countries. Earlier, Western incursions into China had met with no resistance because long years of peace had lulled China's military power to sleep. Later, when China was again intruded upon, her military potential had been revived, but because of domestic difficulties she could not direct it against the external foe. Now, however, the internal disease was on the point of being cured. If the small countries of Korea and Japan could prohibit Christianity and close their doors to the foreigners, surely China, with her vastly greater strength, could do the same. Hsüeh suggested, therefore, that an immediate ban be placed upon foreign missionary activities and that commercial relations also be severed at the first opportunity. If this proposal were unacceptable, he urged that a written agreement be established permitting foreign commerce but prohibiting foreign preaching. If this too

would not do, as a last resort a treaty might be drawn up
clearly authorizing Chinese officials to apply the laws to
Chinese subjects.[120]

Hsüeh Fu-ch'eng's diagnosis of the missionary problem
was penetrating and to the point. But his solutions, with the
possible exception of the last, were too extreme to be acceptable to the foreigner, and probably found little sympathy
from such statesmen as Li Hung-chang in 1869. In 1870, on
the other hand, as the crisis anticipated by Hsüeh came
perilously close to materializing, Ting Jih-ch'ang, Tseng
Kuo-fan, and the members of the Tsungli Yamen became
more aware than ever of the dangers inherent in foreign
missionary activity, and they came forward with suggestions
which, though less immoderate and more realistic than
Hsüeh's, were similarly urgent in tone.

# CHAPTER 9

# THE TIENTSIN CATASTROPHE

IN THE wake of the rising tide of antiforeign feeling which spread over large portions of China toward the close of the 1860's, and in a climate of increasing French harshness under the aegis of Count de Rochechouart, the Tientsin Massacre exploded like a bombshell on the afternoon of June 21, 1870, nearly causing another China war and becoming for several months almost the sole preoccupation of French and Chinese diplomats.[1] Tientsin, a treaty port situated southeast of Peking at the junction of the Grand Canal and Peiho, was, perhaps more than any other Chinese city, ripe for an explosion. It was here that the humiliating treaties of 1858 had been negotiated; here British and French troops had been quartered from 1860 to 1863, leaving behind, at least in the French case, "a legacy of bitter feelings." It was in Tientsin that the French authorities occupied a former imperial villa as their consulate; and here French missionaries, in June 1869, solemnly consecrated the cathedral of Notre Dame des Victoires on the site of a razed Chinese temple. As H. B. Morse has commented, with studied understatement: "It is not too much to say that, at Tientsin, the French nation and French . . . missionaries were detested."[2]

In this highly inflammable setting, the anti-Christian writings of 1869–1870 served to stimulate and activate suspicions, fears, and resentments among the credulous inhabitants of the city. Chihli governor-general Tseng Kuo-fan, in his re-

port on the origins of the Massacre, listed five concrete
sources of popular suspicion: (1) the general aura of secrecy
which enveloped the management of the orphanage of the
Sisters of St. Vincent de Paul in Tientsin; (2) the fact that
people who went to the orphanage for medical treatment
occasionally refused to return home; (3) the common practice of the sisters of taking in children and adults who were
on the verge of death, in order to administer extreme unc-
tion; (4) the popular belief that mothers and children received by the Catholics lived in separate quarters and sometimes did not see each other for the span of a year; and (5)
a rash of kidnapings which had broken out in Tientsin in
the spring of 1870 and in which the Church had been implicated. These sources of suspicion were compounded by
the outbreak in June of an epidemic in the Catholic orphanage, which added significantly to the already high death rate
of this institution. When the bodies of two of the victims
were disinterred and were found to have decayed in an abnormal fashion, wild rumors spread in all directions.[3]

The kidnaping item bears further comment. Early in June
a number of Chinese were arrested on kidnaping charges,
summarily tried, and executed by the local authorities. For
some time it had been asserted by the Chinese, and widely
believed by the non-Catholic foreign population in Tientsin,
that these kidnapings had been inadvertently encouraged by
the imprudence of the Catholic sisters. The latter, according
to the American minister, Frederick F. Low, finding "that
the Chinese were averse to placing children in their charge
. . . offered a certain sum per head for all the children
placed under their control . . . it being understood that a
child once in their asylum no parent, relative, or guardian
could claim or exercise any control over it." Low went on
to express his belief in the assertion that the Catholics were

also "in the habit of holding out inducements to have children brought to them in the last stages of illness, for the purpose of being baptized *in articulo mortis.*" [4] When, on June 18, another kidnaper, Wu Lan-chen, was arrested and confessed to having sold the children he stole to one Wang San, who served as janitor for several of the Catholic establishments in Tientsin, tension in the city neared the breaking point.

On June 19 the Tientsin taotai called on the local French consul, Henri Fontanier, to discuss the situation. Fontanier, according to his own account, had no difficulty demonstrating to the taotai that the accusations against the Church were groundless, but he agreed, according to the Chinese version, to hold an investigation into the activities of Wang San. Later on the same day the Tientsin magistrate also paid Fontanier a visit and, in an angry encounter, insisted on the truth of Wu Lan-chen's charges and demanded an immediate investigation into the conditions prevailing at the Catholic church and orphanage. Fontanier, accusing the magistrate of being the instigator of all the trouble, broke off the discussion and informed Ch'ung-hou, the ranking Chinese official of the area, of the magistrate's conduct. On the following day, Ch'ung-hou intervened personally and, paying a friendly call on Fontanier, got him and Father Claude-Marie Chevrier to agree to a joint Sino-French inquiry into Wu Lan-chen's testimony. On the morning of the twenty-first, at the appointed hour, the local authorities conducted Wu to the Catholic church where his testimony was disproved point by point. Chevrier then went to Ch'ung-hou's yamen to discuss measures by which the people and converts could in the future be made to live together peacefully. The two men agreed that all deaths due to sickness occurring in the Catholic establishments of the city should be reported to the

Chinese authorities, so that the authorities could confirm the deaths and observe the burials. They also agreed that the names of persons who studied with, or were raised by, the Catholics should be reported to the officials, permitting the latter to investigate these persons, with a view to dispelling popular suspicions.[5]

A serious disturbance apparently having been nipped in the bud, Ch'ung-hou began to draft a proclamation to pacify the inhabitants of the city. Shortly after noon, however, he was suddenly informed that a brawl had begun at the Catholic church between some converts and a group of bystanders. Just as he was deputing soldiers to quell the riot, the French consul arrived at the yamen and Ch'ung-hou went out to greet him. Fontanier, accompanied by his chancellor, M. Simon, was armed with two pistols and in an ugly mood. Upon seeing Ch'ung, he began to use abusive language and, in an act of incredible folly, shot at the Chinese official, fortunately without hitting him. Fontanier was then seized by the onlooking attendants, and Ch'ung-hou, finding it "inconvenient" to wrangle with him further, withdrew for the moment into the yamen. The consul then entered and, shouting furiously, started to make a shambles of the room's contents. When his fury had abated somewhat and he prepared to go, Ch'ung-hou advised him that since popular feeling was enraged and a mob of several thousand Chinese — including members of the gentry and official classes — had gathered in the streets outside, he had best not leave the yamen. The Frenchman, according to Ch'ung, replied that he was not afraid of the Chinese common people and angrily stalked out into the crowd. Outside Fontanier encountered the Tientsin magistrate, purportedly on his way back from having suppressed the disturbance at the church. The consul again fired his pistols, missing the magistrate, but fatally wounding one of his attendants.[6]

Whether the hideous atrocities which followed were premeditated, as the "immense majority" of contemporary foreigners seemed to feel,[7] or not, they were now inevitable. Fontanier and Simon were ripped open on the spot. The crowd then plundered and set fire to the French consulate, the orphanage, the church, and other Catholic properties, and killed and savagely mutilated every Frenchman that could be found. Catholic sisters were stripped naked, their eyes gouged out, their breasts cut off, and their bodies violated, before being burned alive. Catholic priests were subjected to equally horrible fates. By nightfall further plundering and destruction had been visited upon four English and American chapels, and the final toll in lives stood at "between thirty and forty" Chinese converts and twenty-one foreigners, including two French officials, ten nuns, and two priests.[8]

The Tientsin Massacre represented the culmination of a decade of Sino-foreign friction revolving around Christian missionary activities. More broadly, it symbolized the tragic end of a mighty effort, on the part of Restoration (and certain foreign) officials, to build and revitalize a Confucian state which would be capable of responding effectively to the impact of the modern West. As Mary Wright has remarked: "At a time when responsible Western diplomats were summoning every reserve of wisdom to allay Chinese suspicion, one French consul closed his eyes to everything except France's role as protector of the Church. At a time when high Chinese officials were eating wormwood to avoid international incidents, one stubborn district magistrate closed his eyes to everything except the swell of local Chinese feeling against missionaries. In an afternoon a decade's work was undone."[9]

TSENG KUO-FAN'S MANAGEMENT
OF THE TIENTSIN CASE

During the hot summer months following the outbreak at
Tientsin, there was considerable unrest in other parts of the
empire. Rumors were rampant, and churches were either
destroyed or their destruction threatened at Tengchow and
Chefoo in Shantung; Kwangping and Chengting in Chihli;
Nanking, Shanghai, and Chinkiang in Kiangsu; Wu-ch'eng
and Fuchow in Kiangsi; Canton; and elsewhere.[10] Universal
alarm was experienced in foreign circles,[11] and the cry for
vengeance (or justice, as the missionaries preferred to call
it) was widespread.[12] Warships from other Far Eastern ports
were rapidly dispatched to the Tientsin area. The Chinese,
for their part, began to mobilize troops and call retired
generals back into active service.[13] In this feverish atmosphere of fear and tension, Tseng Kuo-fan, aging and just
recovering from a serious illness, was once again called upon
to save China in her hour of need. The difficulties that
Tseng encountered in his efforts to reconcile the opposing
demands of extremists on both the Chinese and foreign sides
proved nothing short of gigantic.

The Tientsin outbreak, in addition to furnishing a dramatic climax to the rising crescendo of antiforeign activity
in the late 1860's, also provided a proper outlet for the
pent-up hostilities of the more xenophobic wing of the
Chinese bureaucracy — a group whose views on foreign
affairs had been repeatedly and successfully rebuffed during
the preceding decade by the Tsungli Yamen and the throne.
One of the leaders of this group, Prince Ch'un, set the tone
for the ensuing attack in a memorial presented on June 29,
eight days after the Massacre. The memorial outlined four
points which Prince Ch'un requested the emperor to submit

to the Tsungli Yamen and to Tseng Kuo-fan for their consideration. These were that (1) the Tientsin populace should
not be punished, but should be soothed, so that its aroused
determination might be encouraged; (2) the local officials
of Tientsin should not be carelessly dismissed or transferred,
and any action taken against them should accord with popular opinion; (3) secret preparation should be made for
China's maritime defense; and (4) the barbarians in the
capital should be placed under close surveillance. Prince
Ch'un concluded: "We cannot stop them [the foreigners]
from coming [to China]. The important thing is that, though
they do come, we remain undaunted. We cannot prevent
them from wishing to fight. The important thing is that
even though they do fight, we have no cause for worry." [14]
It is worthy of note that in this memorial Prince Ch'un
placed great stress on the classical Chinese notion that the
strength of the state rests chiefly upon the support of the
people. To punish the people in order to appease the foreigner, therefore, would be to destroy the foundations of the
Confucian polity.

The main themes in Prince Ch'un's uncompromising
stand were echoed in mid-July by a subchancellor of the
Grand Secretariat, Sung Chin. Sung felt that the throne (in
an earlier edict on the Tientsin case) had lodged too much
blame with the common people, and he feared that they
would be alienated as a result. He placed particular emphasis upon the fact that the people had always been able
to live at peace with those foreign countries which concentrated on trade, but that with France, which stressed religion, they had been in constant conflict. The foreigners,
Sung continued, were basically afraid of the Chinese, and
if they used gunboats in this case it would only be to pressure China into a satisfactory settlement. Therefore, if China
prepared her defenses and took a strong stand, she would

have no trouble in getting her own way. But if she pursued a policy of accommodation, the righteous indignation of the people would be hard to control, and it would be France and her missionaries who would in the end suffer most.[15]

On July 19, Grand Secretary Kuan-wen presented a memorial on behalf of a clerk in the Grand Secretariat, Li Ju-sung, in which a still more inflexible stand was taken against any compromise in the Tientsin case. Again, the emphasis was on maintaining the support of the people: "If [the throne] opposes the barbarians but wins the confidence of the people, it still has the people as a means of controlling the barbarians. But if it forfeits popular trust to win over the barbarians, it has no way of controlling the people and also no way of governing the barbarians." Li Ju-sung realized that China was in no position at this time to expel the foreigner. But he strongly advocated expulsion as the long-range goal toward which she should direct her efforts. For the present, he suggested that China sever relations with France as a sign of the emperor's sympathy with the people.

Two days after the presentation of Li Ju-sung's memorial, a censor in charge of the Honan circuit, Ch'ang-jun, voiced his opinion on the Tientsin affair. Ch'ang's argument was somewhat novel. The biggest problem in China's foreign relations was, in his view, the corrupting influence of the French missionaries and their heterodox doctrines. (He seems to have been firmly convinced that the malpractices popularly attributed to the missionaries were true.) The harmful effects of this influence were felt not only by the Chinese people but also, indirectly, by those foreign countries whose chief interest in China was commercial. For the people of China transferred their suspicions of the missionary to the merchant, thereby impeding trade. Ch'ang therefore suggested that Tseng Kuo-fan and the Tsungli Yamen be instructed to engage, in conjunction with the foreign powers, in negotiations with France, clearly explaining to her that, because of the difficulties involved in enforcing the treaty article on preaching, this article should be formally rescinded, the churches throughout China destroyed, and all missionaries sent home.

Tseng Kuo-fan's forthright and unbiased management of the Tientsin case, against this backdrop of intense antiforeign feeling and in spite of his own antiforeign leanings, was a remarkable testimony to both his ability as a statesman and his courage as a man. His first memorial (presented on June 29) outlined the policies that China should pursue. Hostilities were to be avoided if at all possible, and in the official investigations two things were to be determined with complete impartiality: the precise connection, if any, between the Catholic church at Tientsin and the rash of kidnapings which had taken place in the city in the spring of 1870; and whether or not there was any truth to the widespread rumors that the missionaries extracted eyes and hearts from Chinese.[16]

Three weeks later (July 23), Tseng's famous report on his investigation of the case was presented to the throne. Tseng noted that the charges which had been leveled against the Tientsin missionaries were similar to rumors which had been circulated some years earlier in Hunan and Kiangsi, and more recently in Yangchow, Tienmen (Hupeh), Taming (Chihli), and Kwangping (Chihli). The truth or falsity of these rumors had, however, never been determined. Tseng therefore took advantage of this occasion to make it plain that his investigations had revealed absolutely no firm evidence supporting any of these charges, and, going a step further, requested the court to expose the entire fabrication to the empire, both to pacify the foreigners and to dispel the suspicions of the gentry and populace.[17]

In a supplementary memorial, presented on the same day,

Tseng noted that he had received a communication from the French representative, Rochechouart, threatening hostilities if the lives of the Tientsin prefect and magistrate and of the unruly brigadier general, Ch'en Kuo-jui (who in the foreigners' eyes was the principal suspect in the case),[18] were not immediately forfeited. Tseng, of course, felt that for the two officials, whose role in the instigation of the incident had not been proved, a punishment of such severity was entirely unwarranted. Nevertheless, because of Rochechouart's insistence and because the officials in question had indeed been unable to prevent the incident from breaking out, he requested that they be dismissed from their posts and delivered over to the Board of Punishments for trial. Tseng further stated that he knew of no evidence connecting Ch'en Kuo-jui with the case. But since the general was in Peking at this time, he suggested that the Tsungli Yamen interrogate him.

In view of subsequent Chinese hostility to Tseng's management of this case, it is important to note the reaction of the throne to Tseng's two memorials. In general, they met with overwhelming approval. An edict to the Grand Secretariat reviewed Tseng's first memorial at length and commented that, since the rumors about the Catholics had been proved false, in the future the people of the empire need have no suspicions in this regard. A further edict dismissed the Tientsin prefect and magistrate from their posts and ordered their trial and punishment. A third edict sanctioned the general policy being pursued by Tseng—a policy which was at bottom conciliatory and which sought to ward off hostilities. At the same time, however, the throne warned that the foreigners were cunning by nature, that "when they gained one step, they would advance another step." If China yielded to their demands in everything, where would it end? In short, China's desire was to prevent hostilities, but she must not sell her soul in the process. The most urgent task for the present was to take defense measures and prepare for any eventuality.[19]

Meanwhile, the pressures acting on Tseng mounted from all sides. The French, with gunboats stationed at Taku, continued to press their impossible demands, and repeated proclamations failed to have any effect in quieting the Tientsin populace. By July 24 Tseng was forced to bed again, owing to a relapse, and the throne commanded Kiangsu governor Ting Jih-ch'ang to go at once to Tientsin to assist him in managing the case.[20]

Tseng's task was further complicated by the continuing efforts of the extreme antiforeign wing in Peking to block any rapprochement with the French. On July 25 Prince Ch'un memorialized, defending the innocence of Ch'en Kuo-jui.[21] Some weeks later, in late August, a Board of Rites junior metropolitan censor, Hu Yü-yün, openly criticized Tseng Kuo-fan's management of the case. Tseng, he felt, had failed to dispel the suspicions of either the Chinese or the foreigners, and popular opinion was becoming more clamorous every day. The reason for this situation, in Hu's view, was that Tseng had been unable to deal properly with the two Chinese originally implicated in the kidnaping charges — Wang San and Wu Lan-chen. According to Tseng's own testimony, Wang had originally confessed to these charges but had then retracted his confession and gone free.[22] If, Hu Yü-yün commented,

neither Chinese nor foreigner is able to find out what he testified and what he retracted, how are the minds of the Chinese and the foreigners to be set at rest, and their suspicions dispelled? On the one hand, the foreigners suspiciously say: "It is not likely that Wang San confessed. This talk of confession is a sure [sign] that Tseng Kuo-fan is shielding the common people." On the other hand, the gentry and populace suspiciously say: "It is not likely that Wang San retracted his confession. This talk of retraction is a sure [sign] that Tseng Kuo-fan is ingratiating himself with the foreigners."

Hu Yü-yün concluded by requesting the emperor to issue orders for Wang San and Wu Lan-chen to be forwarded in custody to the capital, where the high metropolitan officials could try and sentence them on the basis of the facts.

Aside from its direct criticism of Tseng's management, the significant point about Hu Yü-yün's memorial is the emphasis placed on Wang San and Wu Lan-chen as the "key factors" in the Tientsin case, when in actual fact they had long since ceased to be of primary importance. This might be regarded as an indication of incredible naïveté on the part of Hu. It seems more likely, however, that by exaggerating the significance of the two commoners, Hu hoped vastly to oversimplify the actual problems involved in the management of the Tientsin case and thereby place Tseng Kuo-fan — in view of his inability to conclude it — in a still less favorable light.

Several days after Hu Yü-yün's memorial, Tseng's management of the case was subjected to more veiled criticism by an expositor of the Hanlin Academy, Yüan Pao-heng (1826–1878). Yüan's memorial consisted of five proposals. Three of these concerned defense preparations which had already been ordered by the throne. A fourth, highly reminiscent of Prince Ch'un's earlier proposals, urged that the spirit of the Tientsin populace be bolstered and consolidated rather than stifled and suppressed. "It is indeed to be feared that those who have managed cases involving the barbarians have been overly cautious. They have indulged the barbarians to excess, but have been too busy to trouble themselves concerning popular opinion." If, by repressing the Tientsin populace too severely, its spirit became disunified and its sense of purpose divided, the foreigners would become still more unscrupulous in their conduct. At this point even if it wished once again to rely upon the strength of the people, the throne would find that popular morale could no longer be aroused. And worse still, who could guarantee that popular anger would not again burst forth? Yüan Pao-heng's fifth point was that indemnities should not be frivolously granted in the Tientsin case because China needed the money for military and other purposes.[23]

Yüan Pao-heng's memorial was presented at a time when extensive efforts were being made at Tientsin to round up suspects and try them. Tseng reported on August 26 that thirty-seven persons had already been arrested and that rewards were being offered for information regarding others. At the same time, he proposed that the principals in the case be sentenced to capital punishment and the accessories to exile.[24] It is evident then that Yüan Pao-heng's strong advocacy of lenient treatment for the Tientsin populace ran directly counter to Tseng's policies. In addition to the indirect criticism of Tseng implied in this stand, it symbolized the continuing opposition of diehard elements in the north to a conciliatory settlement of the Tientsin case.

At this point it is well to emphasize the fact that the Chinese court not only condoned a conciliatory settlement, but actually insisted upon it. When Tseng, on September 10, reported the arrests of seven or eight persons, on whom there was enough evidence to warrant capital punishment, it was the throne which, overruling Li Hung-chang, decided that if the foreigner were to be pacified a still larger number of executions would have to take place.[25] Again, it was the throne which, on the recommendation of the Board of Punishments, finally sentenced the two Tientsin officials to lifelong exile in Heilungkiang.[26]

The throne, however, was more or less immune to criticism, and it was upon Tseng that the brunt of the anti-foreign opposition fell. In a letter which was reportedly distributed throughout the empire, the Grand Secretariat clerk, Ts'ang-chih, suggested to Tseng in no uncertain terms that by requesting punishment for the prefect and magistrate of Tientsin he had betrayed both his country and his reputation.[27] Although opposition to Tseng's policy centered in the Peking-Tientsin area, it was voiced elsewhere as well. The British consul at Hankow wrote, toward the end of 1870, that the local literati "were said to have been much incensed against Tseng Kwo Fan for having given up criminals to execution, and honorary tablets erected in Hu-nan to him are stated to have been torn down."[28]

Emotionally and perhaps even philosophically sympathetic to the views of the antiforeign elements, and yet clearly aware of the compromises that China had to make in her intercourse with the foreign powers, Tseng was a torn and embittered man. As far back as July, after recommending that the Tientsin officials be delivered over to the Board of Punishments, he had written to Li Hung-chang that he felt "conscience-stricken within and in opposition to public opinion without."[29] In September, after the threat of war with France had subsided, Tseng submitted a long memorial to the throne in which he sought to assuage his conscience by pleading for leniency in the punishment of the two Tientsin officials. At the same time, he noted the strong criticism that had everywhere been voiced with reference to his earlier memorial clearing the Catholics of the charge that they extracted eyes and hearts from Chinese subjects. The world, Tseng now wrote after reflecting on the matter, did contain people who committed such crimes. Indeed, the penal statutes had a special section dealing with them. Since, moreover, it was universally known that the Church often took in bad subjects, how could it be guaranteed that such villains did not enter the Church and then use it as a shield for their activities? [30]

The ill will that Tseng Kuo-fan's management of the Tientsin case incurred in northeastern China placed the Chinese court in an embarrassing position. Ordinarily, in such circumstances, wise politics would have warranted Tseng's transfer to a post elsewhere in the empire. But in view of his unique position as China's most eminent elder statesman and her national hero of but a few years past, to transfer him in good conscience would require an excellent excuse.

This excuse materialized in a most unexpected fashion. On August 22, the governor-general at Nanking, Ma Hsin-i, while walking back to his yamen, was knifed by an assassin. Ma died the following day. The throne, as soon as it heard the news, ordered Tseng Kuo-fan, upon the completion of his management of the Tientsin case, to return to his old post at Nanking with the honorable mission of conducting further investigations into Ma Hsin-i's assassination and of maintaining peace and order in Kiangsu province. Thus was found a face-saving solution to a very awkward situation.[31]

A few remarks on the circumstances surrounding the assassination of Ma Hsin-i would not be entirely irrelevant. According to the official reports, Ma's murderer, Chang Wen-hsiang, had once been a Taiping rebel, after which he had become an agent of pirates off the coast of Chekiang, many of whom Ma Hsin-i had executed as governor of that province. In addition, he was alleged to have had a personal grievance against Ma because the latter ignored Chang's complaints against his own wife. Finally, he had been forced to close his pawnshop in Ningpo as a result of Ma's energetic campaign against usurers. For these reasons, it was claimed, Chang was urged by his piratical friends to take revenge against Ma.[32]

At the time of the investigations, many Chinese officials found it difficult to believe that Ma Hsin-i's death had been caused by purely personal grievances or that Chang Wen-hsiang had been the only person involved. Apparently, however, none of the rumors that promptly began to circulate in Chinese circles attempted to establish any connection between the assassination and Ma's past conduct toward the missionaries. Such a connection was, nevertheless, widely speculated upon by the foreigners of the time.[33]

From the moment Ma Hsin-i succeeded Tseng Kuo-fan as Nanking governor-general (November 1868) until his death, Ma's relations with the Catholic missionaries in Nanking had been unusually amicable. Some Jesuit missionaries believed him to be the same person who, as a young official years before, had, after being critically wounded by rebels, requested and received baptism in a Jesuit hospital in Shanghai. In any event he was, in the words of a later Jesuit historian, "exempt from the xenophobia which the majority of his colleagues displayed at the time, and invariably showed, in his relations with French diplomats and missionaries, a fairness and benevolence as much appreciated as they were rare."[34]

Ma Hsin-i's conciliatory attitude toward the missionaries was clearly demonstrated in action. In December 1869 he readily assented to Rochechouart's demands in connection with the Anking and Kienteh incidents of that year (although it is only fair to add that these demands were seconded by French gunboats and, while Ma acceded to them, he was none too happy over it).[35] Moreover, on December 28 and January 2, he issued two proclamations — one announced the settlement of the Anhwei cases and the exclusion of the literati instigators from the government examinations; the other publicized the toleration clauses of the

French treaty — which were "as favorable as possible to the Christian religion." [36]

In the summer of 1870 the governor-general demonstrated in a still more emphatic manner his determination to enforce the treaties. During the spring of this year Nanking was flooded with inflammatory leaflets accusing the missionaries of the usual atrocities and calling for their extermination. In April, Ch'en Kuo-jui, the same man who became the bête noire of the French in the Tientsin case, was reported to have arrived in the city and to have assumed direction of antiforeign activities in cooperation with the treasurer of the province. With the convening of the government examinations in June, the excitement reached a new peak. The distributors of leaflets stepped up their activities; Buddhist monks sold talismans to the masses to protect them against the sorcery of the Europeans; and crosses were drawn on streets, doors, and rooftops to stop the kidnaping of children.

At this point the Catholics, in order to establish their innocence of the charges voiced against them, requested the prefect of Nanking to visit their establishment along with as many officials as he chose. The prefect, evidently new at his post and ignorant of the risks he ran in complying with the missionaries' request, visited the Catholic residence on June 11 and made a thorough inspection of the premises. Finding no bodies of dead infants inside, he immediately made a report to Ma Hsin-i. The governor-general, according to the Jesuits, thereupon placed the city under martial law, dispatched one hundred men from his personal guard to protect the missionaries, and had proclamations issued everywhere attesting to the innocence of the Catholics and prohibiting the circulation of false rumors. That evening, moreover, five criminals were beheaded, and Ma issued an announcement to the effect that these were the only persons guilty of the kidnapings that had taken place during the preceding days.[37]

The strong action taken by Ma Hsin-i on this occasion restored order in the southern capital and averted what seems to have had all the makings of a "Nanking Massacre." At the same time, however, his action undoubtedly alienated those members of the gentry and official classes who had taken the lead in exciting hatred against the missionaries. Whether or not this alienation had anything to do with Ma's assassination cannot be known with certainty until the whole incident has been carefully reviewed. One other event, however, did occur which may lend weight to the proposition that some connection existed. Shortly after Ma's death, the prefect of Nanking, upon whose initiative the charges against the Catholics had first been exposed, was found hanging in his yamen. The cause of death was officially announced as suicide. But, according to the Jesuits in Nanking, the official charged with the investigation of the matter was none other than the provincial treasurer who had reportedly been in league with Ch'en Kuo-jui earlier.[38]

The price ultimately exacted from the Chinese for the Tientsin case was a stiff one, but it might well have been stiffer had not fate intervened. The Tientsin prefect and magistrate, as we have seen, were sentenced to lifelong exile. Eighteen Chinese were beheaded, and another twenty-five sentenced to hard labor on the frontiers. For foreign lives lost, a total indemnity of 280,000 taels was paid (250,000 to France, 30,000 to Russia),[39] while additional sums of 210,000 and 2,500 taels were transmitted to the French and British respectively to compensate for property damage.[40] Finally, on October 18, Ch'ung-hou left for France on an official mission of apology.[41]

Rochechouart, all through the negotiations of the summer

of 1870, adhered to his tough, belligerent approach. But the news of the Massacre did not arrive in Europe until July 25, six days after the declaration of hostilities between France and Prussia, and the news of the Franco-Prussian War did not reach Peking until August 4, weeks after Rochechouart had presented his demand for the execution of the two Tientsin officials and Ch'en Kuo-jui.[42] Consequently, Rochechouart's July ultimatum,[43] on which French honor had been staked, could not be backed up by force, and the Chinese never acceded to it. France had overextended herself again in China owing to one of those fateful accidents of history — the lack of direct telegraphic communication between Peking and Europe. And her prestige plummeted to a new low when the news of her defeat in Europe, at the hands of a comparatively little known power, reached the Chinese capital.

### THE AFTERMATH OF THE TIENTSIN MASSACRE: THE TSUNGLI YAMEN PROPOSALS OF 1871

In July 1870, as we have already seen, a censor by the name of Ch'ang-jun, arguing that missionary activity was injurious to commerce, proposed that negotiations be undertaken with France, with a view to rescinding formally the treaty articles on preaching, destroying the churches throughout China, and sending all missionaries home. The throne ordered Tseng Kuo-fan to comment upon Ch'ang-jun's proposal. Tseng replied, several days later, that during the previous year when he had been in Peking he had suggested to Wen-hsiang that Catholic missionaries should not be permitted to establish orphanages. Wen-hsiang, however, had stated forcefully that the orphanages could not be prohibited. "If," Tseng now reasoned, "orphanages cannot be

prohibited, how much more impossible would it be to prohibit missionary activities?" [44]

In late September, Ting Jih-ch'ang (who by this time was
managing the Tientsin affair along with Tseng) submitted
a memorial on the missionary problem. Ting began by making a clear distinction between Protestantism and Catholicism. The members of the former religion minded their
own business and did not fight with the non-Christian population. China had no bone to pick with them. The Catholic
missionaries, however, although their original intentions
were not bad, failed to distinguish between loyal and dis-
loyal subjects and took people in on a grand scale, "finding
power in numbers." Ignorant people who were involved in
lawsuits or who owed money flocked to the religion, where
they obtained foreign protection. This procedure was apparently so common that a saying had gained currency: "Before people join the religion they are still as mice, but once
having joined they become as tigers." It was for this reason,
according to Ting, that the hatred of the common people
grew deeper by the day, and the reputation of the missionaries suffered in proportion. Ting suggested that, at the
impending treaty revision negotiations (referring to the
French Treaty of Tientsin which was subject to revision
after October 1870), it should be agreed that missionaries
were not to take in bad subjects or interfere in lawsuits. He
further requested that orders be sent to the high provincial
authorities to select local officials with care, choosing men
who, when it was appropriate to grant protection to the
Christians, would do so earnestly, but who would not be
afraid vigorously to take issue with them when the demands
of justice so required. [45]

Four days after the presentation of Ting Jih-ch'ang's requests, Tseng Kuo-fan sent in a memorial which analyzed
the missionary problem in much the same terms but went

a good deal further in its specific remedies. Tseng observed that China had always enjoyed peaceful relations with those foreign countries engaged in trade. France alone, because of her missionary activities, had repeatedly stirred up trouble. Similarly, the Chinese people had been able to get along amicably with Buddhism, Taoism, Islam, and even Protestantism. Of all the teachings, only Catholicism created interminable difficulties. Tseng then went on to summarize the abuses that his colleague, Ting Jih-ch'ang, had noted, drawing a parallel between the privileged position of the convert and that of the favorite son. The favorite son, because of his parents' protection, was despised by his brothers and fellow villagers, as a result of which he himself came to ruin, dragging his family down with him. The protection offered him was the very instrument of his destruction. Similarly, if China went on granting protection to converts in accordance with the laws of recent years, but failed to consider ways in which these laws might be altered, in the end there would surely be a day of reckoning. Tseng therefore proposed that all Catholic churches and charitable institutions be placed under the jurisdiction of the local officials; that whenever anyone was either received into these institutions or died within them, it should be reported to the authorities, the latter being permitted to go inside to conduct investigations; that when kidnaped persons were brought to the church, the victims' families should be given the opportunity to identify and redeem them; and that in cases of litigation involving Christian and non-Christian subjects, the missionaries should not be allowed to interfere on behalf of their converts.[46]

The suggestions of both Ting and Tseng were referred to the Tsungli Yamen, which reported the results of its deliberations on October 18. The Yamen felt that Ting's suggestion of ordering the provincial authorities to appoint

local officials of superior caliber "really got to the crux of
the matter." But with regard to the more specific items proposed by Tseng it had little to say, except that it would
seize upon the first opportunity to do whatever it could.[47]

As it turned out, this opportunity was not long in coming.
With Sino-French treaty revision negotiations in the offing,
France's position in China had deteriorated considerably as
a result of her inability to enforce her original demands following the Tientsin Massacre, the capitulation of Napoleon
III in September 1870, and reports in a Shanghai newspaper
of French anticlerical decrees at home.[48] These circumstances, together with the recent dramatization at Tientsin
of the explosive forces underlying the missionary question
and the increasing awareness on the part of responsible
Chinese officials of its seriousness, coalesced during the
winter of 1870–71 to encourage the Tsungli Yamen to make
one last attempt to find a workable solution to the manifold
problems presented by the Christian missionary enterprise.

This took the form of a circular letter and eight draft
regulations, which were transmitted to each of the foreign
powers on February 9, 1871. The circular began by observing that the original object of the treaties between China
and the West had been to ensure a permanent situation
which would be advantageous to both sides and injurious
to neither. Unfortunately, the events of recent years had conclusively shown that this object was not being fulfilled.
"Foreign trade," the Yamen wrote, "has given rise to no differences between China and the foreign countries. But the
abuses spread in connection with foreign missionary activities have been excessive." The Roman Catholic religion, in
particular, far from living up to its stated aim of exhorting
people to virtue, had proven a constant source of trouble for
the Chinese. Since the missionary problem was one which

affected the interests of peace and commerce, it was urgently necessary to devise an effective plan for coping with it.

The circular then drew the familiar contrast between the quality of the earlier converts to Catholicism and those of more recent vintage, finding in this one reason why the religion had fallen into disrepute. After briefly summarizing the abuses commonly identified with the "modern" Church, the Yamen pointed out that the common people of China had not yet learned to distinguish between Protestantism and Catholicism, grouping both under the latter designation, and that they were also ignorant of the distinction among the different countries of the West, simply calling them all foreign countries. Consequently, when disturbances broke out, *all* foreigners in China were equally endangered. That this was so could not be more tragically illustrated than by the recent events at Tientsin (in which Protestants and Russians had suffered along with French Catholics). Moreover, the Yamen continued, although the final settlement of the Tientsin case was near at hand, the measures that had been adopted — punishment of the local officials, decapitation of the principal culprits, and payment of indemnities and reparations — were only half measures designed to meet the immediate situation but giving no consideration to the solution of the long-range problem.

The core of this problem, in the Yamen's view, was the extraterritorial status of the foreign missionary. According to what it had heard, missionaries, regardless of nationality, traditionally abided by the laws and customs of the countries in which they labored and did not enjoy an independent status. If the missionaries in China would adhere to this code, their undertakings might be carried on in peace, without giving rise to acts of violence and slander. If, furthermore, the missionaries would make plain to the people the nature of their calling, and act in accordance with their teachings, the common people would be on good terms with them and the officials would be able to give them effective protection. Unfortunately, the circular dolefully added, the behavior of the missionaries who now came to China was at variance in every respect with this mode of conduct, and as long as the missionaries continued to be "like so many independent hostile states within another state," the preservation of peaceful relations and the avoidance of the antagonism of the officials and people would remain a quixotic hope at best.

The Yamen concluded its circular by conjuring up a vision of bigger and even more terrible disturbances, culminating in an uncontrollable mass uprising, if the existing state of affairs was not somehow altered. As one possible contribution toward this end it proposed eight articles for the regulation of missionary activities. Since in many instances these articles did little more than elaborate upon proposals which we have already examined in previous chapters, they will be summarized here in only the briefest form.

*Article 1.* Because of the popular suspicion that they engender, Catholic orphanages should be completely abolished. If this be deemed inadmissible, they should in the future be permitted to take in Christian children only, the identity of the child and the dates of his admission and departure from the orphanage being reported to the Chinese authorities and placed on record. Non-Christian children, whose families are unable to provide proper care for them, should be entrusted to specially appointed members of the gentry class.

*Article 2.* In order to reconcile the practices of Christianity with native standards of propriety and to remove from the minds of Chinese the feeling that foreigners are lewd and indecent in their behavior, Chinese women should henceforth be prohibited from entering foreign churches and female missionaries should no longer be permitted to labor in China.

*Article 3.* All missionaries should be placed under the control of the local officials. They should respect Chinese laws and customs and should not be permitted to set themselves apart as independent entities, usurp official authority, damage people's reputations, or revile Confucianism. Converts, on the other hand, should be on an equal footing with ordinary Chinese in all matters and should be prohibited from relying on their religion to evade government labor service or the payment of taxes and rents. Litigation involving Christian and non-Christian Chinese should be decided exclusively by the local officials. If the missionaries interfere in any way they should be sent back to their own countries.

*Article 4.* Where Chinese and foreigners live together in the same area, the law should be applied in an equitable manner. Once punishment has been inflicted with reference to any particular case, the missionaries should not bring forward additional pecuniary claims extraneous to the case or demand compensation from innocent gentry and merchants who are not immediately involved. Nor should they be allowed to conceal or otherwise protect converts who are guilty of crimes. Those missionaries who persist in doing this should either be forced to undergo the same punishment as the guilty convert or leave China.

*Article 5.* The passports issued to French missionaries should specify the province and prefecture to which they intend to go, after which the missionaries should not be allowed to travel elsewhere. If passports are transferred to Chinese who then pose as missionaries, or if they are used for any other unlawful purposes, the Chinese involved should be severely punished and the missionary expelled from China. Holders of passports should not be permitted to go to places where rebels are active or to provinces in which military operations are being carried on.

*Article 6.* Since the aim of the missionaries is to exhort people to virtue, they should make certain prior to receiving Chinese into the religion that the latter are upright persons who have never transgressed the law. In accordance with the Chinese practice regarding monasteries, the names of all members of the religion should be registered with the local *pao-chia* organization. Within a fixed time, after receiving a convert, a separate report ought to be made to the local authorities, specifying the date of entry into the religion, the convert's native place, and the nature of his livelihood up to that time, and attesting to the fact that he has not previously violated the law and then changed his name. When converts die or change residence, this too should be announced to the authorities. Converts who commit unlawful acts should be immediately expelled from the Church. The missionaries should submit monthly or quarterly statements to the authorities, who in turn should be authorized to make monthly or quarterly inspection tours of Church establishments, following the procedure applied to Buddhist and Taoist institutions.

*Article 7.* Missionaries should faithfully adhere to the established institutions and customs of China. They should not make unauthorized use of official seals or submit official communications (*chao-hui*) to any of the yamens. If they wish to apply to the authorities with reference to some matter involving themselves personally, but unconnected with the lawsuits of their converts, they should use the petition (*ping*) form of correspondence, as do the Chinese literati. Similarly, when calling on Chinese officials of high or low rank, they should adopt the same ceremonial forms used by the literati and treat these officials politely. On no account should they be permitted freely to barge into the yamens and disrupt public business.

*Article 8.* In the interests of peace on the local scene, missionaries should not be allowed to designate any building they please as formerly confiscated Church property and, regardless of the building's importance to the Chinese people, demand its return. Before property transactions are made or buildings erected, moreover, the parties concerned should lay the matter before the local authorities to make sure that there is no conflict with Chinese geomantic notions (*feng-shui*). If the authorities agree to the transaction and it is not opposed by the local population, permission should then be given to procced in accordance with the convention signed in 1865.

Amplifying most of the above articles, the Tsungli Yamen drew upon the corpus of missionary cases of the 1860's to illustrate the grievances it sought to eradicate. In closing, it suggested that the grievances mentioned constituted only a sampling of those that could have been cited. If something was not immediately done to excise the cancer, its growth would become uncontrollable and the setback to peace and friendly relations irretrievable. The Yamen professed ignorance as to whether or not the missionaries would be willing to accept its proposals. But if they would not, either because they felt them too constraining or in conflict with the regulations of their religion, the Yamen had only one suggestion: that the missionaries carry on their vocation elsewhere, but not in China. In any case, the Yamen was at pains to point out, the enclosed regulations were not meant to constitute a prohibition of missionary operations but, rather, a means of averting disaster before it was too late.[49]

The Tsungli Yamen's circular and draft regulations are of great importance for two reasons. First, they provide a summary statement of those aspects of the missionary enterprise which were of greatest irritation to the Chinese. This statement, moreover, as prejudiced and one-sided as it may have seemed to some, was based on an empire-wide view of the missionary question and on an accumulation of factual data which unquestionably exceeded that at the disposal of any other institution of the time, foreign or Chinese. Second, the Tsungli Yamen's proposals, by stimulating far-reaching discussion among foreign diplomats and missionaries, served to bring into sharp focus the wide area of mutual misunderstanding and disagreement that persisted between Chinese and foreigner at the end of a troubled decade of missionary activity under the new treaties.

## Foreign reaction to the Chinese proposals

The American and British replies to the Chinese government's proposals were communicated in March and June 1871, respectively. Although fairly moderate in tone, they were plainly opposed to the majority of the items and tended to belittle a problem which, to the Chinese, was a major source of concern.[50] Since the Chinese proposals were obviously directed at the French protectorate in particular, Rochechouart's reply was delayed until he had received instructions from Paris (which in turn wished to sound out Britain's views) and was not communicated until November. The French reply was very much stronger than either the British or the American, rejecting outright all of the articles and questioning whether they had even been seriously intended by the Chinese government.[51]

If, after China's "unsatisfactory" management of the Tientsin case, the foreign powers were in no mood to grant concessions in the sphere of missionary activities, the missionaries themselves were positively repelled by the thought. The most detailed and authoritative Catholic refutation of the Tsungli Yamen's proposals was a pamphlet by the

French missionary, Félix Gennevoise, published anony-
mously in Rome by the Imprimerie de la Propagande in
1872. Not to be outdone by the Tsungli Yamen, Gennevoise's rebuttal was a veritable masterpiece of harsh and
uncompromising invective.

Gennevoise charged that the control over Catholic orphanages desired by the Chinese authorities would be tyrannical at best. Moreover, he denied the Yamen's claim that
these institutions were shrouded in secrecy and suspicion
and contended that, if only Christian children were permitted to enter them, it would be tantamount to abolishing
them altogether since it was almost unheard-of for converts to abandon their offspring. The proposal to prohibit
Chinese women from entering churches and foreign women
from working in China, the missionary continued, was a
violation of the religious liberty proclaimed by the Chinese
government and manifested the "infernal hatred" of this
government for Christianity. He conceded that the separa-
tion of the sexes was strictly observed in China — in defer-
ence to which Catholic chapels were already segregated. But
in the same breath he suggested that this very reserve provided positive proof of Chinese immorality.

The Chinese government, Gennevoise went on, could not
be serious in charging that missionaries had set themselves
up as independent entities, resisted the authorities, and
denigrated Confucius, or that Chinese converts — who were
the most loyal subjects in the empire — sometimes refused
to pay taxes. The only occasions on which missionaries interfered in lawsuits involving Christians and non-Christians
were when the former were persecuted because of their religion. They did, however, frequently act as judges in cases
involving Christians only, the venality of Chinese officials
making this a virtual necessity. Gennevoise defended the
right of missionaries to travel throughout the empire and

denied that they ever used their passports to engage in illegal traffic of any kind. Although it was already stipulated in the treaties that passports could not be issued for rebel-held regions, to extend this restriction to territories in which government military operations were being conducted would mean that the Chinese government could refuse passports for almost the entire land.

The conduct of new converts, he continued, was always examined before they were admitted into the religion. But since Christianity was a religion of mercy and pardon, it was impossible to turn away all who had committed some crime in the past. Gennevoise rejected, as an open invitation to persecution, the suggestion that lists of converts be submitted to the local authorities and, relative to the proposal that Chinese officials be permitted to make periodic inspections of Church establishments, commented: "Better an open persecution than this unwarranted intervention of the mandarins in the affairs of religion; to oblige the missionaries to receive them in the churches is as ridiculous as it is tyrannical."

Missionaries, according to Gennevoise, never usurped the privilege of using official seals and, when visiting the yamens, always studiously observed the proper etiquette. But to compel them to use the petition form of communication when addressing officials was asking too much, since it would reduce missionaries to the level of the common people and lower literati.

With regard to the final Chinese proposal, that missionaries no longer be permitted to claim any properties they pleased, Gennevoise retaliated that the treaties clearly stipulated that former Church properties were to be restored to their original owners. The fact that these properties occasionally happened to include buildings which in the meantime had been converted into temples or official residences did not in any way affect the issue at hand. When compensation was due, he continued, the transaction was always made in common accord with the officials. But if, in all their property transactions, the missionaries had to defer to the Chinese superstition of *feng-shui* and to local popular sentiment, it would be an easy matter for the Chinese authorities to prevent all transactions.

The whole of the Chinese government's proposals, Gennevoise concluded, was nothing but a long series of calumnies, in which every effort had been made to coat bad faith with an appearance of benevolent intent. The missionary abuses cited, far from being representative, were the only ones the Chinese had been able to find — or rather invent. And the sole object and desire of the authors was to expel from China all who preached the Christian religion.[52]

The responses of other Catholic missionaries to the Chinese proposals were no less uncompromising than Gennevoise's. The Italian priest, Raimondi, regarded them as "truly unheard-of," and felt the situation to be so threatening that he urged a meeting of all the bishops in China.[53] The vicar apostolic of Peking, Louis Delaplace, who also advocated such a meeting, upon studying the document, was alarmed to find in it "so many calumnies, lies, atrocious suppositions, etc." and felt that, if it were to be made public, a terrifying reaction against missionaries and converts might well result.[54] Again, Monsignor Chauveau, the vicar apostolic of Tibet, was convinced that this "official document, emanating from so high, calculated with such deliberateness, published with so much éclat and solemnity," would by its very nature become immortal in China.[55]

Since the Tsungli Yamen's circular and draft regulations appeared to be aimed chiefly at Catholic missionaries, Protestants did not get quite so stirred up about them. The ever outspoken Griffith John, it is true, remarked: "These demands strike at the very root of Christian missions in China, and they will, if complied with, close every church, chapel, and school in the land." [56] But the memorandum was a two-edged sword from the point of view of other Protestants. And more than a few of these, finding in it confirmation of their own prejudices against the Catholic missionary enterprise, took a considerably more moderate stand.[57]

During the discussions on the revision of the French treaty, the French representative, L. de Geofroy, in April 1874 transmitted to the Chinese government a set of seven proposals to alleviate the difficulties attending missionary activities in the interior. The French proposals, however, conceded little to the Chinese point of view, and in May the Tsungli Yamen countered with its own proposals which were, in all fundamentals, the same as the eight put forward in 1871.[58] Neither side was willing to compromise; the treaty revision negotiations eventually collapsed; and the Chinese proposals were at last consigned to the oblivion that the foreigners felt they so justly deserved.

If the Tientsin Massacre symbolized the tragic end of one era in Chinese history,[59] the airing of views on the missionary question in the early 1870's portended the tragic beginning of the next. In remarking on the history of the Massacre, S. Wells Williams observed that it combined "as many of the serious obstacles in the way of harmonizing Chinese and European civilizations as anything which ever occurred."[60] Certainly this statement is equally applicable to the debate on the missionary question that took place following the Massacre—a debate that revealed in clearest terms the profound gulf still existing between Chinese and Western concepts of law, religious liberty, society, and man.

When viewed in this perspective, it would appear just as myopic to brand the Chinese proposals as a tissue of lies as to charge the foreign missionaries with callous indifference to Chinese sensibilities. Each side operated on premises that it believed to be universally valid, and both were caught up in a clash of cultures over which neither had much control.

# CHAPTER 10

# CHINESE XENOPHOBIA AND THE FOREIGN MISSIONARY

IN THE preceding chapters an attempt has been made to explore some of the problems that resulted from the intrusion of the "modern" foreign missionary into "traditional" Chinese society. Clearly one of the most serious problems to emerge during the 1860's was the political one. The Chinese government, weak and plagued by internal revolt, had to cater to the prejudices of the gentry and populace if the dynasty was to survive. But for the very same reason it also had to cater to the demands of the foreigner. Unfortunately, these two commitments, especially insofar as they impinged upon Sino-foreign relations in the Chinese interior, were basically incompatible. Popular support all too often was conditioned upon defiance of the treaties and, conversely, the treaties in many cases could be implemented in the interior only at the expense of popular support. Satisfaction could not be given to either side without seriously endangering the position of the dynasty. And although in any particular case this dilemma might be circumvented through delaying tactics, shifting responsibility from higher to lower echelons of the Chinese administration, and such, in the long run no real solution could be found.

Although this political problem was particularly acute during the Restoration period, as long as the conflicting forces of Chinese xenophobia and foreign imperialism remained alive and potent, the problem continued to plague the Chinese government at all levels. During the Yangtze valley antiforeign disturbances of the early 1890's, the presiding local authorities were confronted with this same dilemma, and they exhibited the same range of responses. Some officials, in compliance with the treaties, tried to protect the foreigners and suppress the rioters, in which case they were, without exception, censured and attacked by the Chinese populace. Others, choosing the easier way out, sat by and allowed the riots to run their course.[1] Chang Chih-tung (1837–1909), who was charged with the management of the cases, gave expression to the same insoluble problem that in the 1860's had been voiced in connection with the punishment of the unruly Kweichow commander, T'ien Hsing-shu. If, Chang remarked, Chou Han, the chief instigator of the Yangtze disturbances, was punished too severely, public opinion in Hunan (Chou's province) would be incensed; if he was punished too lightly, the foreigners would be outraged.[2]

The debilitating effect of this political problem was again made glaringly apparent in the Boxer uprising of 1900,[3] which played the same symbolic role with regard to the dying Ch'ing dynasty that the Tientsin Massacre had to the T'ung-chih Restoration. To support the virulently antiforeign Boxers meant to risk war with all the foreign powers. But to suppress them was to run the equal danger of alienating the more xenophobic elements at the Chinese court. The throne vacillated at first and then cast its lot with the Boxers. But a number of powerful provincial officials, including Chang Chih-tung and the aging Li Hung-chang and Liu K'un-i, ignored the throne's declaration of hostilities, thereby saving southeastern China from a war that could have materially altered China's destiny. With this act of defiance, the dilemma with which the Chinese government had wrestled for more than half a century finally reached its climax. Power was no longer concentrated in one center that could claim to represent Chinese officialdom as a whole but, rather, in a plurality of centers that held widely divergent views on how China's problems were to be met. This split between the provinces and the throne was irrevocable, and the authority of the imperial government was weakened beyond repair.

If we go a step further, it becomes apparent that this political problem, however significant, was derivative in nature. Underlying it was the much larger issue of Sino-Western cultural conflict, as concretized, for us, in the mutual misunderstanding that existed between the foreign missionary and the Chinese intellectual. On the missionary's side, this antagonism resulted from two closely interwoven circumstances. First, truism that it seems, the missionary was a Westerner and, as such, was governed in thought and action by the values and presuppositions of his civilization. At the same time, however, he was something more than a Westerner. Inevitably, he became a hybrid of sorts, a Westerner-in-China. This does not mean that, as in the case of the early Jesuits, he became enamored of China; with few exceptions, the opposite seems to have been much more the case. What it does mean is that, by the mere fact of his immediate presence in a Chinese context, he took on certain attributes which he would not have had in a Western context. Modern students of Chinese history have all too often focused on the process of Western impact and Chinese response, to the neglect of the reverse process of Chinese impact and Western response. The missionary who came to China found himself confronted with frustrations and hostilities which he could hardly have envisaged before coming and which transformed him, subtly but unmistakably, into a *foreign* missionary. His awareness (one might indeed say resentment) of this metamorphosis, together with his fundamental dissatisfaction with things as they were in

China — a dissatisfaction which, at least in the religious sphere, provided him with his raison d'être in the first place — greatly conditioned the missionary's response to the Chinese setting. He was eminently concerned with the souls of the Chinese and in many cases grew to love the Chinese as people. But this very concern and affection reinforced in him the driving urge to bring light and remove darkness. And this impelled him, almost of necessity, to adopt a critical and often intolerant posture toward much of Chinese *culture*.

At least as crucial as the foreign missionary's attitude toward Chinese culture was the Chinese intellectual's attitude toward Christianity and its bearers — an attitude which, with very few exceptions, ranged from callous indifference to impassioned hatred. Although this attitude was brought to a head and popularized by the events of 1840–1860, its roots were deep and in evidence as far back as the early seventeenth century. As intriguing as it might be to do so, I have studiously avoided any "metaphysical" explanations of its causes, such as the stock charge that the Chinese are basically unsusceptible to religious experience as understood in the West. My impression is that the Chinese response to Christianity was conditioned not by metaphysics but by history and that, to gain a fuller understanding of it, one would have to make an extensive study of Chinese intellectual history, devoting special attention to Chinese attitudes toward foreign ideas during various periods.

In Chapter 1 this hostile attitude was traced up to the writing of the *Pi-hsieh chi-shih* in the early 1860's and was approached within the framework of the traditional Chinese heterodoxy-orthodoxy antithesis. Other writings coming after the *Pi-hsieh chi-shih* continued, to a greater or lesser degree, to follow this pattern.[4] At the same time, however, a radically new departure was taken in the Chinese anti-Christian tradition — one which in all its variety has remained dominant up to the present day. The essentially new ingredient in this development was the realization by some Chinese that there were forces in the West itself which were hostile to Christianity or, if not to Christianity, at least to the Christian missionary enterprise. From here it was but a short step to the appropriation of these new forces and their assimilation into the domestic anti-Christian tradition.

One of the earliest illustrations of this development was a short essay by a Chekiang literatus, Yang Hsiang-chi (1825–1878). Writing sometime between 1855 and 1878, Yang attacked Christianity from the viewpoint of modern Western science. In a manner reminiscent of the antireligious forays of kindred spirits in the West, he pointed enthusiastically to the contradictions between the principle of gravitation and various statements made in the Book of Genesis and Milton's *Paradise Lost,* concluding that if Christianity were unable to reconcile these contradictions it could not be worth much as a teaching.[5]

One of modern China's pioneering journalists and reformers, Wang T'ao,[6] was another who, at a relatively early date, made use of the intra-Western critique of Christianity. In spite of his long and intimate association with the Protestant missionary-translator, James Legge, Wang appears to have been a vigorous opponent of the Christian missionary enterprise, feeling, not unjustifiably, that it had forced its way into China.[7] In a brief piece written before 1883, he noted the recent rise in France and England of Positivism (*Pu-ssu-tieh-ni-chiao*). This teaching, according to Wang, was utterly opposed to both Protestantism and Catholicism. Its adherents did not worship God, nor did they recognize such doctrines as retribution beyond the grave. Rather, they regarded the search for truth and the verification of facts as man's most important responsibilities. Conceiving them in these terms, Wang was quite taken with the Positivists and likened them to true "disciples of the ancient sages." [8]

A variation on this general approach was taken by Yen Fu (1853–1921), the famous translator. The first work translated by Yen, in the early 1890's, was a book by the English correspondent, Alexander Michie, entitled *Missionaries in China*.[9] Michie, although apparently committed to the Christian religion, was a persistent and forceful critic of many of the practices followed by missionaries in China. By making the book available to a Chinese audience, therefore, Yen Fu made it abundantly clear that Westerners were not unanimously uncritical of Christian missionary operations.[10]

In the twentieth century, as Chinese intellectuals became increasingly more attuned to the whole range of recent Western thought, the arguments voiced against Christianity became correspondingly more varied and Western-oriented. The predominant belief in the 1920's was that Christianity, along with other religions, was superstitious and had no place in a modern world ruled by science. This was the conviction shared by such diverse leading figures as Hu Shih, Ch'en Tu-hsiu, and Ts'ai Yüan-p'ei.[11] Gradually, however, it was superseded in importance by another argument nurtured by the twin forces of nationalism and Marxism-Leninism. One application of the Leninist theory of imperialism which has had support from patriotic Chinese of all political hues is the notion that the Christian missionary enterprise was inseparable from other more obvious forms of Western imperialism. The present-day Chinese Communist view of the missionary as a political agent of the imperialist powers is but an extension and refinement of this attitude.[12]

Such views differ from "premodern" anti-Christian thought both in the nature of the arguments used and in the sources drawn upon. These differences, however, are counterbalanced to some extent by continuities in the Chinese anti-Christian tradition. One such continuity has been the belief that Christianity is irrational and superstitious — unworthy of the attention of serious-minded people. This theme is found in the earliest anti-Christian writings. It was strongly echoed in the 1920's. And it remains a basic component of the Marxist outlook in contemporary China. Another motif has been the notion that the missionary was a foreign political agent. This may indeed be consciously formulated policy on the part of the Communists. But it was genuinely believed by many nineteenth-century Chinese and constituted the keystone of Yang Kuang-hsien's attack two centuries earlier. Finally, there has, I think, been an emotional-psychological continuity, the intangible of deep-seated resentment. The Chinese Communists, by ejecting the foreign missionary and bringing strong pressure to bear upon the native Church to sever all connections with the West, have given dramatic fulfillment to a wish that was cherished in vain by numerous Chinese of the nineteenth century. Although Communist actions in this regard have unquestionably been dictated, in small or large part, by considerations of Realpolitik, it would be difficult to deny that they have also been influenced, perhaps significantly, by bitter resentment against a long history of foreign interference in Chinese affairs, a history in which the Christian missionary was inextricably involved.

## THE ROLE OF THE MISSIONARY

The pages of this book have repeatedly been addressed to one or the other of two interrelated phenomena: first, the growing tide of Chinese antiforeignism after 1860 and, second, the progressive deterioration after this date of the Chinese government's position at all levels. Because both developments played a major part in bringing about the transformation of the traditional order in China, it is important that my concluding remarks characterize with as much precision as possible the role which the foreign missionary played in connection with them.

The fundamental causes of Chinese antiforeignism in the modern era may well have been in the nature of intangibles, such as resentment against the unwanted intrusion of the West as a whole; the natural tendency of any society which has been seriously disturbed by internal disorders to seek an external scapegoat which it can hold responsible for all its woes; and, last but not least, the strong tradition of Chinese ethnocentrism which, it will be remembered, had been vented against Indian Buddhism long before it was unleashed against European Christianity.

My concern, however, is less with the roots of Chinese antiforeignism as such than with the fact of its spectacular growth in the latter half of the nineteenth century. Here, I would submit, the foreign missionary played a critical role. In part, this was a simple consequence of the missionary's immediate presence in the Chinese interior. He was the first foreigner to leave the treaty ports and venture into the interior in large numbers and, for a long time, virtually the only foreigner whose field of day-to-day operations extended over the length and breadth of the Chinese empire. For a large segment of the Chinese population in the nineteenth century, therefore, the missionary was the only concrete manifestation of the foreign intrusion and, as such, the only flesh-and-blood object against which opposition to this intrusion could be directed. If missionaries had not entered the interior in large numbers after 1860, it is all but certain that antiforeignism would still have been a prominent theme in the writings of China's intellectuals, as it had been to a lesser degree for centuries past. But it is highly unlikely

that it would have become the widespread social phenomenon that it did until many years had gone by, and it would
have been quite impossible for it to have been manifested
in such a violent manner. In effect, then, however one
chooses to view the underlying origins of nineteenth-century Chinese antiforeignism, the foreign missionary — by
the mere fact of his presence in the interior — played a decisive part both in popularizing and in activating this force.

This conclusion is considerably strengthened when we
recall the many ways in which the missionary of this era
made his presence felt on the local Chinese scene. By in-
dignantly waging battle against the notion that China possessed a monopoly of all civilization and, more particularly,
by his attack on many facets of Chinese culture itself, the
missionary directly undermined the cultural hegemony of
the gentry class. Similarly, by virtue of his privileged position under the new treaties and the simple fact that he was
literate, he posed an effective threat to the gentry's dominant
position in the social sphere. The members of Chinese
officialdom, to the extent that they shared the intellectual
and emotional commitments of the gentry, were equally resentful of the missionary's onslaught against cherished Chinese values. But more directly angering to the official was
the missionary's extraterritorial status in the interior and
his deliberate and frequently tactless abuse of this status.

Lastly, the Chinese populace at large, despite the contemporary foreigner's sanguine view to the contrary, proved
itself to be intensely antiforeign in numerous instances. For,
although the people were not directly threatened by the missionary, in the sense that the gentry and official were, they
had ample cause to take umbrage against him. The missionary's attack on such practices as ancestor worship and
idolatry offended all Chinese, not merely the elite. Moreover, it was the hapless commoner who often had to foot the

bill for the indemnities that the missionary demanded following antiforeign incidents. The ordinary Chinese, again, was irritated by the unscrupulousness that not a few of his fellows exhibited after becoming converts, and he was profoundly bewildered by the strange ways of the foreigner within his midst, providing fertile ground for the gentry propaganda which, in these pages, we have so often had occasion to examine. In sum, although it was the Chinese intellectual who undoubtedly furnished most of the inspiration and impetus for Chinese hostility to Christianity after 1860, there is ample evidence to indicate that this hostility was not the monopoly of any one class, but the common property of all.

The missionary then — partly by the mere fact of his presence in the Chinese interior and partly by the manner in which he made his presence felt there — clearly played a major role in encouraging the growth of Chinese antiforeignism after 1860. Moreover, to the extent that the progressive weakening and eventual breakdown of the Chinese government's political authority was a consequence of its inability to cope with this antiforeignism, the missionary must again be charged with a heavy share of the responsibility. It is essential that this last point be made absolutely clear. The collapse of Ch'ing political authority in the late nineteenth and early twentieth centuries was due not to any one factor alone but to a multiplicity of factors operating together. In this study I have been concerned with only one of these: Chinese xenophobia at the grassroots level and the total inability of the Chinese government to carry out the new treaties effectively in the face of this xenophobia.

At the local and provincial levels, as we have seen, the Chinese official was faced with a variety of equally unsatisfactory alternatives. If he chose to accommodate the foreign missionary, he enraged the sensibilities of the gentry, the populace, and the more xenophobic of his fellow officials, and thereby crippled his future effectiveness as an official. If he elected to oppose the foreign missionary, he aroused the anger of the foreigner and, if the matter was sufficiently grave, risked punishment by the throne. Confronted with this dilemma, many a Chinese official tried to circumvent it by doing nothing. But this, too, proved to be entirely unacceptable to the foreigner and a source of considerable embarrassment to the Chinese central government, in particular the Tsungli Yamen. The Yamen, in turn, by earnestly seeking to carry out the treaties after 1860, alienated the gentry and populace of the interior and progressively weakened its position vis-à-vis large segments of the provincial bureaucracy. At the same time, however, because of its ultimate failure to carry out the treaties effectively, its standing in the eyes of the foreign powers steadily deteriorated as the years went by. At all levels of the Chinese bureaucracy, in short, the effort to implement the new treaties in the Chinese interior was a self-destructive one, corroding the authority of the provincial official if successful and damaging the position of the Tsungli Yamen if unsuccessful.

It remains only to determine the degree to which Sino-foreign friction in the interior after 1860 involved the foreign missionary, as opposed to other foreign forces on the local scene. During the decade of the sixties, the missionary was virtually the only representative of foreign influence in the Chinese interior. But, as the Ch'ing dynasty drew to a close, other foreigners, to an ever-increasing extent, made their way into the interior for either business or pleasure. Nevertheless, even at this point, the record indicates that friction involving the missionary was far more extensive than that involving any other type of foreigner. In the Tsungli Yamen (and after 1901 in the Wai-wu-pu) archives, the number of volumes dealing with missionary difficulties from 1860 to 1909 — nine hundred and ten, *not* including the materials on the Boxer uprising — is more than double that for any other subject category in the sphere of Sino-foreign relations over a comparable span of time.[13] Most of the other categories, moreover, have little to do with Sino-foreign relations in the Chinese interior, and the one that most clearly does — mining affairs in the provinces — is represented by only eighty-six volumes of materials, less than one tenth of the number concerning missionary difficulties.

This evidence, however indirect, lends strong support to the contention that, on the foreign side, the missionary remained the most prominent source of Sino-foreign friction in the Chinese interior right up to the end of the Ch'ing. And as this friction was a significant factor in the ultimate downfall of the dynasty, the part played by the missionary in bringing about this downfall cannot be disputed.

# APPENDIX I

# INCIDENTS MENTIONED
# IN TEXT, 1861–1870

| Date | Place | Sect | Christians killed Foreign | Chinese | Punished Officials | Others | Reparations |
|------|-------|------|---------|---------|-----------|--------|-------------|
| 1861 | Kweichow: Chao-chia-kuan | C | 0 | 4 | 0 | 0 | 0 |
| 1862 | Kweichow: Kaichow | C | 1 | 4 | 7 | 0 | Tls. 12,000 |
| 1862 | Kiangsi: Nanchang | C | 0 | 0 | 0 | 0 | Tls. 17,000 |
| 1862 | Hunan: Siangtan (Changsha fu) | C | 0 | 5 | 0 | 0 | — |
| 1862 | Hunan: Hengchow | C | 0 | 0 | 1 | 0 | — |
| 1862 | Yunnan: Chaotung | C | 0 | 0 | 2 | — | — |
| 1862 | Szechwan: Tatsu | C | 0 | 0 | 1 | 0 | 0 |
| 1863 | Szechwan: Chungking | C | 0 | 0 | 0 | 0 | Tls. 150,000 |
| 1863 | Fukien: Fuan | C | 0 | 0 | — | — | — |
| 1864 | Kiangsi: Kweiki | C | 0 | 0 | — | — | — |
| 1864–65 | Kweichow: Hingi (Hsing-i) | C | 0 | 4 | 0 | 0 | 0 |
| 1864–65 | Kweichow: Puan | C | 0 | — | — | — | — |
| 1865 | Hunan: Hengchow | C | 0 | 0 | — | — | — |
| 1865 | Kweichow: Yungning (Anshun fu) | C | 0 | 6 | 0 | 1(1) | Tls. 800 |
| 1865 | Szechwan: Yuyang | C | 1 | 1 | 0 | 13(1) | Tls. 80,000 |
| 1866 | Honan: Luyi | C | 0 | 0 | 0 | 0 | — |
| 1866 | Kweichow: Anshun | C | 0 | 3 | 1 | — | — |
| 1866 | Honan: Tungpeh (T'ung-po [Nanyang fu]) | C | 0 | 0 | 0 | — | — |
| 1866 | Honan: Wuan | C | 0 | 1 | — | — | — |
| 1866–68 | Honan: Nanyang | C | 0 | 0 | — | — | — |
| 1867 | Chekiang: Siaoshan | P | 0 | 0 | 0 | 0 | 0 |
| 1867–70 | Kwangtung: Luichow | C | 0 | 8 | 0 | 0 | — |
| 1868 | Kiangsu: Yangchow | P | 0 | 0 | 2 | 2 | Tls. 3,326 |
| 1868 | Fukien: Taiwan | PC | 0 | — | 5 | — | $ 3,167 |
| 1869 | Szechwan: Yuyang | C | 1 | 39 | 0 | 7(2) | Tls. 30,000 |
| 1869 | Anhwei: Anking | PC | 0 | 0 | 4 | 15 | $ 5,735 |
| 1869 | Anhwei: Kienteh | C | 0 | 23 | — | — | — |
| 1869 | Kwangsi: Pokpah (Po-pai) | C | 0 | 1 | — | — | — |
| 1869 | Fukien: Ch'uan-shih-shan | P | 0 | 0 | 0 | 0 | 0 |
| 1869 | Chihli: Yungnien | C | 0 | 0 | 0 | 1 | Tls. 100 |
| 1869 | Hupeh: Tienmen | C | 0 | 0 | 0 | 3 | Tls. 5,700 |
| 1869 | Kweichow: Tsunyi | C | — | 29 | 10 | 3(1) | Tls. 80,000 |
| 1869–70 | Kiangsi: Luling, Kweiki, Anjen, Tehhwa, etc. | C | 0 | 2 | — | — | Tls. 6,000 |
| 1870 | Chihli: Tientsin | PC | 21 | — | 2 | 43(18) | Tls. 492,500 |
| | Total | | 24 | 130 | 35 | 88(23) | Tls. 877,426 $ 8,902 |

The above table is concerned only with incidents as such, and not with
the numerous missionary cases of the 1860's which did not involve property
damage or personal injury. The statistics are derived from a multitude of

sources and probably contain some minor inaccuracies. A dash has been inserted where reasonably reliable information is lacking. The parenthetical figures in the "Punished" column indicate the number of Chinese sentenced to capital punishment. "C" and "P" of course refer to "Catholic" and "Protestant." The figures given in the "Reparations" column represent monetary transfers only, not the total value of reparations in any particular case (which would have to include the buildings, sites, and other properties frequently transferred to the foreigner to compensate for injuries sustained). Characters for place names may be found in Glossary I; G. M. H. Playfair, *The Cities and Towns of China: A Geographical Dictionary*, 2nd ed. (Shanghai, 1910); H. C. Tien, Ronald Hsia, and Peter Penn, *Gazetteer of China* (Hong Kong, 1961). In romanizing place names, whenever possible I have followed the recognized forms given in the latter work. For the few instances in which a place name is not given in *Gazetteer of China*, the Wade-Giles spelling is used.

# APPENDIX II

# THE ORIGIN OF THE
## *Pi-hsieh chi-shih*

THE PROBLEM involved in determining the origin of the *Pi-hsieh chi-shih* results largely from the fact that different editions of this work seem to have been put out in different places under different titles. One such edition, an undated version of the shorter *Pi-hsieh shih-lu* — translated by the Shantung missionaries as *Death Blow to Corrupt Doctrines* — claims in the text proper to have been penned by "the most heartbroken man in Jaochow" (Kiangsi). A contemporary English consul, P. J. Hughes, on the other hand, reported that the *Pi-hsieh shih-lu* or a work similar to it was "understood to have been written . . . by Tang-chi-shêng [T'ang Chi-sheng]," the "Commissioner of Finance" of Hupeh in the early 1860's.[1] Again, the Chinese authorities in the Wu-ch'eng, Kiangsi, missionary case of 1870 claimed that the work was composed jointly by persons from Canton and Sihsien, Anhwei.[2] (This last piece of evidence must be viewed with some caution, however, since the edition of the *Pi-hsieh shih-lu* which was involved in the Wu-ch'eng case was the one claiming to have been written by a Kiangsi man. If this was acknowledged, it would of course have reflected adversely on the authorities of the province.) Finally, to complicate matters still further, a similarly entitled work, *P'i-hsieh shih-lu*,

[1] Dispatch of Sept. 29, 1870, *PP*, China, No. 1 (1871), p. 161. (The Chinese characters for T'ang's name are furnished in the original copy of Hughes' dispatch in the Foreign Office Archives, Ser. 17, Vol. 610.) This is perhaps the basis for Couling's statement (regarding the text translated by the Shantung missionaries, i.e., the *Pi-hsieh shih-lu*) that "the author was said to be T'ang Tzû-shêng, Fantai of Hupei, who distributed it gratis to officials in 1862" (*Encyclopaedia Sinica*, I, 140).

[2] Communication of taotai Ching-fu, enclosed in British communication of TC 9/9/24 (Oct. 18, 1870), in TYCT (Shantung-Britain), pp. 4696b–4700b. See also *PP*, China, No. 1 (1871), p. 162.

is reported to have been composed by the gentry of Hunan in the fall of 1862.[3]

All of these references, with the exception of the last, are concerned with the derivative *Pi-hsieh shih-lu.* Evidence relating to the origin of the parent work, the *Pi-hsieh chi-shih,* in every instance suggests that the author was a Hunanese, possibly of high standing. Griffith John reported in the early 1890's that the "Death Blow to Corrupt Doctrines" (the original Chinese text of either the *Pi-hsieh shih-lu* or the *Pi-hsieh chi-shih* — John does not specify which) was widely ascribed to P'eng Yü-lin,[4] a native of Hengyang, Hunan, and (on the basis of considerable independent evidence) one of the most zealously antiforeign Chinese of his generation.[5] On the other hand, the

[3] Dispatch from Hunan governor Mao Hung-pin, TC 2/5/24 (July 9, 1863), in TYCT (Hunan-France), p. 2484a–b. I have not seen the *P'i-hsieh shih-lu;* nor have I seen any other references to the work.

[4] Letter of Dec. 29, 1891, in *Anti-Foreign Riots,* p. 214. John had earlier reported that the author was one Ts'ui Wu-tzu, on the basis of a claim made by Chou Han, the leading instigator of the antiforeign riots of 1890–1891 (letter of Dec. 8, 1891, *ibid.,* p. 211). The attribution of the authorship of the work to P'eng Yü-lin is seemingly confirmed by the anonymous author-translator of *Cause of the Riots,* who remarks (p. 21) that P'eng was "the reputed author of the notorious Death blow to Corrupt Doctrines." This, however, cannot be taken as independent corroboration of John's speculations, which were well enough publicized at the time to be familiar to all interested foreigners. Indeed, it is quite possible, given John's preoccupation with antiforeign literature and the fact that Hankow was his base of operations, that he himself was the author of *Cause of the Riots,* which was published in Hankow.

[5] The scholar-official, Hsia Hsieh, states that in 1855 P'eng led his troops in the destruction of a Catholic church in Kiangsi and then had it converted into a temple for the gods of rain and water. See Hsia Hsieh, 21:1b–2. In referring to the same incident, the French representative in 1861 added that P'eng had the watchman of the church summarily executed when the old man refused to obey P'eng's command to renounce the religion. See French note to the Tsungli Yamen, HF 11/10/8 (Nov. 10, 1861), in TYCT (Kiangsi-France), pp. 2026–2027. In 1884 P'eng submitted a memorial in which, after reviewing the evils commonly associated with Christianity, he suggested three measures for quietly getting rid of the religion: separate registration of converts, the placing of distinguishing signs on the doors of convert homes, and the enforcement of a distinctive style of dress for all Christians. See memorial of June 14, 1884, in P'eng Yü-lin, 5:18b–19b. Further indication of P'eng's extreme xenophobia was displayed, finally, in December 1883, when a proclamation reportedly authorized by him led to the destruction of a large number of Christian chapels in the Canton

Chinese Catholic scholar, Fang Hao, basing himself on the highest authority, claims that the *Pi-hsieh chi-shih* was brought together and printed by the military headquarters of another famous Hunanese, Tseng Kuo-fan, with the special object of encouraging opposition against the Christianity-tainted Taipings.[6] These two assertions seem to be in contradiction with one another, but this is not necessarily the case. P'eng and Tseng were both outstanding leaders of the Hunan Braves — the regional force which performed such an important role in putting down the rebels — and if, as suggested by Fang, the *Pi-hsieh chi-shih* was indeed conceived as part of an ideological program for combating the rebels, both men could have been indirectly associated with it. (In this connection it is worth noting that the pages of the *Pi-hsieh chi-shih* are liberally sprinkled with references linking the rebels with the foreign religion.[7])

Finally, and perhaps most significant of all, there is textual evidence within the *Pi-hsieh chi-shih* itself which, though not pointing to any particular person, strongly implies an author of Hunanese extraction. In the "An-cheng" section the author usually does not hesitate to furnish the names of people and places. However, at one point, when recounting an incident which took place in Changsha, Hunan, he says that because he himself has personal knowledge of the matter in question he will avoid the disgrace to the family name which would result from a disclosure of identities.[8] At another point in this same section the author describes the experiences of two Changsha men in Lichow (Hunan) and then remarks: "they returned home [to Changsha] and told me this in great detail." [9] Another

---

area. A recent study supports the view that this proclamation was in fact attributable to P'eng either directly or indirectly. See Lloyd Eastman, "The Kwangtung Anti-Foreign Disturbances during the Sino-French War," pp. 11–12, 17–18. See also the references to this incident made by contemporary foreigners: Timothy Richard, in *Records of the General Conference*, p. 410; the anonymous author of *Cause of the Riots*, p. 21.

[6] Fang Hao, p. 50. In a letter to the author, Oct. 8, 1962, Father Fang wrote that these assertions were made to him some years ago by Ch'en Yüan, perhaps the foremost Chinese authority on the history of Christianity in China.

[7] See *PHCS, chüan-shang*, p. 3; *chüan-chung*, p. 20b; *et passim*.

[8] *Ibid., chüan-hsia*, p. 19.

[9] *Ibid.*, p. 17b.

incident which took place in Changsha was related to the author by "very many people." [10]

The "An-cheng" section consists of over fifty items in all. Approximately half of these are derived from written sources and half from eyewitness accounts. Of the latter type, eleven out of nineteen items in which place names are given either occurred in Hunan (largely in the Changsha area) or were told to the author by a person from Hunan, while the remaining eight items are for the most part associated with the neighboring provinces of Hupeh and Kiangsi. It is interesting to compare this with the corresponding section of the *Pi-hsieh shih-lu*. The portion based on written sources is very similar in the two works. (Of the "cases" in the *Pi-hsieh chi-shih* for which a written source with title is given, sixteen out of twenty-two are reproduced in the *Pi-hsieh shih-lu* with only minor alterations in content and sequence.) But the *Pi-hsieh shih-lu* contains only five stories based on oral reports, of which one alone is identified with a specific place (Siangtan, Hunan).

A final piece of internal evidence suggesting that the *Pi-hsieh chi-shih* was composed by a Hunanese, possibly from the Changsha area, is provided in the section on militia defense. In the first place, this section is obviously the work of a man with considerable knowledge of the mechanics of organizing a local militia. By 1861, the year in which the *Pi-hsieh chi-shih* was first produced, Hunan was well ahead of the other provinces in the mastery of this art. Secondly, the emphasis on naval militia and river customs strongly suggests that the author had in mind a geographical situation dominated by water transportation. This again would be highly applicable to much of Hunan, including Changsha, which is situated on the largest riverway in the province, the Siang. Taken alone, such evidence is highly circumstantial and is quite relevant to other Chinese provinces as well. But when viewed in the context of all the other factors noted above, it may have significance.

From all this evidence, some conclusions can be tentatively drawn regarding the origin of the *Pi-hsieh chi-shih* and its derivatives. First, as has been suggested several times, it is almost certain that the *Pi-hsieh chi-shih* was an original compilation and that the *Pi-hsieh shih-lu* was derived from it. The former,

[10] *Ibid.*, p. 11b.

with the exception of one section (dated 1862), was completed in 1861 in the form in which we now have it. Moreover, it contains two prefaces in which the author describes the contents of the work, his motivations for compiling it, the time it took him to write it (five successive afternoons and evenings), and so on. The *Pi-hsieh shih-lu*, on the other hand, is much shorter than the *Pi-hsieh chi-shih*, contains no prefaces, and, although undated, from internal evidence can be presumed to have been first published toward the middle of the 1860's or later. Its derivative nature is all but proved, finally, by a postface concerning the compilation of none other than the parent *Pi-hsieh chi-shih*.[11]

Second, and more important, although the exact identity of the author of the *Pi-hsieh chi-shih* can only be guessed at, there is considerable evidence pointing to the conclusion that he was a native of Hunan province (very likely from the Changsha area) and that, in one way or another, he was intimately involved in militia activities. The various editions of the derivative *Pi-hsieh shih-lu*, on the contrary, may well have been edited and compiled by non-Hunanese scholars, and printed and reprinted in areas outside of Hunan. This would account for the various reports that it was a product of Hupeh, Kiangsi, Anhwei, and Kwangtung. It would also account for the omission in the "An-cheng" section of the *Pi-hsieh shih-lu* of almost all the items in the corresponding section of the parent work specifically relating to Hunan — items which would naturally be most effective in stirring up the emotions of Hunanese.

---

[11] This postface, although providing no substantive information concerning the origin of the *PHCS*, praises its author warmly. At one point, moreover, the author of the postface establishes the fact that at the time of writing the Taiping rebels had just been put down while the Nien had yet to be overcome, thus suggesting that the *Pi-hsieh shih-lu* was printed sometime between 1864 and 1868. This tallies with the fact that the work, as far as I am aware, is not mentioned in Chinese or foreign sources until 1869–1870 (see *Pi-hsieh shih-lu*, pp. 25–26).

# NOTES

## ABBREVIATIONS USED IN NOTES

AEC   Archives des Affaires Étrangères, Chine, Vols. 38–47 (Ministère des Affaires Étrangères), filed in the search room at the Quai d'Orsay, Paris.

CAPM   *Chiao-an shih-liao pien-mu* (A bibliography of Chinese source materials dealing with local or international cases involving Christian missions), comps. Wu Sheng-te and Ch'en Tseng-hui (Peiping, 1941).

HJAS   *Harvard Journal of Asiatic Studies.*

IWSM   *Ch'ou-pan i-wu shih-mo* (The complete account of our management of barbarian affairs; Peiping, 1930). Tao-kuang period, 80 *chüan;* Hsien-feng period, 80 *chüan;* T'ung-chih period, 100 *chüan.*

MC   *Les Missions catholiques: Bulletin hebdomadaire illustré de l'Œuvre de la Propagation de la Foi* (Lyon, 1868 et seq.).

PHCS   *Pi-hsieh chi-shih* (A record of facts to ward off heterodoxy; 1871 ed.).

PP   *Parliamentary Papers* (Blue Books).

TYCT   Tsung-li ko-kuo shih-wu ya-men ch'ing-tang (The archives of the Tsungli Yamen: clean files), deposited at the Institute of Modern History, Academia Sinica, Taipei, Taiwan. The portion of TYCT dealing with missionary difficulties from 1860 to 1870 is being prepared for publication, but lack of funds may postpone it indefinitely. In citing this source I have tried to use a system that will facilitate reference either to the original archives or to the same materials in published form. Both lunar and Western dates are given, along with the Chinese province and foreign power immediately concerned. Page numbers refer only to the original archives.

HF   Hsien-feng reign, 1851–1861.

KH   Kuang-hsü reign, 1875–1908.

TC   T'ung-chih reign, 1862–1874.

TK   Tao-kuang reign, 1821–1850.

# NOTES

THE TWO excerpts facing p. 3 of text are taken from the following sources: Letter to the directors of the London Missionary Society, 1869, quoted in R. Wardlaw Thompson, *Griffith John: The Story of Fifty Years in China* (London, 1908), p. 254; *Yung-cheng shang-yü* (Edicts of the Yung-cheng Emperor; 1741), *ts'e* 9:15a-b (under Yung-cheng 5th year, 4th month).

CHAPTER 1. THE ANTI-CHRISTIAN TRADITION IN CHINESE THOUGHT

1. See *CAPM*, pp. 12–38, 199–203. I have relied extensively on this extremely useful bibliography, which catalogues materials on well over 300 cases.

2. *Annales de la propagation de la foi, recueil périodique* (Lyon, 1842 et seq.), 39:383 (1867). Father Leboucq, S.J., wrote, in a letter of Jan. 18, 1870, that in Hokien fu, Chihli, Christian subjects placed about 50 lawsuits connected with religious matters in the hands of the missionaries *each year* (*Annales*, 42:343 [1870]). Again, Jesuit missionaries wrote, in 1869, that in the area of Kiangyin hsien, Kiangsu, a month did not pass in which some persecution did not take place (*La Compagnie de Jésus en Chine: Le Kiang-nan en 1869, relation historique et descriptive par les missionnaires* [Paris, preface dated 1869], p. 160). In Kweichow missionaries and converts were attacked almost incessantly throughout the decade of the sixties (see Adrien Launay, *Histoire des missions de Chine: Mission du Kouy-tcheou* [Paris, 1907–1908], II, 74–191, 325–402, 541–589).

3. J. J. M. de Groot, *Sectarianism and Religious Persecution in China: A Page in the History of Religions*, 2 vols. (Amsterdam, 1903–1904), is the pioneering Western work in the field and is an invaluable storehouse of materials. Nevertheless, it is openly biased in its approach, only partly devoted to the study of anti-Christian thought and action, and based almost exclusively on imperial edicts. For Chinese surveys of late Ming-early Ch'ing anti-Christian thought, see n. 28 below.

4. In the *Lun-yü*, bk. 2, Chap. 16, Confucius says: "The study of strange doctrines [*i-tuan*] is injurious indeed!" (James Legge, *The Chinese Classics*, rev. 2nd ed., Oxford, 1893–1895, I, 150). Waley's

rendering attempts to retain more of the original figure: "He who sets to work upon a different strand destroys the whole fabric." The "different strand" (*i-tuan*) is the opportunistic Way of the world as opposed to the moral Way (Arthur Waley, *The Analects of Confucius,* 3rd ed., London, 1949, p. 91).

Most Chinese dictionaries give, as the locus classicus for *hsieh,* the *Ta Yü mo* section of the *Book of History.* This section, however, is generally regarded as being a later addition. *Hsieh* appears in the *Book of Songs* (*Lu-sung* section) and in *Lun-yü* (*wei-cheng* section) with the probable connotation of "evil" or "depravity." But Mencius, to the best of my knowledge, was the first person to use the term unequivocally as an opprobrious label for unorthodox schools of thought. See Legge, *The Works of Mencius* (*The Chinese Classics,* Vol. II, 1895), bk. 3, Pt. 2, Chap. 9, pp. 282–284.

*Tso-tao,* which seems to be somewhat less common than either *i-tuan* or *hsieh,* appears to have been first used in the *wang-chih* section of the *Book of Rites.*

5. Hsün Chi's anti-Buddhist thought, along with that of Ku Huan and Fan Chen, is treated in Kenneth Ch'en, "Anti-Buddhist Propaganda during the Nan-ch'ao," *HJAS,* 15:166–192 (1952). For early applications of the "heterodoxy" terminology to Buddhism, see E. Zürcher, *The Buddhist Conquest of China: The Spread and Adaptation of Buddhism in Early Medieval China,* 2 vols. (Leiden, 1959), I, 27, 52, 183, 265. For a survey and analysis of early Chinese anti-Buddhist thought and a discussion of the *hua-hu* theory (which had a later parallel in the common Chinese view that Christianity was an offshoot of Buddhism), see *ibid.,* Vol. I, Chaps. 5 and 6.

6. Kenneth Ch'en, "Anti-Buddhist Propaganda," pp. 185, 187, 191–192 (quote from p. 191).

7. Arthur F. Wright, "Fu I and the Rejection of Buddhism," *Journal of the History of Ideas,* 12:33–47 (1951). For a listing of Western translations of Fu I's writings, see Hans H. Frankel, comp., *Catalogue of Translations from the Chinese Dynastic Histories for the Period 220–960* (Berkeley, 1957), pp. 183–184.

8. Arthur F. Wright, *Buddhism in Chinese History* (Stanford, 1959), pp. 86–96.

9. This discussion of Han Yü's memorial is based primarily on James R. Hightower's translation in Edwin O. Reischauer, *Ennin's Travels in T'ang China* (New York, 1955), pp. 221–224. Other translations of Han Yü's writings are listed in Frankel, pp. 191–193, 223–224.

10. Arthur F. Wright, *Buddhism in Chinese History,* p. 97.

11. For the Chinese texts of these laws, along with English translations, see de Groot, I, 137–140.

12. *Ibid.*, I, 140. I have revised de Groot's translation somewhat.

13. For a brief discussion of the different editions of the *Sacred Edict*, see Arthur W. Hummel, ed., *Eminent Chinese of the Ch'ing Period*, 2 vols. (Washington, D.C., 1943, 1944), I, 329.

14. Chang Chung-li, *The Chinese Gentry: Studies on Their Role in Nineteenth-Century Chinese Society* (Seattle, 1955), pp. 65, 199–200.

15. I have used the popular edition of the *Sacred Edict* put together by Wang Yu-p'u, entitled *Sheng-yü kuang-hsün chih-chieh* (A colloquial explanation of the *Sacred Edict*), 2 *chüan* (n.d., original preface 1724), *shang-chüan*, pp. 50–52. The text of the seventh sermon, with translation, is also in de Groot, I, 244–248.

16. I have here modified Waley's translation somewhat; see Waley, pp. 130–131.

17. This edict was delivered on the dual occasion of the Buddha's birthday and the presentation of gifts to the throne by a Portuguese envoy who sought greater leniency for missionaries. It is in *Yung-cheng shang-yü*, *ts'e* 9:13–15b (under Yung-cheng 5th year, 4th month). For an English translation of the entire edict by T. Watters, see *The Chinese Recorder and Missionary Journal*, 4:225–227 (1872).

18. Huang Yü-pien, *P'o-hsieh hsiang-pien* (A detailed refutation of heterodoxy), 1:28a-b. This work, consisting of a *chüan-shou* and 4 *chüan* in 2 *ts'e*, has prefaces dated 1834 and 1839; it was reprinted in 1883 by the Tartar general at Kingchow, Hupeh.

19. Mary C. Wright, *The Last Stand of Chinese Conservatism: The T'ung-chih Restoration, 1862–1874* (Stanford, 1957), p. 132.

20. Some of these beliefs were subjected to critical examination by the eminent early-Ch'ing scholar, Huang Tsung-hsi, in his *P'o-hsieh lun* (A discourse on the refutation of heterodoxy), in *Chao-tai ts'ung-shu* (Collection of Ch'ing dynasty works; Shen-yung-t'ang ed., 1919), *ts'e* 66, *chüan* 15. Huang deals with such subjects as accessory sacrifices (*ts'ung-ssu*), the supreme ruler, or lord (*shang-ti*), the soul (*hun-p'o*), and hell (*ti-yü*). For a critical reference to Christianity, see *ibid.*, 15:4. For an examination of Huang's anti-Christian thought, see Ch'en Shou-i, "Ming-mo Ch'ing-ch'u Yeh-su-hui-shih ti ju-chiao-kuan chi ch'i fan-ying" (The Jesuits' conception of Confucianism in the late Ming and early Ch'ing and its repercussions), *Kuo-hsüeh chi-k'an* (The journal of Sinological studies), 5.2:58–59 (1935).

21. *P'o-hsieh hsiang-pien*, 3:6b–7. See also Huang's critical references to such practices as popular gatherings, monetary collections, and the indiscriminate mixing of the sexes, *ibid.*, 1:28, 3:7, *et passim*.

22. When in the 1860's a censor proposed that, of the temples destroyed during the recent rebellions, only those devoted to the gods of the soil be rebuilt, the *North-China Herald* commented: "It is worthy of note that the reasons urged for this step are entirely of a

political character, viz., the prevention of large gatherings of the people" (quoted from M. Wright, *The Last Stand,* p. 133).

23. See Vergilius Ferm, ed., *An Encyclopedia of Religion* (New York, 1945), pp. 334, 552.

24. Hsü Chi-yü, *Ying-huan chih-lüeh* (A brief description of the oceans' circuit; 1850 ed.), 6:29b; see also *ibid.,* 6:39b.

25. The early history of Christianity in China is summarized in Latourette, pp. 46-77.

26. For a survey of the persecutions directed against the Catholics prior to 1800 and a detailed examination of the general persecution of 1784-1785, see Bernward H. Willeke, *Imperial Government and Catholic Missions in China During the Years 1784-1785* (St. Bonaventure, New York, 1948).

27. This work is sometimes referred to by the title, *Sheng-ch'ao p'o-hsieh chi.* I have used here a Japanese reprint of the *P'o-hsieh chi* dated 1855 and consisting of 8 *chüan* in 8 *ts'e.*

28. Chinese scholars who have investigated the late Ming–early Ch'ing opposition to Western religion and culture have relied heavily on the *P'o-hsieh chi.* See, e.g., Chang Wei-hua, "Ming-Ch'ing chien Chung-Hsi ssu-hsiang chih ch'ung-t'u yü ying-hsiang" (The ideological conflict between China and the West during the late Ming and early Ch'ing, and its effect), *Hsüeh-ssu* (Study and thought), 1.1:19-24 (Jan. 1942); a second article by the same author, "Ming-Ch'ing chien Fo-Yeh chih cheng-pien" (The dispute between Buddhists and Christians during the late Ming and early Ch'ing), *ibid.,* 1.2:12-17 (Jan. 1942); Ch'en Shou-i, "Ming-mo Ch'ing-ch'u Yeh-su-hui-shih ti ju-chiao-kuan chi ch'i fan-ying," pp. 49-64; and Ch'üan Han-sheng, "Ming-mo Ch'ing-ch'u fan-tui hsi-yang wen-hua ti yen-lun" (Criticisms of Western culture voiced during the late Ming and early Ch'ing), in Li Ting-i et al., eds., *Chung-kuo chin-tai-shih lun-ts'ung* (Collection of essays on modern Chinese history), 1st Ser., 10 vols. (Taipei, 1956), II, 227-235.

Chang Wei-hua, in his two articles, draws on a second collection of anti-Christian writings that I have been unable to examine, entitled *P'i-hsieh chi* (An anthology of writings exposing heterodoxy). See *Hsüeh-ssu,* 1.1:22, 1.2:15-16.

29. Shih Ju-ch'un, "T'ien-hsüeh ch'u-p'i" (A preliminary refutation of the doctrines of Catholicism), *P'o-hsieh chi,* 8:26a-b.

30. Lin Ch'i-lu, "Chu-i lun-lüeh" (A short discourse on the suppression of the barbarians), *ibid.,* 6:3.

31. *Ibid.,* p. 3a-b.

32. The fact that the anti-Christian writings of Buddhists form an important part of the *P'o-hsieh chi* merely serves to underscore this point. See, e.g., the essay by Shih T'ung-jung, entitled "Yüan-

tao p'i-hsieh shuo" (Using the original way to refute heterodoxy), *ibid.*, 8:3–20. A more striking example of the relativity of the Chinese notion of heterodoxy could hardly be found. "Yüan-tao" was originally the title of a famous essay by Han Yü, in which the T'ang polemicist sought to revive the "original (or true) way" of Confucius and Mencius in order to attack the then widely prevalent heterodoxies of Buddhism and Taoism. In Shih's essay, however, the "original way" is taken to include Buddhism and Taoism as well as Confucianism, and is used to rebut the new heterodoxy of Catholicism (see, e.g., Shih's defense of "*our* Buddha" against the "slanders" of Matteo Ricci, 8:11b; italics mine).

33. Huang Wen-tao, "P'i-hsieh chieh" (A commentary on the refutation of heterodoxy), *ibid.*, 5:19b, 20b.

34. "Na-huo hsieh-tang hou kao-shih" (The proclamation issued after the arrest of the heterodox parties), *ibid.*, 2:23a-b.

35. See Yang's biography in Hummel, II, 889–892.

36. Substantial selections from the *Pu-te-i* were included in the following works, among others: Wei Yüan, *Hai-kuo t'u-chih* (An illustrated gazetteer of the maritime countries), 1st ed. (1844), 15:25–32; the expanded 3rd ed. of the same work (1852), 27:8–15; Hsia Hsieh (pseud. Chiang-shang chien-sou), "Hua-Hsia chih chien" (The gradual deterioration of China), in his *Chung-Hsi chi-shih* (A record of Sino-Western affairs; 1st preface 1851, 2nd preface to rev. ed. 1859, last preface 1865, title page dated 1868), 2:6–9b; *PHCS, chüan-shang*, pp. 9–15; *Pi-hsieh shih-lu* (A true record to ward off heterodoxy; n.d., comp. anon.), pp. 13b–18b. The selections from Yang Kuang-hsien in the *Hai-kuo t'u-chih, PHCS*, and *Pi-hsieh shih-lu* are more or less identical. Moreover, they present most of the important elements in Yang's attack. For these reasons, and because all three works had a wide circulation during the nineteenth century, I have based my discussion of Yang's ideas on the selections in *PHCS*, giving cross references to the original *Pu-te-i* (1929 photolithographic ed.).

37. Hummel, II, 890. See also *PHCS, chüan-shang*, p. 9a-b; Yang Kuang-hsien, *shang-chüan*, pp. 8b–9b. A theory similar to Li Tsu-po's was adhered to by some of his Jesuit contemporaries known as the Figurists. See Arnold H. Rowbotham, *Missionary and Mandarin: The Jesuits at the Court of China* (Berkeley, 1942), pp. 122–123.

38. *PHCS, chüan-shang*, pp. 10–14, esp. pp. 10a-b, 11a-b, 14. See also Yang Kuang-hsien, *shang-chüan*, pp. 11b–22b, esp. pp. 11b–12b, 16a-b, 22a-b.

39. See Chang's biography in Hummel, I, 65–66.

40. Chang Yü-shu, *Wai-kuo chi*, in *Chao-tai ts'ung-shu*, *ts'e* 104:9b–10.

41. See Hummel, I, 453.

42. *Ming-shih,* Chung-hua shu-chü ed. (Shanghai, 1933), 326:10b–11.

43. See Hummel, I, 453; II, 895.

44. Tung Han, *Ch'un-hsiang chui-pi* (Scribblings by Tung Han), in Wu Chen-fang, ed., *Shuo-ling* (Collection of miscellaneous writings of early Ch'ing authors; 1702–1705), *chüan* 20 *(hou-chi),* pp. 14–15b.

45. See Chang's biography in Hummel, I, 51–52.

46. See Antonio Sisto Rosso, *Apostolic Legations to China of the Eighteenth Century* (South Pasadena, 1948); Rowbotham, Chaps. 9–12.

47. Chang Po-hsing, *Cheng-i-t'ang chi* (A collection of writings from the Cheng-i-t'ang; 1876), *chüan* 1 *(hsia),* pp. 40b–41b. For other memorials similar in content to Chang's see Hsia Hsieh, *chüan* 2, *passim;* Chang Ju-lin and Yin Kuang-jen, *Ao-men chi-lüeh* (A brief record of Macao; Kiangsu, 1880), *shang-chüan,* pp. 33b–36.

48. For Chang Po-hsing's memorial, see *Ao-men chi-lüeh, hsia-chüan,* pp. 52–53.

49. See, e.g., Ch'en Lun-chiung, *Hai-kuo wen-chien lu* (A record of things seen and heard among the maritime nations; preface 1730), in *Chao-tai ts'ung-shu, ts'e* 55. *Chüan* 1 of this work contains "geographical" lore about various countries, including Holland, Spain, and France; *chüan* 2 contains maps of these countries. For an example of early Chinese lore about Christianity, based on the practices of Spanish Catholics in the Philippines, see *ibid.,* 1:15. Still earlier Chinese works on the West are listed and briefly summarized in John K. Fairbank and Teng Ssu-yü, *Ch'ing Administration: Three Studies* (Cambridge, Mass., 1960), pp. 180–185.

50. See, e.g., *Ao-men chi-lüeh, hsia-chüan,* pp. 24–29b. This was frequently done in later works also, a good illustration being the *Hai-lu* (A maritime record; preface 1820). The *Hai-lu* was written by a Cantonese literatus, Yang Ping-nan, on the basis of the oral account given him by a blind interpreter, Hsieh Ch'ing-kao, who had traveled abroad from 1782 to 1795. It has been reprinted numerous times and contains, in the section on Portugal, a brief account of the sacraments, among them marriage and confession, as well as burial practices. Throughout this account Buddhist terminology is used for such words as "priest" *(ta ho-shang* or *seng),* "church" *(miao),* and "preaching" *(shuo-fa).* See the annotated edition by Feng Ch'eng-chün, *Hai-lu chu* (Peking, 1955), pp. 64–66. See also Kenneth Ch'en, *"Hai-lu:* Forerunner of Chinese Travel Accounts of Western Countries," *Monumenta Serica,* 7:208–226 (1942).

51. *Ao-men chi-lüeh, hsia-chüan,* p. 51a-b.

52. See Wang's essay, "Ko-kuo chiao-men shuo" (A discussion of the religious sects of various countries), in his *T'ao-yüan wen-lu wai-pien* (Supplement to *T'ao-yüan wen-lu;* Hong Kong, 1883), 7:22b–24;

also in *Huang-ch'ao ching-shih-wen hsü-pien* (Supplement to the *Huang-ch'ao ching-shih-wen*), comp. Ko Shih-chün (Shanghai, 1888), 112:12b–13. See also the view of Wei Yüan (below, this chapter) and of the compiler of *Chiao-wu chi-lüeh* (A summary record of church affairs; pub. by order of Governor-General Chou Fu, Anhwei, 1905), *li-yen* (introduction). The latter work has been partially translated by Jérôme Tobar in *Kiao-ou ki-lio; "Résumé des affaires religieuses" publié par ordre de S. Exc. Tcheou Fou: Traduction, commentaire & documents diplomatiques, appendices contenant les plus récentes décisions* (Variétés sinologiques, No. 47; Shanghai, 1917).

53. It is possible, incidentally, that Chang and Yin were familiar with the *P'o-hsieh chi*, since they reproduce (*shang-chüan*, pp. 36b–37b) one of the items in that work — the *"P'o-hsieh chi hsü"* (A preface to the *P'o-hsieh chi*), by Chiang Te-ching (see *P'o-hsieh chi*, 3:1–3). In general, however, the *P'o-hsieh chi* seems to have exerted little influence on Chinese anti-Christian thought and was not rediscovered by Chinese scholars until comparatively recent times.

54. The origin of the charge that foreign priests gouged out the eyes of dying converts for alchemical purposes remains obscure. The charge was alluded to earlier (1724) by a certain Wu Te-chih of Hupeh (see Hsia Hsieh, 2:19a-b; and Li Ting-i, *Chung-kuo chin-tai shih* [Modern Chinese history], 7th ed., Taipei, 1959, p. 206). The Japanese scholar, Yazawa Toshihiko, traces it back to the late Ming, when the Portuguese were accused by many Chinese of kidnaping Chinese children and roasting and eating their flesh (see Yazawa Toshihiko, "Chōkō ryūiki kyōan no kenkyū" [The antiforeign riots of 1891], *Kindai Chūkoku kenkyū* [Studies on modern China], No. 4:113–114 [Tokyo, 1960]).

55. Chang Chen-t'ao, *Ao-men t'u-shuo* (An illustrated discussion of Macao), in *Hsiao-fang-hu-chai yü-ti ts'ung-ch'ao* (Collection of geographical works from the Hsiao-fang-hu studio), comp. Wang Hsi-ch'i (1877–1897), *ts'e* 48:315b; Chang Chen-t'ao, *Ao-men hsing-shih lun* (A discussion of conditions in Macao), *ibid.*, p. 320; Chang Chen-t'ao, *Chih-yü Ao-i lun* (On controlling the barbarians of Macao), *ibid.*, p. 331.

56. *Ssu-k'u ch'üan-shu tsung-mu* (An annotated bibliography of books in the *Ssu-k'u ch'üan-shu*; I-wen yin-shu-kuan photolithographic ed., Taipei, n.d.), pp. 2502, 2503 (original ed., 125:28a-b, 29b).

57. Willeke, pp. 47, 89, 146–147, 166.

58. See John K. Fairbank, *Trade and Diplomacy on the China Coast: The Opening of the Treaty Ports, 1842–1854,* 2 vols. (Cambridge, Mass., 1953), I, 48–51.

59. Willeke, p. 165, states that the laws against Christianity were

enforced even more strictly during the Chia-ch'ing period (1796–1820). See also de Groot, II, 387–405, 470–486.

60. See Wei's biography in Hummel, II, 850–852.

61. See Dorothy Ann Rockwell, "The Compilation of Governor Hsü's *Ying-huan chih-lüeh*," *Papers on China*, 11:1–28 (Harvard University, East Asian Research Center, 1957); Teng Ssu-yü and John K. Fairbank, *China's Response to the West: A Documentary Survey, 1839–1923* (Cambridge, Mass., 1954), pp. 29–35; and Fairbank, *Trade and Diplomacy*, pp. 178–183.

62. *Hai-kuo t'u-chih*, 1st ed., 15:1–17b (quote from p. 4b); 3rd ed., 26:1–8b (quote from p. 4b), 13b–22b. The 3rd ed., just prior to the discussion of the Nestorian Tablet, inserts several items taken from Hsü Chi-yü's *Ying-huan chih-lüeh* and other works which are not found in the 1st ed.

63. See Hsü's biography in Hummel, I, 316–319.

64. *Hai-kuo t'u-chih*, 1st ed., 15:17b–18; 3rd ed., 27:1a-b. Wei's account of both of these anecdotes departs somewhat from the original, in which, for example, Hsü Kuang-ch'i is not specifically mentioned; see Wen Ping, *Lieh-huang hsiao-shih* (A sketch of the last Ming emperor), in *Ming-chi pai-shih* (An unofficial history of the late Ming; Shanghai: Commercial Press, 1912), *chüan* 6 (*ch'u-pien*), p. 3a-b.

65. The Chinese (and Japanese) practice of compelling people to tread on the cross in order to determine the extent of their commitment to Christianity was still widely followed in the 1860's, as later chapters will indicate. The history of this apostasy test is examined in detail in Fang Hao, "Ch'ing-tai chin-i T'ien-chu-chiao so shou Jih-pen chih ying-hsiang" (Japanese influence on the proscription of Catholicism during the Ch'ing dynasty), in *Fang Hao wen-lu* (Essays of Fang Hao; Shanghai, 1948), pp. 47–65.

66. See Yü's biography in Hummel, II, 936–937.

67. *Hai-kuo t'u-chih*, 1st ed., 15:21a-b, 22b–24b; 3rd ed., 27:4a-b, 6–8. See also *Ao-men chi-lüeh, hsia-chüan*, p. 53a-b; Yü Cheng-hsieh, *Kuei-ssu lei-kao* (Selected short pieces of Yü Cheng-hsieh; Shanghai, 1957), pp. 582–585.

68. *Hai-kuo t'u-chih*, 1st ed., 15:44–45; 3rd ed., 27:29–30.

69. *Ibid.*, 3rd ed., 27:31a-b.

70. See Hsü's biography in Hummel, I, 309–310.

71. Hsü Chi-yü, 3:37b, 40b–41; 6:29b, 39a-b; 7:36b–37.

72. *Ibid.*, 6:29b, 39b. See also the section on Spain where Hsü takes note of the great power of the religious hierarchy, which silenced all heretics by burning them at the stake (7:20).

73. *Ibid.*, 4:12b; 5:3b–4, 7b; 6:29b, 39b; 7:38b, 43. See also, in this connection, Ch'en Ch'i-yüan, *Yung-hsien-chai pi-chi* (Miscellaneous notes from the Yung-hsien studio; Shanghai, 1925), 5:6b–7.

74. See Liang's biography in Hummel, I, 503–505.

75. This argument against Christianity was not a new one. See Huang Chen, "Ch'ing Yen Chuang-ch'i hsien-sheng p'i T'ien-chu-chiao shu" (A letter to Mr. Yen Chuang-ch'i refuting Catholicism), in *P'o-hsieh chi*, 3:9a-b.

76. The original of Liang's book is unfortunately not accessible. But a summary of it, containing an excerpt of some length, is available in Hsien Yü-ch'ing, "Liang T'ing-nan chu-shu lu-yao" (On the writings of Liang T'ing-nan), *Ling-nan hsüeh-pao* (Lingnan journal), 4.1:142–143 (Canton, 1935).

77. The extent and character of Christianity's influence on the Taipings are examined in detail in Eugene Boardman, *Christian Influence upon the Ideology of the Taiping Rebellion, 1851–1864* (Madison, 1952).

78. Wang T'ao, himself a sometime rebel sympathizer, stated: "When [Protestant missionaries] came and went among the [rebels], appearing to be coreligionists, the gentry and people in the coastal areas took them to be in collusion with the rebels and became deeply angered. This is the origin of the popular criticism that they [the missionaries] have attracted" ("Ch'uan-chiao" [The propagation of Christianity], in Wang's *T'ao-yüan wen-lu wai-pien*, 3:3b). Typical of the Protestant missionaries who did visit the rebels was Griffith John. See his accounts of these visits in Thompson, pp. 71, 127–149.

79. Latourette, pp. 360, 405.

80. D. MacGillivray, ed., *A Century of Protestant Missions in China* (Shanghai, 1907), chart following p. vii.

81. Latourette, p. 329.

82. The several portions of the *PHCS* were published at different times. I have used here an 1871 reprint in the Harvard-Yenching collection. The first preface is dated 1861, the second preface and one of the sections, 1862. In addition, the work in its various forms went through *at least* 3 other editions. I have examined in the Toyo Bunko collection an 1886 edition which is virtually identical with that of 1871. The edition of the derivative *Pi-hsieh shih-lu* used here is undated. Professor Sasaki Masaya was kind enough to show me a photostatic copy of another edition published shortly after the Tientsin Massacre of June 1870.

83. *Death Blow to Corrupt Doctrines: A Plain Statement of Facts*, tr. Tengchow missionaries (Shanghai, 1870). This work professes on its title page to have been published by the gentry and the people. The translators, whom Samuel Couling identifies as John L. Nevius, Calvin Mateer, and J. B. Hartwell (*Encyclopaedia Sinica*, 2 vols., Shanghai, 1917, I, 140), omitted the title of the original Chinese text. But the library of the Academia Sinica in Taiwan has a copy of the

*Pi-hsieh shih-lu,* and comparison reveals that the *Death Blow* is unquestionably a translation of it. Contemporary notices of the translation appeared in *The Chinese Recorder and Missionary Journal,* 3:254–255 (1871), and in the *North-China Herald,* Nov. 1, 1870, pp. 324–325. The latter review states, in part: "The book has been written by a man of high ability, encouraged by the authorities, widely circulated among the educated, and by them communicated to the ignorant. It is a true firebrand of war."

84. Shantung, Kiangsi, and Honan. *PP,* China, No. 1 (1871), pp. 162, 198–199; Tsungli Yamen letter to Shantung governor Ting Paochen, Kiangsi governor Liu K'un-i, superintendents of trade Tseng Kuo-fan and Li Hung-chang, TC 9/9/29 (Oct. 23, 1870), in TYCT (Shantung-Britain), pp. 4710–4712b; 2 letters from Ting Pao-chen to the Tsungli Yamen, TC 9/intercalary 10/4 (Nov. 26, 1870), *ibid.,* pp. 4715–4719; letter from Liu K'un-i to the Yamen, TC 9/11/12 (Jan. 2, 1871), *ibid.,* pp. 4720–4722; Tsungli Yamen letter to Honan governor Ch'ien Ting-ming, TC 12/6/14 (July 8, 1873), *ibid.* (Honan-France), unpaginated; letter from Ch'ien Ting-ming to the Yamen, TC 12/intercalary 6/3 (July 26, 1873), *ibid.,* unpaginated. See also Timothy Richard's speech, "Relation of Christian missions to the Chinese government," in *Records of the General Conference of the Protestant Missionaries of China, Held at Shanghai, May 7–20, 1890* (Shanghai, 1890), p. 411; and Gilbert Reid's comment, in *ibid.,* p. 584.

85. Letter from Henry Blodget to N. G. Clark, Oct. 24, 1870, quoted in Fairbank, "Patterns behind the Tientsin Massacre," p. 502.

86. Letter to E. B. Drew, Oct. 12, 1870, quoted in H. B. Morse, *The International Relations of the Chinese Empire,* 3 vols. (London, 1910–1918), II, 235n.57.

87. *PP,* China, No. 1 (1871), p. 166 (for "Nevins" read Nevius throughout).

88. See *Death Blow,* preface, pp. v–vi, where the circulation of the work in Shantung is discussed in almost the same terms. See also the correspondence concerning the *Pi-hsieh shih-lu* in TYCT (Shantung-Britain), pp. 4672–4722.

89. *Records of the General Conference,* pp. 410, 584.

90. Petition of the residents of Nanyang hsien, enclosed in letter of Honan governor Li Ho-nien to Tsungli Yamen, TC 7/12/18 (Jan. 30, 1869), in TYCT (Honan-France), p. 4957b.

91. French communication of July 25, 1873, summarized in *Ch'ing-chi ko-kuo chao-hui mu-lu* (A catalogue of the communications sent by the various nations during the late Ch'ing; Peiping, 1935), Fa-kuo, No. 287. See also the French communications of TC 12/6/8 (July 2,

1873) and TC 12/intercalary 6/2 (July 25, 1873), in TYCT (Honan-France), unpaginated.

92. Consul Hughes to Wade, Kiukiang, Sept. 29, 1870, *PP*, China, No. 1 (1871), pp. 160–161. This book is identified as the "Pi-hsieh-shi-lu" on p. 162. See also TYCT (Shantung-Britain), pp. 4672–4722.

93. Griffith John, letter of Jan. 27, 1892, in *The Anti-Foreign Riots in China in 1891* (Shanghai, 1892), p. 220.

94. See Tseng's biography in Hummel, II, 751–756.

95. See Appendix II.

96. Latourette, pp. 364, 375; see also *ibid.*, pp. 389, 495.

97. See, e.g., Liang Ch'i-ch'ao, *Wu-hsü cheng-pien chi* (The *coup d'état* of 1898; Chung-hua shu-chü ed., 1954), Appendix 2, p. 130; Wang Wen-chieh, *Chung-kuo chin-shih-shih shang ti chiao-an* (A study of the religious persecutions in modern Chinese history; Foochow, 1947), pp. 24–25.

98. Of the 72 cases dealt with by Wang Wen-chieh (covering 1856–1898), only 3 actually took place in Hunan. On the other hand, 34 took place in Szechwan and Kweichow where there were many missionary residences, particularly Catholic. This ratio is well substantiated by TYCT, in which materials concerning Hunan are very meager, while those concerning Szechwan and Kweichow abound.

99. See, e.g., the 2 Hunan writings which helped to ignite the Kiangsi incident of 1862 and which were widely circulated elsewhere all through the 1860's (see Chap. 3, n. 31); the placards (demanding the death penalty for all missionaries) which were a partial cause of the Hunan incidents of 1862 (French communication, TC 1/4/6 [May 4, 1862], in TYCT [Hunan-France], p. 2347a-b); the public petition circulated by the people of Hengchow, Hunan, late in 1862 to explain the causes of the Hengchow riots of April of that year (reproduced in *Pi-hsieh shih-lu*, pp. 19–25, and tr. in *Death Blow*, pp. 50–62); the *P'i-hsieh shih-lu* (reportedly written by the gentry of Hunan), which set off an anti-Christian incident in Yungchow, Hunan, early in 1863 (dispatch from Hunan governor Mao Hung-pin to Tsungli Yamen, TC 2/5/24 [July 9, 1863], in TYCT [Hunan-France], p. 2484a-b); the numerous inflammatory pieces reported to have been circulated in Hengchow in 1865 (letters of Bishop Navarro, Hengchow fu, Feb. 2, 1865 and Feb. 16, 1866, in *Annales*, 39:99–104 [1867]); the hostile notice publicly distributed by the gentry and populace of Hunan in the fall of 1876 (enclosed in French dispatch to Tsungli Yamen, KH 2/10/20 [Dec. 5, 1876], in TYCT [Hunan-France], unpaginated); the series of anonymous writings circulated in Yungchow, Hunan, early in the 1880's (noted in Hunan governor Li Ming-ch'ih's letter to the Yamen, KH 7/9/29 [Nov. 20, 1881], *ibid.*, unpaginated); and items quoted in *Anti-Foreign Riots*, e.g., the book by the leading in-

stigator of the Yangtze valley riots of the early 1890's, Chou Han, *Kuei-chiao kai-ssu* (Death to the devils' religion). For a contemporary analysis of the Hunan publications of the early nineties, based on 25 (!) anti-Christian and antiforeign pamphlets and tracts, see *The Hunan Tracts of China, Which Produced the Anti-Christian and Anti-Foreign Riots of 1891, Analysed by a Shocked Friend* (Shanghai, 1892). *The Cause of the Riots in the Yangtse Valley: A "Complete Picture Gallery"* (Hankow, 1891) contains "an exact reproduction" of one of the inflammatory picture books which was widely circulated in Hunan during the early 1890's, entitled *Chin-tsun sheng-yü pi-hsieh ch'üan-t'u* (Heresy exposed in respectful obedience to the Sacred Edict: A complete picture gallery).

100. *PHCS, chüan-shang,* pp. 1b-2; see also p. 3b. Cf. corresponding section of *Pi-hsieh shih-lu,* p. 1a-b.

101. *PHCS, chüan-shang,* p. 2; see also p. 4b, where the swallowing of the menses of virgins is described as a means of acquiring the spirit of youth.

102. *Ibid.,* pp. 3–4b. Cf. corresponding section of *Pi-hsieh shih-lu,* pp. 3b–4.

103. Of the 8 or so sources that I have checked, the excerpts in the *PHCS* are faithful reproductions of the originals.

104. *PHCS, chüan-chung,* pp. 3b–4.

105. This section was written in 1862 and inserted by the author in the *PHCS* 1862 edition.

106. Whether or not this is more than coincidence is impossible to determine without knowing the title and edition of the original Chinese work to which John referred in his letter as the "Death Blow to Corrupt Doctrines." John may have been familiar only with the *Pi-hsieh shih-lu* which does not contain the "P'i-po hsieh-shuo" section. According to Alexander Wylie, the *Yüeh t'ien-lu chih-ming* was published in Hankow in 1862. See Wylie, *Memorials of Protestant Missionaries to the Chinese: Giving a List of Their Publications, and Obituary Notices of the Deceased* (Shanghai, 1867), p. 238.

107. *PHCS, chüan-chung,* pp. 16, 20a-b, 21a-b, 21b–22.

108. *Ibid., chüan-hsia,* pp. 4, 6, 13a-b, 17b. See also *Pi-hsieh shih-lu,* pp. 10–11b, where the first 2 of these incidents are reproduced.

109. The name, Hung-chin tsei, ordinarily refers to a secret society which rebelled during the late Yuan dynasty and also stirred up trouble in the Canton area in the 1850's. It is possible, however, that the author's usage of the name here refers to the Taipings. This is suggested in the concluding section on the Ko-lao-hui (Elder Brother Society), in which he remarks: "Otherwise the poison will spread endlessly, robber bands will appear everywhere, and before the disaster of the Hung-chin tsei has been put down that of the Ko-lao-hui will

commence" (*PHCS, fu-chüan*, p. 15a-b). In 1861, when this section of the *PHCS* was purportedly written, the "disaster" mentioned would appear to refer to the Taiping rebellion, which was put down three years later.

110. *PHCS, fu-chüan*, pp. 7–12.

111. See, e.g., the inflammatory piece enclosed in Honan governor Li Ho-nien's letter to the Tsungli Yamen, TC 7/8/30 (Oct. 15, 1868), in TYCT (Honan-France), pp. 4940–4942; the memorial of Prince Ch'un, Feb. 17, 1869, *IWSM:TC*, 64:10b–11. In both cases it was proposed that popular militia units be established to uphold orthodoxy and protect against the inroads of the foreign religion.

112. Two recent examples bear witness to this truth. During the McCarthy era in the United States, many people in government service were accused of being security risks because of their alleged homosexuality or addiction to other forms of sexual aberrancy. Still more recently, the *New York Times* noted the arrest and imprisonment of seven members of an "underground religious group in the Chuvash Autonomous Republic" in the Soviet Union. One of the charges reported in a Soviet newspaper was that the sect members "went so far as to dissuade boys and girls from marrying at the same time as they arranged orgies among themselves" (see *New York Times*, Aug. 16, 1959, p. 6).

CHAPTER 2. CHINA, CHRISTIANITY, AND THE
FOREIGN POWERS IN 1860

1. See the biographies of Li and Yang in Hummel, I, 452–454 and II, 894–895

2. See John F. Cady, *The Roots of French Imperialism in Eastern Asia* (Ithaca, 1954), p. 295 *et passim*.

3. The fullest and most scholarly account is in a recent book by the Chinese Catholic scholar, Wei Tsing-sing, *La Politique missionnaire de la France en Chine, 1842–1856: L'Ouverture des cinq ports chinois au commerce étranger et la liberté religieuse* (Paris, 1960). Unfortunately I saw this book too late to make more than passing reference to it here. See also A. A. Dorland, "A Preliminary Study of the Role of the French Protectorate of Roman Catholic Missions in Sino-French Diplomatic Relations" (M.A. thesis, Cornell University, 1951); H. M. Cole, "Origins of the French Protectorate over Catholic Missions in China," *The American Journal of International Law*, 34:473–491 (1940); Henri Cordier, *Histoire des relations de la Chine avec les puissances occidentales, 1860–1902* (Paris, 1901–1902), II, 625–648.

4. See *IWSM:TK*, 73:2, 30b, for the Chinese texts of one of Ch'i-ying's memorials and the edict of Dec. 14, 1844. For the Chinese

text of the edict of Feb. 20, 1846, see *Chiao-wu chi-lüeh, shou-chüan*, p. 4a-b. For foreign translations of some of these documents see Alexander Michie, *China and Christianity* (Boston, 1900), pp. 183–189; Tobar, pp. 8–9; and S. Couvreur, tr. and comp., *Choix de documents: Lettres officielles, proclamations, édits, mémoriaux, inscriptions . . . texte chinois avec traduction en français et en latin*, 3rd ed. (Hokien, Chihli, 1901), pp. 111–113. See also Cady, pp. 48–56, 60–64.

5. Cady, pp. 77–86, esp. pp. 85–86.

6. *Ibid.*, Chap. 7.

7. For a detailed recitation of events see Adrien Launay, *Histoire des missions de Chine: Mission du Kouang-si* (Paris, 1903), Chap. 3, and his *Supplément à l'histoire de la Mission du Kouang-si*, pp. 1–21.

8. See Cady, Chaps. 11–12, 14–15; Henri Cordier, *L'Expédition de Chine de 1857–58: Histoire diplomatique, notes et documents* (Paris, 1905); H. Cordier, *L'Expédition de Chine de 1860: Histoire diplomatique, notes et documents* (Paris, 1906).

9. The chief official advocate of a powerful union between the Cross and Tricolor appears to have been the French minister in China, M. de Bourboulon. The French foreign minister in 1859 wrote to Bourboulon: "I do not think that we shall be able to give to the protection of religious interests in China, the character that seems to you it might be useful to give it." Dorland, pp. 158–162 (quote from p. 161).

10. Cady, pp. 241, 256. For the text of Gros's secret supplementary instructions, see Cordier, *L'Expédition de 1860*, pp. 124–131.

11. The French text of this article may be found in many works. See, e.g., Cordier, *Histoire des relations*, I, 26, 53–54, and William Frederick Mayers, ed., *Treaties between the Empire of China and Foreign Powers* (Shanghai, 1877), pp. 62–63. For the Chinese text of the article, see *IWSM:HF*, 28:21, and other works cited in *CAPM*, p. 164.

12. For the Chinese text of the article, see *IWSM:HF*, 67:19b–20, and other works cited in *CAPM*, p. 164. For the French text, see Cordier, *Histoire des relations*, I, 53, and Mayers, p. 73.

13. Just who was ultimately responsible for this interpolation remains a matter of speculation. Latourette and the Jesuit historian, J. de La Servière, suggest that the interpreter may have been the French missionary, Louis Delamarre. In the most recent study addressed to the question, the Chinese Catholic scholar, Wei Tsing-sing, attributes it to Delamarre without hesitation. A. A. Dorland refutes this and attributes the drafting of the Chinese text to the other French interpreter at the time, Baron de Méritens, on the basis of Méritens' own admission in his *Notes upon Mr. Wade's Memorandum regarding the Revision of the Treaty of Tientsin* (Hong Kong, 1871), p. 4. (I

have been unable to examine Méritens' work.) John F. Cady implicates Baron Gros in the matter, suggesting that he connived at the discrepancy in wording "in order to avoid divulging in the published official French text the full scope of the exactions levied in the passports in favor of the French missionaries. Otherwise British and Americans would claim the same privileges." See Latourette, p. 276; J. de La Servière, S. J., *Histoire de la mission du Kiang-nan: Jésuites de la province de France (Paris) (1840–1899)*, 2 vols. (Zikawei, Shanghai, preface dated 1914), II, 21; Dorland, pp. 172–174; Wei Tsing-sing, pp. 456–459; Cady, p. 255.

14. The friction which resulted from this discrepancy in texts was only partly removed by the Berthemy Convention of 1865 (see Chap. 5).

15. Cady, p. 254. See also Cordier, *Histoire des relations*, I, 60–63.

16. Although this was technically true, the Protestants seem to have been given a considerable amount of trouble by the local officials when they attempted to rent or purchase land in the interior. The memorials of British missionaries to Minister Alcock, at the time discussions were taking place concerning the revision of the British Treaty of Tientsin, all requested that the privileges and rights granted to the French missionaries be specifically incorporated into the British treaty, in order to avoid ambiguity and prevent further obstructiveness on the part of the authorities. See *PP, Memorials addressed by Chambers of Commerce in China to the British Minister at Peking, on the subject of the Revision of the Treaty of Tien-tsin*, pp. 16–17, 34, 38, 39–41.

17. The Catholics were overjoyed with the allied victories of 1858–1860 (Latourette, p. 306), while in Protestant circles, according to Latourette (p. 359), "No one of influence . . . seems to have questioned seriously the consistency of entering the Empire in the wake of armed forces and under the protection of treaties."

18. Latourette, pp. 318–329, 405–406, 479. The number of Catholics that Latourette (p. 328) gives for Fukien in 1870 is 400,000. Contemporary Catholic sources give 40,000, which is no doubt closer to the truth. See *Annales*, 39:217 (1867); *MC*, 2:378 (1869).

19. By and large, I have accepted Mary Wright's view that the real, if not "official," end of the T'ung-chih Restoration came in 1870 with the Tientsin Massacre and the rejection of the Alcock Convention (*The Last Stand*, pp. 7, 299). For a fuller discussion of the meaning of the Chinese concept of "restoration," see the excellent account in *ibid.*, Chap. 4.

20. See Prince Kung's biography in Hummel, I, 380–384; Wen-hsiang's in *ibid.*, II, 853–855; and Kuei-liang's in *ibid.*, I, 428–430. Although Wen-hsiang was nominally second to Prince Kung in the

Tsungli Yamen, he was often in fact its acting head and was praised by Robert Hart as "one of the ablest, fairest, friendliest, and most intelligent Mandarins ever met by foreigners" (R. Hart, *"These from the Land of Sinim": Essays on the Chinese Question,* London, 1901, p. 68). Alexander Michie regarded him as "the most conscientious as well as the most liberal-minded statesman that China has produced during the sixty years of foreign intercourse" (*The Englishman in China during the Victorian Era, as Illustrated in the Career of Sir Rutherford Alcock, K.C.B., D.C.L., Many Years Consul and Minister in China and Japan,* Edinburgh and London, 1900, II, 374–375).

21. Memorial received on Jan. 13, 1861, *IWSM:HF,* 71:17b–26. This long memorial has been translated in part in Teng and Fairbank, pp. 47–49, 73–74.

22. See *IWSM:HF,* 72:27–36; M. Wright, *The Last Stand,* p. 224. On the organization and development of the Tsungli Yamen, see S. M. Meng, *The Tsungli Yamen: Its Organization and Functions* (Cambridge, Mass., 1962); Banno Masataka, "Sōrigamon no setsuritsu katei" (The process of establishing the Tsungli Yamen), *Kindai Chūkoku kenkyū,* No. 1:1–105 (Tokyo, 1958); Banno Masataka, " 'Sōrigamon' setsuritsu no haikei" (The background of the establishment of the Tsungli Yamen), *Kokusaihō gaikō zasshi* (The journal of international law and diplomacy), 51:360–402, 506–541 (1952); 52:89–111 (1953).

23. M. Wright, *The Last Stand,* pp. 227–228.

24. Martin had been working on this translation since the early sixties. Prince Kung and Wen-hsiang, who were enthusiastic about the project, appointed a commission of 4 Chinese scholars to assist him in preparing the final manuscript. See W. A. P. Martin, *A Cycle of Cathay, or China, South and North, with Personal Reminiscences* (New York, 1896), pp. 221–222, 233–235; Immanuel C. Y. Hsü, *China's Entrance into the Family of Nations: The Diplomatic Phase, 1858–1880* (Cambridge, Mass., 1960), pp. 125–138; M. Wright, *The Last Stand,* pp. 237–238.

25. The most important of these schools was the T'ung-wen kuan, established in Peking in 1862. On its history and development, see Knight Biggerstaff, "The Tung Wen Kuan," *Chinese Social and Political Science Review,* 18.3:307–340 (Oct. 1934). The curricula of these schools quickly expanded beyond the study of foreign languages (see M. Wright, *The Last Stand,* pp. 241ff).

26. Teng and Fairbank, pp. 47–48.

27. Letter to Hunan governor Mao Hung-pin, TC 1/5/20 (June 16, 1862), in TYCT (Hunan-France), pp. 2351–2354. The same policy is outlined in the Yamen's letter of TC 1/7/18 (Aug. 13, 1862) to Mao,

*ibid.*, p. 2374a-b. In response to the first letter, Mao issued a proclamation to the people of Changsha and Siangtan in which he emphasized that, though it was perfectly all right for people who didn't believe in Christianity to discourage their relatives from joining the religion, it was not all right for them to violate the laws or take the law into their own hands. If crimes were committed by Christians, these should be duly reported to the authorities along with evidence. See the text of this proclamation, enclosed in Mao's letter of TC 1/7/15 (Aug. 10, 1862), *ibid.*, pp. 2368–2370, and Mao's memorial of July 8, 1862, in *IWSM:TC*, 7:15.

28. Teng and Fairbank, p. 48.

29. M. Wright, *The Last Stand*, p. 226.

30. This statement is based on a reading of almost all published Tsungli Yamen memorials dealing with missionary affairs during the sixties and of the imperial responses accompanying them.

CHAPTER 3. GENTRY OPPOSITION TO CHRISTIANITY

1. J. Hudson Taylor, *China's Spiritual Need and Claims*, 5th ed. (London, 1884), pp. 47–48; also pp. 3, 11–12.

2. Nicolas Broullion, S.J., *Mémoire sur l'état actuel de la mission du Kiang-nan, 1842–1855, suivi de lettres relatives à l'insurrection 1851–1855* (Paris, 1855), p. 154.

3. François-Xavier Leboucq, *Monseigneur Edouard Dubar de la Compagnie de Jésus, évêque de Canathe, et la mission catholique du Tche-ly-sud-est, en Chine* (Paris, preface dated 1879), pp. 338–345.

4. Letter, Sept. 15, 1862, in *Annales*, 39:211 (1867). See also André-Marie [Meynard], *Missions dominicaines dans l'Extrême Orient*, 2 vols. (Paris, 1865), I, 251–252.

5. Dated Shanghai, Sept. 1, 1857, quoted in Thompson, p. 65.

6. William Muirhead, *China and the Gospel* (London, 1870), p. 59.

7. Letter of Oct. 5, 1856, in Thompson, pp. 59–60. See also Leboucq, pp. 371–376.

8. *The Chinese Recorder and Missionary Journal*, 4:155 (1871).

9. Letter to the directors of the London Missionary Society, 1869, in Thompson, p. 256.

10. Muirhead, pp. 67–68.

11. *Compagnie de Jésus*, p. 9; see also Broullion, p. 5.

12. Broullion, p. 5.

13. Muirhead, pp. 64–65.

14. John Macgowan, "Remarks on the Social Life and Religious Ideas of the Chinese," in D. Matheson, *Narrative of the Mission to*

*China of the English Presbyterian Church,* 2nd ed. (London, 1866), pp. 106–116; see also Griffith John's letter to the directors of the London Missionary Society, 1869, in Thompson, pp. 252–254.

15. *Compagnie de Jésus,* pp. 22–23. The vicar apostolic of Kweichow, Louis Faurie, wrote in the "Journal de la mission du Kouy-Tcheou," July 20, 1864: "They are veritable children, these Chinese, but shrewd children who oppress as soon as they feel themselves to be the stronger. It is thus with them in all classes of society and with regard to all kinds of matters" *(Annales,* 38:88 [1866]). See also Muirhead, p. 126.

16. See Paul A. Cohen, "Missionary Approaches: Hudson Taylor and Timothy Richard," *Papers on China,* 11:29–62 (1957); and Peter Duus, "Science and Salvation in China: The Life and Work of W. A. P. Martin," *ibid.,* 10:97–127 (1956).

17. Timothy Richard, *The New Testament of Higher Buddhism* (Edinburgh, 1910), pp. 49, 131; see also Richard's speech, "Relation of Christian Missions to the Chinese Government," in *Records of the General Conference,* p. 412.

18. This discussion of the gentry is based largely on Chang Chungli, esp. pp. 3–70. See also Ch'ü T'ung-tsu, *Local Government in China under the Ch'ing* (Cambridge, Mass., 1962), Chap. 10.

19. The most notable example of this among the Protestants was the China Inland Mission, most of whose members wore Chinese dress. For a sampling of their views on the question, see *The Occasional Papers of the "China Inland Mission"* (London, 1872), 1–2:84–85, 95, 101, 134–135 (1868).

20. Chengtu Tartar general Ch'ung-shih, toward the middle of the decade, attributed the numerous anti-Christian outbreaks in Szechwan chiefly to the jealousy and antagonism aroused among the gentry (and populace) by the extensive intercourse which the missionaries of the province (especially Eugène Desflèches) had with the local authorities and the influence they were able to exert in the yamens (letter to Tsungli Yamen, TC 4/10/20 [Dec. 7, 1865], in TYCT [Szechwan-France], pp. 2742–2744).

21. Father Leboucq of eastern Chihli lent his good offices to the Chinese government during its campaign against the rebels of Shantung and Chihli in the early years of the T'ung-chih reign, for which he was decorated by the emperor (see Chap. 7). Faurie of Kweichow appears to have advised the authorities of that province in a variety of military matters during the 1860's (see the laudatory memorial of the governor-general of Yunnan and Kweichow, Lao Ch'ung-kuang, Jan. 6, 1866, in *IWSM:TC,* 37:50b, and the partial French translation in Launay, *Histoire des missions de Chine: Mission du Kouy-tcheou,* Paris, 1907–1908, II, 340).

22. M. Wright, *The Last Stand*, p. 146; Michie, *China and Christianity*, pp. 129–132.

23. Letter to the directors of the London Missionary Society, 1869, quoted in Thompson, pp. 255–256.

24. For examples in Kiangsi and Hunan, see below in the present chapter and Chap. 1, n. 99. In Kweichow "numerous pamphlets" were circulated in the early sixties, one of which was *Summons to the People for the Repression of the Brigands of the European Religion* (see comments on, and partial French translation of, this pamphlet in Launay, *Kouy-tcheou*, II, 25–28). In April 1864, Mgr. Aguilar, coadjutor of Fukien, wrote that the pagans of that province had "distributed horrible pamphlets against the Christian religion in profuse amounts" (letter of Apr. 14, 1864, *Annales*, 39:208 [1867]). A local militia leader in eastern Chihli is reported to have written, in January 1864, a piece of writing ordering his braves and the populace at large to harass, by all possible means, those who evinced a desire to embrace the Christian religion (letter of Leboucq, July 29, 1864, *ibid.*, 37:61–62 [1865]). Again, during the same year, "scurrilous placards" led to the maltreatment of one of Griffith John's native assistants in a small town near Hankow, Hupeh (Thompson, p. 206), while in the following year the vicar apostolic of Hupeh wrote of anti-Christian booklets circulated by the literati of Hwangchow prefecture, just east of Hankow (letter of Mgr. Zanoli, July 29, 1865, in *Annales*, 39:95 [1867]). In the fall of 1865, the murder of Father François Mabileau in Yuyang chou, Szechwan, was immediately preceded by the posting of a placard calling for the extermination of the Catholics (report of the vicar apostolic of eastern Szechwan, Desflèches, Oct. 19, 1865, in *IWSM:TC*, 35:32b). In the following year a placard appeared in the Shanghai papers which reportedly had been "posted extensively" in Honan (*PP*, China, No. 9 [1870], pp. 25–26). And in Kanchow, Kiangsi, during the same year, two manifestoes were circulated calling for the burning of the Christian literature which had recently been distributed in the area, before ignorant people were misled by it (texts enclosed in dispatch from British minister Alcock to the Tsungli Yamen, TC 6/3/16 [Apr. 20, 1867], in TYCT [Kiangsi-Britain], pp. 5813b–5817). For examples of anti-Christian literature circulated later in the decade, see the end of Chap. 8.

25. This interaction between popular suspicions and rumors generated by inflammatory literature was clearly noted by Li Hung-chang in connection with the Tienmen, Hupeh, missionary case of 1869. See his letter to Tseng Kuo-fan, July 3, 1870, in *Li Wen-chung-kung ch'üan-chi* (The collected works of Li Hung-chang), 165 *chüan* (Shanghai: Commercial Press, 1921), *chüan* 10 (*p'eng-liao han-kao*), p. 8. For a critical summary of the sources of friction resulting from Catho-

lic practices, see Paul Boell, *Le Protectorat des missions catholiques en Chine et la politique de la France en Extrême-Orient* (Paris, 1899), pp. 15–23.

26. Hsia Hsieh, 21:5a-b; Chiang T'ing-fu, comp., *Chin-tai Chung-kuo wai-chiao shih tzu-liao chi-yao* (Selected materials on modern Chinese diplomatic history), 2nd ed., 2 vols. (Taipei, 1959), II, 76–77; memorial of Kiangsi governor Shen Pao-chen, Apr. 25, 1862, in *IWSM:TC*, 5:27b–28.

The Nanchang case of 1862 is hardly dealt with in Western sources. Chinese materials, aside from Hsia Hsieh's account, are found chiefly in *IWSM:TC* (see *CAPM*, pp. 12–13, 199); Chiang T'ing-fu, II, 73–84; and TYCT (Kiangsi-France), which has over 130 folio pages on the case.

27. Hsia also took an interest in the more traditional areas of Chinese scholarship. His published works included a study of the tables in the *Han-shu* (*Chiao Han-shu pa-piao*); a work on phonology (*Shu-yün*); and a history of the Ming (*Ming t'ung-chien*).

28. For a brief biographical note on Anot, see J. van den Brandt, *Les Lazaristes en Chine, 1697–1935: Notes biographiques* (Peiping, 1936), p. 48. This is a useful work for identifying the European names of Catholic missionaries whose Chinese names are known. See also, for this purpose, the two books by Joseph de Moidrey, S.J., *Confesseurs de la foi en Chine, 1784–1862* (Shanghai, 1935) and *La Hiérarchie catholique en Chine, en Corée et au Japon (1307–1914)* (Variétés sinologiques, No. 38, Zikawei, Shanghai, 1914); and *Cheng-chiao feng-pao* (In homage to the orthodox [Roman Catholic] religion), comp. by the Chinese priest Huang Po-lu, 3rd ed. (Shanghai, 1904), pp. 145–146b.

29. Hsia Hsieh, 21:2–4; Chiang T'ing-fu, II, 74–76. See also the memorial of acting Kiangsi governor Li Huan, Apr. 2, 1862, in *IWSM:TC*, 5:4b–5b.

30. Hsia Hsieh, 21:4; Chiang T'ing-fu, II, 76.

31. The original texts of these writings were enclosed by Kiangsi governor Shen Pao-chen in his letter to the Tsungli Yamen, TC 1/3/16 (Apr. 14, 1862), in TYCT (Kiangsi-France), pp. 2040b–2049b. The same pieces, in part or in entirety, were also circulated in Kwangping fu, Chihli, in 1864 (French communication of TC 3/4/13 [May 18, 1864], *ibid.* [Chihli-France], pp. 1369–1374b); Kanchow and other places in Kiangsi in 1866 (British communication of TC 6/3/16 [Apr. 20, 1867], *ibid.* [Kiangsi-Britain], pp. 5803–5813b); Ningpo (Chekiang) and numerous places in Kiangsu in 1868 (Tseng Kuo-fan's dispatch to the Yamen, TC 7/9/2 [Oct. 17, 1868], *ibid.* [Kiangsu-France], pp. 5333–5337); and "throughout the empire" in 1869 (Morse, II, 235–236, and Cordier, *Histoire des relations*, I, 336–340, both of

which contain partial translations). The Tsungli Yamen was quick to expose some of the more blatant falsehoods in the Hunan pieces (letter to Shen Pao-chen, TC 1/4/14 [May 12, 1862], in TYCT [Kiangsi-France], pp. 2053b–2054).

32. Memorials of Shen Pao-chen, Apr. 25, 1862, *IWSM:TC*, 5:27a-b; and June 23, 1862, *ibid.*, 6:47b.

33. Thus, following the Nanchang incident, some of the inhabitants of the city, in an interview with representatives of Governor Shen Pao-chen, were asked whether the missionaries' practice of rearing abandoned children was not a good thing, to which they replied: "Locally, our rearing of abandoned children is limited to taking in and nursing the newly born. But in their orphanage the boys and girls bought are all over ten *sui*. Do you think that their purpose is to rear children or to avail themselves of this as a pretext for cutting out their vital organs and severing their limbs [to sell for medicinal purposes—a crime punishable by death in the Ming code]?" (see *ibid.*, 12:33b).

34. Shen Pao-chen showed a clear awareness of this interaction (*ibid.*, 6:47b–48).

35. Hsia Hsieh, 21:4a-b; Chiang T'ing-fu, II, 76.

36. M. Wright, *The Last Stand*, p. 146.

37. See Shen Pao-chen's memorial of Apr. 25, 1862, *IWSM:TC*, 5:27b; Hsia Hsieh, 21:5; Chiang T'ing-fu, II, 76.

38. Hsia Hsieh, 21:5a-b; Chiang T'ing-fu, II, 77. For a somewhat different translation of Shen's remark, see A. Michie, *Missionaries in China* (Tientsin, 1891), p. 61. The author discusses the Nanchang case briefly. For a contemporary Chinese critique of Shen's handling of the Nanchang case, together with recommendations on how such cases should be managed, see Kuo Sung-tao's letter to Tseng Kuo-fan, 1862, in *Yang-chih shu-wu ch'üan-chi* (The collected works of Kuo Sung-tao; 1892), *chüan* 10 (*wen-chi*), pp. 17b–18b; also in Chiang T'ing-fu, II, 78–79.

39. It is indicative of the general confusion in the Chinese mind at this time as to the different forms of Christianity that Mao, at the very moment he is expounding on this confusion, mistakenly identifies the rebel religion with a corrupt form of Catholicism rather than with Protestantism (see Mao's memorial of Feb. 2, 1863, *IWSM:TC*, 12:22b). In this regard, see also Ch'en Ch'i-yüan, 4:5b.

40. Letter to Tsungli Yamen, TC 1/7/15 (Aug. 10, 1862), in TYCT (Hunan-France), p. 2366a-b.

41. Navarro, letter of Sept. 6, 1862 (Peking), in *Annales*, 35:424 (1863).

42. See the French communication of TC 1/4/6 (May 4, 1862), in TYCT (Hunan-France), p. 2347a-b. According to the French repre-

sentative, the piece in question was posted by the provincial judge of Hunan. Governor Mao, however, denied this charge. See Mao's letter to the Yamen, TC 1/7/8 (Aug. 3, 1862), *ibid.*, pp. 2354b–2355b. See also *Ch'ing-chi ko-kuo chao-hui mu-lu,* Fa-kuo, No. 56.

43. Navarro, letter of Sept. 6, 1862 (Peking), in *Annales,* 35:422–429 (1863). (The quotation is from p. 425.) See also the French communication of TC 1/5/16 (June 12, 1862), in TYCT (Hunan-France), pp. 2348b–2349b; and Mao Hung-pin's memorials of July 8, 1862, and Feb. 2, 1863, in *IWSM:TC,* 7:14b–15 and 12:24b respectively.

44. That the Tsungli Yamen and the throne were acutely conscious of this was expressly indicated. See, e.g., edict of Apr. 25, 1862, *IWSM:TC,* 5:29; edict of June 23, 1862, *ibid.,* 6:49b; Tsungli Yamen memorial of Oct. 17, 1862, *ibid.,* 9:20b.

45. For the complete text of the French demands, originally transmitted on Oct. 6, see *ibid.,* 9:22–25. For the French-drafted proclamation, see *ibid.,* 9:25–26b.

46. For the text of Shen's commentaries on the French demands, dated Feb. 3, 1863, see *ibid.,* 12:31–33; for Mao's, dated Feb. 2, 1863, see *ibid.,* 12:23b–26b.

47. See the proclamation drafted by the French and transcribed on Oct. 17, 1862, *ibid.,* 9:25a-b; French communication, transcribed on same date, *ibid.,* 9:30–32b; French communication, transcribed on Jan. 4, 1863, *ibid.,* 11:17b–18; French communication, transcribed on Feb. 10, 1863, *ibid.,* 12:50a-b.

48. See the following edicts in *IWSM:TC*: Apr. 25, 1862 (5:29), June 23, 1862 (6:49b), Oct. 17, 1862 (9:21a-b), Jan. 4, 1863 (11:17a-b), Feb. 10, 1863 (12:48b–49b), Apr. 25, 1863 (15:4b–5).

49. See the following memorials of Shen Pao-chen in *ibid.*: June 23, 1862 (6:48b–49), Feb. 3, 1863 (12:27a-b), June 23, 1863 (16:18b). For the texts of the interview with the populace and of one of the placards circulated by the gentry which called upon the populace forcibly to prevent the return of the Catholic missionaries to Nanchang, see *ibid.,* 12:33–35; Chiang T'ing-fu, II, 82–84. For translations of these two documents, see Paul A. Cohen, "The Hunan-Kiangsi Anti-Missionary Incidents of 1862," *Papers on China,* 12:20–22 (1958).

50. Mao, memorial of June 29, 1863, *IWSM:TC,* 16:19b–21.

51. See French communication to Tsungli Yamen, TC 3/8/11 (Sept. 11, 1864), in TYCT (Hunan-France), p. 2494a-b, and summary of same in *Ch'ing-chi ko-kuo chao-hui mu-lu,* Fa-kuo, No. 118.

52. Shen, memorial of Aug. 18, 1863, *IWSM:TC,* 18:19b–20; *Annales,* 39:452 (1867). For background on the Wu-ch'eng case, see the French communication of HF 11/10/8 (Nov. 10, 1861), in TYCT (Kiangsi-France), pp. 2026–2027.

53. Letter of Sept. 6, 1862, Peking, in *Annales*, 35:425, 427, 429–430 (1863).

54. This is the only biographical information I have been able to find on Hsia. See *Hsin-chien hsien-chih* (The Sinkien hsien gazetteer; 1871), comps. Tu Yu-t'ang, Ch'eng P'ei, et al., *chüan* 33 (*k'o-ti*), p. 26b.

55. Hsia Hsieh, 21:5; Chiang T'ing-fu, II, 76.

56. Hsia Hsieh, 21:6b–7; Chiang T'ing-fu, II, 78. Shen Pao-chen, in his memorial of June 23, 1862 (*IWSM:TC*, 6:48), also gives an account of this matter, which differs somewhat from Hsia Hsieh's. From our standpoint the most significant discrepancy is that Shen gives only Hsia T'ing-chü's surname. This, for all intents and purposes, concealed Hsia's identity completely and protected him from any punishment in connection with the case. Liu Yü-hsün's name was not mentioned in any of the memorials dealing with the case.

57. Shen, memorial of June 23, 1862, *IWSM:TC*, 6:48a-b. The French representative, Kleczkowski, explained these mysterious articles in his communication of Oct. 17, 1862, *ibid.*, 9:32.

58. *Hsü pei-chuan chi* (Supplementary collection of tombstone biographies), comp. Miao Ch'üan-sun (1893), 37:21b–22. Liu's biography is also in *Chiang-hsi t'ung-chih* (A general gazetteer of Kiangsi), comps. Li Wen-min et al. (1881), 140:47b–48.

59. W. L. Bales, *Tso Tsungt'ang, Soldier and Statesman of Old China* (Shanghai, 1937), pp. 101, 130, 135.

60. In one of the interviews that Shen Pao-chen's friends had with members of the Nanchang populace, the people stated in part: "The Taipings are all Catholic converts. [The missionaries] insist on preaching in the city and nearby places. If they lure the Taipings into entering [the city], will it not mean the end for ourselves and our families?" (see *IWSM:TC*, 12:33b).

61. The distinction between the upper and the lower gentry is discussed and defined in Chang Chung-li, pp. 6–8.

62. Chang Chung-li, p. 116, states: "The total number of civil and military officials at the capital and in the provinces has been given as approximately 27,000. Of this number, approximately 20,000 were civil officials, and 7,000 were military officers. Among the civil officials, approximately 2,000 were key regional and local officials, and 1,500 were key educational officials."

63. M. Wright, *The Last Stand*, p. 125.

64. As in all things proverbial there were, of course, exceptions. See Chap. 7.

65. The support of the gentry was obtained by the state in two primary ways: by means of the examination system which served as

a magnificent vehicle for indoctrinating the gentry with Confucian principles; by strictly safeguarding the legal and economic privileges of the class. On the official's dependence upon gentry support, see M. Wright, *The Last Stand,* pp. 128–129.

66. In most cases during the 1860's officials were severely punished only if they played a somewhat more active role in combating the Christians. Thus, as we have seen, no officials were punished in the Nanchang case. In connection with the Hunan cases, three local officials were deprived of their official insignia because of failure to prevent the riots and inability, once the riots had occurred, to suppress them. But by managing the cases satisfactorily, two of these officials redeemed themselves and were restored to rank the following year. See Mao Hung-pin's memorials of July 8, 1862 (*IWSM:TC,* 7:15a-b) and June 29, 1863 (*IWSM:TC,* 16:20b–21).

67. Two more such cases which took place in Yangchow and Anking later in the decade are dealt with in Chap. 7.

68. In addition to the Nanchang and Siangtan cases, I have come across 5 instances in the sixties in which relatively serious incidents occurred in connection with examinations. These were the Hengchow and Yuyang (Szechwan) incidents of 1865, the Yangchow incident of 1868, and the Anking and Luling (Kiangsi) cases of 1869. In all of these except the Luling incident there is definite evidence of the role played by inflammatory anti-Christian literature. Undoubtedly there were also many minor disturbances that took place in connection with examinations. Thus the English Protestant missionary, David Hill, reported in a letter of May 3, 1869, that he had encountered "a rather stormy reception" the previous year in Hwangchow fu, Hupeh, as a result of the examinations being held there (see W. T. A. Barber, *David Hill, Missionary and Saint,* 3rd ed., London, 1899, p. 93).

69. Letter of Dec. 27, 1869, *Occasional Papers,* 3–4:360 (1870).

70. Letter to M. L. Guerrin, Yéou-yang, Oct. 23, 1868, in *MC,* 2:114–115 (1869). The potential dangers at examination time were so evident that they could, in certain circumstances, be exploited by Chinese officials in their relations with the missionaries. In the negotiations for the settlement of the Tsunyi incident of 1869, the Kweichow governor, Tseng Pi-kuang, reportedly warned the missionary, Léonard Vielmon, that if he did not submit to Tseng's propositions, he would expose himself to "new misfortunes which were almost inevitable, at the moment when all the literati in the province were coming to the capital to pass the examinations" (Launay, *Kouytcheou,* II, 564).

71. Letter to Tsungli Yamen, TC 4/10/20 (Dec. 7, 1865), in *TYCT* (Szechwan-France), p. 2741b.

72. Memorial of Feb. 10, 1870, *IWSM:TC,* 71:2a-b, 3, 4a-b.

73. *North-China Herald,* July 7, 1870, p. 3.

74. Memorial of Hunan governor Yün Shih-lin, Aug. 31, 1864, *IWSM:TC,* 27:42b–43.

75. See the report of one of the missionaries, J. W. Williamson, to the British authorities, enclosed by Wade in his communication of Feb. 23, 1870, in *Wen-hsien ts'ung-pien* (Collectanea from the Historical Records Office), 46 *ts'e* (Peiping, 1930–1943), *chi* 31 (*chiao-an shih-liao*), p. 5b; also in *Ch'ing-chi chiao-an shih-liao* (Historical materials on missionary cases in the late Ch'ing; Peiping, 1937), 1:32.

76. See Chap. 8, n. 114, and Chap. 9, n. 7.

77. Fairbank, "Patterns behind the Tientsin Massacre," pp. 497–499. The Yangchow case is also dealt with in Chaps. 7–8.

78. Launay, *Kouy-tcheou,* II, 553. Chien Yin appears to have been known also by the name Kien Tse-ko (or -ho). According to the missionary Bouchard, his troops took a leading part in the destruction and pillaging of the Catholic church in Tsunyi (*ibid.,* p. 556). Father Vielmon, in a letter to the French legation, Kouy-yang, Aug. 17, 1870, remarked: "Kien-in, as I have often said, is the author of the Tsunyi persecution" (*ibid.,* p. 580).

79. See Li's memorial of Jan. 20, 1870, *IWSM:TC,* 70:28b; and Ch'ung's memorial of July 8, 1870, *ibid.,* 73:5b.

80. The private letters of figures like Li Hung-chang, Tseng Kuo-fan, and Liu K'un-i, which one might expect to shed light in this area, actually add very little to the content of these officials' memorials. See Li's letters on the Szechwan and Kweichow cases of 1869, in Li Hung-chang, *p'eng-liao han-kao, chüan* 9; Tseng's letters on the Tientsin case, in *Tseng Wen-cheng-kung ch'üan-chi* (The collected writings of Tseng Kuo-fan), 174 *chüan* (1876), *shu-cha, chüan* 32–33; and Liu's letters on the Kiangsi difficulties of 1869–1870, in *Liu K'un-i i-chi* (The collected works of Liu K'un-i), 6 vols. (Peking, 1959), *shu-tu, chüan* 14.

CHAPTER 4. OFFICIAL OPPOSITION TO CHRISTIANITY

1. Letter of Seckinger, May, 1868, in *MC,* 1:83 (1868). See also La Servière, II, 139ff.

2. Letter from Fenouil to Mgr. Ponsot, Feb. 24, 1868, in *MC,* 1:115 (1868).

3. Letter of Mgr. Louis de Castellazo, Nov. 2, 1865, in *Annales,* 39:86 (1867).

4. French note to Tsungli Yamen, TC 4/1/17 (Feb. 12, 1865), in TYCT (Fukien-France), p. 2924.

5. See, e.g., the letter of Mgr. Chiais, vicar apostolic of Shensi, Sept. 19, 1864, in *Annales,* 39:89 (1867); the letter of Mgr. Pinchon,

vicar apostolic of northern Szechwan, Sept. 20, 1868, *MC*, 2:23 (1869).

6. See below in the present chapter. The vicar apostolic of northern Szechwan, Pinchon, claimed that the officials of that province published "the blackest calumnies" against the Christians. See *MC*, 2:23 (1869).

7. Letter from David Hill, Dec. 1, 1869, in Barber, pp. 105–106.

8. *Compagnie de Jésus*, pp. 118ff.

9. *MC*, 1:54 (1868). La Servière, II, 145, reports the seizure of a Jesuit father in Yingshan, Hupeh, by the subprefect in charge of the area. The priest showed the official his passport and the proclamation of religious toleration. The official, however, took no cognizance of these documents. And as soon as the missionary was released and had left the area, the officials and gentry directed a severe persecution against the native Christians for having "invited the head of the European religion" to their district.

10. Letter from Mgr. Anouilh, vicar apostolic of western Chihli, Jan. 16, 1866, in *Annales*, 39:442–443 (1867).

11. See, e.g., the communication addressed by the French minister, Bellonet, to the Tsungli Yamen, originally dated July 25, 1866, presented to the throne on Aug. 27, 1866, in *IWSM:TC*, 43:34b; La Servière, II, 130–131.

12. Letter of David Hill, May 3, 1869, in Barber, p. 101. See also Launay, *Kouy-tcheou*, II, 570; Cordier, *Histoire des relations*, I, 334–335.

13. On the decline in effectiveness of the *pao-chia* system as a control mechanism, see Hsiao Kung-chuan, *Rural China: Imperial Control in the Nineteenth Century* (Seattle, 1960), Chap. 3.

14. The T'ien Hsing-shu case is covered extensively on the French side in Launay, *Kouy-tcheou*, Vol. II. Published Chinese materials (almost exclusively in *IWSM:TC*) are listed in *CAPM*, pp. 15–19, 199. TYCT (Kweichow-France) contains well over 200 folio pages on the case.

15. The causes of unrest, in the opinion of Hu Lin-i (1812–1861), who had served as a prefect in Kweichow in the early 1850's, were maladministration, inadequate military force, and discrimination against the non-Chinese Miao tribes. The disorders were prolonged, no doubt, chiefly because the allocation of government resources — civil, military, and financial — was concentrated in other parts of the empire where revolt was more serious (see M. Wright, *The Last Stand*, p. 118).

16. See P'eng's biography in Hummel, II, 617–620.

17. These facts are extracted from T'ien's biography in the *Ch'ing-shih kao* (Draft history of the Ch'ing dynasty), comps. Chao Erh-hsün

et al., Lien-ho shu-tien photolithographic ed. (Shanghai, 1942), II, 1383–1384.

18. Edict to the Grand Secretariat, Aug. 21, 1862, in *IWSM:TC*, 8:40a-b. See also the criticisms of T'ien voiced by Ch'ung-shih and Lao Ch'ung-kuang, quoted in the Tsungli Yamen memorial of Aug. 21, 1862, in *ibid.*, pp. 37–38, 39a-b.

19. T'ien's disobedience of imperial orders is noted in the edict of Aug. 21, 1862, *ibid.*, p. 40b. For a long description of T'ien and his behavior see the excerpt from the diary of the Kweichow bishop, Louis Faurie, Apr. 29, 1861, in *Annales*, 34:417–424 (1862). See also the communication of the French chargé d'affaires, Kleczkowski, transcribed on Feb. 6, 1863, in *IWSM:TC*, 12:42b; Launay, *Kouy-tcheou*, II, 69; and J. H. Castaing, *Vie de Mgr. Faurie, membre de la Société des Missions Étrangères, vicaire apostolique du Kouy-tcheou (Chine)* (Paris, 1884), p. 233.

20. Launay, *Kouy-tcheou*, II, 48–51; Castaing, pp. 235–237.

21. Kleczkowski also severely reproached Faurie for using a violet-colored sedan chair on this visit (see his letter of Dec. 21, 1861, in Launay, *Kouy-tcheou*, II, 52). One of the Kweichow missionaries, Lions, expressed serious misgivings about the tactfulness of such elaborate proceedings, which he felt could only excite the jealousy of the literati and officials (*ibid.*).

22. These incidents are recounted in Launay, *Kouy-tcheou*, II, 60–73; Castaing, pp. 237–258.

23. Launay, *Kouy-tcheou*, II, 110–111 (italics mine). Kleczkowski negotiated this settlement with Lao Ch'ung-kuang, who at the time was governor-general at Canton and who had been delegated by the Chinese government to deal with the case. For details of this incident and background information, see *ibid.*, pp. 74ff; Faurie's letter to the French legation, transcribed in *IWSM:TC*, 6:41–42b; and Castaing, pp. 259–280. The terms of the settlement are itemized in Kleczkowski's long letter of Dec. 21, 1861, to Faurie (Launay, *Kouy-tcheou*, II, 110–112). According to a Tsungli Yamen memorial of June 19, 1862, T'ien Hsing-shu, when first questioned about the case, wrote that in a province where rebels were constantly being attacked by government forces it was quite impossible to make distinctions between Christian and non-Christian rebels (*IWSM:TC*, 6:33).

24. The title of the pamphlet was *Chiu-chieh pao-hsün* (Valuable advice on how to ward off calamity). See Faurie's letter to the French legation, transcribed in *IWSM:TC*, 6:42b. In a Tsungli Yamen memorial of Mar. 28, 1865, it was attributed to a former expectant taotai, Miao Huan-chang (*ibid.*, 31:21). I have been unable to determine the contents of this pamphlet.

25. This letter was also signed by the then governor of Kweichow, Ho Kuan-ying. The missionaries found out about its existence from a Christian clerk in the Kiensi chou yamen (Launay, *Kouy-tcheou,* II, 113), a leakage which, incidentally, was sternly reprimanded by the throne (edict of June 19, 1862, *IWSM:TC,* 6:37b–38). A copy of the letter was transmitted by the French legation to the Tsungli Yamen and was transcribed in *ibid.,* 6:43b–44. Whether or not this was an exact replica of the original cannot, of course, be known with certainty. See Ch'ung-shih's comments on both this letter and the anti-Christian pamphlet reprinted by T'ien Hsing-shu (memorial of Mar. 22, 1863, in *ibid.,* 13:15).

26. This succession of events is pieced together from the account in Launay, *Kouy-tcheou,* II, 120–127, and from Faurie's letter to Kleczkowski, *IWSM:TC,* 6:42b–43. See also Castaing, pp. 281–304.

27. Launay, *Kouy-tcheou,* II, 113, asserts that whatever seeming connection there may have been between these two events there were no known documents proving it.

28. Faurie, letter to French legation, transcribed in *IWSM:TC,* 6:41b. For details of this incident, see Launay, *Kouy-tcheou,* I, 485–517, and Castaing, pp. 187–192.

29. Memorials of Feb. 6, 1863, *IWSM:TC,* 12:38b–39, 39b–40.

30. Edict to the Grand Secretariat, Aug. 21, 1862, *ibid.,* 8:40a-b; Tsungli Yamen memorial, Jan. 18, 1863, *ibid.,* 11:27. For the full Chinese text of Kleczkowski's demands, see *ibid.,* 11:29b–31.

31. See Kleczkowski's communication (transcribed Feb. 6, 1863, in *ibid.,* 12:42–43b), in which he details to the Chinese government the secret machinations by which T'ien sought to disengage himself from any responsibility for the Kaichow case. These machinations had been recounted to the French legation by the missionary, Vielmon, who had been delegated by Faurie to go to Peking to seek redress. The throne's recognition of this intrigue in the Kweichow capital was clearly voiced in its edict of Feb. 6, 1863 (*ibid.,* 11:41a-b).

32. Launay, *Kouy-tcheou,* II, 140–141, 170; Castaing, p. 307.

33. The demands voiced by Faurie were limited exclusively to material reparations (Launay, *Kouy-tcheou,* II, 136–137). See also the position of the missionary Mihières (*ibid.,* p. 166).

34. This analysis is borne out by the Tsungli Yamen's confidential note to the French representative, Nov. 12, 1864, *IWSM:TC,* 29:11a-b.

35. This statement is based on a careful reading of almost all published Chinese official documentation dealing with missionary cases during the 1860's, and on a fairly comprehensive survey of the TYCT.

36. See, e.g., the following documents in *IWSM:TC:* Tsungli Yamen memorial, Jan. 18, 1863 (11:27–28); Yamen communication to France, same date (11:31b–33b); Yamen memorial, Jan. 30, 1863 (12:

11a-b); edict of Feb. 6, 1863 (12:40b–42); edict of Apr. 11, 1863 (14:11b–12); Yamen memorial, June 8, 1863 (15:43a-b); edict of same date (15:44b–45b); edict, Aug. 27, 1863 (18:37a-b); edict, Sept. 27, 1863 (19:17b); Yamen memorial, Dec. 4, 1863 (21:51b).

37. The French text of Berthemy's communication and demands is in Launay, *Kouy-tcheou,* II, 162–163; for the Chinese text, presented to the throne on June 8, 1863, see *IWSM:TC,* 15:46–47b. The relaxation of the French position was no doubt due in part to Berthemy's awareness that the Chinese government's resistance to French demands was not motivated simply by ill will, but also by fear of furnishing ammunition to the party hostile to its policy. See Berthemy's dispatch to the French foreign minister, June 12, 1863, in AEC, 39:47a-b (May-Dec. 1863).

38. See Faurie's letter to Berthemy, Oct. 9, 1863, in Launay, *Kouy-tcheou,* II, 180; Chinese text in *IWSM:TC,* 21:62b–65.

39. See the two letters of Chang and Lao, transcribed Dec. 4, 1863, in *IWSM:TC,* 21:59b–61, 65–68. For Berthemy's letter to Faurie, see Launay, *Kouy-tcheou,* II, 183. The throne's approval of the recommendations of Lao and Chang, dated Feb. 10, 1864, is in *IWSM:TC,* 23:1b. See also the edict to the Grand Secretariat announcing T'ien's sentence, Mar. 28, 1865, in *ibid.,* 31:23b–24. This edict also contains the other punishments meted out in the case. For a French translation, see Launay, *Kouy-tcheou,* II, 183–184. For the memorial of Lao Ch'ung-kuang and Chang Liang-chi (Oct. 24, 1864) officially recommending the punishments eventually carried out, see *IWSM:TC,* 28:42b–46b. Berthemy's note giving official French sanction to the punishment of T'ien recommended by the Chinese was quoted by the Tsungli Yamen in its memorial of Mar. 28, 1865, in *ibid.,* 31:20b.

40. See the edict of Mar. 28, 1865, *ibid.,* 31:24; the Tsungli Yamen memorial and edict of Oct. 12, 1865, *ibid.,* 35:10b–12b; Ch'ung-shih's memorial of Nov. 18, 1865, *ibid.,* 37:1a-b.

41. Ch'ung-shih memorial, Aug. 2, 1866, *ibid.,* 42:66a-b. See also the memorial of Shensi governor Liu Jung, in which he discusses the route T'ien will take through Shensi (*ibid.,* 42:72b).

42. See T'ien's biography in *Ch'ing-shih kao,* II, 1384.

43. See Tso's memorial, Sept. 23, 1867, and the imperial response, Sept. 29, 1867, in *Tso Wen-hsiang-kung ch'üan-chi* (The collected writings of Tso Tsung-t'ang; 1890), *tsou-kao,* 22:45–46, 48a-b. The throne's firm resolve to see T'ien punished was evinced earlier in its strong rejection of Hunan governor Yün Shih-lin's request that T'ien be permitted to lead troops in Hunan (see Yün's memorial of Mar. 19, 1864, in *IWSM:TC,* 23:24b–25b, and the edict of the same date, *ibid.,* 23:25b–26b).

T'ien was apparently released from his exile in 1873 and permitted to return to his home in Hunan, where he died four years later. See his biography in *Ch'ing-shih kao*, II, 1384.

44. See, e.g., the memorial of the famous scholar-official, Hung Liang-chi (1746–1809), in *Ch'ing wen-hui* (Collection of Ch'ing literature; Taipei, 1960), p. 956. As late as 1891, Griffith John, noting the aura of authority lent to anti-Christian writings by virtue of their inclusion of the *Sacred Edict*, wrote: "Has the time not come when the Chinese Government should be asked by the Foreign Powers to expunge from the *Shêng-yü* its very hostile reference to Christianity . . . ?" (*Anti-Foreign Riots*, p. 215).

45. Latourette, p. 307. For the Sino-French correspondence over this question, which took place between TC 6/6/15 (July 16, 1867) and TC 6/7/4 (Aug. 3, 1867), see TYCT (*t'ung-hsing chiao-wu*), pp. 3874–3891b.

46. The Yamen may have had in mind here a case that occurred early in the decade in which a Chinese Christian, claiming to represent the French missionary Anot, rushed into a Kiangsi yamen dressed as a foreigner and created quite a stir among the local officials. See the letter of the acting governor of Kiangsi, Li Huan, to the Yamen, TC 1/3/3 (Apr. 1, 1862), in TYCT (Kiangsi-France), p. 2149.

47. The text of the Yamen's proposals was transcribed on Oct. 17, 1862 (*IWSM:TC*, 9:27b–29b). See also the Yamen communication to the French representative, TC 1/8/10 (Sept. 3, 1862), in TYCT (Hunan-France), pp. 2386b–2389; *ibid.* (Kiangsi-France), pp. 2075–2077b.

48. *IWSM:TC*, 9:33b. This was the only response ever made by the French to the Yamen proposals. See Yamen communication to the French, TC 6/11/5 (Nov. 30, 1867), in TYCT (Shansi-France), p. 4773b.

49. Memorial seen on Mar. 22, 1863, *IWSM:TC*, 13:16–17.

50. Memorials seen on Apr. 11, 1863, *ibid.*, 14:15b–17.

CHAPTER 5. THE MISSIONARY'S ABUSE OF HIS POSITION

1. E.g., the Jesuit authors of *Compagnie de Jésus* (pp. 20–24), after lauding the gunboat exploits of the British and French toward the end of the decade (see Chap. 8), explicitly approved a policy of "recourse to the cannon" whenever the Chinese failed to render prompt and strict justice. See also the comments of another Jesuit, Father Ravary, in a letter of Dec. 3, 1868, *MC*, 2:108 (1869).

The Catholic attitude toward the use of force to further their interests was also indicated by their almost ecstatic appreciation of the Anglo-French invasions of 1858–1860. See, e.g., the views of the vicar apostolic of Kiangnan, Languillat, in L'Abbé Appert, ed., *Mgr. Lan-*

*guillat, évêque de Sergiopolis, vicaire apostolique de Kian-nan (Nan-kin), chanoine d'honneur de la Cathédrale de Chalons* (Chalons, 1867), p. 8; and those of the vicar apostolic of Manchuria, E. Vérolles, in his letter of July 2, 1866, *Annales,* 39:301–302 (1867).

The Protestants of the 1860's seem to have been somewhat less unanimous in their opinions regarding the merits of using force to defend missionary interests. But they all accepted enthusiastically their new treaty rights, which had been won by force, and many of them insisted that their governments take strong action against any infringements of these rights. See, e.g., Griffith John's letter of July 30, 1858, in Thompson, p. 79; the view of David Hill, in Barber, pp. 101–102; that of William Muirhead, in Muirhead, pp. 74–75, 77, 135; and that of John Chalmers, in *The Chinese Recorder and Missionary Journal,* 4:155–158 (1871).

2. These indemnities were collected for the following cases: (1) the Chungking case of 1863 in which a Catholic church was pillaged and converts' homes destroyed — 150,000 taels (see the joint memorial of Chengtu Tartar general Ch'ung-shih and Szechwan governor-general Lo Ping-chang, Feb. 24, 1865, in *IWSM:TC,* 31:6b; this large indemnity was also intended to compensate the Church for previously confiscated properties); (2) the Yuyang chou case of 1865 in which a French missionary, Mabileau, and a native priest were killed, and the Catholic church and converts' homes destroyed — 80,000 taels (see joint memorial of Ch'ung-shih and Lo Ping-chang, July 27, 1867, *ibid.,* 49:53b); (3) the case of 1869, also in Yuyang chou, in which the Catholic missionary Rigaud and numerous converts were killed, and the church destroyed — 30,000 taels (see the memorial of Assistant Grand Secretary and Hu-kuang governor-general Li Hung-chang, Feb. 11, 1870, in *ibid.,* 71:6; this memorial is dated Feb. 2, 1870, in Li Hung-chang, *tsou-kao,* 16:1).

3. These fears were raised with specific reference to Szechwan by the Tsungli Yamen secretary, Chou Chia-mei, in a letter to Prince Kung, 1869. See Chou's collected writings, *Ch'i-pu-fu-chai ch'üan-chi* (A collection of writings from the Ch'i-pu-fu studio), 8 *ts'e* (Honan, 1895), *chüan* 2 (*cheng-shu*), pp. 31–32b. The French representative, Rochechouart, also thought the "principal reason" for the antagonism harbored by the population of Szechwan against Christianity to be "the enormous sums paid to Mgr. Desflèches by the district of Yuyang . . . sums levied on the people and distributed by the Bishop to his Christians." See his dispatch to Paris, Dec. 1, 1869, in AEC, 46:146 (Sept.-Dec. 1869).

4. See the dispatch of the French representative, Berthemy, to the Foreign Ministry, Jan. 20, 1864, in *ibid.,* 40:4a-b (1864).

5. In June 1869, when the Jesuit missionary Leboucq called on

Tseng Kuo-fan, the aging administrator told Leboucq that the Catholics openly offended the opinions and beliefs of the populace in demanding temples and other public monuments as reparations, and then converting them into churches. See Leboucq's letter of Jan. 18, 1870, in *Annales,* 42:334 (1870).

6. La Servière, II, 32–34.

7. Letter of Mgr. Anouilh, Tching-Ting-Fou, Mar. 10, 1862, in *Annales,* 34:375 (1862). See also *MC,* 1:134 (1868) and the Chinese materials on this case in TYCT (Chihli-France), pp. 517–543.

8. See the memorial of the censor, Chu Hsüeh-tu, Aug. 27, 1866, in *IWSM:TC,* 43:41b–42; the memorial of the Tsungli Yamen, Sept. 15, 1866, *ibid.,* 44:1–3b; the statement of the subprefect, Huang Wei-hsüan, Dec. 16, 1867, *ibid.,* 53:15b; and the extensive materials on this case, dating from HF 10/9/4 (Oct. 17, 1860) to TC 13/12/24 (Jan. 31, 1875), in TYCT (Chihli-France). See also C. Martin, "Notes sur le Massacre de Tien-tsin," in H. Cordier, ed., *Revue de l'Extrême-Orient* (Paris, 1887), II, 110.

9. See Honan governor Li Ho-nien's dispatch to the Tsungli Yamen, Sept. 1867, in *Chiao-wu chi-yao* (Selected documents on church affairs), comp. Hsü Chia-kan, 4 *chüan* (Hupeh, 1898), *chüan* 3 (*shang*), p. 24a-b; the Yamen's communication to France, Nov. 23, 1869, in *IWSM:TC,* 69:31b; and the account of the Honan missionary, Peyralbe, in his letter of Feb. 16, 1868, in *MC,* 1:140 (1868). For further discussion of this case, see Chap. 7.

10. Letter of Jan. 16, 1866, in *Annales,* 39:441–442 (1867).

11. See Dorland, pp. 197–200 (trans. by Dorland); Cordier, *Histoire des relations,* I, 63–67. For a severely critical appraisal of Guillemin's conduct in this affair, see Baron Gros's report of Dec. 13, 1860, in Wei Tsing-sing, p. 462.

12. See Launay, *Kouy-tcheou,* II, 339, 576.

13. For the Chinese texts of Faurie's communication, dated TC 7/11/3 (Dec. 16, 1868), and the Tsungli Yamen's angry response to the French representative, dated TC 7/11/13 (Dec. 26, 1868), see TYCT (Kweichow-France), pp. 7551–7555b. For the French versions see Launay, *Kouy-tcheou,* II, 384–385. See also the Yamen's circular memorandum of 1871 in which Faurie's action is cited as an instance of the usurpation of official prerogatives by missionaries (transcribed on Sept. 1, 1871, in *IWSM:TC,* 82:23b). The Kweichow bishop was sharply reprimanded by the French chargé d'affaires, Rochechouart. See the latter's dispatch to Paris, Jan. 30, 1869, in AEC, 45:27b–28 (Jan.-Aug. 1869); and his letter to Faurie, Jan. 7, 1869, *ibid.,* 45:33a-b.

14. This was early in 1867 and is not to be confused with the case of the spurious 10 articles which erupted in 1866 in Szechwan and which also involved Pinchon (see Chap. 6). On the 1867 case, see

the following documents in TYCT (Szechwan-France): letter from Ch'ung-shih to Tsungli Yamen, TC 6/4/11 (May 14, 1867), p. 6317a-b; Yamen letter to Szechwan governor-general Lo Ping-chang, TC 6/4/27 (May 30, 1867), pp. 6318–6319b; letter from Ch'ung-shih to the Yamen, TC 6/7/3 (Aug. 2, 1867), pp. 6350–6355.

15. *IWSM:TC*, 82:23b.

16. E.g., a French missionary referred to himself as "your younger brother" in a letter to the governor of Shansi (Tsungli Yamen letter to Hunan governor Mao Hung-pin, TC 1/7/18 [Aug. 13, 1862], in TYCT [Hunan-France], pp. 2374b–2375); the bishops of Honan (Baldus) and Hupeh, on separate occasions, used official forms in corresponding with the officials of these provinces (Tsungli Yamen letter to Honan governor Chang Chih-wan, TC 2/9/17 [Oct. 29, 1863], *ibid.* [Honan-France], pp. 1791b–1792b; letter in reply from Chang, TC 2/12/20 [Jan. 28, 1864], *ibid.*, pp. 1793b–1796b).

17. In 1869, e.g., the superior of Kwangsi, S. Mihières, was officially deputed by the French chargé d'affaires, Rochechouart, to investigate and negotiate a settlement of the anti-Christian incidents which had taken place earlier that year in Yuyang, Szechwan (see Li Hung-chang's memorial of Jan. 3, 1870, transcribed on Jan. 20, in *IWSM:TC*, 70:24; the letter of the Szechwan missionary, L. Blettery, Sept. 23, 1869, in *MC*, 3:20 [1870]).

18. Hsüeh Fu-ch'eng, in a letter to Li Hung-chang in 1869, discussed at length the abuses resulting from this interference. See Hsüeh Fu-ch'eng, *Yung-an ch'üan-chi* (Collected works of Hsüeh Fu-ch'eng), Tsui-liu-t'ang ed. (Shanghai, 1897), *chüan* 2 (*wen-pien*), pp. 28b–30b. See also the following memorials in *IWSM:TC*: the governor of Anhwei, Ch'iao Sung-nien, Mar. 19, 1866 (39:27–28); the governor of Kiangsi, Liu K'un-i, May 29, 1866 (41:43b); the Tartar general at Canton, concurrently Canton governor-general, Jui-lin, and the Kwangtung governor, Chiang I-li, Oct. 25, 1866 (44:32b); the governor-general of Shensi and Kansu, Tso Tsung-t'ang, Nov. 20, 1867 (51:23b); Jui-lin, Dec. 10, 1867 (52:21); the governor of Kiangsu, concurrently acting Hu-kuang governor-general, Li Han-chang, Dec. 16, 1867 (52:35b–36); the governor of Fukien, Li Fu-t'ai, Dec. 31, 1867 (55:36b–37b); the governor of Hupeh, concurrently acting governor of Kiangsu, Kuo Po-yin, Dec. 31, 1867 (55:41); the acting governor-general of Chihli, Kuan-wen, Jan. 16, 1868 (56:14b–15).

19. The clause in Article 13 which proved most difficult to draft, interestingly enough, was the last one invalidating all previously issued official prohibitions of Christianity. The phrasing initially demanded by the French would have mentioned the abolition of all *imperial edicts* previously directed against Christianity. This, however, would have run counter to Chinese tradition and was strongly objected

to by the Chinese negotiators. The final wording of the clause circumvented this ticklish question quite simply by invalidating all writings against the Christian religion which had been previously published in China "by order of the government." The throne's sanctity was thus preserved. See Cordier, *L'Expédition de 1857–58,* pp. 429–431.

20. Latourette, p. 310.

21. Letter of July 29, 1864, in *Annales,* 37:58–59 (1865).

22. Protocol and propriety were important to the Chinese. The Tsungli Yamen, in its missionary memorandum of 1871, stated: "When [missionaries] visit high Chinese officials, they should observe the same formalities required of Chinese literati in *their* visits with these officials. When they request audiences with local officials they should, again, observe these formalities, meeting with them politely. They must not barge into the yamens and disrupt public business" (*IWSM:TC,* 82:23b).

23. Letter of Jan. 18, 1870, in *Annales,* 42:342–343 (1870).

24. Others named in this regard were Octave and Anouilh of Chihli and Hannibal of Shantung. See Émile Becker, *Un Demi-siècle d'apostolat en Chine: Le Révérend père Joseph Gonnet de la Compagnie de Jésus,* 3rd ed. (Hokien, 1916), pp. 121–122.

25. Chou Chia-mei, *chüan* 2 (*cheng-shu*), p. 31a-b. For a missionary refutation of Chou's charge (which, incidentally, was repeated in the Tsungli Yamen memorandum of 1871), see the letter of Pinchon, Chengtu, July 16, 1872, in *MC,* 4:632–633 (1872). Chou also accused Desflèches of interference in connection with the Yuyang case of 1865 (undated letter to Ch'ung-shih, in Chou Chia-mei, 2:24a-b). Desflèches' propensities in this regard were also noted by Ch'ung-shih in his letter to the Tsungli Yamen, TC 4/10/20 (Dec. 7, 1865), in TYCT (Szechwan-France) pp. 2742–2744.

26. Wei Tsing-sing, pp. 540–545. Rochechouart accused Desflèches of making no distinction between good and bad converts and of desiring, "more than anything else in the world . . . to see [his converts] become the occasion of lucrative lawsuits" (*ibid.,* p. 540). See also Cordier's assertion (*Histoire des relations,* I, 429) that Desflèches and Faurie of Kweichow, through their attitude and demands, rendered the management of certain matters very delicate for the French legation.

27. See Hsüeh Fu-ch'eng's letter to Li Hung-chang, 1869, in *Yung-an ch'üan-chi, chüan* 2 (*wen-pien*), p. 29. See also the following memorials in *IWSM:TC:* the acting governor of Kweichow, Chang Liang-chi, Aug. 25, 1865 (34:15) and Dec. 31, 1865 (37:39b); Shen Pao-chen, Dec. 16, 1867 (53:7); Li Hung-chang, Dec. 31, 1867 (55:16).

28. See, e.g., the memorial of Ch'ung-shih's younger brother,

Ch'ung-hou, Dec. 21, 1867, *IWSM:TC*, 54:20b; the memorial of Ch'ung-shih, Apr. 11, 1863, *ibid.*, 14:15b–16.

29. *Compagnie de Jésus,* pp. 157–158.

30. For foreign documentation on this case, see Launay, *Kouy-tcheou*, II, 216–324, and Castaing, pp. 337–392. Chinese documentation is available chiefly in *IWSM:TC, chüan* 34, 37–38, 42 (see *CAPM,* pp. 22–23), and TYCT (Kweichow-France).

31. There is no account in Western languages. In Chinese, see the comprehensive account in Ling T'i-an, *Hsien-T'ung Kuei-chou chün-shih shih* (A history of military affairs in Kweichow during the Hsien-feng and T'ung-chih periods), 8 *ts'e* (Shanghai, 1932).

32. Launay, *Kouy-tcheou,* II, 216–221.

33. T'ien's yamen (*prétoire*) was converted by the Catholics into a cluster of establishments, including a large orphanage, several schools, and a pharmacy. There is a reproduction of the floor plan in *ibid.,* Vol. III, Plate V.

34. See the Chinese and French texts of this proclamation in *ibid.,* III, 513, and II, 182, respectively. Faurie, as might be expected, had nothing but the highest praise for the governor-general (see, e.g., *ibid.,* II, 173, 182).

35. *Ibid.,* II, 222–224. According to Faurie, after traveling a short distance, he sent the troops back to Kweiyang with a word of thanks to the governor-general and governor for their solicitude on his behalf.

36. The negotiations entered into by Faurie are recounted in *ibid.,* II, 238–255; Castaing, pp. 337-370.

37. See Faurie's "Journal de la mission du Kouy-Tcheou," July 20, 25, 28, 1864, quoted in *Annales,* 38:86–87, 89–90, 92 (1866). Two of the incidents are recounted with minor variations in Launay, *Kouy-tcheou,* II, 228–231.

38. "Journal," July 20, 1864, quoted in *Annales,* 38:87 (1866). See also Launay, *Kouy-tcheou,* II, 225–233.

39. *Ibid.,* II, 262–322; Castaing, pp. 371–392.

40. "Journal," Nov. 1864, in Launay, *Kouy-tcheou,* II, 263.

41. *Ibid.,* II, 348, 350–351. To Vielmon, Faurie wrote (Tchen-lin, July 21, 1864): "All these individuals have embraced the faith through interest. They have caused much trouble here" (*ibid.,* II, 350).

42. *Ibid.,* II, 275, 287. A French translation of Ch'ien's proclamation is in *ibid.,* II, 288. For the original Chinese text, dated TC 4/12/2 (Jan. 18, 1866), see TYCT (Kweichow-France), p. 3283. Ch'ien Hsün's name, as found in Launay, is Tsien Pe-ya. That these were one and the same person is clearly indicated in Chang Liang-chi's memorial of Aug. 25, 1865, in *IWSM:TC,* 34:13.

43. Launay, *Kouy-tcheou,* II, 308–309, 326–327, 330–331. See Chang

Liang-chi's account of the Yungning incident in his memorial of Apr. 16, 1866, in *IWSM:TC*, 41:22bff.

44. Launay, *Kouy-tcheou*, II, 270, 316, 320. See also *ibid.*, II, 289, 322, 325, 328–329, 334, *et passim*.

45. *Ibid.*, II, 316. Faurie eventually went over Chang's head and got Lao Ch'ung-kuang to sign an order for the arrest of Liu (*ibid.*, II, 318), but Chang refused to countenance the transfer of Ch'ien (*ibid.*, II, 322). See also Chang Liang-chi's two memorials of Aug. 25, 1865 (*IWSM:TC*, 34:13b) and Dec. 31, 1865 (*ibid.*, 37:37a-b), in which he vigorously defends Ch'ien Hsün in particular.

46. See the following memorials of Chang in *IWSM:TC*: Aug. 25, 1865 (34:10b–17), Dec. 31, 1865 (37:36b–40), June 16, 1866 (42:22–23b).

47. Remark by Lions, quoted in Launay, *Kouy-tcheou*, II, 349.

48. Mary Wright remarks that Chang virtually saved the day for Yunnan in 1860 by *negotiating* an eleventh-hour settlement with a rebel leader of the province, Ma Ju-lung (*The Last Stand*, pp. 115–116).

49. This is a remarkable document, of a sort seldom found in Chinese official writings of this period. In addition to defending Faurie, Lao accused Chang Liang-chi of being prejudiced and easily taken in by baseless rumors; of trying to pursue in Kweichow the same cunning tactics he had previously followed in Yunnan, namely, pacifying the rebels in the open while secretly destroying them, and therefore giving rise to endless misery among the inhabitants; of monopolizing official power and secretly countermanding Lao's orders, etc. (memorial, Jan. 6, 1866, in *IWSM:TC*, 37:50–60, esp. pp. 57–59). Significantly, perhaps, Lao did not send in this memorial until after his departure from Kweiyang (Dec. 11, 1865) to take up residence in the normal seat of the Yün-Kuei governor-generalship, Kunming (see Launay, *Kouy-tcheou*, II, 361).

50. Memorial of June 16, 1866, *IWSM:TC*, 42:23.

51. Tsungli Yamen memorial of Sept. 17, 1865, *ibid.*, 34:27b–29. See also the following documents presented by the Yamen with its memorial: the summary of Chang Liang-chi's original memorial, sent to the French minister, in *ibid.*, 34:30–32b; the French minister's letter to the Yamen, *ibid.*, 34:32b–33; Faurie's letter to the French minister (written in April-May 1865, prior to Chang's memorial) in which he accused Chang and other officials of poor administration, *ibid.*, 34:33–34; the Yamen's note to the French minister, *ibid.*, 34:34–35.

52. See Launay, *Kouy-tcheou*, II, 338, 343–345.

53. Letter of J. B. D. Aubry, in *ibid.*, II, 324. In a letter of June 22, 1879, Aubry commented that he knew of only one person who, having been baptized at the time of Vielmon's expedition, had remained a faithful Christian (*ibid.*, II, 324n).

54. Letter to Faurie, Gan-chouen, Sept. 14, 1865, in *ibid.*, II, 324; Castaing, p. 392.

55. Launay, *Kouy-tcheou*, II, 161–162. Mihières, in contrast, defended Kleczkowski (*ibid.*, II, 159).

56. Paris to Berthemy, Feb. 14, 1863, in AEC, 38:33 (Jan.-Apr. 1863).

57. See the following dispatches from Berthemy to Paris: Aug. 2, 1863, *ibid.*, 39:127–128 (May-Dec. 1863); Apr. 25, 1864, *ibid.*, 40:72–74 (1864); May 27, 1864, *ibid.*, 40:95a-b.

58. *Ibid.*, 40:75–78; reproduced in Cordier, *Histoire des relations,* I, 429–430. Baldus, incidentally, like Guillemin, was a forceful advocate of a combined political-religious role for the French missionary. See Wei Tsing-sing, pp. 506–512.

59. Dispatch to Paris, May 27, 1864, in AEC, 40:95b–96 (1864).

60. Becker, pp. 121–122.

61. AEC, 40:79–80 (1864).

62. Cordier, *Histoire des relations,* I, 68–71. For the Chinese text of the Berthemy Convention, see *Cheng-chiao feng-ch'uan* (The propagation of the orthodox [Roman Catholic] religion), comp. Huang Po-lu, 2nd ed. (Shanghai, 1908), p. 120.

63. Thus Hudson Taylor by 1895 had come to feel that in no circumstances was it appropriate for Protestant missionaries to appeal for redress to their governments. See his letter on "Appeals for redress, etc.," *The Chinese Recorder and Missionary Journal,* 26:575–579 (1895). On the Catholic side, see the excerpt from L. E. Louvet's *Les Missions catholiques au XIX^e siècle,* reproduced in *MC,* 23:310 (1891).

CHAPTER 6. CHINESE PROPOSALS FOR THE REGULATION
OF MISSIONARY ACTIVITIES

1. This case, which took place in the summer in Yuyang chou, is dealt with only briefly in the present narrative. The missionary killed was François Mabileau. A native priest was also killed, and the Catholic church and numerous convert homes in Yuyang destroyed. The French exacted 80,000 taels from the Chinese as indemnity.

2. See the following documents in TYCT (Szechwan-France): Ch'ung-shih's letter to the Yamen containing the 14 articles, TC 4/10/20 (Dec. 7, 1865), pp. 2745–2754; Ch'ung's letter to the Yamen, TC 5/7/21 (Aug. 30, 1866), containing an earlier draft of the articles (pp. 2813–2818) and another copy of the final draft (pp. 2820b–2825b); Yamen communication to the French, TC 4/11/28 (Jan. 14, 1866), pp. 2761–2762. French translations of the key documents are in Launay, *Kouy-tcheou,* II, 363–367 (see also Castaing, pp. 409–411). TYCT does

not indicate which 10 articles of the original 14 were selected by the Yamen; Launay does.

3. The Chinese text of Bellonet's communication, dated TC 4/12/4 (Jan. 20, 1866), is in TYCT (Szechwan-France), pp. 2763–2765. The French text, dated Jan. 19, is in AEC, 41:193–194b (Jan. 1865–July 1866), and in Launay, *Kouy-tcheou*, II, 367–368.

4. The text of Bellonet's letter to Faurie is in *ibid.*, II, 368–369.

5. See Bellonet's dispatch to Paris (Jan. 30, 1866) and Paris' reply (May 18, 1866), in AEC, 41:182–184, 243–244 (Jan. 1865–July 1866); see also Dorland, pp. 294–295.

6. Launay, *Kouy-tcheou*, II, 369–371.

7. The French texts of these two notes are in *ibid.*, II, 371–372. The Chinese texts, dated TC 5/5/25 (July 7, 1866) and TC 5/5/28 (July 10, 1866), are in TYCT (Szechwan-France), pp. 2787–2790.

8. See Ch'ung-shih's two letters to the Tsungli Yamen (with enclosures), both dated TC 5/7/21 (Aug. 30, 1866), in TYCT (Szechwan-France), pp. 2807–2832.

9. See the Yamen memorial of Mar. 28, 1866, in *IWSM:TC*, 40:9b–10, and the dispatch of the governor-general of Fukien and Chekiang, Tso Tsung-t'ang, to the Yamen, announcing his receipt of the 10 articles and his intention to put them into immediate effect in Fukien, TC 5/5/6 (June 18, 1866), in TYCT (Fukien-France), pp. 2928–2931.

10. See the Yamen's circular letter of TC 5/10/25 (Dec. 1, 1866) to the high provincial officials, enjoining them to return to the old method of dealing with missionary difficulties "on the basis of reason and in accordance with the treaties" (TYCT [Szechwan-France], pp. 2860–2861).

11. For Bellonet's circular letter of Sept. 25, 1866, announcing the Chinese government's official retraction of the 10 articles, and Faurie's letter of Dec. 18, 1866, see Launay, *Kouy-tcheou*, II, 372–373 (also Castaing, p. 413).

12. Compare this with the distinction implied in the Ming and Ch'ing codes between the practice and propagation of Buddhism (see Chap. 1). The practice of a religion, from the Chinese point of view, was essentially a private matter. But its organized propagation had social and political ramifications and was plainly frowned upon by the state.

13. This series of proposals contained the suggestions for China's domestic reform of two of the most enlightened Englishmen in China during this era, Robert Hart and Thomas Wade. Hart's "spectator's memorandum" was presented to the Tsungli Yamen on Nov. 6, 1865, Wade's memorandum on Mar. 5, 1866 (see M. Wright, *The Last Stand*, pp. 263–268).

14. For Ch'iao's memorials, dated Mar. 19, 1866, see *IWSM:TC*, 39:27–29; for the Tsungli Yamen's memorial of Mar. 28, 1866, see *ibid.*, 40:8b–10; for Liu's memorial of May 29, 1866, see *ibid.*, 41:43–44.

15. Launay, *Kouy-tcheou*, II, 372.

16. See Biggerstaff's excellent summary of this correspondence, "The Secret Correspondence of 1867–1868: Views of Leading Chinese Statesmen Regarding the Further Opening of China to Western Influence," *The Journal of Modern History*, 22:122–136 (1950), esp. pp. 132–135, which deal with the missionary question.

17. Tseng Kuo-fan's reply somehow got into foreign hands and was accurately summarized and reviewed in the *North-China Herald* on June 13, 1868 (M. Wright, *The Last Stand*, p. 272). For an extended account of the treaty-revision negotiations and a summary of Chinese and foreign views on the various issues, see *ibid.*, Chap. 11.

18. *IWSM:TC*, 50:34b–35.

19. See M. Wright, *The Last Stand*, pp. 243–246.

20. Yang's memorial, submitted on his behalf by the Censorate, in *IWSM:TC*, 49:13–24b; edict in reply, *ibid.*, 49:24b–25b.

21. Memorandum submitted by Censorate on Yang's behalf, *ibid.*, 49:32b–33b.

22. See, e.g., the Tsungli Yamen's letter to Hunan governor Mao Hung-pin, TC 1/5/20 (June 16, 1862), in TYCT (Hunan-France), pp. 2351–2354, in which its view of Christianity is clearly set forth.

23. This possibility has been suggested in Biggerstaff, "The Secret Correspondence," pp. 133–134.

24. The portions of the memorials of these officials that deal with the missionary question are all in *IWSM:TC*, as follows: Tso Tsung-t'ang, Nov. 20, 1867 (51:19, 22b–23b); Jui-lin, Dec. 10, 1867 (52:20b–21); Ting Pao-chen, Dec. 14, 1867 (52:27); Li Han-chang, Dec. 16, 1867 (52:35b–36b); Shen Pao-chen, Dec. 16, 1867 (53:4b, 7a-b); Tseng Kuo-fan, Dec. 18, 1867 (54:3b–4b); Ying-kuei, Dec. 20, 1867 (54:10b–11); Liu K'un-i, Dec. 20, 1867 (54:13b); Ch'ung-hou, Dec. 21, 1867 (54:20b–21); Wu T'ang, Dec. 28, 1867 (55:4b–5); Li Hung-chang, Dec. 31, 1867 (55:16–17 — cf. the similar passage in a memorial attributed to Li and dated Dec. 1, 1867, in Michie, *The Englishman in China*, II, 187); Ma Hsin-i, Dec. 31, 1867 (55:28a-b); Li Fu-t'ai, Dec. 31, 1867 (55:36b–37b); Kuo Po-yin, Dec. 31, 1867 (55:41a-b); Kuan-wen, Jan. 16, 1868 (56:14b–16).

25. See Immanuel Hsü, p. 165, for a translation of this passage from Shen's memorial.

26. *IWSM:TC*, 53:15a-b, 19a-b, 25b–26.

27. M. Wright, *The Last Stand*, p. 275.

28. *Ibid.*, p. 261. This view apparently came to be shared by the

Tsungli Yamen. The British minister, Alcock, on the basis of two interviews with the members of the Yamen in May 1869, reported to Clarendon (on May 20, 1869) that he was convinced "that the subject which most preoccupied them, as of primary importance, was the residence of missionaries inland, and especially the location of the Roman Catholic missions under a French protectorate" (*PP*, China, No. 5 [1871], p. 394).

29. *IWSM:TC*, 56:14b–15.

30. *CAPM* lists only one missionary case for 1867 — a minor incident involving two China Inland Mission missionaries in Siaoshan hsien, Chekiang. Wang Wen-chieh notes no cases at all for this year.

31. A contemporary official, Wang Chih-ch'un, recorded an audience which Tseng apparently had with the Empress Dowager on Sept. 30, 1870:

Empress Dowager: "The foreigners certainly are cause for worry. The churches are always making a nuisance of themselves."

Tseng: "The foreigners are indeed cause for worry . . . The incidents which have occurred everywhere of late have all been prompted by the churches. The converts mistreat commoners who have not accepted the religion; the missionaries shield the converts; the churches give free rein to the missionaries; and the officials are unable to exercise control. Hereafter when we exchange treaties we must negotiate strict provisions concerning missionary activities. Then only will things be set aright." See Wang Chih-ch'un, *Fang-hai chi-lüeh* (A brief record of maritime defense; 1880), 2:33.

CHAPTER 7. OFFICIAL ACCOMMODATION OF THE FOREIGN MISSIONARY

1. Cordier, *Histoire des relations,* I, 345–346, gives a French translation of Ch'ung-hou's proclamation. See also Leboucq, pp. 200–206, 286–288; Rochechouart to Paris, Jan. 30, 1869, in AEC, 45:24b–25 (Jan.-Aug. 1869).

2. Letter of Octave, Aug. 2, 1865, in *Annales,* 39:383 (1867). See also Leboucq's letter of Jan. 18, 1870, *ibid.,* 42:343 (1870).

3. An astounding number of legal cases involving religious persecution seem to have occurred in the 1860's in this part of Chihli (see Chap. 1, n. 2).

4. The Fuan case occurred in 1863. See the letter of Mgr. Calderon, Apr. 14, 1864, in *Annales,* 39:206–209 (1867), and the documentation, spanning the period TC 1–3 (1862–1864), in TYCT (Fukien-France), pp. 2904–2927b.

5. Consul Medhurst's dispatch to British minister Alcock, Chinkiang, Sept. 3, 1868, *PP*, China, No. 2 (1869), p. 10. See also *MC,* 1:205 (1868), and *Occasional Papers,* 3–4:220–222 (1869). The Chin-

kiang incident is also recounted in Tseng Kuo-fan's dispatch (with enclosures) to the Tsungli Yamen, TC 7/8/4 (Sept. 19, 1868), in TYCT (Kiangsu-Britain), pp. 5089–5098. For other Chinese materials dealing with the case, dating from TC 7/8/9 (Sept. 24, 1868) to TC 7/10/24 (Dec. 6, 1868), see *ibid.*, pp. 5114–5242.

6. *IWSM:TC*, 12:33–34.

7. There is an abundance of materials on the Nanyang case in TYCT (Honan-France), beginning in TC 1 (1862) and spanning the remainder of the decade. See also Chap. 5, n. 9, above.

8. Some of these incidents are summarized in a long dispatch from Honan governor Li Ho-nien to the Tsungli Yamen, Aug.-Sept. 1867, in *Chiao-wu chi-yao, chüan* 3 (*shang*), pp. 22–32b.

9. See Li Ho-nien's letter to the Tsungli Yamen, TC 6/12/4 (Dec. 29, 1867), in TYCT (Honan-France), p. 4904a-b. In an earlier letter to the Yamen, dated TC 6/7/8 (Aug. 7, 1867), Li enclosed one of the petitions of the Nanyang gentry class signed by 144 individuals including an expectant hsien magistrate, 2 *chin-shih,* and 12 *chü-jen* (see *ibid.,* pp. 4826–4833b).

10. These writings were enclosed in a letter from Li Ho-nien to the Tsungli Yamen, TC 7/8/30 (Oct. 15, 1868), in *ibid.,* pp. 4940–4942. In the second piece the middle character of the Chinese term for Catholicism (*T'ien-chu-chiao*) is written with the first-tone homonym meaning "to kill" or "to punish," resulting in "heaven-chastised religion" instead of the usual "religion of the Lord of Heaven." Similar substitutions were commonplace in the anti-Christian literature of the late nineteenth century.

11. Quoted in Tsungli Yamen memorial of Nov. 8, 1868, in *IWSM:TC,* 62:1b.

12. Another instance of this phenomenon occurred toward the middle of the sixties in Nanking, where there was opposition to the establishment of a Catholic church. Certain members of the local gentry met with the missionaries to try to work out an agreement, whereupon threats began to circulate to the effect that if the gentry permitted the Christians to enter the city and carry on operations there, the homes of the leading gentry would be burnt down. See the gentry petition enclosed by the acting Liang-Kiang governor-general, Li Hung-chang, in his letter to the Tsungli Yamen, TC 5/13/14 (Apr. 28, 1866), in TYCT (Kiangsu-France), p. 1919b. There are extensive materials on the Nanking case in TYCT (Kiangsu-France) covering the years TC 5–6 (1866–1867).

13. This summary is based on Ying-kuei's memorial of Mar. 30, 1869, in *IWSM:TC,* 65:3–5b. Other Chinese documents on this case are listed in *CAPM,* pp. 33–34. See also *PP,* China, No. 9 (1869).

14. On Pien Pao-shu, who was one of the chief gentry suspects in

the Yangchow case of 1868, see Fairbank, "Patterns behind the Tientsin Massacre," p. 498. Pien Pao-ti's stubbornness and antiforeign sentiments were clearly pointed out by Ying-kuei in his memorial of Mar. 30, 1869, in *IWSM:TC*, 65:4a-b.

15. Interestingly enough, the reason, according to Pien, why the missionaries had not been permitted to have social intercourse with the local officials was the fear that they would use the occasion to make unprincipled demands regarding the legal cases of their converts (see his memorial of Apr. 26, 1869, *ibid.*, 65:21).

16. Memorial of Apr. 26, 1869, *ibid.*, 65:20–21b, and edict to Grand Secretariat, *ibid.*, 65:22.

17. These general comments are based on a close reading of some two dozen of Ch'ung-shih's memorials dealing with missionary cases in the 1860's, together with the imperial responses.

18. These incidents are summarized in Chinese in Wang Wen-chieh, pp. 54–59. The published Chinese materials (chiefly in *IWSM:TC*, chüan 64, 67, 69–71; and in Li Hung-chang, *p'eng-liao han-kao*, chüan 9) are listed in *CAPM*, pp. 30–32, 201. TYCT (Szechwan-France), containing about 450 folio pages on the case, provides, from the Chinese side, the most detailed and thorough coverage. The missionary side is presented in *Annales*, 42:113–136 (1870) and 43:83–95 (1871); *MC*, 2:113–115, 121–124, 129–130, 260, 313–316 (1869), and 3:19–20, 29–30, 36–38, 49–50, 109 (1870). See also the French translation of two Chinese documents concerning the case in C. Martin, "Notes sur le Massacre de Tien-tsin," pp. 127–128 (reproduced in Cordier, *Histoire des relations,* I, 332–334).

19. See, e.g., the letter of Mgr. Desflèches, Feb. 13, 1869, in *MC,* 2:129 (1869); the letter of the Szechwan missionary Provot, Mar. 19, 1869, in *Annales,* 42:124–125 (1870); and the following French communications in *IWSM:TC*: Mar. 20, 1869 (64:30b–31, 37–38b); Nov. 6, 1869 (69:7). Chang P'ei-ch'ao had also been implicated in the earlier killing of the missionary Mabileau (see n. 20 below).

20. See, e.g., Li's letter to Governor Ying-han, Dec. 29, 1869, in Li Hung-chang, *p'eng-liao han-kao*, 9:28b; his letter to Szechwan governor-general Wu T'ang, Jan. 5, 1870, *ibid.*, 9:30; and his joint memorial (with Ch'ung-shih and Wu T'ang) of Jan. 20, 1870, in *IWSM:TC*, 70:25. Li, in his investigation of this case, rejected the missionary contention that Chang P'ei-ch'ao had played a principal role in it. Published Chinese materials on the Mabileau case of 1865 are listed in *CAPM*, pp. 23, 199. See also TYCT (Szechwan-France). Wang Wen-chieh, pp. 51–54, gives a brief summary in Chinese. The French side is presented in a letter of the Szechwan missionary, Paul Perny, Shanghai, Jan. 16, 1866, in *Annales,* 38:302–313 (1866).

21. See Chou Chia-mei, *chüan* 2 (*cheng-shu*), pp. 30–37. This letter

is reproduced in *Huang-ch'ao hsü wen-hsien t'ung-k'ao* (Supplement to the Ch'ing *Wen-hsien t'ung-k'ao*), comp. Liu Chin-tsao, 320 *chüan* (1905), 316:37b–46b, and in *Huang-ch'ao cheng-tien lei-tsuan* (Classified compendium of Ch'ing documents on administrative affairs), comp. Hsi Yü-fu, 500 *chüan* (Shanghai, 1903), 490:9–12.

22. Seven Chinese were punished (two with death), and a 30,000 tael indemnity was exacted by the French. The Chinese priest, T'an Ch'un-ch'ing, on the other hand, seems to have escaped interrogation altogether by going to Europe (see the joint memorial of Li Hung-chang, Wu T'ang, and Ch'ung-shih, Jan. 20, 1870, in *IWSM:TC*, 70:27b). The different positions taken in these cases by the missionaries and the French legation are worth noting. The missionaries, according to the French chargé (Rochechouart), were completely dissatisfied with his handling of the affair and wanted him, above and beyond seeking redress for the murder of Rigaud and the damage done French establishments, to involve himself in the conflicts that had been raging in Szechwan between the native Christians and the populace. Rochechouart was firmly opposed to this, regarding it as unwarranted interference in Chinese affairs. See his dispatches to Paris of Mar. 21, 1870, in AEC, 47:78–81b (Jan.-June 1870); and Apr. 2, 1870, AEC, 47:118b–119.

23. The particulars in this account are based upon Taylor's statement of Aug. 31, 1868, the veracity of which was sworn to by Taylor and 3 other missionaries who witnessed the Yangchow proceedings (*PP*, China, No. 2 [1869], p. 3ff). See also Taylor's long letter to the "Friends of the Mission," Chin-kiang-fu, Sept. 10, 1868, in *Occasional Papers*, 3–4:188–212 (1868).

24. Fairbank, "Patterns behind the Tientsin Massacre," pp. 483–485, presents and analyzes the main facts in the management of this case. Summaries are in Morse, II, 226–228; Cordier, *Histoire des relations*, I, 277–279; and Wang Wen-chieh, pp. 35–37. The documentation on the foreign side is very extensive. In addition to *PP*, China, No. 2 (1869), see *PP*, China, No. 10 (1869); *Wen-hsien ts'ung-pien, chi 29 (chiao-an shih-liao)*, pp. 4b–14b; *Ch'ing-chi chiao-an shih-liao*, 1:5–15; and the letters of missionary participants, in *Occasional Papers*, 3–4:188ff. For the Chinese documentation, see *CAPM*, pp. 29–30, and TYCT (Kiangsu-Britain), TC 7–8 (1868–1869), in which there are well over 200 folio pages on the Yangchow case.

25. The inevitable difficulties they had in renting the property are recounted in Williamson's letter of Apr. 13 and Meadows' letter of May 16, 1869, in *Occasional Papers*, 3–4:307–317 (1869), and in Williamson's further letter of Aug. 31, 1869, *ibid.*, 3–4:338–341.

26. Letters from Williamson, Nov. 16, 1869, and from Mrs. Meadows, Nov. 19, *ibid.*, 3–4:360–368. The same ground is covered, with

some variations in detail, in Williamson's report to the acting British minister, Wade. This report was enclosed by Wade in his communication to the Chinese government, dated Feb. 23, 1870, in *Wen-hsien ts'ung-pien, chi* 31 *(chiao-an shih-liao),* pp. 5b–7b, and in *Ch'ing-chi chiao-an shih-liao,* 1:31b–33b.

27. See Wade's 2 communications to the Tsungli Yamen dated Feb. 23 and Mar. 7, 1870, in *Wen-hsien ts'ung-pien, chi* 31 *(chiao-an shih-liao),* pp. 4–8, and *Ch'ing-chi chiao-an shih-liao,* 1:30–34b; Anhwei governor Ying-han's letter to the Yamen, TC 9/3/8 (Apr. 8, 1870), in TYCT (Anhwei-Britain), p. 5599b; Ma Hsin-i's letter to the Yamen, TC 9/3/19 (Apr. 19, 1870), *ibid.,* pp. 5604–5606.

CHAPTER 8. FRANCE, BRITAIN, AND THE MISSIONARY PROBLEM

1. The general remarks on British policy in this and the preceding paragraph are largely based on Nathan A. Pelcovits' excellent study, *Old China Hands and the Foreign Office* (New York, 1948), Chap. 1. See also M. Wright, *The Last Stand,* pp. 23–33.

2. See Dr. and Mrs. Howard Taylor, *Hudson Taylor and the China Inland Mission: The Growth of a Work of God,* 7th ed. (London, 1925), Pts. 1–3.

3. Alcock to Lord Stanley, Peking, Oct. 12, 1868, in *PP,* China, No. 2 (1869), pp. 31–32.

4. See Fairbank, "Patterns behind the Tientsin Massacre," pp. 484–485; and *PP,* China, No. 10 (1869), pp. 8–10, 13–17.

5. Published Chinese language documentation on the Taiwan case is listed in *CAPM,* pp. 30, 200–201. TYCT (Fukien-Britain) contains almost 500 folio pages on this case alone. For British documentation, see *PP,* China, No. 3 (1869). For a summary of the main facts, see Wang Wen-chieh, pp. 121–123. The diplomatic aspect is briefly treated in Fairbank, "Patterns behind the Tientsin Massacre," pp. 486–489.

6. See *PP,* China, No. 2 (1869), p. 48; *PP,* China, No. 3 (1869), pp. 6, 10, 18; *IWSM:TC,* 62:31; Fairbank, "Patterns behind the Tientsin Massacre," pp. 486–487.

7. *PP,* China, No. 3 (1869), p. 53; *IWSM:TC,* 65:7–9b; Fairbank, "Patterns behind the Tientsin Massacre," p. 487.

8. Minute by Hammond, quoted in Pelcovits, p. 53.

9. See *ibid.,* pp. 53–56. The full text of the Clarendon Declaration is in *PP,* China, No. 1 (1869), pp. 1–2.

10. Clarendon to Alcock, Jan. 14, 1869, in *PP,* China, No. 2 (1869), pp. 63–64.

11. Clarendon to Alcock, Feb. 23, 1869, in *PP,* China, No. 3 (1869), pp. 21–22. See also M. Wright, *The Last Stand,* pp. 30–31; Fairbank, "Patterns behind the Tientsin Massacre," pp. 488–489; the Tsungli

Yamen memorial of May 30, 1869, in *IWSM:TC*, 65:25b–26; Pelcovits, p. 56.

12. Clarendon to Alcock, Jan. 28, 1869, in *PP*, China, No. 2 (1869), pp. 76–77.

13. Pelcovits, pp. 56–57, 309n.80.

14. Clarendon to Alcock, Apr. 23, 1869, in *PP*, China, No. 9 (1869), p. 5.

15. Alcock to Stanley, Sept. 11, 1868, in *PP*, China, No. 2 (1869), p. 26.

16. Alcock to Caine, Jan. 12, 1869, in *PP*, China, No. 8 (1869), p. 3. Alcock was, nevertheless, willing to request that 1 or 2 gunboats be temporarily stationed on the Yangtze to cope with emergencies (*ibid.*, pp. 3–4).

17. Alcock to Stanley, Jan. 13, 1869, *ibid.*, p. 1; Clarendon to Alcock, Mar. 30, and Apr. 19, 1869, *ibid.*, pp. 4–5.

18. *Hansard's Parliamentary Debates*, 3rd Ser., Vol. 194 (Mar. 9, 1869), pp. 934–942. See also Thompson, pp. 245–248 (the *Times* article is quoted on pp. 245–246).

19. *Occasional Papers*, 3–4:287–294 (1869).

20. Thompson, pp. 249–250.

21. In his communication to Clarendon of Oct. 1, 1869, he remarked: "I cannot, without a total disregard of history, hope that missionaries will accomplish more with the Chinese race in this nineteenth century than has been effected with far more ample means, and under more favourable conditions, in the West during the preceding eighteen. What 30,000 pulpits and preachers cannot do in Great Britain at the present day, is not likely, as far as human means are concerned, to be accomplished by 200 or 300 teachers of an alien race, and of different and conflicting sects and rival churches, however earnest and devoted may be the men. And on the chance of this, or some miraculous intervention, a Government may well be permitted to hesitate before it sacrifices a vast commerce on which the greatness and power of the nation mainly depends, and with it the influence of all the material elements of civilization which follow in its train" (*PP*, China, No. 9 [1870], p. 14).

22. Although it is true that Alcock was personally opposed to the entry of Protestant missionaries into the interior, he realized that there was little that could be done to prevent it. But he felt that the situation might be much improved if the missionaries would ask for residence in the interior as a privilege and not demand it as a right. See his communication to Clarendon, Mar. 12, 1869, in *PP*, China, No. 9 (1870), pp. 2–4.

23. See also Griffith John's lengthy critique (1869) of Alcock's views, in Thompson, pp. 257–269.

24. Text in Mayers, pp. 12–13.

25. *PP,* China, No. 9 (1870), pp. 17–39, esp. pp. 17, 20, 27–28, 32, 34, 35–39. See Clarendon's strong endorsement of the "restrictive policy" in his communication to Alcock, May 19, 1869, in *ibid.,* p. 4, and Hammond's advice to British missionaries in his letter to the Bishop of Victoria, Nov. 13, 1869, in *ibid.,* pp. 13–14.

26. Mary Wright stresses this point (*The Last Stand,* pp. 39, 226–227).

27. For the original text of this note, dated TC 8/5/17 (June 26, 1869), see TYCT (*t'ung-hsing chiao-wu*), pp. 3893–3894b; *IWSM:TC,* 82:13–14. For varying English translations, see *PP,* China, No. 9 (1870), p. 12; and *PP,* China, No. 1 (1872), pp. 13–14.

28. Alcock to Clarendon, July 31, 1869, in *PP,* China, No. 9 (1870), p. 5.

29. *IWSM:HF,* 71:18b, tr. in Teng and Fairbank, p. 48.

30. Memorial of Dec. 16, 1867, *IWSM:TC,* 53:7.

31. M. Wright, *The Last Stand,* p. 34.

32. *Documents diplomatiques* (Ministère des Affaires Étrangères), No. 8 (1867), "Exposé des affaires politiques et commerciales," p. 16; No. 11 (Jan. 1869), "Exposé des affaires politiques et commerciales," p. 13; No. 13 (Nov. 1869), "Exposé des affaires . . . ," pp. 14–15.

33. *Ibid.,* p. 14.

34. Alcock, in his communication to Lord Stanley, Sept. 11, 1868, remarked: "I believe one of the chief occupations of the French Legation here, consists in pressing claims for redress, and making reclamations on their [Roman Catholic missions'] behalf" (*PP,* China, No. 2 [1869], p. 26). Alcock's statement is fully borne out by the French Foreign Ministry archives which, for the 1860's at least, give far more coverage to missionary difficulties than to any other single subject.

35. Letter of Dec. 27, 1862, Peking, in Launay, *Kouy-tcheou,* II, 151–152.

36. See Cordier, *Histoire des relations,* I, 262, for an appreciation of both Berthemy and Bellonet.

37. Communications of Oct. 19, 1865 and Sept. 3, 1866, in *IWSM:TC,* 35:31a-b, 43:30b–31. See also the Tsungli Yamen's somewhat worried response to the first communication, *ibid.,* 35:26–29.

38. Letter of Mar. 10, 1866, in La Servière, II, 141–142.

39. Presented to the throne on July 18, 1866, in *IWSM:TC,* 42:56b–57.

40. Presented to the throne on Aug. 27, 1866, *ibid.,* 43:29b–37.

41. Along with Li Hung-chang, Lo Ping-chang — an able and responsible official who had rendered great services to the throne in the 1850's and 1860's — seems to have possessed qualities peculiarly irritating to the French. Several years earlier Kleczkowski had placed him in a class with the greatest foreign bête noire of them all, Yeh

Ming-ch'en, and branded him as the arch villain of China. See his note to the Tsungli Yamen, TC 1/10/2 (Nov. 23, 1862), in TYCT (Kweichow-France), p. 3059b; TYCT (Szechwan-France), pp. 2529b–2530b.

42. See La Servière, II, 135ff. See also Chap. 7, n. 12.

43. AEC, 41:263–270b, 275–280b (Jan. 1865–July 1866). Completely out of patience with France's conciliatory policy in China, Bellonet in the months immediately ahead repeatedly urged Paris to adopt a more belligerent line of conduct. See his dispatches of Sept. 1, 1866, in ibid., 42:13b–14 (Aug. 1866–July 1867); Oct. 1, 1866, ibid., 42:27a-b; Dec. 10, 1866, ibid., 42:153a-b.

44. The Chinese documentation on the Korean case is listed in CAPM, pp. 27–28. See also M. Wright, "The Adaptability of Ch'ing Diplomacy: The Case of Korea," The Journal of Asian Studies, 17:363–381 (1958). Since this case took place outside the Chinese cultural context, its diplomatic aspect — which involved the Chinese government because of China's traditional suzerainty over Korea — is all that is touched on here.

45. IWSM:TC, 42:54a-b.

46. M. Wright, "The Adaptability of Ch'ing Diplomacy," p. 377. See also Cordier, Histoire des relations, I, 269–272.

47. Documents diplomatiques, No. 8 (1867), "Exposé des affaires politiques et commerciales," p. 16.

48. Cordier, Histoire des relations, I, 269.

49. See Lallemand's critical appraisal of Bellonet's tactics in his dispatch to Paris, July 2, 1867, in AEC, 42:282b–284b (Aug. 1866–July 1867).

50. Cable of Sept. 10, 1867, in Cordier, Histoire des relations, I, 273. See also C. Martin, "Notes sur le Massacre de Tien-tsin," p. 89.

51. See Cordier, Histoire des relations, I, 341, for a brief biographical note on Rochechouart. See also Julien de Rochechouart, Excursions autour du monde: Pékin et l'intérieur de la Chine (Paris, 1878), pp. 353–355.

52. See his dispatches to Paris of Jan. 30, 1869, in AEC, 45:27–28 (Jan.–Aug. 1869), critical of the Société des Missions Étrangères in general and Faurie in particular; Dec. 1, 1869, ibid., 46:146a-b (Sept.–Dec. 1869), critical of Gennevoise; Apr. 2, 1870, ibid., 47:118b–119 (Jan.–June 1870), critical of the Société des Missions Étrangères in general and of Huc in particular; Apr. 24, 1870, ibid., 47:145a-b, critical of the Société des Missions Étrangères.

53. See, e.g., his dispatches to Paris of Mar. 2, 1869, ibid., 45:34b–35 (Jan.–Aug. 1869); Mar. 4, 1869, ibid., 45:36b; Sept. 5, 1869, ibid., 46:8b–9b (Sept.–Dec. 1869).

54. Rochechouart to Paris, Mar. 18, 1870, ibid., 47:76a-b (Jan.–June 1870).

55. Presented to throne on Mar. 20, 1869, in *IWSM:TC*, 64:33a-b.

56. *Ibid.*, 64:28b, 33b–38b.

57. Cordier, *Histoire des relations,* I, 340–341; Rochechouart, pp. 320–321.

58. Launay, *Kouy-tcheou*, II, 565; Tsungli Yamen memorial of Oct. 9, 1869, *IWSM:TC*, 68:3–4; Yamen memorial, Oct. 17, 1869, *ibid.*, 68:6b.

59. Rochechouart to Paris: dispatches of June 20 and Aug. 21, 1869, in AEC, 45:199, 238a-b (Jan.–Aug. 1869).

60. Tsungli Yamen memorial, Oct. 17, 1869, *IWSM:TC*, 68:7; and French communication, *ibid.*, 68:10b.

61. *Ibid.*, 68:8b–9b. For the French text of Rochechouart's memorial, see AEC, 46:88b–89b (Sept.–Dec. 1869). The reactions of various members of the diplomatic corps in Peking are related by Rochechouart in his dispatch of Oct. 23, 1869, *ibid.*, 46:81–85.

62. *IWSM:TC*, 68:8a-b.

63. Presented to the throne on Nov. 6, 1869, in *ibid.*, 69:5–7.

64. Rochechouart, p. 331. See also his dispatches to Paris of Dec. 1, 1869, in AEC, 46:143b–144 (Sept.–Dec. 1869); Mar. 18, 1870, *ibid.*, 47:75–76b (Jan.–June 1870).

65. Paris to Rochechouart, Dec. 24, 1869, *ibid.*, 46:202a-b (Sept.–Dec. 1869). See also the letter from the minister of marine to the foreign minister, Dec. 23, 1869, *ibid.*, 46:191–192; the foreign minister's reply to the minister of marine, Dec. 24, 1869, *ibid.*, 46:206a-b; Paris' telegram to Rochechouart, Nov. 1, 1869, *ibid.*, 47:72 (Jan.–June 1870).

66. Memorial of Nov. 23, 1869, and edict in response, *IWSM:TC*, 69:25b–28b; Tsungli Yamen communication to French, *ibid.*, 69:28b–33.

67. Joint memorial of Li, Ch'ung-shih, and Wu T'ang, received on Jan. 20, 1870, *ibid.*, 70:27b (dated Jan. 3 in Li Hung-chang, *tsou-kao*, 15:50ff). See also Li's dispatch to the French consul, Jan. 1870, in *Chiao-she yüeh-an tse-yao* (Selected documents on agreements and cases pertaining to foreign intercourse), comp. Wang P'eng-chiu, 8 *chüan* (1900), 3:19ff; and other sources listed in *CAPM*, p. 32.

68. See Li's letters of Dec. 11, 1869, to taotai Cheng P'u-hsiang and taotai T'u Lang-hsien, in Li Hung-chang, *chüan* 9 (*p'eng-liao han-kao*), pp. 27–28; his memorial, received Jan. 20, 1870, *IWSM:TC*, 70:29b–30.

69. See his own rather amorphous account (Rochechouart, p. 329ff); Cordier, *Histoire des relations,* I, 342–344; La Servière, II, 168–171.

70. Li, memorial of Feb. 2, 1870, received by the throne, Feb. 11, in *IWSM:TC*, 71:5–6b. See also Liu's memorial of Feb. 10, 1870, *ibid.*, 71:3b.

71. Paris to Rochechouart, Feb. 17, 1870, in AEC, 47:62b (Jan.–June 1870).

72. Father Pfister, letter of Jan. 6, 1870, MC, 3:94–95 (1870). See also the comment of the Jesuit, Victor Launay, letter of Mar. 16, 1870, in *ibid.*, 3:171.

73. See Wade's communication of Mar. 21, 1870, *IWSM:TC*, 71:34b–36; the Tsungli Yamen memorial and edict of the same date, *ibid.*, 71:32b–34.

74. Cordier, *Histoire des relations*, I, 344.

75. Communications of May 21 and June 4, 1870, in *Ch'ing-chi ko-kuo chao-hui mu-lu*, Fa-kuo, Nos. 252, 256; Tsungli Yamen memorial of May 25, 1870, *IWSM:TC*, 72:12b–13; Launay, *Kouy-tcheou*, II, 575ff. According to the French, the difficulty in removing Tseng was that he had formerly served as Prince Kung's tutor (*ibid.*, II, 576).

76. Tsungli Yamen memorial, May 25, 1870, *IWSM:TC*, 72:11b–13b.

77. M. Wright, *The Last Stand*, p. 147.

78. See, e.g., the following Tsungli Yamen memorials in *IWSM:TC*: June 19, 1862 (6:34–35); Oct. 19, 1865 (35:26–29; very critical of Szechwan local officials); Aug. 27, 1866 (43:29); Nov. 8, 1868 (62:2a-b; coupled with injunction that officials must keep the gentry and populace in line); Oct. 17, 1869 (68:7a-b); Mar. 21, 1870 (71:30, 33a-b; critical of the ineptness of local officials who can neither prevent nor suppress disturbances); May 25, 1870 (72:13b).

79. See, e.g., the Tsungli Yamen memorial of Oct. 18, 1870, *ibid.*, 77:33b–34b, in which the adroit selection of competent local officials by the governors-general and governors is regarded as the crux of the issue.

80. M. Wright, "The Adaptability of Ch'ing Diplomacy," pp. 378–379.

81. See Tsungli Yamen communication to England, May 30, 1869, *IWSM:TC*, 65:28–29b; Yamen memorial of Mar. 21, 1870, *ibid.*, 71:30a-b.

82. Letter to Hunan governor Mao Hung-pin, TC 1/5/20 (June 16, 1862), in TYCT (Hunan-France), p. 2353b.

83. Memorial of Ying-han, Dec. 8, 1869, *IWSM–TC*, 70:5b; memorial of Ma Hsin-i, Jan. 21, 1870, *ibid.*, 70:33a-b, 34a-b. When Count de Rochechouart visited Nanking in late December, Ma told him frankly that it would be unfortunate if he were to insist upon going to Anking while the examinations were still in progress. Rochechouart stopped outside the city on Jan. 2, but did not enter, and left the next day (*ibid.*, 70:36a-b).

84. See the Tsungli Yamen memorial of Aug. 21, 1862. *ibid.*, 8:39b–

40; the joint letter of Lao Ch'ung-kuang and Chang Liang-chi, Dec. 4, 1863, *ibid.*, 21:66a-b; the edicts of Mar. 19, 1864 (*ibid.*, 23:26b) and Apr. 19, 1864 (*ibid.*, 23:40b–41). The edict of Mar. 19 ordered Hunan governor Yün Shih-lin to see to it that T'ien, who at this time had crossed the border into Hunan, was immediately conducted to Szechwan to await punishment. Significantly, the edict warned Yün against divulging these orders to the local gentry of Hunan or to the secretaries in his yamen who were, of course, also Hunanese.

85. See Li's memorial of Jan. 20, 1870, *ibid.*, 70:25; and Chou's letter of 1869 to Prince Kung, in Chou Chia-mei, *chüan* 2 (*cheng-shu*), pp. 31–32.

86. *IWSM–TC,* 12:34–35. Even prior to the circulation of this notice, a Honan censor, Tseng Hsieh-chün, had suggested to the throne the dire consequences that might result from compliance with the French demands (memorial of May 26, 1862, *ibid.*, 5:58b–59).

87. Letter from Liu K'un-i, TC 6/4/14 (May 17, 1867), in TYCT (Kiangsi-France), pp. 5823–5830b.

88. Letter to Tsungli Yamen, July 5, 1870, in Liu K'un-i, V, 2316–2317. See also Liu's letter to the Yamen, TC 5/2/9 (Mar. 25, 1866), in TYCT (Kiangsi-France), pp. 2193–2194b. In his letter of July 1870, Liu made it very clear that it was not the foreigner in general who was detested by the Nanchang gentry and populace, but only the French missionary.

89. M. Chagot, "Préfecture de Loui-tcheou," in A. Launay, *Histoire des missions de Chine: Mission du Kouang-tong, monographies des districts par les missionnaires* (Paris, 1917), pp. 194–195; letters of missionaries involved, in *MC,* 2:90–92, 421 (1869), 3:108–109, 313–314 (1870).

90. Navarro, letter of Nov. 10, 1862, Peking, in *Annales,* 35:431 (1863).

91. Memorial of Hunan governor Yün Shih-lin, Aug. 31, 1864, *IWSM:TC,* 27:42b–43. For "Fang An-chih" (who was Anot's Chinese assistant) read "Fang-lai-yüan" (Navarro) throughout.

92. Navarro's letters of Feb. 2, 1865, and Feb. 16, 1866, in *Annales,* 39:99–104 (1867); letter from Hunan governor Li Han-chang to Tsungli Yamen, TC 4/8/23 (Oct. 12, 1865), in TYCT (Hunan-France), p. 2503b.

93. *MC,* 3:206, 242 (1870).

94. It is worth noting that this "paper war" could, under certain conditions, be directed against foreign elements other than the Christians. A proclamation which emanated from Ichang, Hupeh, in April 1869, was clearly aimed not at the foreign missionary but at the foreign merchant and announced a system of rewards and punishments designed to encourage the inhabitants of the prefecture to resist foreign

commercial encroachment. See Foreign Office Archives, Ser. 682, Vol. 26.

95. See his letter from Wun-chau-fu, Feb. 26, 1868, in *Occasional Papers*, 1–2:147 (1868). A translation of one of these handbills which was specifically directed at Stott is appended to his letter (*ibid.*, 1–2:148–150).

96. For translations of both placards, see Seckinger's letter of May 1868, *MC*, 1:83–84 (1868). The Chinese text of one of them was enclosed in Tseng Kuo-fan's dispatch to the Tsungli Yamen, TC 7/9/21 (Nov. 25, 1868), in TYCT (Kiangsu-France), pp. 5360–5361. Other materials on the Hwaian case, dating from TC 7/10/18 (Dec. 1, 1868) to TC 8/7/5 (Aug. 12, 1869), are in *ibid.*, pp. 5378–5410.

97. The two writings in question were the Hunan manifesto that had first been circulated in 1862 in Nanchang (see Chap. 3), and a pamphlet (which I have not seen) entitled *Hsing-hsin pien*. Languillat claimed that the distribution of the two writings began in the spring of 1868 when 3000 copies were printed in Changchow and passed out to the literati who had assembled there for the government examinations. See Tseng Kuo-fan's letter to the Tsungli Yamen, TC 7/9/2 (Oct. 17, 1868), in TYCT (Kiangsu-France), pp. 5333–5337; and the Yamen's reply to Tseng instructing him to prohibit the two writings, TC 7/9/12 (Oct. 27, 1868), TYCT (Kiangsu-France), pp. 5338–5339.

98. On the notices circulated in Ch'uan-shih-shan, see the memorial of the governor-general of Fukien and Chekiang, Ying-kuei, Mar. 30, 1869, in *IWSM:TC*, 65:4–5. On those circulated in Yangchow and Nanyang, see Chap. 7.

99. A translation of this placard appeared in the *North-China Herald*, Oct. 31, 1868, pp. 529–530. See also *MC*, 1:206 (1868).

100. *Compagnie de Jésus*, pp. 136–137.

101. Letter of Father Ravary, Shanghai, July 1, 1869, in *Annales*, 42:15–16 (1870).

102. See the following documents: the memorial of acting Anhwei governor Ying-han, Dec. 8, 1869, *IWSM:TC*, 70:3b–4b; the Chinese texts of the two communications of acting English minister Wade (Feb. 23 and Mar. 7, 1870) and the report of one of the English missionaries involved (presented with Wade's communication of Feb. 23), in *Wen-hsien ts'ung-pien, chi* 31 (*chiao-an shih-liao*), pp. 4b, 6, 8. La Servière, II, 173, attributes the Anking incident in part to "this campaign of pamphlets."

103. Letter of Father Leboucq, Jan. 18, 1870, in *Annales*, 42:331 (1870). Tseng's troops were reported by Leboucq (*ibid.*) to have amassed in "Pao-lin-fou," evidently an error for Paoting prefecture, which in French romanization would be written "Pao-tin-fou."

104. *MC*, 2:298–299 (1869).

105. *Ibid.*, 2:323.

106. Letter of Father Gennevoise, Shanghai, Dec. 1, 1869, *ibid.*, 3:29–30 (1870). Gennevoise summarizes the contents of the pamphlet.

107. Letter of Father Foucard, Feb. 16, 1870, *ibid.*, 3:249–250.

108. Launay, *Kouy-tcheou*, II, 541–552, summarizes these. See also Wang Wen-chieh, pp. 59–63.

109. The foreign documentation on this case is in Launay, *Kouy-tcheou*, II, 552–589. The Chinese official documentation (chiefly in *IWSM:TC*, *chüan* 68–74, 78, 80, and in Li Hung-chang, *p'eng-liao han-kao*, *chüan* 9) is listed in *CAPM*, pp. 34–37, 202. There is also considerable coverage in TYCT (Kweichow-France).

110. The Chinese text of this manifesto was enclosed by the governor of Kweichow, Tseng Pi-kuang, in his letter to the Tsungli Yamen, TC 8/7/14 (Aug. 21, 1869), in TYCT (Kweichow-France), pp. 7603–7605. For a French translation, see Launay, *Kouy-tcheou*, II, 566–567. See also *MC*, 2:410–411 (1869).

111. This second piece of writing, exposing "a new conspiracy more diabolical than the first," was posted sometime later. "The delicacy of the French language," however, did not permit a translation of this "infernal piece." See letter from Vielmon to Faurie, Nov. 25, 1869, in Launay, *Kouy-tcheou*, II, 567. A brief summary of this last piece is in *MC*, 3:81–82n (1870). It may or may not be the same as a Tsunyi manifesto listing ten evils of the Catholic religion which Tseng Pi-kuang enclosed, along with the first Tsunyi piece, in his letter to the Tsungli Yamen, TC 8/7/14 (Aug. 21, 1869), in TYCT (Kweichow-France), pp. 7591–7595.

112. Early in 1870 the missionary Jean Lebrun was attacked in the vicinity of Tsunyi. In the spring of this year another missionary, Bodinier, was also attacked along with many native Christians. See Launay, *Kouy-tcheou*, II, 575–577; also *MC*, 3:195, 321–322 (1870).

113. For a summary of the Hunan writings see Chap. 3. On their circulation in other places throughout the decade, see Chap. 3, n. 31. In the early months of 1870 an inflammatory writing that appears to have been influenced by the Hunan manifesto was widely posted in Taming prefecture, Chihli. The Taming manifesto was directed primarily at the English and might best be characterized as an antiforeign piece rather than an exclusively anti-Christian one. See Wade's communication to the Tsungli Yamen, TC 9/9/2 (Mar. 3, 1870), in TYCT (Chihli-Britain), pp. 4343–4347; the Yamen's letter to Tseng Kuo-fan, TC 9/2/5 (Mar. 6, 1870), *ibid.*, pp. 4348–4349; and Ch'ung-hou's letter to the Yamen, TC 9/2/25 (Mar. 26, 1870), *ibid.*, pp. 4351–4355b.

114. After discussing the widespread antiforeign incidents of the late sixties, the Jesuit authors of *Compagnie de Jésus* wrote (p. 18): "One sees from all this detail that if there was not perfect agreement

among the mandarins of the eighteen provinces, there was at least a secret signal given, and it is this which must not be forgotten." See also, in this regard, Chap. 9, n. 7.

115. The British consul at Hankow remarked that the hatred of the Hankow literati for Christianity may well have been intensified by Rochechouart's expedition. See "Report on Trade of Hankow for the Year 1870" (Enclosure No. 1 in Consul Caine's dispatch to the Foreign Office, Hankow, May 27, 1871), Foreign Office Archives, Ser. 17, Vol. 597.

116. Prince Ch'un (I-huan) was Prince Kung's half-brother and father of the Kuang-hsü Emperor (r. 1875–1908). See his biography in Hummel, I, 384–386.

117. See Prince Ch'un's memorial, Feb. 17, 1869, in *IWSM:TC,* 64:10b–11; the Tsungli Yamen's memorial, *ibid.,* 64:20–21. Wo-jen's proposals are referred to in the Yamen memorial.

118. In Alcock's dispatch of May 20, 1869, to Clarendon, he observed that the members of the Tsungli Yamen had asked him if Britain would be willing to restrict her missionaries to the port cities. Alcock replied that although his government was fully aware of the disadvantages attending inland missionary activities, as long as missionaries of other nationalities freely enjoyed the privilege of inland residence it would be difficult to apply a different and more restrictive rule to British subjects (*PP,* China, No. 5 [1871], pp. 394–395).

119. See Hsüeh's biography in Hummel, I, 331–332.

120. Hsüeh Fu-ch'eng, *Yung-an ch'üan-chi, chüan* 2 (*wen-pien*), pp. 28b–30b (quotation from p. 28b).

CHAPTER 9. THE TIENTSIN CATASTROPHE

1. The published Chinese documentation on the Tientsin incident (some 275 items, many of which are from *IWSM:TC, chüan* 72–78) is listed in *CAPM,* pp. 38–49, 203–205. For a selection of important documents, see Chiang T'ing-fu, II, 84–104. For an illuminating contemporary Chinese account, see Wang Chih-ch'un, 2:27–33b. British and foreign official documentation is in *PP,* China, No. 1 (1871). For Western summaries, see Morse, Vol. II, Chap. 12, and Cordier, *Histoire des relations,* Vol. I, Chaps. 23–26. (Cordier's is the more complete of the two and is based extensively on French documentary sources. Morse's summary, however, is somewhat more balanced.) Other primary and secondary sources are noted in M. Wright, *The Last Stand,* p. 392n.185, and Fairbank, "Patterns behind the Tientsin Massacre," pp. 480–511. TYCT coverage of the case, consisting of four slim *ts'e* on the involvement of Russia, America, Belgium, and Germany, and nothing at all on that of

France and Britain, is very disappointing. Undoubtedly the bulk of the TYCT materials were at some point either lost, destroyed, or borrowed and not returned. Chinese scholars with whom I have spoken feel that they were possibly deliberately destroyed by the Chinese government.

A book, and a very interesting one at that, could be written on the Tientsin Massacre. I deal only with certain aspects of it here.

2. Morse, II, 241.

3. Joint memorial of Tseng and Ch'ung-hou, July 21, 1870, *Tseng Wen-cheng-kung ch'üan-chi, chüan* 35 (*tsou-kao*), pp. 30b–31b (also in Chiang T'ing-fu, II, 92–93). The most complete and accurate text of this famous memorial is the one in Tseng's collected works. The *IWSM:TC* rendering (73:23–26) is significantly abbreviated. The complete text, with a number of obvious errors, is also in *Huang-ch'ao hsü-ai wen-pien* (Compendium of Ch'ing essays on statecraft), comp. Yü Pao-hsüan, 80 *chüan* (Shanghai, 1903), 54:15–17. For additional Chinese versions, see *CAPM*, p. 40. There is a French translation in Couvreur, pp. 125–137. English versions are in *PP*, China, No. 1 (1871), pp. 126–127, and in *Papers Relating to the Foreign Relations of the United States, 1870*, pp. 370–371.

Tseng, in this memorial, notes the interaction between popular suspicions and inflammatory anti-Christian literature.

4. *Papers Relating to the Foreign Relations of the United States, 1870*, pp. 355–356. See also S. Wells Williams, *The Middle Kingdom: A Survey of the Geography, Government, Literature, Social Life, Arts, and History of the Chinese Empire and Its Inhabitants*, rev. ed., 2 vols. (New York, 1901), II, 700.

5. See Fontanier's letter to Rochechouart, Tien-Tsin, June 21, 1870, in Cordier, *Histoire des relations*, I, 351–352; Ch'ung-hou's memorial of June 23, 1870, *IWSM:TC*, 72:22b–23b (also in Chiang T'ing-fu, II, 85).

6. See Ch'ung-hou's memorial of June 23, 1870, *IWSM:TC*, 72:23b–24 (also in Chiang T'ing-fu, II, 85–86); Cordier, *Histoire des relations*, I, 352–353.

7. Father Pfister, S.J., wrote to Mgr. Languillat on June 16, five days before the Tientsin outbreak: "I am inclined to believe that there exists a plot, and that our enemies would like to extricate themselves from us by exciting the people to drive us out" (*Annales*, 42:417 [1870]). A letter to the *Shanghai Evening Courier*, July 20, 1870, stated: "That the massacre at Tientsin, and the outrages which preceded it in other parts of the Empire are in some way connected, can hardly be questioned by any one well acquainted with these matters" (*The Tientsin Massacre: Being Documents Published*

*in the "Shanghai Evening Courier," from June 16th to Sept. 10th, 1870,* 2nd ed., Shanghai, n.d., pp. 76–77). Another foreigner remarked: "the opinion that the massacres were only a partial realization of a vast programme having for its object the extermination of foreigners in general, is shared by the immense majority, I should almost say, by the totality of European and American residents" (M. le Baron de Hübner, *A Ramble Round the World, 1871,* tr. Lady Herbert, 2 vols., London, 1874, II, 359).

8. See Cordier, *Histoire des relations,* I, 353–357; Morse, II, 246; Ch'ung-hou's memorial of June 23, 1870, *IWSM:TC,* 72:24 (also in Chiang T'ing-fu, II, 86); *Tientsin Massacre, passim.*

9. M. Wright, *The Last Stand,* p. 297.

10. On the disturbances or near disturbances in Kwangping and Chengting, see Tseng Kuo-fan's dispatch to the Tsungli Yamen, TC 9/7/5 (Aug. 1, 1870), in TYCT (Chihli-France), pp. 4367–4369b *et passim,* and the French communication of TC 9/8/1 (Aug. 27, 1870), *ibid.,* pp. 4392–4393b *et passim.* On the rumors and kidnaping charges that were rife in Shanghai, Nanking, and other places, see the correspondence between Kiangsu governor Ting Jih-ch'ang and the Yamen, TC 9/7/4 (July 31, 1870) and TC 9/7/6 (Aug. 2, 1870), in *ibid.* (Kiangsu-France), pp. 5414–5419b. See also Morse, II, 247–248.

11. A letter from J. L. Nevius to the American vice-consul at Tengchow, S. A. Holmes, Aug. 29, 1870, requesting immediate evacuation by gunboat, reveals the tense atmosphere which prevailed among foreigners:

"We have credible grounds for believing that official communications were received here some time back from Tsen-quo-fan [Tseng Kuo-fan], and from the Governor of the Province calling upon the authorities and the people to make arrangements for massacring Foreigners generally some time this fall." See Foreign Office Archives, Ser. 228, Vol. 493.

12. Morse, II, 249–250.

13. Memorials and edicts concerning Chinese military preparations are listed and briefly summarized in M. Wright, *The Last Stand,* pp. 392–393n.191. As the danger of war subsided in September 1870, the frequency of such memorials and edicts declined sharply, virtually ceasing in October.

14. *IWSM:TC,* 72:34–36 (also in Chiang T'ing-fu, II, 87–88).

15. Two memorials of July 12, 1870, *IWSM:TC,* 73:8–11. Sung's antiforeign sentiments were further suggested by his proposal in 1872 that the Foochow Shipyard be abolished (see M. Wright, *The Last Stand,* p. 372n.107).

16. For Li Ju-sung's memorial, see *IWSM:TC,* 73:16b–20 (also

in Chiang T'ing-fu, II, 89–91); for Ch'ang-jun's memorial, see *IWSM:TC*, 73:21–22b; for Tseng's memorial of June 29, see *ibid.*, 72:31–33.

17. Chiang T'ing-fu, II, 92–93. Note also Tseng's admonition to the Tientsin gentry and populace in *Tseng Wen-cheng-kung tsa-chu ch'ao* (Miscellaneous writings of Tseng Kuo-fan), *ts'e* 8 of Chiang Te-chün, comp., *Ch'iu-shih-chai ts'ung-shu* (Compilation of writings from the Ch'iu-shih studio; 1891), pp. 36–37b. Tseng again firmly discounted the rumors about the Catholics in his memorial of July 27, 1870, *IWSM:TC*, 73:44b–45.

18. See Ch'en's biography in Hummel, I, 89–90; a critical summation of his career in Hsüeh Fu-ch'eng, *Yung-an pi-chi* (Miscellaneous notes by Hsüeh Fu-ch'eng; Shanghai, 1917), 2:15–17b; and the discussion of his role in the Tientsin incident in Fairbank, "Patterns behind the Tientsin Massacre," pp. 507ff.

19. Memorial of July 21, 1870, transcribed on July 23, in *IWSM:TC*, 73:26–27; edicts of July 23, *ibid.*, 73:27–28b. See also a fourth edict ordering the governors-general and governors of the coastal provinces to instruct the military commanders under them to prepare their troops for the eventuality of war (*ibid.*, 73:29a-b).

20. See Tseng's two memorials, received on July 27, 1870, *ibid.*, 73:46a-b, 48; Ch'ung-hou's memorial, received on July 26, 1870, *ibid.*, 73:39b–40, and the imperial edicts of the same date, *ibid.*, 73:41, 43.

21. *Ibid.*, 73:33–34. See also Fairbank, "Patterns behind the Tientsin Massacre," pp. 507ff.

22. See Tseng's memorial, received on July 27, *IWSM:TC*, 73: 45b–46.

23. For Hu Yü-yün's memorial, received on Aug. 22, 1870, see *ibid.*, 75:2–3; for Yüan Pao-heng's memorial, received Aug. 26, 1870, see *ibid.*, 75:10–13b, esp. pp. 10b–11.

24. Joint memorial of Tseng and Board of Works president Mao Ch'ang-hsi, received on Aug. 28, 1870, in *ibid.*, 75:15–16. By Sept. 10 Tseng reported the arrests of over 80 suspects, 7 or 8 of whom were deserving of capital punishment (*ibid.*, 76:12b–13).

25. For Tseng's report, see *ibid.*, 76:12b. Li Hung-chang's memorial — expressing the view that 7 or 8 executions were a stern enough warning to would-be violators of the treaties, and that if more persons were put to death it would arouse popular resentment — was received on Sept. 15, 1870 (*ibid.*, 76:20a-b). The main argument in the edict in response to Li's memorial was that since China absolutely refused to administer capital punishment to the two Tientsin officials, the only way to appease the foreigners was to sentence to death a number which approximated more closely the number of foreigners killed (*ibid.*, 76:21a-b).

26. Edict of Oct. 5, 1870, *ibid.*, 77:14b, in response to the Board of Punishments memorial of the same date (*ibid.*, 77:13–14).

27. The Chinese text of this letter is in the Foreign Office Archives, Ser. 228, Vol. 944. The supporting English-language documentation is in *ibid.*, Vol. 505 (Dispatch No. 41, Hankow, Nov. 21, 1871).

28. See "Report on Trade of Hankow for the Year 1870" (Enclosure No. 1 in Consul Caine's dispatch to the Foreign Office, Hankow, May 27, 1871), *ibid.*, Ser. 17, Vol. 597.

29. Letter of July 21, quoted in Li's memorial of Aug. 7, 1870, *IWSM:TC*, 74:3. See also Wang Chih-ch'un, 2:31.

30. Memorial of Sept. 24, 1870, *IWSM:TC*, 76:38b–41b.

31. The edict ordering Tseng to his new post is in *Tung-hua lu* (Tung-hua records), comp. Wang Hsien-ch'ien (Peking, 1887), *chüan* 86 (TC), p. 39b. This interpretation of Tseng's transfer is also adhered to by Fang Chao-ying in his biography of Ma Hsin-i in Hummel, I, 556.

32. The investigation into Ma's murder and the various possible reasons for it are reviewed by Fang Chao-ying in Hummel, I, 555–556.

33. Thus, Medhurst, the British consul at Shanghai, in his report on the assassination, wrote: "it is quite within the compass of possibility that the act has been committed in revenge for the active and determined measures which Ma adopted last year against the military students of Ganking[Anking]-fu with a view to compelling them to produce the two ringleaders in the attack upon the missionary establishments of that city." Medhurst went on to predict that if this hypothesis were true it would "have the effect of causing the well-disposed towards us to lose heart, while it will embolden those amongst the officials and literati who do not favour foreign relations to persist in their efforts to incense the mass of the population against us." Dispatch to Wade, Aug. 25, 1870, *PP*, China, No. 1 (1871), p. 121 (also p. 156). See also La Servière, II, 181; Cordier, *Histoire des relations*, I, 371–372; *MC*, 3:325 (1870).

34. La Servière, II, 162–163.

35. See Ma's memorial of Jan. 21, 1870, *IWSM:TC*, 70:32–36b; see also La Servière, II, 169–170.

36. La Servière, II, 170. For an exultant missionary appraisal of the Dec. 28 proclamation, see *MC*, 3:94–95 (1870). The Chinese texts of these proclamations (one of which was issued jointly with Anhwei governor Ying-han) are in *Cheng-chiao feng-ch'uan*, pp. 18–20; they were also enclosed in Ma Hsin-i's letters to the Tsungli Yamen of TC 8/12/6 (Jan. 7, 1870), in TYCT (Anhwei-France), pp. 5527–5528b, and TC 8/12/23 (Jan. 24, 1870), *ibid.*, p. 5570a-b. For French

translations of the Dec. 28 proclamation, see *MC,* 3:94 (1870); C. Martin, "Notes sur le Massacre de Tien-tsin," pp. 130–131; Cordier, *Histoire des relations,* I, 372. See also *Occasional Papers,* 3–4:404–407 (1870).

37. This account is based primarily on La Servière, II, 172–175. See also the letter (dated June 16, 1870) of one of the Jesuits who witnessed these events, Pfister, in *MC,* 3:291–292 (1870).

38. The provincial treasurer, Mei Ch'i-chao, had good reason to hate foreign missionaries. Early in 1862, after he had persecuted the Christians in his prefecture, the missionary, M. Lemaître, aided by a French gunboat, forced him to make "humiliating reparations." See La Servière, II, 173–174, 180.

39. The portion allotted to the Catholic Church was 130,000 taels. Mgr. Delaplace, on Jan. 3, 1871, announced his unwillingness to accept it. But the sum had already been deposited with the treasurer of the mission at Shanghai, who refused to part with it. See Cordier, *Histoire des relations,* I, 388n.1; Morse, II, 258n.96.

40. See the Tsungli Yamen memorial of Oct. 22, 1870, *IWSM:TC,* 77:42–43b. On the British indemnity, see the Foreign Office Archives, Ser. 17, Vol. 612, *passim.* On punishments meted out to commoners, see the edict to the Grand Secretariat, Oct. 5, 1870, *IWSM:TC,* 77:15; the joint memorial of Tseng Kuo-fan, Li Hung-chang, and Ch'eng-lin, Oct. 9, 1870, *ibid.,* 77:18a-b; the edict of same date, *ibid.,* 77:19b–20; the memorial of Tseng Kuo-fan, Oct. 12, 1870, *ibid.,* 77:22b–23b; the edict of same date, *ibid.,* 77:23b; Cordier, *Histoire des relations,* I, 383–386; Morse, II, 257–258.

41. See the Tsungli Yamen memorial of June 28, 1870, suggesting such a mission to the throne, and the imperial edict in response ordering Ch'ung-hou to go to France, in *IWSM:TC,* 72:29b–31. See also Knight Biggerstaff, "The Ch'ung-hou Mission to France, 1870–1871," *Nankai Social and Economic Quarterly,* 8.3:633–647 (Oct. 1935); Cordier, *Histoire des relations,* Vol. I, Chap. 28.

42. Morse, II, 254–255; Cordier, *Histoire des relations,* I, 374.

43. The chargé, in a bit of somewhat unconvincing diplomatic hairsplitting, later denied that he had issued an ultimatum and asserted that he had merely "insisted on certain points" (*ibid.,* I, 387).

44. Edict of July 21, 1870, *IWSM:TC,* 73:23, and Tseng's memorial of July 27, 1870, *ibid.,* 73:45b. See also Tseng's dispatch to the Tsungli Yamen, TC 7/9/21 (Nov. 5, 1868), in TYCT (Kiangsu-France), p. 5343b; Yamen dispatch to Tseng, TC 7/10/18 (Dec. 1, 1868), *ibid.,* p. 5379a-b.

45. Memorial seen on Sept. 20, *IWSM:TC,* 76:32b–34b.

46. Memorial seen on Sept. 24, *ibid.,* 76:40–41b.

47. *Ibid.,* 77:32–34b.

48. Rochechouart reported to Paris his suspicion that the timing of the Tsungli Yamen circular had been partly conditioned by these reports (Dorland, p. 309).

49. *IWSM:TC*, 82:14–25b. For other Chinese texts of the circular and regulations (presented to the throne on Sept. 1, 1871), see *Chiao-wu chi-yao, chüan 2 (chang-ch'eng)*, pp. 22–35; *Chiao-wu chi-lüeh, chüan 3 (chang-ch'eng)*, pp. 6–15b; and other sources listed in *CAPM*, p. 171.

Full or partial English and/or French translations are in the following sources, among others: *PP*, China, No. 3 (1871), pp. 1–16; *PP*, China, No. 1 (1872), pp. 4–13; Michie, *China and Christianity*, pp. 190–225; Cordier, *Histoire des relations*, I, 417–429; C. Martin, "Notes sur le Massacre de Tien-tsin," pp. 131–138; [Félix Gennevoise], *Le Mémorandum chinois, ou violation du traité de Peking, exposé et réfutation par un missionnaire de Chine* (Rome, 1872), pp. 20–71; Prosper Giquel, *La Politique française en Chine depuis les traités de 1858 et de 1860* (Paris, 1872), pp. 51–70; Launay, *Kouy-tcheou*, III, 23–33; Castaing, pp. 650–656; *MC*, 4:45–48 (1871); *Chinese Recorder and Missionary Journal*, 4:141–148 (1871); *Papers Relating to the Foreign Relations of the United States, 1871*, pp. 99–107.

50. The American reply was communicated by Low to the Chinese government on Mar. 20, 1871, and is in *Papers Relating to the Foreign Relations of the United States, 1871*, pp. 107–110; *PP*, China, No. 1 (1872), pp. 25–28. Low's reply was fully approved by the State Department and was regarded as "wise and judicious" by President Grant (see the dispatch from J. C. B. Davis to Low, Washington, Oct. 19, 1871, *PP*, China, No. 1 [1872], pp. 29–30).

The British reply of June 1871 was transmitted by Wade and is in *PP*, China, No. 1 (1872), pp. 14–17. The Foreign Office, in an independent statement on the Tsungli Yamen proposals, took a stand which, if anything, was even more critical than that taken by Wade. The Office regarded the draft regulations as "cumbrous and impractical" and felt that the treaties already afforded sufficient remedy for what was "the gist of the accusations brought forward," namely, the assumption by missionaries of a protective jurisdiction over Chinese converts (see the dispatch from Earl Granville to Wade, Foreign Office, Aug. 21, 1871, in *PP*, China, No. 1[1872], pp. 18–20).

According to Wade, the Yamen's proposals had originally been secretly submitted to him for preliminary comment. The British representative expressed frank chagrin that before his criticisms could be voiced the Yamen had, in its impatience, circulated the proposals among the other powers. His delay in answering the circular (and the flavor of his answer too?) was therefore attributable "in no small part to the discouragement I have felt at discovering, in this instance, as so frequently before, that my advice, even when asked for, has little chance of being attended to" (*PP*, China, No. 1 [1872], pp. 14–17).

51. The text of the French reply is in Cordier, *Histoire des relations*, I, 430–435. See also Launay, *Kouy-tcheou*, III, 51–54; *MC*, 4:220–222 (1872).

52. Gennevoise, pp. 32–71.

53. The text of his circular letter of May 8, 1871, is in Launay, *Kouy-tcheou*, III, 34–35. The reunion never materialized.

54. Letter to Osouf, Aug. 2, 1871, *ibid.*, III, 35. According to Gennevoise (pp. 72–73), the Chinese circular and regulations were in fact posted in all 18 provinces by the officials.

55. Launay, *Kouy-tcheou*, III, 36.

56. "The Chinese Circular on Foreign Missions," *Chinese Recorder and Missionary Journal*, 4:149 (1871). Severe criticisms were also voiced by A. Williamson and Carstairs Douglas in the pamphlet, *Analysis of the Circular of the Chinese Government* (London, 1871).

57. See, e.g., the series of letters by "W. M." (William Muirhead?) in *Chinese Recorder and Missionary Journal*, 4:158–165 (1871); Williams, II, 708–709.

58. Launay, *Kouy-tcheou*, III, 54-69, gives the chief documents in this exchange.

59. The Chinese Communists' position on the Tientsin Massacre deserves a word in passing. Differences in terminology aside, their judgments concerning the events are, ironically enough, almost identical with those of the more militant conservatives (Li Ju-sung, Prince Ch'un, Sung Chin, etc.) of the time. Fontanier's death at the hands of the "broad masses" was fully justified; the charges of hypnotism and murder in the Catholic orphanage were proved by the investigations; the Ch'ing authorities complied slavishly with the foreigners' demands; and Tseng Kuo-fan — everybody's bête noire in the Tientsin case — by "sacrificing the people in order to fall in with the imperialists" betrayed his country and established the noxious precedent of "using severe punishments to suppress the patriotic people."

The Tientsin Massacre also marks an important turning point in Chinese Communist historiography. Before the Massacre, in the Communist historians' view, the leaders in the struggle against the foreigner were the members of the ruling "feudal landlord class," the officials and gentry. These opposed the missionary movement, first, because the missionaries represented a flagrant attack on their monopoly of political authority and, second, because the tenets of Christianity conflicted at many points with the "feudal tradition" and "feudal conventions and customs" of China. With the Massacre, however, leadership in the struggle gravitated into the hands of the toiling propertyless masses. The aim of the struggle now was "to oppose imperialist aggression" and save the Chinese people; the sharp edge of the struggle was directed not only against the foreign aggressor, but also against the traitorous Ch'ing ruling class. This new trend culminated in the Sino-French War of 1885. See, e.g., Hu Sheng, *Ti-kuo-chu-i yü Chung-kuo cheng-chih* (Imperialism and Chinese politics; Peking, 1952), Chap. 2, esp. pp. 56, 64, 69–70; Li Shih-yüeh, "Chia-wu chan-cheng ch'ien san-shih nien chien fan yang-chiao yüntung" (The movement against the foreign religion during the thirty years prior to the war of 1894), in *Li-shih yen-chiu* (Historical research), No. 6:5, 7, 14 (1958); Hsieh Hsing-yao, "How did imperialism use religion for aggression on China?" *Jen-min jih-pao* (Peking), Apr. 13, 1951, tr. in *Current Background* (American Consulate General, Hong Kong), No. 68, Apr. 18, 1951.

60. Williams, II, 706.

1. The responses of the local officials to these riots are analyzed in Yazawa Toshihiko, "Chōkō ryūiki kyōan no ichi kōsatsu" (The attitude of Chinese officials toward the antiforeign riots in 1891), *Kindai Chūkoku kenkyū*, No. 1:107–136 (Tokyo, 1958).

2. *Chang Wen-hsiang-kung ch'üan-chi* (The collected writings of Chang Chih-tung; 1928), 137:1.

3. See Chester C. Tan, *The Boxer Catastrophe* (New York, 1955), esp. Chaps. 3 and 4.

4. See, e.g., Sung Yü-jen, *T'ai-hsi ko-kuo ts'ai-feng chi* (An account of some of the customs of the Occidental countries), in *Hsiao-fang-hu-chai yü-ti ts'ung-ch'ao, tsai-pu-pien, ts'e* 79. Lao Nai-hsüan's survey of Christianity in China, *Hsi-chiao yüan-liu* (The origins and history of the Western religion), summarizes the reasons why the religion was regarded by Chinese as heterodox (in *Chiao-wu chi-yao, chüan* 4 [*tsa-lu*], pp. 68b–69b).

5. Yang Hsiang-chi, "Yang-chiao so yen to pu ho Hsi-jen ko-chih hsin-li lun" (A discussion of the discrepancies between the statements of the Western religion and the new principles of Western science), in *Huang-ch'ao ching-shih-wen hsü-pien*, 112:11b–12. Yang was branded by the English missionary, Joseph Edkins, as "a full blown materialist." It was Edkins who wrote the synopsis of *Paradise Lost* on which Yang based his information (see his discussion and partial translation of Yang's essay in *Records of the General Conference*, pp. 561–565).

6. See Wang's biography in Hummel, II, 836–839.

7. See Wang's essay on the propagation of Christianity, "Ch'uan-

chiao," in *T'ao-yüan wen-lu wai-pien,* 3:2b–6b. See also H. McAleavy, *Wang T'ao: The Life and Writings of a Displaced Person* (London, 1953), p. 21.

8. Wang T'ao, "Chi Pu-ssu-tieh-ni-chiao" (A note on Positivism), in *T'ao-yüan wen-lu wai-pien,* 6:9b–10b.

9. Michie's book, published in Tientsin in 1891, was translated by Yen Fu under the title *Chih-na chiao-an lun* (A discussion of missionary difficulties in China). I have not seen the translation.

10. Another early example of the use of Western literature to cast aspersions on Christianity is found in Chang Tzu-mu, *Ying-hai lun* (A discussion of the circuit of the seas), in *Hsiao-fang-hu-chai yü-ti ts'ung-ch'ao, ts'e* 60, pp. 483–495. From the Protestant missionary weekly, *Wan-kuo kung-pao* (Review of the times), started by Young J. Allen in 1868, Chang cites certain passages recounting the anti-Catholic measures taken by Bismarck in Germany and by Giovanni Lanza and Quintino Sella in Italy. He also mentions a book by Prime Minister Gladstone which takes the Catholics to task (see Chang, pp. 485b–486, 494).

11. See Kiang Wen-han, *The Chinese Student Movement* (New York, 1948), Chap. 2.

12. See, e.g., Ting Tse-liang, *Li-t'i-mo-t'ai: i-ko tien-hsing ti wei ti-kuo-chu-i fu-wu ti ch'uan-chiao-shih* (Timothy Richard: A typical missionary in the service of imperialism; Peking, 1951); Li Shih-yüeh, "Chia-wu chan-cheng ch'ien san-shih nien chien fan yang-chiao yün-tung," pp. 1–15; and Hsieh Hsing-yao, "How did imperialism use religion for aggression on China?"

13. See the pamphlet printed by the Institute of Modern History, Academia Sinica, *Publications from the Chinese Diplomatic Archives* (Taipei, n.d.), pp. 2–5. During the 1860's alone, the materials in TYCT concerning missionary difficulties total more than 8000 folio pages. For the longer period, the number of volumes (*ts'e*) per subject category is as as follows:

| | |
|---|---|
| Missionary activities and cases (1860–1909) | 910 |
| Diplomatic representation by various powers (1860–1907) | 437 |
| Leaseholds and concessions (1860–1911) | 433 |
| Maritime defense (1860–1911) | 384 |
| Korean relations (1864–1910) | 362 |
| Border affairs and defense (1861–1911) | 230 |
| Establishment, revision, and exchange of treaties with various powers (1860–1911) | 220 |
| Mining affairs in the various provinces (1865–1911) | 86 |

# REFERENCE
# MATTER

# BIBLIOGRAPHY

The works cited below are those that I have examined. For the characters of Chinese titles mentioned in the text or notes but not included here, see Glossary I. Chinese sources that are better known by their titles than by their compilers are listed by title.

AEC: Archives des Affaires Étrangères, Chine, Vols. 38-47. Ministère des Affaires Étrangères; filed in the search room at the Quai d'Orsay, Paris. Ministry correspondence and other documents relating to Sino-French relations from 1863 to 1870.

Ai-ju-lüeh 艾儒略 (Giulio Aleni). Chih-fang wai-chi 職方外紀 (Notes supplementary to the geography of the ancients). 5 chüan; 1623.

Analysis of the Circular of the Chinese Government. London, 1871; 21 pp.

Annales de la propagation de la foi, recueil périodique. Lyon, 1842 et seq.

Anti-Foreign Riots in China in 1891, The. Shanghai, 1892; 304 pp.

Appert, L'abbé, ed. Mgr. Languillat, évêque de Sergiopolis, vicaire apostolique de Kian-nan (Nankin), chanoine d'honneur de la Cathédrale de Chalons. Chalons, 1867; 19 pp.

Archives des Affaires Étrangères, Chine, see AEC.

Bales, W. L. Tso Tsungt'ang, Soldier and Statesman of Old China. Shanghai, 1937; 436 pp.

Banno Masataka 坂野正高. "'Sorigamon' setsuritsu no haikei"總理衙門設立の背景 (The background of the establishment of the Tsungli Yamen); Kokusaiho gaiko zasshi 國際法外交雜誌 (The journal of international law and diplomacy), 51.4:360-402 (Aug. 1952); ibid., 51.5:506-541 (Oct. 1952); ibid., 52.3:89-111 (June 1953).

------"Sorigamon no setsuritsu katei" 總理衙門の設立過程 (The process of establishing the Tsungli Yamen); Kindai Chukoku kenkyu 近代中國研究 (Studies on modern China), No. 1:1-105 (Tokyo, 1958).

Barber, W. T. A.  David Hill, Missionary and Saint.  3rd ed.; London, 1899; 337 pp.

Becker, Émile.  Un Demi-siècle d'apostolat en Chine:  Le révérend père Joseph Gonnet de la Compagnie de Jésus.  3rd ed.; Hokien, 1916; 268 pp.

Biggerstaff, Knight.  "The Tung Wen Kuan," Chinese Social and Political Science Review, 18.3:307-340 (Oct. 1934).

------"The Ch'ung-hou Mission to France, 1870-1871," Nankai Social and Economic Quarterly, 8.3:633-647  (Oct. 1935).

------"The Secret Correspondence of 1867-1868: Views of Leading Chinese Statesmen Regarding the Further Opening of China to Western Influence," The Journal of Modern History, 22:122-136 (1950).

Boardman, Eugene Powers.  Christian Influence upon the Ideology of the Taiping Rebellion, 1851-1864.  Madison, 1952; 188 pp.

Boell, Paul.  Le Protectorat des missions catholiques en Chine et la politique de la France en Extrême-Orient.  Paris, 1899; 71 pp.

Brandt, J. van den.   Les Lazaristes en Chine, 1697-1935: Notes
    biographiques.   Peiping, 1936; 321 pp.

Broullion, Nicolas, S. J.    Mémoire sur l'état actuel de la mission
    du Kiang-nan, 1842-1855, suivi de lettres relatives à
    l'insurrection 1851-1855.   Paris, 1855; 487 pp.


Cady, John F.   The Roots of French Imperialism in Eastern Asia.
    Ithaca, 1954; 322 pp.

CAPM: Chiao-an shih-liao pien-mu 教案史料編目 (A
    bibliography of Chinese source materials dealing with local
    or international cases involving Christian missions), comp.
    Wu Sheng-te 吳盛德 and Ch'en Tseng-hui 陳增輝.
    Peiping, 1941; 227 pp.

Castaing, J. H.   Vie de Mgr. Faurie, membre de la Société des
    Missions Étrangères, vicaire apostolique du Kouy-tcheou
    (Chine).   Paris, 1884; 674 pp.

Cause of the Riots in the Yangtse Valley, The:  A "Complete
    Picture Gallery."  Hankow, 1891.   Contains a reproduction,
    with translation, of the inflammatory pictorial tract,
    Chin-tsun sheng-yü pi-hsieh ch'üan-t'u 謹遵聖諭辟邪
    全圖 (Heresy exposed in respectful obedience to the
    Sacred Edict:  a complete picture gallery); 32 full-page
    colored illustrations; and an English introduction, 27 pp.

Chang Chen-t'ao 張甄陶.   Ao-men t'u-shuo 澳門圖説
    (An illustrated discussion of Macao); in Hsiao-fang-hu-
    chai yü-ti ts'ung-ch'ao, ts'e 48.

------Ao-men hsing-shih lun 澳門形勢論 (A discussion of
    conditions in Macao); in Hsiao-fang-hu-chai yü-ti ts'ung-
    ch'ao, ts'e 48.

------Chih-yü Ao-i lun 制馭澳夷論 (On controlling the barbarians of Macao); in Hsiao-fang-hu-chai yü-ti ts'ung-ch'ao, ts'e 48.

Chang Chih-tung 張之洞 . Chang Wen-hsiang-kung ch'üan-chi 張文襄公全集 (The collected writings of Chang Chih-tung). 229 chüan; 1928.

Chang Chung-li. The Chinese Gentry: Studies on Their Role in Nineteenth-Century Chinese Society. Seattle, 1955; 250 pp.

Chang Ju-lin 張汝霖 and Yin Kuang-jen 印光任 . Ao-men chi-lüeh 澳門紀略 (A brief record of Macao). 2 chüan; Kiangsu, 1880.

Chang Po-hsing 張伯行 . Cheng-i-t'ang chi 正誼堂集 (A collection of writings from the Cheng-i-t'ang). 1876.

Chang Tzu-mu 張自牧 . Ying-hai lun 瀛海論 (A discussion of the circuit of the seas); in Hsiao-fang-hu-chai yü-ti ts'ung-ch'ao, ts'e 60.

Chang Wei-hua 張維華 . "Ming-Ch'ing chien Chung-Hsi ssu-hsiang chih ch'ung-t'u yü ying-hsiang" 明清間中西思想之衝突與影響 (The ideological conflict between China and the West during the late Ming and early Ch'ing, and its effect); Hsüeh-ssu. 學思 (Study and thought), 1.1:19-24 (Jan. 1942).

------"Ming-Ch'ing chien Fo-Yeh chih cheng-pien" 明清間佛耶之爭辯 (The dispute between Buddhists and Christians during the late Ming and early Ch'ing); Hsüeh-ssu, 1.2:12-17 (Jan. 1942).

Chang Yü-shu 張玉書 . Wai-kuo chi 外國紀 (A record of foreign countries); in Chao-tai ts'ung-shu, ts'e 104.

Chao-tai ts'ung-shu 昭代叢書 (Collection of Ch'ing dynasty works).
　　Original comp. Chang Ch'ao 張潮, enlarged by Yang Fu-chi
　　楊復吉 , rev. by Shen Mou-te 沈楙德; 1st ed. 1697, rev.
　　ed. 1833, 1919 Shen-yung-t'ang ed. used here.

Ch'en Ch'i-yüan 陳其元 . Yung-hsien-chai pi-chi 庸閒齋筆
　　記 (Miscellaneous notes from the Yung-hsien studio).
　　12 chüan; Shanghai, 1925.

Ch'en, Kenneth. "Hai-lu: Forerunner of Chinese Travel Accounts
　　of Western Countries," Monumenta Serica, 7:208-226
　　(1942).

------"Anti-Buddhist Propaganda during the Nan-ch'ao,"
　　Harvard Journal of Asiatic Studies, 15:166-192 (1952).

Ch'en Lun-chiung 陳倫炯. Hai-kuo wen-chien lu 海國聞見
　　錄 (A record of things seen and heard among the maritime
　　nations; 1st preface 1730); in Chao-tai ts'ung-shu, ts'e 55.

Ch'en Shou-i 陳受頤 . "Ming-mo Ch'ing-ch'u Yeh-su-hui-shih
　　ti ju-chiao-kuan chi ch'i fan-ying" 明末清初耶穌會士
　　的儒教觀及其反應　　(The Jesuits' conception
　　of Confucianism in the late Ming and early Ch'ing and its
　　repercussions); Kuo-hsüeh chi-k'an 國學季刊 (The
　　journal of Sinological studies), 5.2:1-64 (1935).

Cheng-chiao feng-ch'uan 正教奉傳 (The propagation of the
　　Orthodox [i.e., Roman Catholic] religion), comp.
　　Huang Po-lu 黄伯祿 . 2nd ed.; 2 vols.; Shanghai, 1908.

Cheng-chiao feng-pao 正教奉褒 (In homage to the Orthodox
　　[i.e., Roman Catholic] religion), comp. Huang Po-lu 黄
　　伯祿 . 3rd ed.; Shanghai, 1904.

Chiang-hsi t'ung-chih 江西通志 (A general gazetteer of Kiangsi),
    comp. Li Wen-min 李文敏 et al. 180 chüan; 1881.

Chiang-shang chien-sou, see Hsia Hsieh.

Chiang Te-ching 蔣德璟. "P'o-hsieh chi-hsü" 破邪集序
    (A preface to the P'o-hsieh chi); P'o-hsieh chi, 3:1-3.

Chiang T'ing-fu 蔣廷黻, comp.   Chin-tai Chung-kuo wai-chiao
    shih tzu-liao chi-yao 近代中國外交史資料輯要
    (Selected materials on modern Chinese diplomatic history).
    2nd ed.; 2 vols.; Taipei, 1959.

Chiao-an shih-liao pien-mu, see CAPM.

Chiao-she yüeh-an tse-yao 交涉約案摘要 (Selected documents
    on agreements and cases pertaining to foreign intercourse),
    comp. Wang P'eng-chiu 王鵬九. 8 chüan; 1900.

Chiao-wu chi-lüeh 教務紀略 (A summary record of church
    affairs).   Chüan-shou and 4 chüan; pub. by order of
    Governor-General Chou Fu 周馥, Anhwei, 1905.

Chiao-wu chi-yao 教務輯要 (Selected documents on church
    affairs), comp. Hsü Chia-kan 徐家幹. 4 chüan; Hupeh,
    1898.

Chinese Recorder and Missionary Journal, The.   Foochow,
    1868-1872; Shanghai, 1874 et seq.

Ch'ing-chi chiao-an shih-liao 清季教案史料 (Historical
    materials on missionary cases in the late Ch'ing), Vol. 1.
    Peiping, 1937.

Ch'ing-chi ko-kuo chao-hui mu-lu 清季各國照會目錄
    (A catalogue of the communications sent by the various
    nations during the late Ch'ing). 4 ts'e; Peiping, 1935.

Ch'ing-shih kao 清史稿 (Draft history of the Ch'ing dynasty), comp. Chao Erh-hsün 趙爾巽 et al. 2 vols.; Shanghai, 1942.

Ch'ing-wen-hui 清文彙 (Collection of Ch'ing literature), comp. Chu Hsiu-hsia 祝秀俠 and Yüan Shuai-nan 袁帥南. Taipei, 1960; 1890 pp.

Chou Chia-mei 周家楣. Ch'i-pu-fu-chai ch'üan-chi 期不負齋全集 (A collection of writings from the Ch'i-pu-fu studio). 8 ts'e; Honan, 1895.

Ch'ou-pan i-wu shih-mo, see IWSM.

Ch'ü T'ung-tsu. Local Government in China under the Ch'ing. Cambridge, Mass., 1962; 360 + 50 pp.

Ch'üan Han-sheng 全漢昇. "Ming-mo Ch'ing-ch'u fan-tui hsi-yang wen-hua ti yen-lun" 明末清初反對西洋文化的言論 (Criticisms of Western culture voiced during the late Ming and early Ch'ing); in Li Ting-i 李定一 et al., eds., Chung-kuo chin-tai-shih lun-ts'ung 中國近代史論叢 (Collection of essays on modern Chinese history), 1st ser., II, 227-235. Taipei, 1956.

Cohen, Paul A. "Missionary Approaches: Hudson Taylor and Timothy Richard," Papers on China, 11:29-62. Harvard University, East Asian Research Center, 1957.

------"The Hunan-Kiangsi Anti-Missionary Incidents of 1862," Papers on China, 12:1-27 (1958).

Cole, H. M. "Origins of the French Protectorate over Catholic Missions in China," The American Journal of International Law, 34:473-491 (1940).

Compagnie de Jésus en Chine, La: Le Kiang-nan en 1869, relation historique et descriptive par les missionnaires. Paris, preface dated 1869; 317 pp.

Cordier, Henri. Histoire des relations de la Chine avec les puissances occidentales, 1860-1902. 3 vols.; Paris, 1901-1902.

------L'Expédition de Chine de 1857-58: Histoire diplomatique, notes et documents. Paris, 1905; 478 pp.

------L'Expédition de Chine de 1860: Histoire diplomatique, notes et documents. Paris, 1906; 460 pp.

Couling, Samuel. The Encyclopaedia Sinica. 2 vols.; Shanghai, 1917.

Couvreur, S., S.J., tr. and comp. Choix de documents: Lettres officielles, proclamations, édits, mémoriaux, inscriptions... texte chinois avec traduction en francais et en latin. 3rd ed.; Hokien, Chihli, 1901; 560 pp.


Death Blow to Corrupt Doctrines: A Plain Statement of Facts. Tr. of the Pi-hsieh shih-lu by Tengchow missionaries. Shanghai, 1870.

Documents diplomatiques, 1867, 1869. Ministère des Affaires Étrangères.

Dorland, A.A. "A Preliminary Study of the Role of the French Protectorate of Roman Catholic Missions in Sino-French Diplomatic Relations." M.A. thesis, Cornell University, 1951.

Duus, Peter. "Science and Salvation in China: The Life and Work of W.A.P. Martin," Papers on China, 10:97-127 (1956).

Eastman, Lloyd, "The Kwangtung Anti-Foreign Disturbances during
the Sino-French War," Papers on China, 13:1-31 (1959).

Fairbank, John K.   Trade and Diplomacy on the China Coast:
The Opening of the Treaty Ports, 1842-1854.  2 vols.;
Cambridge, Mass., 1953.

------"Patterns behind the Tientsin Massacre," Harvard Journal
of Asiatic Studies, 20:480-511 (1957).

Fairbank, John K. and Teng Ssu-yü.  Ch'ing Administration: Three
Studies. Cambridge, Mass., 1960; 218 pp.

Fang Hao 方豪 .  "Ch'ing-tai chin-i T'ien-chu-chiao so shou
Jih-pen chih ying-hsiang" 清代禁抑天主教所受
日本之影響 (Japanese influence on the proscription
of Catholicism during the Ch'ing dynasty); Fang Hao wen-lu
方豪文錄 (Essays of Fang Hao), pp. 47-65.  Shanghai,
1948.

Feng Ch'eng-chün 馮承鈞.  Hai-lu chu 海錄注 (An annotation
of the Hai-lu).  Peking, 1955.

Ferm, Vergilius, ed.   An Encyclopedia of Religion.  New York,
1945; 844 pp.

Foreign Office Archives.   Foreign Office correspondence and
other documents, in both Chinese and English, relating
to Anglo-Chinese relations particularly during the late
1860's and early 1870's.  Filed in Public Record Office,
London.

Frankel, Hans H., comp.   Catalogue of Translations from the
Chinese Dynastic Histories for the Period 220-960.
Berkeley, 1957; 295 pp.

[Gennevoise, Félix]. Le Mémorandum chinois, ou violation du
traité de Peking, exposé et réfutation par un missionnaire
de Chine. Rome, 1872.

Giquel, Prosper. La Politique française en Chine depuis les
traités de 1858 et de 1860. Paris, 1872.

Groot, J.J.M. de. Sectarianism and Religious Persecution in
China: A Page in the History of Religions. 2 vols.;
Amsterdam, 1903-1904.


Hansard's Parliamentary Debates, 3rd ser., Vol. 194 (1869).

Hart, Robert. "These from the Land of Sinim": Essays on the
Chinese Question. London, 1901; 254 pp.

Hsia Hsieh 夏燮 (pseud. Chiang-shang chien-sou 江上蹇叟 ).
Chung-Hsi chi-shih 中西紀事 (A record of Sino-Western
affairs). 24 chüan; first preface dated 1851, second preface
to rev. ed. 1859, last preface 1865, title page 1868.
Chüan 2, "Hua-Hsia chih-chien" 猾夏之漸 (The gradual
deterioration of China); chüan 21, "Chiang-Ch'u ch'u-chiao"
江楚黜教 (The expulsion of Catholicism from Kiangsi
and Hunan).

Hsiao-fang-hu-chai yü-ti ts'ung-ch'ao 小方壺齋輿地叢鈔
(Collection of geographical works from the Hsiao-fang-hu
studio), comp. Wang Hsi-ch'i 王錫祺 84 ts'e;
1877-1897.

Hsiao Kung-chuan. Rural China: Imperial Control in the Nineteenth
Century. Seattle, 1960; 783 pp.

Hsieh Hsing-yao. "How did imperialism use religion for
aggression on China?" Jen-min jih-pao 人民日報

(Peking), Apr. 13, 1951, tr. in Current Background, No. 68, Apr. 18, 1951 (American Consulate General, Hong Kong).

Hsien Yü-ch'ing 冼玉清. "Liang T'ing-nan chu-shu lu-yao" 梁廷柟著述錄要(On the writings of Liang T'ing-nan); Ling-nan hsüeh-pao 嶺南學報 (Lingnan journal), 4.1:119-154 (1935).

Hsin-chien hsien-chih 新建縣志 (The Sinkien hsien gazetteer), comp. Tu Yu-t'ang 杜友棠, Ch'eng P'ei 承霈, et al. 99 chüan; 1871.

Hsü Chi-yü 徐繼畬. Ying-huan chih-lüeh 瀛環志略 (A brief description of the oceans' circuit). 10 chüan; 1850 (preface dated 1848).

Hsü, Immanuel C.Y. China's Entrance into the Family of Nations: The Diplomatic Phase, 1858-1880. Cambridge, Mass., 1960; 255 pp.

Hsü pei-chuan chi 續碑傳集 (Supplementary collection of tombstone biographies), comp. Miao Ch'üan-sun 繆荃孫. 86 chüan; 1893.

Hsüeh Fu-ch'eng 薛福成. Yung-an ch'üan-chi 庸盦全集 (Collected works of Hsüeh Fu-ch'eng). 21 chüan; Tsui-liu-t'ang ed., Shanghai, 1897.

------Yung-an pi-chi 庸盦筆記 (Miscellaneous notes by Hsüeh Fu-ch'eng). 6 chüan; Shanghai, 1917.

Hu Sheng 胡繩. Ti-kuo-chu-i yü Chung-kuo cheng-chih 帝國主義與中國政治 (Imperialism and Chinese politics). Peking, 1952; 222 pp.

Huang-ch'ao cheng-tien lei-tsuan 皇朝政典類纂 (Classified
    compendium of Ch'ing documents on administrative affairs),
    comp. Hsi Yü-fu 席裕福. 500 chüan; Shanghai, 1903.
Huang-ch'ao ching-shih-wen hsü-pien 皇朝經世文續編
    (Supplement to the Huang-ch'ao ching-shih-wen), comp.
    Ko Shih-chün 葛士濬. 120 chüan; Shanghai, 1888.
Huang-ch'ao hsü-ai wen-pien 皇朝蓍艾文編 (Compendium of
    Ch'ing essays on statecraft), comp. Yü Pao-hsüan 于寶軒.
    80 chüan; Shanghai, 1903.
Huang-ch'ao hsü wen-hsien t'ung-k'ao 皇朝續文獻通考
    (Supplement to the Ch'ing Wen-hsien t'ung-k'ao), comp.
    Liu Chin-tsao 劉錦藻. 320 chüan; 1905.
Huang Chen 黃貞. "Ch'ing Yen Chuang-ch'i hsien-sheng p'i
    T'ien-chu-chiao shu" 請顏壯其先生闢天主教書
    (A letter to Mr. Yen Chuang-ch'i refuting Catholicism);
    P'o-hsieh chi, 3:8-21b.
Huang Tsung-hsi 黃宗羲. P'o-hsieh lun 破邪論 (A discourse
    on the refutation of heterodoxy); Chao-tai ts'ung-shu, ts'e 66,
    chüan 15.
Huang Wen-tao 黃問道. "P'i-hsieh chieh" 闢邪解 (A commentary
    on the refutation of heterodoxy); P'o-hsieh chi, 5:19-22.
Huang Yü-pien 黃育楩. P'o-hsieh hsiang-pien 破邪詳辯
    (A detailed refutation of heterodoxy). Chüan-shou and 4
    chüan; Kingchow, Hupeh, 1883 (prefaces dated 1834 and
    1839).
Hübner, M. le Baron de. A Ramble Round the World, 1871, tr.
    Lady Herbert. 2 vols.; London, 1874.

360

Hummel, Arthur W., ed.  Eminent Chinese of the Ch'ing Period.
2 vols.; Washington, D.C., 1943, 1944.

Hunan Tracts of China, Which Produced the Anti-Christian and
Anti-Foreign Riots of 1891, Analysed by a Shocked Friend,
The.  Shanghai, preface dated 1892; 6 pp.

IWSM: Ch'ou-pan i-wu shih-mo 籌辦夷務始末  (The complete
account of our management of barbarian affairs).  Peiping,
1930.  Tao-kuang period, 80 chüan;  Hsien-feng period,
80 chüan; T'ung-chih period, 100 chüan.

Kiang Wen-han.  The Chinese Student Movement.  New York,
1948; 176 pp.

Kuo Sung-tao 郭嵩燾 .  Yang-chih shu-wu ch'üan-chi 養知書
屋全集 (The collected works of Kuo Sung-tao).
55 chüan; 1892.

Lao Nai-hsüan 勞乃宣 .  Hsi-chiao yüan-liu 西教源流
(The origins and history of the Western religion); Chiao-wu
chi-yao, chüan 4 (tsa-lu), pp. 54-70b.

La Servière, J. de, S.J.  Histoire de la mission du Kiang-nan:
Jésuites de la province de France (Paris) (1840-1899).
Zikawei, Shanghai, preface dated 1914.  Of three projected
volumes only two were published, covering 1840-1878.

Latourette, Kenneth S.  A History of Christian Missions in China.
New York, 1929; 930 pp.

Launay, Adrien.  Histoire des missions de Chine: Mission du
Kouang-si (together with Supplément).  Paris, 1903;
447 + 38 pp.

------Histoire des missions de Chine: Mission du Kouy-tcheou. 3 vols.; Paris, 1907-1908.

------Histoire des missions de Chine: Mission du Kouang-tong, monographies des districts par les missionnaires. Paris, 1917; 207 pp.

Leboucq, François-Xavier [Prosper]. Monseigneur Édouard Dubar de la Compagnie de Jésus, évêque de Canathe, et la mission catholique du Tche-ly-sud-est, en Chine. Paris, preface dated 1879; 491 pp.

Legge, James. The Chinese Classics, Vols. I and II. Rev. 2nd ed.; Oxford, 1893-1895.

Li Hung-chang 李鴻章. Li Wen-chung-kung ch'üan-chi 李文忠公全集 (The collected works of Li Hung-chang). 165 chüan; Shanghai, 1921.

Li Shih-yüeh 李時岳. "Chia-wu chan-cheng ch'ien san-shih nien chien fan yang-chiao yün-tung" 甲午戰爭前三十年間反洋教運動 (The movement against the foreign religion during the thirty years prior to the war of 1894); Li-shih yen-chiu 歷史研究 (Historical research), No. 6:1-15 (1958).

Li Ting-i 李定一. Chung-kuo chin-tai shih 中國近代史 (Modern Chinese history). 7th ed.; Taipei, 1959; 266 pp.

Liang Ch'i-ch'ao 梁啟超. Wu-hsü cheng-pien chi 戊戌政變記 (The coup d'état of 1898). Chung-hua shu-chü ed., 1954.

Lin Ch'i-lu 林啟陸. "Chu-i lun-lüeh" 誅夷論略 (A short discourse on the suppression of the barbarians); P'o-hsieh chi, 6:1-7.

Ling T'i-an 凌惕安. Hsien-T'ung Kuei-chou chün-shih shih
咸同貴州軍事史 (A history of military affairs in
Kweichow during the Hsien-feng and T'ung-chih periods).
8 ts'e; Shanghai, 1932.

Liu K'un-i 劉坤一. Liu K'un-i i-chi 劉坤一遺集 (The
collected works of Liu K'un-i). 6 vols.; Peking, 1959.


MacGillivray, D., ed. A Century of Protestant Missions in China
(1807-1907), Being the Centenary Conference Historical
Volume. Shanghai, 1907; 677 pp.

Macgowan, John. "Remarks on the Social Life and Religious Ideas
of the Chinese," in D. Matheson, Narrative of the Mission
to China of the English Presbyterian Church. 2nd ed.;
London, 1866; 151 pp.

Martin, C. "Notes sur le Massacre de Tien-tsin," in H. Cordier,
ed., Revue de l'Extrême-Orient, 2:89-138 (Paris, 1887).

Martin, W. A. P. A Cycle of Cathay, or China, South and North,
with Personal Reminiscences. New York, 1896; 464 pp.

Mayers, William Frederick, ed. Treaties between the Empire of
China and Foreign Powers, together with Regulations for the
Conduct of Foreign Trade.... Shanghai, 1877; 225 pp.

MC: Les Missions catholiques: Bulletin hebdomadaire illustré de
l'Oeuvre de la Propagation de la Foi. Lyon, 1868 et seq.

McAleavy, H. Wang T'ao: The Life and Writings of a Displaced
Person. London, 1953; 40 pp.

Meng, S. M. The Tsungli Yamen: Its Organization and Functions.
Cambridge, Mass., 1962.

[Meynard], André-Marie. Missions dominicaines dans l'Extrême-
Orient. 2 vols.; Paris, 1865.

Michie, Alexander. Missionaries in China. Tientsin, 1891; 63 pp.

------China and Christianity. Boston, 1900; 232 pp.

------The Englishman in China during the Victorian Era, As Illus-
trated in the Career of Sir Rutherford Alcock, K.C.B.,
D.C.L., Many Years Consul and Minister in China and
Japan. 2 vols.; Edinburgh and London, 1900.

Ming-shih 明史 (History of the Ming dynasty). 336 chüan;
Shanghai, 1933.

Missions catholiques, Les: Bulletin hebdomadaire illustré de
L'Oeuvre de la Propagation de la Foi, see MC.

Moidrey, Joseph de, S.J. La Hiérarchie catholique en Chine,
en Corée, et au Japon (1307-1914) (Variétés sinologiques,
No. 38). Zikawei, 1914; 301 pp.

------Confesseurs de la foi en Chine, 1784-1862. Shanghai, 1935;
210 pp.

Morse, Hosea B. The International Relations of the Chinese
Empire. 3 vols.; London, 1910-1918.

Muirhead, William. China and the Gospel. London, 1870; 305 pp.


"Na-huo hsieh-tang hou kao-shih" 拿獲邪黨後告示 (The
proclamation issued after the arrest of the heterodox
parties); P'o-hsieh chi, 2:21-24.

Nan-ch'ang hsien-chih 南昌縣志 (The Nanchang hsien gazetteer),
comp. Liu Yü-hsün 劉于潯 and Yen I 燕毅. 36 chüan;
1870.

Nan-huai-jen 南懷仁 (Ferdinand Verbiest). K'un-yü t'u-shuo 坤
輿圖說 (An illustrated discussion of the earth); in Ch'ien
Hsi-tso 錢熙祚 and sons, comps., Chih-hai 指海
(Compendium of writings of various periods), ts'e 91. 1936 ed.

New York Times, The. 1959.

North-China Herald and Supreme Court and Consular Gazette, The.
Shanghai, 1868-1870.

Occasional Papers of the "China Inland Mission," The, Vols. I-IV
(Jan. 1866-May 1870). Publ. as bound book, London, 1872.

Papers Relating to the Foreign Relations of the United States,
1870-71. Washington, D.C.: Department of State.

Parliamentary Papers, see PP.

Pelcovits, Nathan A.    Old China Hands and the Foreign Office.
New York, 1948; 349 pp.

P'eng Yü-lin 彭玉麟.  P'eng Kang-chih-kung tsou-kao 彭剛
直公奏稿 (The memorials of P'eng Yü-lin).  8 chüan;
1891.

PHCS:  Pi-hsieh chi-shih 辟邪紀實 (A record of facts to ward
off heterodoxy).  1871 ed. used here (first preface dated
1861, second preface and one section dated 1862), 4 chüan
in 1 ts'e; I have also seen an 1886 ed. in the Toyo Bunko,
Tokyo.  Sections cited:

"T'ien-chu hsieh-chiao chi-shuo" 天主邪教集説
(A compilation of the teachings of the heterodox
Christian religion).

"T'ien-chu hsieh-chiao ju Chung-kuo k'ao-lüeh" 天主
邪教入中國考略    (A brief examination
of the entrance of the heterodox Christian religion
into China).

"P'i-po hsieh-shuo" 批駁邪説(A critique of
heterodox doctrines).

365

"An-cheng"案證(Evidence from cases).

"Pi-hsieh ko" 辟邪歌(A ballad to ward off heterodoxy).

"T'uan-fang-fa"團防法 (Measures for militia defense).

Pi-hsieh chi-shih, see PHCS.

Pi-hsieh shih-lu 辟邪實錄 (A true record to ward off heterodoxy).
N. d. ; 30 folio pp. ; I have also seen in Japan a photostatic copy
of an ed. dated 1870.

Playfair, G. M. H.   The Cities and Towns of China: A Geographical
Dictionary.  2nd ed.; Shanghai, 1910; 582+76 pp.

P'o-hsieh chi 石破邪集 (An anthology of writings exposing heterodoxy),
comp. Hsü Ch'ang-chih 徐昌治.  8 chüan; 1855 Japanese
block-print ed. (preface dated 1640).

PP:  Parliamentary Papers (Blue Books).
Memorials Addressed by Chambers of Commerce in China
to the British Minister at Peking, on the Subject of
the Revision of the Treaty of Tien-tsin, Presented to the
House of Commons by Command of Her Majesty, in
Pursuance of the Address Dated February 24, 1868.

China, No. 1 (1869).  Correspondence Respecting the
Relations between Great Britain and China.

China, No. 2 (1869).  Correspondence Respecting the
Attack on British Protestant Missionaries at Yang-chow-
foo, August 1868.

China, No. 3 (1869).  Correspondence Respecting Missionary
Disturbances at Che-foo and Taiwan (Formosa).

China, No. 8 (1869).  Correspondence with Sir Rutherford
Alcock Respecting Missionaries at Hankow, and the State
of Affairs at Various Ports in China.

China, No. 9 (1869). Papers Respecting the Proceedings of
Her Majesty's Ship "Janus" at Sharp Peak Island, near
Foo-chow-foo.

China, No. 10 (1869). Further Correspondence Respecting
the Attack on British Protestant Missionaries at Yang-
chow-foo, August 1868.

China, No. 9 (1870). Correspondence Respecting Inland
Residence of British Missionaries in China.

China, No. 1 (1871). Papers Relating to the Massacre of
Europeans at Tien-tsin on the 21st June, 1870.

China, No. 3 (1871). Circular of the Chinese Government
Communicated by the French Chargé d'Affaires.

China, No. 5 (1871). Correspondence Respecting the
Revision of the Treaty of Tien-tsin.

China, No. 1 (1872). Correspondence Respecting the
Circular of the Chinese Government of February 9, 1871,
Relating to Missionaries.

Publications from the Chinese Diplomatic Archives. Taipei, n.d.;
18 pp.


Records of the General Conference of the Protestant Missionaries
of China Held at Shanghai, May 7-20, 1890. Shanghai, 1890;
744 pp.

Reischauer, Edwin O. Ennin's Travels in T'ang China. New York,
1955; 341 pp.

Richard, Timothy. The New Testament of Higher Buddhism.
Edinburgh, 1910; 275 pp.

Rochechouart, Count Julien de. Excursions autour du monde:
Pékin et l'intérieur de la Chine. Paris, 1878; 355 pp.

Rockwell, Dorothy Ann. "The Compilation of Governor Hsü's Ying-huan chih-lueh," Papers on China, 11:1-28 (1957).

Rosso, Antonio Sisto. Apostolic Legations to China of the Eighteenth Century. South Pasadena, 1948; 502 pp.

Rowbotham, Arnold H. Missionary and Mandarin: The Jesuits at the Court of China. Berkeley, 1942; 374 pp.

Sheng-ch'ao p'o-hsieh chi, see P'o-hsieh chi.

Sheng-yü kuang-hsün chih-chieh 聖諭廣訓直解 (A colloquial explanation of the Sacred Edict), comp. Wang Yu-p'u 王又樸. 2 chüan; n.d.

Shih Ju-ch'un 釋如純. "T'ien-hsüeh ch'u-p'i" 天學初闢 (A preliminary refutation of the doctrines of Catholicism); P'o-hsieh chi, 8:26-41b.

Shih T'ung-jung 釋通容. "Yüan-tao p'i-hsieh shuo" 原道闢邪說 (Using the original way to refute heterodoxy); P'o-hsieh chi, 8:3-20.

Ssu-k'u ch'üan-shu tsung-mu 四庫全書總目 (An annotated bibliography of books in the Ssu-k'u ch'üan-shu), comp. Chi Yün 紀昀 et al. 16 vols.; I-wen yin-shu-kuan photo-lithographic ed., Taipei, n.d.

Sung Yü-jen 宋育仁. T'ai-hsi ko-kuo ts'ai-feng chi 泰西各國采風紀 (An account of some of the customs of the Occidental countries); in Hsiao-fang-hu-chai yü-ti ts'ung-ch'ao, second supplement, ts'e 79.

Tan, Chester C. The Boxer Catastrophe. New York, 1955; 276 pp.

Taylor, Dr. and Mrs. Howard. Hudson Taylor and the China Inland
Mission: The Growth of a Work of God. 7th ed.; London,
1925; 640 pp.

Taylor, J. Hudson. China's Spiritual Need and Claims. 5th ed.;
London, 1884.

Teng Ssu-yü and John K. Fairbank. China's Response to the West:
A Documentary Survey, 1839-1923. Cambridge, Mass.,
1954; 296 pp.

Thompson, R. Wardlaw. Griffith John: The Story of Fifty Years
in China. London, 1908; 552 pp.

Tien, H.C., Ronald Hsia and Peter Penn. Gazetteer of China.
Hong Kong, 1961; 237 pp.

Tientsin Massacre, The: Being Documents Published in the
Shanghai Evening Courier, from June 16th to Sept. 10th,
1870. 2nd ed.; Shanghai, n.d.; 129 pp.

Ting Tse-liang 丁則良. Li-t'i-mo-t'ai: i-ko tien-hsing ti
wei ti-kuo-chu-i fu-wu ti ch'uan-chiao-shih 李提摩太
一個典型的為帝國主義服務的傳教士
(Timothy Richard: a typical missionary in the service
of imperialism). Peking, 1951; 66 pp.

Tobar, Jérôme, S.J., tr. and comp. Kiao-ou ki-lio; "Résumé
des affaires religieuses" publié par ordre de S. Exc.
Tcheou Fou: traduction, commentaire et documents
diplomatiques, appendices contenant les plus récentes
décisions (Variétés sinologiques, No. 47). Shanghai,
1917; 252 pp.

Tseng Kuo-fan 曾國藩. Tseng Wen-cheng-kung ch'uan-chi
曾文正公全集 (The collected writings of Tseng Kuo-fan).
174 chüan; 1876.

------Tseng Wen-cheng-kung tsa-chu ch'ao 曾文正公雜著鈔
(Miscellaneous writings of Tseng Kuo-fan); in Chiang Te-chün 蔣
德鈞, comp., Ch'iu-shih-chai ts'ung-shu 求實齋叢
書 (Compilation of writings from the Ch'iu-shih studio),
ts'e 8. 1891.

Tso Tsung-t'ang 左宗棠. Tso Wen-hsiang-kung ch'üan-chi 左文
襄公全集 (The collected writings of Tso Tsung-t'ang).
100 chüan; 1890.

Tsung-li ko-kuo shih-wu ya-men ch'ing-tang, see TYCT.

Tung Han 董含. Ch'un-hsiang chui-pi 蓴鄉贅筆 (Scribblings
by Tung Han); in Wu Chen-fang 吳震方, ed., Shuo-ling
說鈴 (Collection of miscellaneous writings of early
Ch'ing authors), hou-chi, chüan 20. 1702-1705.

Tung-hua lu 東華錄 (Tung-hua records), comp. Wang Hsien-
ch'ien 王先謙. 252 ts'e (including supplementary section
on T'ung-chih period); Peking, 1887.

TYCT: Tsung-li ko-kuo shih-wu ya-men ch'ing-tang 總理各國
事務衙門清檔 (The archives of the Tsungli Yamen:
clean files), portion dealing with missionary difficulties
and affairs. Deposited in the Institute of Modern History,
Academia Sinica, Taipei. These materials are arranged
by province and then by the foreign power concerned. The
section covering 1860 to 1870 is being prepared for
publication.


Waley, Arthur. The Analects of Confucius. 3rd ed.; London,
1949; 268 pp.

Wang Chih-ch'un 王之春. Fang-hai chi-lüeh 防海紀略
(A brief record of maritime defense). 2 chüan; 1880.

370

Wang T'ao 王韜 .    T'ao-yüan wen-lu wai-pien 韜園文錄外
編 (Supplement to the T'ao-yüan wen-lu).    10 chüan;
Hong Kong, 1883.    Essays cited:
"Chi Pu-ssu-tieh-ni-chiao" 紀卜斯迭尼教 (A note
on Positivism), 6:9b-10b.
"Ch'uan-chiao" 傳教 (The propagation of Christianity),
3:2b-6.
"Ko-kuo chiao-men shuo" 各國教門説 (A discussion
of the religious sects of various countries), 7:22b-24;
also in Huang-ch'ao ching-shih-wen hsü-pien, 112:
12b-13.

Wang Wen-chieh 王文杰 . .  Chung-kuo chin-shih shih shang ti
chiao-an 中國近世史上的教案 (A study of the
religious persecutions in modern Chinese history).
Foochow, 1947; 146 pp.

Wei Tsing-sing.    La Politique missionnaire de la France en Chine,
1842-1856:  L'ouverture des cinq ports chinois au commerce
étranger et la liberté religieuse.  Paris, 1960; 653 pp.

Wei Yüan 魏源.    Hai-kuo t'u-chih 海國圖志 (An illustrated
gazetteer of the maritime countries).  1844 ed., 50 chüan;
1852 ed., 100 chüan.

Wen-hsien ts'ung-pien 文獻叢編 (Collectanea from the Historical
Records Office).  46 ts'e; Peiping, 1930-1943.

Wen Ping 文秉 .    Lieh-huang hsiao-shih 烈皇小識 (A sketch
of the last Ming emperor ); in Ming-chi pai-shih 明季稗
史 (An unofficial history of the late Ming), ch'u-pien,
chüan 6.  Shanghai, 1912.

Willeke, Bernward H.   Imperial Government and Catholic Missions
in China during the Years 1784-1785.  St. Bonaventure,
New York, 1948; 227 pp.

Williams, S. Wells.   The Middle Kingdom: A Survey of the
Geography, Government, Literature, Social Life, Arts, and
History of the Chinese Empire and Its Inhabitants.   Rev.
ed.; 2 vols.; New York, 1901.

Wright, Arthur F.   "Fu I and the Rejection of Buddhism," Journal
of the History of Ideas, 12:33-47 (1951).

------Buddhism in Chinese History.  Stanford, 1959; 144 pp.

Wright, Mary Clabaugh.   The Last Stand of Chinese Conservatism:
The T'ung-chih Restoration, 1862-1874.  Stanford, 1957;
426 pp.

------"The Adaptability of Ch'ing Diplomacy: The Case of Korea,"
The Journal of Asian Studies, 17:363-381 (1958).

Wylie, Alexander.   Memorials of Protestant Missionaries to the
Chinese: Giving a List of Their Publications, and Obituary
Notices of the Deceased.  Shanghai, 1867; 331 pp.


Yang Hsiang-chi 楊象濟.   "Yang-chiao so yen to pu ho Hsi-jen
ko-chih hsin-li lun" 洋教所言多不合西人格致
新理論(A discussion of the discrepancies between the
statements of the Western religion and the new principles
of Western science); Huang-ch'ao ching-shih-wen hsü-pien,
112:11b-12.

Yang Kuang-hsien 楊光先 .   Pu-te-i 不得已  (I could not do
otherwise).  2 ts'e; 1929 photolithographic ed.

Yang Ping-nan 楊炳南 .   Hai-lu 海錄(A maritime record).
2 chüan; 1820.

Yazawa Toshihiko 矢澤利彦. "Chōkō ryuiki kyōan no ichi
 kōsatsu" 長江流域教案の一考察 (The attitude
 of Chinese officials toward the antiforeign riots in 1891);
 Kindai Chūkoku kenkyū, No. 1:107-136 (Tokyo, 1958).

------"Chōkō ryuiki kyōan no kenkyu" 長江流域教案の研究
 (The antiforeign riots of 1891); Kindai Chūkoku kenkyū,
 No. 4:109-158 (Tokyo, 1960).

Yung-cheng shang-yü 雍正上諭 (Edicts of the Yung-cheng
 Emperor), comp. Chang T'ing-yü 張廷玉 et al.          •
 24 ts'e; 1741.

Yü Cheng-hsieh 俞正燮. Kuei-ssu lei-kao 癸巳類稿
 (Selected short pieces of Yü Cheng-hsieh). Shanghai,
 1957; 616 pp.


Zürcher, E. The Buddhist Conquest of China: The Spread and
 Adaptation of Buddhism in Early Medieval China. 2 vols.;
 Leiden, 1959.

# GLOSSARY I

## NAMES, TERMS, AND TITLES

Chang Chen-t'ao 張甄陶

Chang Chih-tung 張之洞

Chang Chih-wan 張之萬

Chang Ju-lin 張汝霖

Chang Liang-chi 張亮基

Chang P'ei-ch'ao 張佩超

Chang Po-hsing 張伯行

Chang Wen-hsiang 張汶祥

Chang Yü-shu 張玉書

Ch'ang-jun 長潤

Chao-chia-kuan 罩家關

chao-hui 照會

Ch'en Kuo-jui 陳國瑞

Ch'en Tu-hsiu 陳獨秀

Ch'en Yüan-i 陳原益

cheng 正

cheng-chiao 正教

Cheng P'u-hsiang 鄭圃香

cheng-tao 正道

Ch'eng-lin 成林

Chi Yün 紀昀

Ch'i-ying 耆英

Chiang I-li 蔣益澧

chiao-an 教案

Chiao Han-shu pa-piao

校漢書八表

Ch'iao Sung-nien 喬松年

chieh-mien ch'ao-sheng

潔面朝聖

chien-sheng 監生

Chien Yin 褰闉

Ch'ien Hsün 錢壎

Ch'ien Ting-ming 錢鼎銘

Chih-na chiao-an lun

支那教案論

Chin-chih shih-wu hsieh-shu

禁止師巫邪術

chin-shih 進士

Ching-fu 景福

ching-shui 經水

Chiu-chieh pao-hsün

救刦寶訓

Chou Chia-mei 周家楣

Chou Han 周漢

Chu Hsüeh-tu 朱學篤

Ch'uan-shih-shan 川石山

374

Ch'un 醇
chung-hsing 中興
Ch'ung-cheng lu 崇正錄
Ch'ung-hou 崇厚
Ch'ung-shih 崇實
chü-jen 舉人

Fan Chen 范縝
Fang An-chih 方安之
Feng-t'u kuang-wen 風土廣聞
Fu Hsi 伏羲
Fu I 傅奕

Hai-chung 海鍾
Hai-kuo ssu-shuo 海國四說
Han Ch'ao 韓超
Han Yü 韓愈
Ho Kuan-ying 何冠英
Ho Ta-hai 何大海
hsi-wen 檄文
Hsia Hsieh 夏燮
Hsia T'ing-ch'ü 夏廷榘
hsieh 邪
hsieh-shuo 邪說
Hsing-hsin pien 醒心編
hsiu-ts'ai 秀才
Hsü Ch'ang-chih 徐昌治
Hsü Chi-yü 徐繼畬

Hsü Chih-chien 許之漸
Hsü Kuang-ch'i 徐光啟
Hsüeh Fu-ch'eng 薛福成
Hsün Chi 荀濟
hsün-fu 巡撫
Hu Lin-i 胡林翼
Hu Shih 胡適
Hu-t'u chi 糊塗集
Hu Yü-yün 胡毓筠
Hua T'o 華陀
Huang Tsung-hsi 黃宗羲
Huang Wei-hsüan 黃維煊
Huang Yü-pien 黃育楩
hui chih ch'üan-shen 會之全身
hui chih yüan-shou 會之元首
hun-p'o 魂魄
Hung-chin tsei 紅巾賊
Hung Liang-chi 洪亮吉

I-hsin 奕訢
I-huan 奕譞
i-tuan 異端

jen-hui 仁會
Jui-lin 瑞麟

Ko-lao-hui 哥老會
Ku Huan 顧歡
Ku Yen-wu 顧炎武

kuan-fang 關防
Kuan-wen 官文
Kuang-chien lu 廣見錄
Kuei-chiao kai-ssu 鬼教該死
Kuei-liang 桂良
Kung 恭
kung-hsi 公檄
kung-shih 公事
Kuo Po-yin 郭柏蔭

Lao Ch'ung-kuang 勞崇光
Li Chih-tsao 李之藻
Li Fu-t'ai 李福泰
Li Han-chang 李瀚章
Li Ho-nien 李鶴年
Li Huan 李桓
Li Hung-chang 李鴻章
Li Ju-sung 李如松
Li Ming-ch'ih 李明墀
Li Tsu-po 李祖白
Liang T'ing-nan 梁廷枏
lien-ch'i 連氣
Lin Ch'üan-ch'u 林全初
Liu Hung-k'uei 劉鴻魁
Liu Jung 劉蓉
Liu K'un-i 劉坤一
Liu Yü-hsün 劉于潯
liu-yüan 留元

Lo Ping-chang 駱秉章

Ma Chung 馬忠
Ma Hsin-i 馬新貽
Ma Ju-lung 馬如龍
Mao Ch'ang-hsi 毛昶熙
Mao Hung-pin 毛鴻賓
Mei Ch'i-chao 梅啟照
miao 廟
Miao Huan-chang 繆煥章
Ming t'ung-chien 明通鑑

ni-ming chieh-t'ieh 匿名揭帖

Pa-li-ta 巴利(里)達
pao-chia 保甲
P'eng Yü-lin 彭玉麟
P'i-hsieh chi 闢邪集
P'i-hsieh shih-lu 闢邪實錄
Pien Ch'üeh 扁鵲
Pien Pao-shu 卞寶書
Pien Pao-ti 卞寶第
ping 稟
pu-chin chih chin 不禁之禁
pu-ching 不經
pu k'o hsin yeh 不可信也
Pu-ssu-tieh-ni-chiao 卜斯迭尼教
seng 僧

Shang-ti 上帝
Shen Ch'üeh 沈㴶
Shen Pao-chen 沈葆楨
shen-shih 紳士
sheng-yü 聖諭
sheng-yü lo-fu 聖諭(揄)羅福
shih-t'ien 事天
Shu-yün 述韻
shuo-fa 說法
ssu 寺
Sung Chin 宋晉

ta ho-shang 大和尚
ta-kung 大公
tai-li ch'üan-ch'üan ta-ch'en
　代理全權大臣
Tai Lu-chih 戴鹿芝
T'an Ch'un-ch'ing 譚純鄉
T'ang Chi-sheng 唐際盛
ti-yü 地獄
T'ien 天
t'ien-chu 天主
T'ien-chu-chiao 天主教
t'ien-chu-t'ang 天主堂
t'ien-hsia ti-i shang-hsin jen
　天下第一傷心人
T'ien Hsing-shu 田興恕
T'ien-hsüeh 天學

T'ien-hsüeh ch'uan-kai
　天學傳概
Ting Jih-ch'ang 丁日昌
Ting Pao-chen 丁寶楨
To Wen 多文
Ts'ai Yüan-p'ei 蔡元培
Ts'ang-chih 倉植
Tseng Hsieh-chün 曾協均
Tseng Kuo-fan 曾國藩
Tseng Pi-kuang 曾璧光
tso-tao 左道
Tso Tsung-t'ang 左宗棠
Tso Tsung-te 左宗德
Ts'ui Wu-tzu 崔五子
ts'ung-ssu 從祀
T'u Lang-hsien 涂朗仙
Tung Han 董舍

Wang San 王三
Wang T'ao 王韜
Wei Yüan 魏源
Wen-hsiang 聞香
Wen-hsiang 文祥
Wen Ping 文秉
Wo-jen 倭仁
Wu Chung-hsiang 吳仲翔
Wu Lan-chen 吳蘭珍
Wu T'ang 吳棠

Wu Te-chih 吳德芝

Yang Hsiang-chi 楊象濟
Yang Kuang-hsien 楊光先
Yang T'ing-hsi 楊廷熙
Yang T'ing-yün 楊廷筠
Yeh Ming-ch'en 葉名琛
Yeh-su-chiao 耶穌教
Yeh-su-chiao nan ju Chung-kuo
  shuo 耶穌教難入中國
  說
Yeh Wen-lan 葉文瀾
Yen Fu 嚴復
Yin Kuang-jen 印光任
Ying-han 英翰
Ying-kuei 英桂
Yü-chang shu-yüan 豫章書院
Yü Cheng-hsieh 俞正燮
Yü-k'o 毓科
Yüan Pao-heng 袁保恆
Yüeh hai-kuan chih 粵海關志
Yüeh t'ien-lu chih-ming 閱天路
  指明
Yün Shih-lin 惲世臨

# GLOSSARY II

## CHINESE NAMES OF MISSIONARIES

This glossary has been compiled in part from comparison of Chinese and Western texts dealing with the same events, in part from MacGillivray, van den Brandt, and Moidrey's two books, Confesseurs and La Hiérarchie. It includes only those missionaries whose Chinese names I have been able to determine.

### CATHOLIC

Aguilar, Juste-Alphonse (1814-1874): Chou-ju-ssu-to 周如斯多

Aleni, Giulio (1582-1649): Ai-ju-lüeh 艾儒略

Anot, Antoine (1814-1893): Lo-an-tang 羅安當

Anouilh, Jean-Baptiste (1819-1869): Tung-jo-han 董若翰

Baldus, Jean-Henri (1811-1869): An-jo-wang 安若望

    (An-en-li-ko 安恩理格)

Blettery, Laurent (1825-1898): Hsiang-te-li (li) 向德立 (理)

Calderon, Michel (1803-1883): Kao-mi-ko-erh 高彌格爾

Chapdelaine, Auguste (1814-1856): Ma-ao-ssu-to 馬奧斯多

Chauveau, Joseph-Marie (1816-1877): Ting 丁

Chevrier, Claude-Marie (1821-1870): Hsieh-fu-yin 謝福音

Chiais, Ephisius (1806-1884): Kao-i-chih 高一志

Cosi, Éloi (Eligio) (1819-1885): Ku-li-chüeh 顧立爵

Delaplace, Louis-Gabriel (1820-1884): T'ien-chia-pi 田嘉璧

    (T'ien-lu-ssu 田魯斯)

Desflèches, Eugène J. (1814-1887): Fan-jo-se 范若瑟

Dubar, Édouard A. (1826-1878): Tu-pa-erh-o-tu 杜巴爾厄督

379

Faurie, Louis S. (1824–1871): Hu-fu-li 胡縛理

Fenouil, Jean J. (1821–1907): Ku-fen-lei 古分類

Gilles, Pierre (1829–1869): Chao 趙

Gonnet, Joseph (1815–1895): O-erh-pi-jo-se 鄂爾璧若瑟

Guillemin, Philippe F. Z. (1814–1886): Ming-chi-le 明稽埒

Heude, Pierre (b. 1836): Han-shih-chen 韓石貞

Languillat, Adrien H. (1808–1878): Lang-huai-jen-hou-fu 郎懷
仁厚甫 (Lang-chi-la 郎吉臘)

Leboucq, François-Xavier (Prosper) (b. 1828): Hsü-po-li 徐博理

Lebrun, Jean (b. 1839): Lo-po-en 羅伯恩

Lemaître, Mathurin (1816–1863): Mei-te-erh-cheng-hsin 梅德
爾正心

Lions, François-Eugène (1820–1893): Li-wan-mei 李萬美

Mabileau, François (1829–1865): Ma-pi-le 瑪弼樂

Mihières, Simon (1821–1871): Mei-hsi-man 梅西滿
(Mei-li-hei 梅例黑)

Mouly, Joseph-Martial (1807–1868): Meng-chen-sheng 孟振生

Navarro, Michel (1809–1877): Fang-lai-yüan 方來遠

Néel, Jean-Pierre (1832–1862): Wen-nai-erh 文乃耳
(Wen-jo-wang 文若望)

Pantoja, Didace de (1571–1618): P'ang-ti-wo 龐廸我

Perny, Paul-Hubert (1818–1907): T'ung-wen-hsien 童文獻

Peyralbe, André (1825–1872): Po 白

Pichon, Pierre M. (1816–1871): Ch'in 秦

Pinchon, Jean T. (1814–1891): Hung-kuang-hua 洪廣化

Ponsot, Joseph (1803–1881): Yüan-peng-so 袁細索

Raimondi, Jean-Timoléon (d. 1894): Kao-jo-wang 高若望

Ricci, Matteo (1552–1610): Li-ma-tou 利瑪竇

Rigaud, Jean-François (d. 1869): Li-kuo 李國
  (Li-kuo-an 李國安 )

Schall, J. Adam (1591-1666): T'ang-jo-wang 湯若望

Seckinger, Joseph (1829-1890): Chin-chien-san 金緘三

Tagliabue, François (1822-1890): Tai-chi-shih 戴濟世
  (Ta-li-pu 達里布 )

Verbiest, Ferdinand (1623-1688): Nan-huai-jen 南懷仁

Vérolles, Emmanuel (1805-1878): Fang-chi-ko 方濟各

Vielmon, Léonard (1825-1870): Jen-kuo-chu 任國柱

Zanoli, Eustache G. M. (1831-1883): Ming-hsi-sheng 明希聖

## PROTESTANT

Allen, Young J.: Lin-le-chih 林樂知

Chalmers, John (1825-1899): Chan-yüeh-han 湛約翰

Edkins, Joseph (1823-1905): Ai-yüeh-se 艾約瑟

John, Griffith (1831-1912): Yang-ko-fei 楊格非

Legge, James (1815-1897): Li-ya-ko 理雅各

Martin, William A. P. (1827-1916): Ting-wei-liang 丁韙良

Meadows, James J.: Mi-tao-sheng 宓道生

Morrison, Robert (1782-1834): Ma-li-sun 馬禮遜

Muirhead, William (1822-1900): Mu-wei-lien 慕維廉

Reid, Gilbert: Li-chia-po 李佳白

Richard, Timothy (1845-1919): Li-t'i-mo-t'ai 李提摩太

Taylor, J. Hudson (1832-1905): Tai-te-sheng 戴德生

Williamson, John W.: Wei-yang-sheng 衛養生

Wolfe, John R.: Hu-yüeh-han 胡約翰

# INDEX

# INDEX

Navarro, Michel, 95–96, 98–99, 100, 106, 220
Néel, Jean-Pierre, 118–119
Nevius, J. L., 46
*Ni-ming chieh-t'ieh*, 87
Nien rebellion, 73, 114, 200

Officialdom: dilemma of, 93, 98–99, 104, 184–185, 215, 262–263, 271–273; difficulty of enforcing treaties, 102–103, 170–179; paralysis, 103–104, 180–185; cooperation with missionary, 106; opposition to Christianity, 110–126, 310n9; relation to gentry, 111–113; decay, 112–113; weakness of central government, 113–123, 215–217, 227; proposals to regulate missionary, 123–126, 149–169, 224–228, 247–256; accommodation of Christianity, 170–179, 217–221; extreme antiforeign wing, 234–237, 239–242. *See also* Tsungli Yamen
Opium War, 44, 65
Orphanages, 101, 225, 247; source of popular suspicion, 91–92, 230–231; and Tientsin Massacre, 230–231, 233; Chinese proposals to abolish, 252, 257
Orthodoxy, 4–20; Buddhism as, 6–8; Confucianism as, 7–10, 19–20

Pantoja, Didace de, 32
*Paradise Lost*, 266
Pei-t'ang case, 129, 316n8
*P'ei-wen yün-fu*, 27
P'eng Yü-lin, 114, 278–279
Peterborough, Bishop of, 195
*Pi-hsieh chi-shih*, 45–59, 90, 224, 265; reaction of foreigners to, 45–57; origin, 47–48, 277–281; blends truth and falsehood, 48–50; charges Christians with sexual malpractices, 49–51, 54–55; examines Christian doctrines, 52–54; suggests military force against missionary, 56–57; place in anti-Christian tradition, 58–59
*Pi-hsieh shih-lu*, 45–59, 280–281

Pien Ch'üeh, 89
Picn Pao-ti, 176–177
Pinchon, Jean T., 131, 145, 149, 152–153, 204
*P'o-hsieh chi*, 21–24, 30, 58, 288n32
Positivism, 266
Protestantism, 18, 34–35, 66, 70–71, 248–249, 266
*Pu-ssu-tieh-ni-chiao*, 266
*Pu-te-i*, 24–27, 30, 38, 40

Raimondi, J. T., 220, 259
Reid, Gilbert, 46
Rental of property by Christians, 172, 175–176, 204
Restoration of church property, 67–69, 96–97, 128–130, 155, 255
Ricci, Matteo, 25, 27–28, 32, 289n32
Richard, Timothy, 47, 81, 279
Rigaud, Jean-François, 177, 208
Rites controversy, 29
Rochechouart, Count Julien de, 208–214, 229, 238, 244–247, 256, 315n3, 318n26, 327n22
Roze, Rear Admiral, 206–207
Russia, 200, 246, 251

*Sacred Edict*, 29, 48, 123, 166, 314n44
Schall, Adam, 24–25, 28
Seckinger, Joseph, 221
Sexual crimes, charged against foreigners, 49–51, 54–55, 58, 86, 89–92
Shen Pao-chen, 92–93, 96, 101, 161, 167–168, 172, 200
*Shen-shih*, 77. *See also* Gentry
*Sheng-yü*, 10
*Sheng-yü kuang-hsün*, 11
Sinclair, Consul, 192
Sino-French agreements, 44, 64–66, 68–69. *See also* Treaty of Tientsin
Société des Missions-Étrangères, 70, 131, 136, 141, 208
Somerset, Duke of, 194–195
Spurious ten articles, case of (1866), 149–153, 158, 204; France's view of, 151–152; missionary view of, 152–153
*Ssu-k'u ch'üan-shu tsung-mu*, 32, 38